THE POST-COLONIAL STATES OF SOUTH ASIA

THE POST-COLONIAL STATES OF SOUTH ASIA

Democracy, Development and Identity

Edited by

Amita Shastri
and
A. Jeyaratnam Wilson

Palgrave

THE POST-COLONIAL STATES OF SOUTH ASIA

Copyright © Amita Shastri and A. Jeyaratnam Wilson 2001

Softcover reprint of the hardcover 1st edition 2001 978-0-312-23852-0

All rights reserved. No part of this book may be used or reproduced in any manner whatsoever without written permission except in the case of a brief quotation embodied in critical articles or reviews for information, address:

PALGRAVE, 175 Fifth Avenue, New York, N.Y. 10010

First published by PALGRAVE, 175 Fifth Avenue, New York, N.Y. 10010. Companies and representatives throughout the world. PALGRAVE is the new global imprint of St. Martin's Press, LLC Scholarly and Reference Division and Palgrave Publishers Ltd. (formerly Macmillan Press Ltd.)

First published in the United States of America in 2001

ISBN 978-1-349-63192-6   ISBN 978-1-137-11508-9 (eBook)
DOI 10.1007/978-1-137-11508-9

Library of Congress Cataloguing-in-Publication Data

The post-colonial states of South Asia : democracy, development, and identity / Amita Shastri, A. Jeyaratnam Wilson, editors.
    p. cm.
    Includes bibliographical references and index.

    1. South Asia–Politics and government. 2. Democracy–South Asia. 3. Nationalism–South Asia. 4. South Asia–Economic conditions. I. Shastri, Amita. II. Wilson, A. Jeyaratnam.

DS340 .P67 2000
320.954–dc21
                                                                   00-034493

To my father
Raghunath Sahai Gupta
With love

(A.S.)

To the late
W. H. Morris-Jones
Teacher, scholar and friend

(A.J.W.)

Contents

Acknowledgments xi
List of Contributors xiii

Introduction
    The Post-Colonial States of South Asia: Democracy, Identity, Development and Security 1
    Amita Shastri

PART I DEMOCRACY

Chapter 1
    Political Governance in India: The Challenge of Stability and Diversity 17
    Stanley A. Kochanek

Chapter 2
    The Fragile Base of Democracy in Pakistan 41
    Samina Ahmed

Chapter 3
    Bangladesh: An Unsteady Democracy 69
    D. Hugh Evans

Chapter 4
    Nation-Building in a Demotic State: The Failure of Political Leadership in Sri Lanka 88
    A. Jeyaratnam Wilson

Chapter 5
    The National Political Culture and Institutions in Nepal 114
    Leo E. Rose

PART II IDENTITY

Chapter 6
The Rise of Hindu Nationalism and the Marginalisation of
Muslims in India Today 141
Christophe Jaffrelot

Chapter 7
State, Nation, Identity: The Quest for Legitimacy in
Bangladesh 158
Tazeen M. Murshid

Chapter 8
State Support for Religion in Contemporary Sri Lanka:
Some Ideological and Policy Issues 183
Chandra R. de Silva

Chapter 9
The 'Nationalities' Question in South Asia 196
Raju G.C. Thomas

PART III DEVELOPMENT

Chapter 10
Economic Crisis, Momentary Autonomy and Policy Reform:
Liberalisation in India 1991–95 215
Ronald J. Herring and N. Chandra Mohan

Chapter 11
Liberalising India's Economy: Context and Constraints 241
Vanita Shastri

Chapter 12
Institutional Impediments to Human Development in Pakistan 264
Christopher Candland

PART IV SECURITY

Chapter 13
Creating a Common Home? Indo–Pakistan Relations and the
Search for Security in South Asia 283
Vernon Hewitt

Chapter 14
The Flash-Point of South Asia: Kashmir in Indo–Pakistani
Relations 311
Sumit Ganguly

Contents

Chapter 15
   Pokhran II and After: Consequences of the Indian Nuclear
   Tests of 1998   326
   Ashok Kapur

Index   347

Acknowledgments

Good teachers are found both inside and outside academe. My father, to whom I (Shastri) have dedicated this book, has been influential in teaching me innumerable things, many more than I could possibly identify. His keen and active interest in politics which I witnessed as a child, no doubt, rubbed off to result in the discipline I chose for a career in academe. His lively curiosity about the subject and its concerns struck me even on a recent visit when he wanted to know how the 'mixed' German electoral system worked, and what impact it might have if adopted in India to overcome the growing fragmentation of the party system. The lucidity with which he explained the Kashmir situation to his granddaughter on another occasion would leave many a professional presentation of the subject pale in comparison.

Many of the contributors to this volume are W. H. Morris-Jones' former students or keen readers of his works on India and the other South Asian states. They join me (Wilson) in dedicating this volume as yet another tribute to our great teacher. We hope these essays will be as warmly received by the community of scholars interested in South Asia as a previous volume was which went out of print within a couple of months of its publication. We want to pay our *namaskarams* (thanks/respects) once again because we are convinced that Morris more than deserved these. With regard to the momentous times of the last ten years, he once told a group of students that the end of the Soviet Union and with it the exposure of Communism as an empty ideology were as startling and shocking to him as if Christianity had suddenly come to an end.

We owe a number of debts of gratitude. We are thankful to Joel Kassiola, Dean of Behavioral and Social Sciences, and Richard DeLeon, Chair of the Department of Political Science, at San Francisco State University who provided support for the volume to cover part of the costs of research assistance and indexing the book. We were lucky to have Evan Daniels, Benjamin Rogus and Danah Lee, graduate students at the university,

Acknowledgments

provide excellent research assistance in editing and producing the manuscript. The university also awarded a summer research grant to Shastri to facilitate work on the volume. Tyler Williams did a superb job of building the index. We also wish to express our sincere thanks to Marc Milner, Professor of History at the University of New Brunswick (Canada), and members of his committee for the grant made towards the costs of indexing this book. Debbie Sloan, administrative secretary in the Political Science department at the university, proved herself a veritable Johannes Factotum. Finally, our thanks to Jonathan Price of Curzon for his enthusiasm for the project.

Our respective families were a constant source of support and encouragement. Nilabh was a pillar of strength and optimism. Avantika watched the development of the manuscript with friendly interest. Susili was the wonderful companion she has always been. To each, our heartfelt thanks.

Amita Shastri
Alfred Jeyaratnam Wilson

List of Contributors

Samina Ahmed is Fellow, International Security Program and Science, Technology and Public Policy at the Belfer Center for Science and International Affairs, Harvard University. She has previously worked at the Institute of Regional Studies, Islamabad and the Pakistan Institute of International Affairs, Karachi. Recipient of a number of research awards and grants, she has worked as a Visiting Scholar at Oxford University and as an Associate Researcher at the Stockholm International Peace Research Institute. She is the author of several book chapters and articles. Her latest publications include 'Pakistan's Nuclear Weapons Program: Turning Points and Nuclear Choices', *International Security* (Spring 1999) and a co-edited book, *Pakistan and the Bomb: Public Opinion and Nuclear Options* (1998). Her current research interests focus on issues of South Asian regional security with an emphasis on nuclear proliferation, including an ongoing study on 'The Role of Sanctions and Incentives in Managing South Asian Proliferation'.

Christopher Candland is Assistant Professor in Political Science at Wellesley College, where he teaches development and South Asian politics. The American Institutes of Indian, Bangladesh, Pakistan and Sri Lanka Studies, and the US Fulbright Commission made possible his research in South Asia. His research interests are in labor and community development in South and Southeast Asia. His co-edited volume *Industrial Relations in the Age of Globalization: Labor, State, and Management in Post-Colonial and Post-Communist Economies* is forthcoming.

D. Hugh Evans was educated at the University of London and at the University of Chicago where he was a Fulbright Scholar. He joined the British Foreign and Commonwealth Office in 1985 as a research specialist on South Asia. He has had diplomatic postings in Islamabad (1988–89) and Washington (1995–98). He co-authored an article on democracy in

List of Contributors

Pakistan with Leo Rose which appeared in the *Journal of Democracy* (January 1997).

Sumit Ganguly is Professor of Asian Studies at the University of Texas at Austin. He was previously at Hunter College of the City University of New York. He specializes in the study of ethnic violence, regional security and arms control. His regional foci are primarily South and secondarily Southeast Asia. He has published numerous articles in leading international journals. His research has been supported by grants from the Asia Foundation, the Ford Foundation, the W. Alton Jones Foundation and the United States Institute of Peace. He has been a both a fellow and a guest scholar at the Woodrow Wilson International Center for Scholars in Washington, DC. His most recent book is, *The Crisis in Kashmir: Portents of War, Hopes of Peace* (1997). He is currently at work on a manuscript that seeks to explain political quiescence and ethnic violence in Malaysia and Sri Lanka.

Ronald J. Herring is John S. Knight Professor of International Relations and Professor of Government and Director, Mario Einaudi Center for International Studies, Cornell University, Ithaca, New York. He taught for many years at Northwestern University and for brief periods at the Universities of Chicago, Texas, Washington, and Wisconsin. Herring has been editor of *Comparative Political Studies* and worked with various academic committees of Fulbright, Social Science Research Council, American Council of Learned Societies, American Institute of Indian Studies and MacArthur Foundation, among others. His earliest academic interests were in land relations, on which his book *Land to the Tiller: The Political Economy of Agrarian Reform in South Asia* (1985) won the Graham Prize (London) in 1986. He has recently edited (with Milton Esman) the volume *Carrots, Sticks and Ethnic Conflict: Rethinking Development Assistance* (University of Michigan Press, forthcoming).

Vernon Hewitt is Lecturer in Politics at the University of Bristol. He was born in Leicestershire in 1961 and educated at the University of East Anglia, St Peter's College and Nuffield College, Oxford. He is the author of *The New International Politics of South Asia* (1997) and *Reclaiming the Past? The Search for Political and Cultural Unity in Contemporary Jammu and Kashmir* (1995). He has contributed essays on Indian politics, South Asian political institutions, ethnic formation and ethnic conflicts in the region since 1947. His current research interests concern the rise of the BJP in India and the ideology of Hindutva.

Christophe Jaffrelot is Research Fellow at the Centre d'Etudes et de Recherches Internationales, Paris, where he teaches South Asia politics. He

List of Contributors

has recently published *The Hindu Nationalist Movement and Indian Politics, 1925 to 1990* (1996, 1999), and co-edited (with Thomas B. Hansen), *The BJP and the Compulsions of Politics in India* (1998). His current research is on the rise of the lower castes in North Indian politics and B.R. Ambedkar, about whom he has written a biography in French. He is editor in chief of *Critique Internationale* (a Paris-based quarterly in international affairs).

Ashok Kapur is Professor of Political Science at the University of Waterloo, Ontario. Born in Lahore, he is a Canadian citizen. He served as a member of the United Nations Committee to study Israeli Nuclear Armament in 1980–81. His publications include *India's Nuclear Option: Atomic Diplomacy and Decision-Making* (1976), *International Nuclear Proliferation: Multilateral Diplomacy and Regional Aspects* (1979), *The Indian Ocean: Regional and International Power Politics* (1983), *Pakistan's Nuclear Development* (1987), the edited volume *Diplomatic Ideas and Practices of Asian States* (1991), *Pakistan in Crisis* (1991), *The South Asian Nuclear Non-Proliferation Debate: Issues, Interests and Strategies of Change* (June 1993), and (with A.J. Wilson) *Foreign Policies of India and Her Neighbors* (1996). His current research deals with security structures in the Asia–Pacific region (including the Persian Gulf and Central Asia) and the changing patterns of foreign relations in the region. This work is supported by the Social Sciences and Humanities Research Council of Canada. His latest book *Pokhran and After* is forthcoming.

Stanley A. Kochanek is Professor at Pennsylvania State University. He has published several books and numerous research articles on the politics of South Asia. He has written *The Congress Party of India: The Dynamics of One-Party Democracy* (1968), *Business and Politics in India* (1974), *Interest Groups and Development: Business and Politics in Pakistan* (1983), *Patron-Client Politics and Business in Bangladesh* (1993), and (with R.L. Hardgrave) *India: Government and Politics in a Developing Nation* (2000, 6th edition). He has had extensive field experience in India as a Senior Fulbright Fellow and a research fellow of the Indian Institute of Indian Studies. He is primarily interested in the role of political parties and interest groups in political systems.

N. Chandra Mohan is Business Editor, *Times of India*. He worked as Senior Researcher for *The Hindu* (1984–90), Senior Assistant Editor at *The Economic Times* (1990–92), and Deputy Editor in *Business India* (1992–97). He was a Parvin Fellow at the Woodrow Wilson School, Princeton University (1989–90). He has researched and written extensively on issues relating to urban and industrial employment in India, India's liberalisation process, and US–Japan trade. His article on

List of Contributors

'Industrial Employment: Some Emerging Trends' was published in *Indian Industrialization* (1992) edited by Ghosh, Subramanian, Eapen and Drabu; and one on 'US-Japan Services Trade: The Anatomy of Persistent American Strength' in *Fortune* (1990).

Tazeen M. Murshid is currently a fellow of the Institute for Advanced Study at Berlin, where she is researching issues of gender and law in colonial and post-colonial South Asia. She is a Senior Lecturer in history and politics, School of Arts and Humanities, University of North London. She has taught at the School of Oriental and African Studies, University of London and is a Research Associate of the Center for South Asian Studies there. She has been Research Fellow and Senior Member at St Antony's College, University of Oxford, where she was awarded the Frere Exhibition for Indian Studies. She has been a Visiting Scholar at the Modern Asia Research Centre, University of Geneva; at Homerton College, University of Cambridge; and at the Asiatic Society of Bangladesh, Dhaka. She has written on intellectual and social history as well as on contemporary political and educational concerns. Her publications include *The Sacred and the Secular: Bengal Muslim Discourses, 1971–1977* (1995); and 'Democracy in Bangladesh: Illusion or Reality?' *Contemporary South Asia* (1995).

Leo Rose is Professor Emeritus of Political Science at University of California at Berkeley and Editor Emeritus of *Asian Survey*. He has also served as member and consultant to the US State Department. He has been the recipient of numerous grants and awards in his long career, including the Sherman Fairchild Distinguished Scholar award. He has researched and published extensively on South Asian international and regional relations and on the politics and foreign policies of the Himalayan states. Amongst the many books he has published are *Politics of Nepal: Persistence and Change in an Asian Monarchy* (with Margaret Fisher, 1970), *Politics of Bhutan* (1977), *War and Secession: Pakistan, India, and the Creation of Bangladesh* (with Richard Sisson, 1989), *Beyond Afghanistan: Pakistan–US Relations* (with Matinuddin Khan, 1990), *The New World Order: Adjusting India–US Relations* (edited with Eric Gonsalves, 1992), and *Afghanistan and Kashmir: The Report of a Joint American–Russian Study* (with Stephen Cohen et al, 1993).

Amita Shastri is Professor of Political Science at San Francisco State University. She was a University Grants Commission Research Fellow, India, and a Pew Faculty Fellow in International Affairs at J.F.K School of Government, Harvard University. She has also been a Research Fellow/Visiting Scholar at California Institute of Technology, University of California at Los Angeles, University of California at Berkeley, and the

List of Contributors

International Center for Ethnic Studies at Colombo. Her research interests focus on the processes of democracy and democratization, political economy of development and ethnic conflict. She has contributed chapters to books, and articles to a variety of international scholarly journals. Recently published were 'Estate Tamils, the Ceylon Citizenship Act of 1948 and Sri Lankan Politics' *Contemporary South Asia* (1999), and 'Transitions to a Free Market: Economic Liberalisation in Sri Lanka', *Round Table* (October 1997).

Vanita Shastri is currently a consultant to the India Program at the Harvard Institute for International Development, Cambridge, Massachusetts. She has taught Political Science at various places, including Delhi University, Clarke University and Salem State College. Her research and publications have explored issues relating to the politics of economic liberalization in India. She recently wrote a development discussion paper with Nirupam Bajpai on the software industry in India (1998), and is currently working on a policy paper on 'Modernization and Development of Ports in Tamilnadu' for the state government of Tamilnadu, India. Vanita is also a trained Indian classical dancer practicing the Odissi style.

Chandra R. de Silva is Professor and Chair of History at Old Dominion University. He was Professor and Chair of History at Indiana State University 1991–98 and at the University of Sri Lanka (Ceylon), Peradeniya, 1962–89. He has held fellowships from the Calouste Gulbenkian Foundation (1970, 1976), the Newberry Library, Chicago(1976) and was Hallsworth Fellow at the University of Manchester in 1982. He has authored and co-edited many books including *The Portuguese in Ceylon* (1972), *Sri Lanka: A History* (1987, 1997), *Education in Sri Lanka* (1990), and *Buddhist Fundamentalism and Minority Identities in Sri Lanka* (1998). He is currently working on a book of documents on the Portuguese encounter with the peoples of Sri Lanka and the Maldives.

Raju Thomas is Allis Chalmers Professor of International Affairs and Professor of Political Science at Marquette University in Milwaukee, Wisconsin. He was Co-Director, Center for International Studies, University of Wisconsin-Milwaukee and Marquette University (1992–97); and has been Visiting Scholar/Research Fellow at various leading universities in the US and UK. He has lectured in or consulted with various agencies of the U.S. and British governments. He worked for British multinational corporations in India (1965–69). He has published numerous articles in professional journals, chapters in edited books, and op-ed pieces in leading newspapers and magazines. His books include *The Defense of India* (1978); *Indian Security Policy* (1986); *South Asian*

Security in the 1990s (1993); and *Democracy, Security and Development in India* (1996). He is the contributing editor or co-editor of *The Great Power Triangle and Asian Security* (1983); *Energy and Security in the Industrializing World* (1990); *Perspectives on Kashmir* (1992); *The South Slav Conflict: History, Religion, Ethnicity and Nationalism* (1996); and *The Nuclear Non-Proliferation Regime: Prospects for the Twenty-First Century* (1998). He is currently writing two books on *Markets and Politics in India* and *Postmortem Yugoslavia*; and co-editing two books titled *India's Nuclear Security* and *Nuclear India in the 21st Century*.

A. Jeyaratnam Wilson was Professor Emeritus of Political Science at the University of New Brunswick, Canada, where he worked from 1972. He previously held the founding Chair in Political Science at the University of Peradeniya, Sri Lanka. He was also the first incumbent of the Foundation Chair of Political Science at the University of New Brunswick, and was elected Chair for three terms (1972–86). He was a Leverhulme Research Scholar at LSE, and Research Fellow at McGill, Manchester, and Columbia Universities. He was Visiting Fellow at St. Anthony's College, and Academic Visitor at Nuffield College, Oxford. He wrote numerous books and articles on Sri Lanka's government and politics.The more recent of his many publications are *The Break-up of Sri Lanka* (1989), *S.J.V. Chelvanayagam and the Crisis of Sri Lankan Tamil Nationalism* (1994). His most recent book was *Sri Lankan Tamil Nationalism: Its Origins and Development in the 19th and 20th Centuries* (2000).

Introduction

The Post-Colonial States of South Asia: Democracy, Identity, Development and Security

Amita Shastri

Five decades after the end of colonial rule, the states of South Asia are still faced with problems related to democratic governance, social identities, development and welfare, and territorial security. The establishment of participatory political and economic processes in the last half century has led to the mobilisation of new social groups with different values from those who came to power in the early post-independence period. This has raised serious issues of state legitimacy and governance on the one hand and a questioning of popular identities on the other. Whether manifested in its extreme form in the violent dissolution of the state after a civil war as in Pakistan over twenty-five years ago, or the traumatic assertion of the rights of the majority ethno-religious group as in Sri Lanka and India in recent years, these issues run as a common thread through the political experience of all South Asian states.

The South Asian states reveal a significant amount of change since the achievement of independence. The evolving relationships between various branches of the state – the civil with the military, the executive with the legislative and judicial, the central with the regional or local – have all contributed to defining the nature and cohesion of the state entity as a whole. There has also been a growing interaction between the original post-colonial form of the state and the broader patterns of political activity and mobilisation as expressed in political parties, regional movements, religious or linguistic groups, and social classes. This has caused an alteration in the dominant ideology of the state on the one hand and a restructuring of the surrounding political environment on the other. Previously dominant groups have been forced to adapt the pursuit of their own interests to the competition and challenges posed by other numerically significant groups now active in the polity. Whether these changes are positive or dysfunctional to the working of each system requires investigation and assessment.

The states in South Asia have a varied geography and history, so that their prospects and performance are not directly comparable. The large state of India formed the core of British imperial power in South Asia which was maintained in the region by both direct and indirect means. The next largest states of Pakistan and Bangladesh are relatively recent creations in the community of states: Pakistan came into formal existence a mere half century ago and Bangladesh only three decades back. The smaller states of Sri Lanka and Nepal also existed as separate entities during the colonial period and were recognised as such by the British, even though Sri Lanka was ruled directly as a colony and Nepal was subject to indirect control. Like Nepal, the micro-states of Bhutan and Maldives acquired modern statehood as a byproduct of the accidents of colonial conquest and strategy of indirect rule. As a result, at independence, India inherited the advantages of an established state structure and of being the recognised legatee of the colonial power on the subcontinent. Pakistan and, to a lesser degree, Bangladesh had to virtually assemble state structures from such fragments of state authority as existed within their territory. Like India, Sri Lanka and Nepal inherited established core structures, but were far weaker in terms of organized political power and material resources than their larger neighbour.

However, the advantage of prior existence in the colonial period primarily led to the establishment of the executive core, coupled with a bureaucracy and military. It included only a limited development of popularly elected legislative and representative structures in India and Sri Lanka. The elites of all states had to, therefore, reckon with and reconfigure their state structures at independence to accommodate a broader role and participation by the people. They had to 'modernise' their political structures and attempted to do so by adopting for their purposes the model they were most familiar with, the Westminster parliamentary system of the departing colonial power.

The success and longevity of the new structures varied in each case. Given their inherited state capacity, India and Sri Lanka worked their democratic parliamentary systems with greater success. Pakistan and, later, Bangladesh rapidly lapsed into extended periods of military rule. The remaining three states in South Asia concentrated on closely managing the transformation of their traditional monarchical systems into more participative ones, a process which has gone farthest in the largest of them, Nepal.

Yet, despite their differences and the ways in which they articulate their national projects, each state in South Asia has in common a serious attempt to succeed *as a state* in perpetuating itself as an established entity. Each state has sought to do this both through maintaining its unity and, less successfully, by creating consent through its claims of championing the interests of its peoples. Towards these ends, the South Asian states have sought to create new means and capacities for shaping democratic legitimacy, national identity, economic development, and territorial integrity.

This has led to certain notable developments. One, through a dialectical process, by the end of this period, it seemed (till the military coup in Pakistan in late 1999) that each of the five larger states had emerged as a functioning democracy. Repeated elections had been held in each which were, by and large, reputed to be 'free and fair'. Diverse political interests and groups had organised together as political parties to compete in elections for power. As a consequence, repeated changes in the party or coalition in government had also taken place. More than that, in each political system two rival political parties or blocs seem to have emerged, which offer intimations of an emerging two major party system and the possibilities of greater electoral stability in the future.

Two, through a process of trial and error, the South Asian states have been developing distinct identities by breaking away from the model of distant, bureaucratised authority that had been instituted by the colonial state in regions under its direct rule. They have attempted to draw greater support from society by invoking and linking indigenous moral and social norms with the formal political institutional structure. In the process, each state has adopted some of the values, norms, and organisational principles of its society – a process which has inevitably been dominated by those of the majority community in each state. This has been a highly contentious process and is, by no means, over.

Three, they have sought to use the power and structures of the state to sponsor a process of economic development to increase state power even while attempting to mobilise and channel the loyalties of the impoverished mass of the people to support the state. Initially the pressures towards centralisation of power and consolidation of state authority favored a more directly-sponsored pattern of development. However, with the limits of the above pattern becoming evident and the growing globalisation of the international economic system, each state has turned to greater dependence on a more open market model for growth.

Four, they have sought to develop their armed capabilities to better defend their interests. Given the asymmetries in the world and regional order, this has translated into a concern by the largest state in the region, India, to keep super power rivalries and cold war conflicts out of the region. In turn, rival states and oppositional regimes in the smaller states have sought to 'borrow power' by allying with larger powers outside the region. This dynamic has imported divisions and fissures from the larger field of international relations into the arena of inter-state relations in the region and into the domestic politics of each state making the successive regimes in each state, their relations with those of the other states, and their overall efforts at regional cooperation an unstable one.

The variety of routes through which the above processes are happening is explored in the various contributions in this volume. A closer look at the South Asian states in the post-colonial era reveals that this process has not been a smooth one. Nor is it stable or complete. The interesting paradox is that even in periods of authoritarian rule, in large part because of that very experience, there have emerged broad-based oppositional movements for democracy which have demanded that alternative civilian elites and political parties be allowed to come to power. However, in giving civilian norms and structures an enhanced role within the state, the South Asian states have been less successful in maintaining soundwalls between secular state institutions and particularistic mobilisation. Moreover, with the state increasingly relying on the strategy of economic liberalisation, it has made common cause with private capital to a greater degree. While this has overcome one of the major divides in each society in the post-independence period between supporters of state-led development versus those supporting economic growth based primarily on private ownership and the market, it has opened up the society to potential fissures created by increasing inequalities in society that market-based growth engenders. Lastly, the end of the cold war and demise of the Soviet Union as a super power has compelled a reappraisal of relationships to be undertaken within and between states in the region, and thrown their relations into a state of flux and realignment.

The contributors to this volume explore the different ways in which the larger states in South Asia – India, Pakistan, Bangladesh, Sri Lanka, and Nepal – have functioned to deal with the demands of various domestic groups and to meet the challenges posed by external actors and forces. In keeping with the central concerns of the volume, we divided the volume into four sections, and asked the contributors to each section to explore particular sets of questions.

DEMOCRACY

The first set of papers look at issues relating to democratic governance. They identify what features of the constitutional structure of the colonial state were incorporated into that of the independent state, and what was created anew. Was the process of constitution-making undertaken in the name of 'the people' which denoted a notion of general collective interest, or was it consciously biased towards particular social groups? What role has leadership played in the process of political development? And, in what way has the mobilisation of new interest groups affected the functioning of the political and the party system?

India's political and democratic system is, in many ways, not only the longest lived[1] of any of the South Asian states, but constitutes an exceptional case in the developing world. Its persistence is particularly remarkable in comparative terms in view of the country's territorial size, huge population, unparalleled diversity, and low level of development. The ideals of its nationalist movement and leadership were important in infusing and defining the post-independence polity. Despite this legacy, as

Stanley Kochanek elaborates, a disturbing deinstitutionalisation of key political structures has taken place in the post-Nehru period, along with growing fragmentation, corruption and criminalisation in Indian politics. Yet, the increasing and active participation of the poor and lower castes in India in the processes of electoral politics and government reflect the expanding feeling of political efficacy that they have acquired which has had a profound effect on Indian politics. It has contributed to the rise to power of non-Congress opposition parties and coalitions at the national level – a change which first occurred in 1977, but which has happened repeatedly in the post-1989 period. The growing assertion of other branches of government and groups in the polity; such as the judiciary, election commission, press, and civic rights groups; is further contributing to the strengthening and vitality of the system.

Writing on Pakistan, Samina Ahmed traces its process of transition from a new and shaky, highly centralised, authoritarian state to a very fragile representative democratic system which was overthrown recently. The rise to power and consolidation in power of the executive and military apparatuses of state, first in the context of the cold war and then of the Afghanistan war, had numerous far-reaching consequences. To name only the most important, it resulted in the growth of regional inequalities and tensions (most dramatically highlighted in the secession of Bangladesh), the continued weakness of civilian political parties and governments even after democratisation in 1988, and one of the worst records of socio-economic inequalities and social development to be found anywhere in the world (a theme which is addressed separately in another chapter in the volume). The declining legitimacy of the political elites, though not of the democratic system *per se*, was manifested in declining voter turnouts at elections. In an effort to shore up their legitimacy, the leadership has sought time and again to use religion (Islam) for political purposes with regressive effect.

The establishment of Bangladesh, which constituted the only successful case of secession in the post-war international order till the dissolution of the Eastern bloc in the late 1980s, laid the foundation for a new representative state. However, as Hugh Evans points out, it was only in 1990 that a multi-party democracy could be considered to have been established in Bangladesh. The country was subject to numerous crises and divisions after its inception, the worst of which seem to have been overcome. The shortage of resources and economic crises in Bangladesh continue to be a recurrent problem, though not as severe as in the early 1970s when it undermined the post-liberation regime. The acute fragmentation and politicisation of the military, evident in numerous actual and attempted coups, has been gradually overcome. Indeed, the professionalisation of the military has proceeded to the point where not only has the military stepped out of politics, but has actively played a neutral mediating and facilitating role along with the judiciary to reconcile conflicts within the sharply divided civilian leadership. With the emergence of two major centrist political parties, the rotation of power to the Awami League after over two decades, the recent agreement to decentralise power (especially to the Chittagong Hill Tracts), and the wide ranging activities of numerous civic groups; Bangladesh has made substantial progress in overcoming some of the worst cleavages in its polity.

A. Jeyaratnam Wilson focuses on the role that political leadership has played in Sri Lanka in contributing to the state of acute hostilities and civil war in which the island finds itself today. Drawing on his personal knowledge of the island and its politics, he makes a comparative assessment of the various heads of government and identifies the choices they had open to them at various junctures to turn Sri Lanka away from becoming the majoritarian demotic state it evolved into. The failure of the leadership in forging or implementing inter-ethnic agreements to resolve conflicts in the plural polity has been particularly tragic given the fact that Sri Lanka has had so many of the other attributes of a representative democratic system and enjoys the distinction in the developing world (along with India and Costa Rica) of having worked through democratic constitutional processes of government continuously since independence. As he emphasises, the process of democratic state-building in a multi-ethnic society is a more complex endeavour than political parties merely competing for power in elections based on the support of the majority group.

Leo Rose traces the evolution of Nepal's traditional monarchical system into an open modern democratic system. In particular, he focuses on the differentiation and roles of the traditional elite groups at the national level vis à vis those exercising power in a subordinate capacity at the regional or local level. As he highlights, with the introduction of a modicum of representation and a more assertive monarchy in the 1950s, the possibilities of inter-elite conflict were heightened as the 'source and force' of politics (the power of social and family connections) did not change much. However, after the 1990 'revolution' to an open democratic system, despite intra-party feuds and parliamentary instability, there is emerging a greater integration of the two levels than before.

IDENTITY

The second set of papers examines issues related to the process of national integration and the creation of political community in various states. As these essays discuss, the ideal of secularism embraced in multi-ethnic South Asia did not imply a total separation of church and state on the Western model, but an attempt to maintain equidistance to all religions, with varying results. The essays examine the redefinition of majoritarian and minority identities that are underway and explore the manner in which the fluid expression of particular identities within the society denote shifting coalitions and bases of power.

In his chapter on India, Christophe Jaffrelot traces the rise of communalism in Indian politics as evidenced by the rise of the BJP and the 'Sangh parivar'. He argues that the principle of secularism, understood as denoting equidistance from all religions, has been unevenly and incompletely implemented in law and practice, so that members of each of the major religious communities find enough cause for complaints of bias in the actions of the state. The competition for power and use of religion to mobilise electoral support by various parties, particularly the BJP, has sharpened communal conflict in the last decade and adversely affected the Muslim and other minority communities.

The conflicts relating to secularism and the rise of communalism have been even more pronounced in the neighboring state of Bangladesh. Tazeen Murshid explores the fluid, and often contradictory, nature of national identity in a territory and population which underwent a series of dramatic changes in its political status in the last half century and more. The attributes of religion, language, culture and territory have been variously emphasised, either singly or in combination, by differing segments of society at different times. The essay demonstrates how the search for legitimacy by successive regimes in Bangladesh has led to the formulation of competing visions of alternative national identities. This has not only engendered conflict within the society, but also led to the rise of the religious right and undermined the influence of the liberal intelligentsia.

An interesting comparative case to the nature of state practice and secularism in South Asia is provided by Sri Lanka – a state in the throes of an extended ethnic civil war. Questioning to what degree the Sri Lankan state can be considered as veering towards 'fundamentalism', as alleged by critics, Chandra R. De Silva analyses the role of the state in Sri Lanka in its relationship to the major religious groups in the mid-1990s. Analysing the constitutional provisions and financial allocations made to the four major religious groups, he shows that the Sri Lankan state seems to conform substantially to the larger regional tradition of following a policy of equidistance of the state towards all religions. Yet, as he points out, the state's policy conceals differences within the state apparatus regarding the nature of the relationship between state and religion – between the protection afforded by the state to religious entities versus individual rights, of efforts to expand the protection and privileges extended to the majority religion, and of state officials subordinating religious organisations or personnel to serve partisan ends.

The political and security dilemmas that have been posed by secessionist or irredentist nationality groups to the existing state structures are discussed by Raju Thomas. Given the ethnic heterogeneity of the leading states in South Asia, and the overlapping and changing nature of nationality identities, Thomas rejects the possibility that an 'objective' redrawing of state boundaries could ever resolve matters, even were such intervention to be attempted by the 'international community' on humanitarian grounds. As the partition of the sub-continent in 1947 and the dismantling of Yugoslavia more recently illustrated only too starkly, such 'solutions' carry unacceptably high costs in terms of breakdown of community, violence, killings and material loss. Instead, he argues that acceptance of existing state boundaries and the cooperation of the existing states through the South Asian Association for Regional Cooperation (SAARC) offers the best means to reconcile such nationality conflicts and to accommodate the overlapping and fluid social identities that are endemic in this region.

DEVELOPMENT

The third section takes a look at how successful the political process has been in assuring the material welfare of its citizens and how governmental performance has affected the legitimacy of state authority. Does the decline of bureaucratically-sponsored development indicate the rise of new social forces? What was the political and economic context for the liberalization of the economy? How successful have the reforms been in terms of generating growth and equity in the South Asian states?

While the policy of economic liberalization was launched in Sri Lanka as early as 1977, it was the adoption and implementation of reforms in 1991 by the largest country, India, that committed the region as a whole to greater integration with the world economy. Ron Herring's chapter points to the paradox of the severity of the 1991 balance of payments crisis in India and the political instability induced in the aftermath of the mid-term polls as providing an exceptional 'moment' of autonomy to the weak newly-elected minority Congress government at the Centre to launch reforms. While a strategic structural shift in favor of the market and private capital was effected in the following period, the pressures that emanated from segments of society hurt or threatened by the new measures were relayed via the media of populist electoral politics to result in a slowdown of reforms. As he argues, the precise nature and scope of the reforms have, inevitably in a vigorous competitive democracy like India's, been shaped by the opportunities presented by the political process. While it is too early to judge their full impact, just as in the period of state-led import-substitutionist development before them, the reforms have been influenced by the interaction of the market with society.

Vanita Shastri's paper, likewise, agrees that economic reforms are best viewed as a 'process' spread over a number of years. Shastri, however, emphasises the fact that the foundations of the reforms were laid in the 1980s. The 'change team' of bureaucrats that was instituted at the time has stood India well in pushing through reforms piecemeal at politically appropriate moments, despite a series of weak minority and coalition governments at the Centre in the 1990s. Notwithstanding this, as both authors agree, the economic reforms have been widely accepted at both the national and the state levels of the Indian polity. On the basis of the limited data available, while the reforms seem to have increased socio-economic inequalities, the context of political and electoral pressures in a vigorous and noisy democracy such as India's has compelled politicians to be cautious in legislating reforms which dislocate large numbers of people. So the 'Indian model of reform' that has emerged has been one that moves forward gradually within a democratic system in a consensus mode.

The legacies of the Nehruvian state thus seem to be several: the institutionalisation of a vigorous, albeit imperfect, participatory system; the concentration of power and a certain technical capacity in the hands of the central bureaucratic elite; and the acculturation of the mass of the people to the promise of socio-economic equality. The important consequences of the relative lack of the same legacies in the next largest state in the region are highlighted in the discussion by Christopher Candland on social development in Pakistan. While the South Asian region is now identified as having a disproportionate number of the poor in the world; due to Pakistan's emphasis on state-led development *in favor* of private sector growth, to the neglect of the increasing socio-economic disparities and considerations of social opportunity for the mass of the population, the impact of such policies have been particularly injurious in Pakistan. The situation was made worse by another legacy of the post-independence period, the prominent role played by the military in the polity in claiming power and economic resources. Coupled with the existence of rampant patronage and corruption, common to all South Asian states but particularly severe in Pakistan, it has created a deep crisis of financial viability and political legitimacy of the state. This pattern of relationships was so entrenched that the successive democratically elected regimes of the post-1988 period proved to be too weak to change it.

SECURITY

The last section of the volume examines issues related to national security and conflicting claims pertaining to territory. What have been the ramifications of disputes relating to territory, ethnic conflict, and military competition for security on the sub-continent? In what manner has the sharp variation in terms of resources, institutional weaknesses, and pressures on elites to gain popular legitimation affected the possibilities for the emergence of relations of co-operation between the South Asian states? To what degree has the changing world context from the cold war to the demise of the Soviet Union, the spread of globalisation, and growing nuclear capabilities of India and Pakistan changed the manner in which the South Asian states interact with each other and with the rest of the world?

In his essay, Vernon Hewitt traces the trajectory of Indo–Pakistan relations over the years with a view to examining the possibilities for regional cooperation between them. He identifies the deep generic hostility between them arising from the very process of state formation and partition as being central to the slow progress the region has made in developing relations of cooperation. The long periods of military rule in Pakistan have also left their legacy in the form of deep institutional factionalism within the Pakistani state between the civil and military structures, the latter working closely with the unaccountable intelligence apparatus (the Inter-Services Intelligence or ISI). Though the civilian leadership attempted to assert control after 1997, the military and intelligence apparatuses remained determined to maintain parallel lines of authority to the civilian wing and sharply opposed the normalisation of relations between Pakistan and India. The problem of asymmetry between the two states in their conception of their legitimate security needs, their resource base and capabilities also accentuates the conflict in perceptions between them. To Hewitt, the best solution lies in having an external power, namely the US, act as guarantor to a collective security regime in South Asia, through which each state could have certain key aspirations and concerns fulfilled.

The central role that Kashmir has played in constituting a 'flashpoint' in these hostilities is explored in further detail by Sumit Ganguly. The complexities surrounding the accession and integration of Kashmir in the Indian union have been exacerbated by the unwillingness of Pakistan to accept the status quo and the entanglement of the Kashmir issue in cold war politics. Giving primacy to domestic factors for the eruption of the insurgency in Kashmir in the late 1980s, Ganguly argues it was in large part due to the shortcomings in the practice of Indian federalism which resulted in attempts by the Central leadership to control events in the province to its own advantage. Support to the Kashmir youth insurgents by the Pakistani ISI and its Islamic mujahiddeen made the insurgents' actions more potent and devastating. In Ganguly's view, the alternative to continued hostility along the border between the two states would be a pragmatic acceptance by both states of the fifty year old Line of Control in Kashmir as the international border.

The asymmetry of the international nuclear order, divided between the nuclear 'haves' and 'have-nots', against which the Indian nuclear tests of May 1998 were a blow and a challenge, is elaborated by Ashok Kapur. Analysing a broad sample of responses to the tests, he demonstrates that there is no consensus among Western decision-makers and scholars as to how the prospects of overt Indian nuclear weaponisation should be treated. He argues that the Indian tests were a carefully considered response to a pattern of Pakistani, Chinese and American provocations in the strategic sphere, and that the much publicised but non-binding nuclear non-proliferation regime has been only imperfectly adhered to by its signatories. In his view, the opposition of Chinese and Indian strategic interests in the Asia-Pacific region cannot be ignored. He asserts that suitable restraints in the nuclear sphere will have to be arrived at through negotiations which take the geo-strategic interests of relevant states into account if such restraints are to be viable.

The essays, individually and collectively, cover a wide array of issues and developments. They will hopefully prove to be stimulating and informative to a broad readership of scholars and laypersons alike. They examine the evolution of the South Asian states beyond the formation of their political centres and efforts of the post-independence elites at state-building. They focus in particular on the challenges that have been posed to those institutions and values by what might be termed as 'the post post-colonial generation' in each society. This generation has no direct links with the colonial period and freedom movement and is looking beyond the post-colonial state in its efforts to construct a fitting structure to express their interests and identity.

◆

Overall, as the South Asian states enter the new millennium, there is reason both for hope and dismay. Much has been accomplished over the last fifty years, but much remains to be done. Putting aside the difficulties created by the military coup in Pakistan, a core representative and democratic structure has been constructed in each state over the preceding five decades. Undergirding this, it might even be argued, two rival political parties or blocs have a tenuous existence in each state which offer intimations of an emerging two major party system and the possibilities of greater electoral stability in the future. The effort to consolidate electoral fortunes by searching for a position in the moderate center will in all likelihood tame the wilder urges to communal extremism. It is now possible to find greater agreement across the political spectrum over the relative merits of market versus state-led development than was the case in the past. The existence of representative structures gives reason for hope that the political process as defined by the broad public will moderate the pace and specifics of economic policies and reform. Consolidation of the political center in each state should also create greater confidence in various regimes in the region to develop closer political, economic and social ties with each other through the SAARC.

And yet the issues and problems that remain to be resolved are also immense. The weakness in political structures range from the need for a greater development of the judicial and court system in India to a reinstauration of the weak democratic representative structures in Pakistan. In all states there is need to hold the political elite, of whatever hue, accountable for their actions, and for the norms of openness and transparency to be better respected in public life for better governance. This holds true with regard to actions taken by ruling regimes against opposition and dissident forces, disbursal of state resources and funds, and the abuse of official power to promote private interests. This would also lighten the burden of accountability which is otherwise placed on the political electoral process, when elections are looked on as the primary means by which rectification of political wrongs might be obtained. Powerful passions and tensions in opposing parties and politicians are unleashed in the competition for power, with violence punctuating the whole process. Yet, despite electoral promises, few political or bureaucratic officials guilty of corruption or abuse of power are brought to book even when they are out of power, increasing public cynicism and alienation.

Issues of identity in these complex plural societies continue to beleaguer each state. Majority nationalism remains as much an effect as a cause of bad, often opportunistic, governance. The temptation to use particularistic symbols and slogans to advantage remains a real temptation to many politicians from the majority community, whether belonging to the ruling party or to the opposition. Reactive mobilisation by minority communities often takes extreme, even secessionist, forms as it did in Sri Lanka, Kashmir, Punjab, and the states of north-eastern India. The use of coercion by the state to suppress such movements gives impetus to the spiral of hostile rhetoric and violent conflict, which can acquire an uncontrollable dynamic of its own. The lack of fair judicial procedures protecting individual and human rights often constitute an important part of the problem. Negotiations and decentralization of control over pertinent aspects of state authority offer other means by which accommodations might be made with minority groups. The difficulty, of course, remains, as with much else in politics, that it is precisely those in power, who benefit from the extant distribution of power, who are likely to be the most reluctant to undermine their own control by agreeing to place restraints on its exercise.

The tasks remaining in the economic realm are only too obvious and have been enumerated with stultifying repetitiveness over the years. Yet, the widespread realisation of the need for greater government intervention to combat mass poverty, disease and illiteracy while exercising caution on government entering the process of economic production, distribution and direct regulation is gaining widespread acceptance in policy circles as the new conventional wisdom.

The strategic environment around and in South Asia remains wanting. Comprehensive and serious disarmament measures have to take into account the existing inequalities in conventional and nuclear power capabilities between the established five nuclear powers and those of other states. The temptation to acquire such capability remains a strong one when a neighboring hostile power has such capability, as the examples of India and China as well as India and Pakistan demonstrated. Just as importantly, the effort to address regional rivalries and hostilities between India and Pakistan have to take into account the current cause for such differences persisting – embedded as it is in the deep conflict of interest between the civilian and military leadership within the Pakistani state. The use of Pakistan by larger non-regional powers as a check on the perceived aggrandizing ambitions of India in the region strengthens the military at the expense of the civilian institutions in Pakistan, maintains a dynamic of instability in the relations between the two largest states in the region, and contributes to heightened tensions in the region. These, in turn, contribute to increased expenditures on arms and a lower channeling of resources to social infrastructural development by both states. The pernicious impact of such policies on the consolidation of representative democratic institutions and groups and on mass economic welfare and standards of living are particularly evident in the case of Pakistan, the smaller and weaker of the two states. Any sincere declarations of support for democracy and for the alleviation of poverty by outside powers could do no better than to start with pressuring undemocratic or arbitrary regimes to adhere to norms of democratic functioning and accountability.

NOTES

1 The introduction of internal self-government and universal franchise in Sri Lanka as early as 1931 was seriously compromised by the restriction of the voting rights of the estate Tamil population before independence. Their exclusion essentially continued in the post-independence period till 1988. For a discussion, see Amita Shastri, 'Estate Tamils, the Ceylon Citizenship Act of 1948 and Sri Lankan Politics', *Contemporary South Asia* 8 (1), 1999: 65–86.

PART I

DEMOCRACY

Chapter 1

Political Governance in India: The Challenge of Stability and Diversity

Stanley A. Kochanek

At midnight on 15 August 1947 British colonial rule over India came to an end in an atmosphere of hope and anticipation. 'Long ago', India's new prime minister Jawaharlal Nehru eloquently proclaimed to the Constituent Assembly, 'we made a tryst with destiny, and now the time has come when we shall redeem our pledge'. Despite considerable political and economic progress, fifty years later as the Indian republic celebrated its Golden Jubilee anniversary, hope had turned to cynicism, anticipation to anxiety, and the country's 'tryst with destiny' appeared to remain unfulfilled. India's dangerous decades seemed to have arrived and the country was faced by a serious crisis of governance. This crisis of governance was reflected in the erosion of its political institutions, new stresses on its federal compact, a breakdown in its national consensus, the decline of national parties, the regionalisation of the party system, increasing political instability, a rising sense of discontent among its increasingly mobilised and politically conscious society, its continued mass poverty and mounting calls for the creation of a second republic. Faced with this growing crisis of governance, it seems pertinent to analyse to what extent India's political system has taken root and what forces have shaped its successes and failures.[1]

ESTABLISHMENT OF THE GOVERNMENTAL FRAMEWORK

Despite the upheaval of Partition, war with Pakistan and the assassination of Mohandas K. Gandhi, the newly independent state moved quickly and decisively to restore order and hammer out a new constitution for free India. The new constitution created a federal, parliamentary framework of governance with a strong center and popular elections based on universal franchise. Although the new governmental system was a transplant and not solely the result of natural evolution; it did have strong local roots in the British legacy, the nationalist elite's commitment to liberal democratic norms, the experience of the nationalist movement, and the pluralism of Indian society.²

Under the constitution, the executive power of the Union was formally vested in the president, but the president was to act primarily as a titular head of state. In both theory and practice, power was concentrated in the hands of the prime minister and the cabinet. The prime minister and cabinet became the focal point of decision making, controlled the bureaucracy and the military, and came to dominate the lower house of the Indian parliament. The constitution also created a supreme court that stood at the apex of a single integrated judicial system with a limited power of judicial review, and laid down a governmental framework for each of India's twenty-five states that reproduced in miniature the organisation of the union government.³

THE EMERGENCE OF EXECUTIVE DOMINANCE

The new constitution came into force on 26 January 1950, and became fully operational following the first general elections of 1951–52. The elections confirmed the overwhelming dominance of the Congress party and the leadership of Prime Minister Jawaharlal Nehru.⁴ By the early 1950s, the collective leadership of party and government that had developed in the immediate post-independence period, had given way to the emergence of Nehru as supreme leader of the party, the government and the nation. The charismatic Nehru commanded the respect of the bureaucracy, the military, the intelligentsia and even the fledgling opposition parties. Despite his overwhelmingly dominant position, however, Nehru worked diligently to construct a viable governmental structure, a national consensus on domestic and foreign policy, and a working relationship with the country's small but vocal political opposition. He also strove to accommodate the broad array of interests within the Congress party and the country as a whole. Nehru's efforts were facilitated by the fact that the Congress, the bureaucracy, the military, the parliament and the judiciary were staffed by a relatively homogenous elite drawn from the urban, Western-educated, upper castes and the existence of an elaborate structure of intermediation in the Congress and the country that linked the newly-elected government with the mass of the population resident in the countryside.

As a result, from the time of its adoption in 1950 until the mid-1960s, the constitutional system created by the Constituent Assembly and dominated by India's nationalist elite worked very well. Nehru and his senior colleagues in the party and the government provided strong and effective leadership at both the central and the state levels. Through a policy of accommodation and reconciliation, they succeeded in managing the potentially divisive issues of states reorganization and the official language question and created a national consensus behind the goals of democracy, secularism, socialism, development planning and a foreign policy of non-alignment. Under the leadership of Nehru and the Congress party, the new governmental system gained legitimacy and respect. The Indian economy experienced a decade of rapid economic growth, and India acquired a global stature in a world deeply divided by the cold war. At the time of his death in May 1964, Nehru bequeathed to his successors a unified nation, a well-organised and disciplined party, an institutionalised political order, a basic consensus on domestic and foreign policy, and a high level of public morality.

However, the first signs of strain in the new republic appeared in the early 1960s even as the Nehru era was drawing to a close and accelerated following his death. In the brief period of five years from 1962 to 1967, India was confronted by the divisive impact of two leadership successions, two wars, two major droughts, rapid inflation, severe recession, political defections and social upheaval. These events resulted in growing popular unrest, an erosion of Congressional support and a split in the party. These challenges were sought to be managed by a populist assault on India's development consensus and governmental institutions by the newly elected prime minister Indira Gandhi, the daughter of Jawarharlal Nehru.

In a desperate effort to confront the crisis facing India and to consolidate her power, Indira Gandhi embarked upon a series of steps designed to restructure the existing political order and concentrate power in her hands. In the succeeding period, she centralised an increasingly federal polity, subordinated the role of the president, created a dependent cabinet, weakened the Congress party, eroded the authority of the courts and politicized the bureaucracy in the name of increased governmental responsiveness and socio-economic justice.[5]

Indira Gandhi's centralisation and personalisation of power and continued Congress dominance, however, were undermined by a series of events that combined to produce a major political crisis. These events included a communist-led peasant revolt in the Naxalbari districts of West Bengal, sharp criticisms of the allegedly corrupt Congress-led governments of Gujarat and Bihar, and the rise of a broad-based Gandhian-style civil disobedience movement lead by Jayaprakash Narayan. While the events in West Bengal, Gujarat and Bihar were localized; the movement led by Jayaprakash Narayan – or J.P., as he was popularly known – took on a national character and was supported by most of India's opposition parties. The J.P. movement called for 'total revolution', a reconstruction of Indian society, and directly challenged Indira Gandhi by calling for her resignation. In the midst of this challenge to her authority, the legitimacy of Indira Gandhi's rule was called into question in June 1975 when the Allahabad High Court found her guilty of violating India's election laws during the 1971 elections. The court's decision further inflamed a growing mass movement demanding that Gandhi step down as prime minister.

Political Governance in India

Indira Gandhi responded to the growing political and economic crisis by declaring a national emergency, suspending democratic rights, introducing press censorship, jailing her opponents, and ruling by decree from 1975 to 1977. During the Emergency, Indira Gandhi attempted to corporatise the society and even appointed a committee to study the feasibility of replacing the existing constitution. In the end, faced by opposition from within her own party, Gandhi decided instead to radically alter the existing system by passing the Forty-Second Amendment which affected fifty-nine clauses of the constitution and strengthened the position of the prime minister in the Indian political system.

Although the democratic character of the Indian political system was restored as a result of Indira Gandhi's defeat and the victory of the Janata Party in the 1977 elections, the crisis of the 1960s and 1970s left a permanent mark on the country's politics and governmental institutions. The crisis eroded the organisational base of the Congress party, ushered in the beginning of coalition and alliance politics, undermined the established institutions of governance, and initiated a process of political decay.[6]

The Janata Party proved to be the first in a series of failed attempts by India's highly fragmented opposition parties to forge a national, centrist alternative to Congress rule. While the Janata coalition agreed on the importance of restoring democratic parliamentary rule, the coalition was able to agree on little else. Torn by personality clashes, ideological contradictions, conflicting interests and endemic factionalism; the Janata Party soon disintegrated. Despite periodic efforts at unity, India's opposition parties remained divided for most of the 1980s.

The breakup of the Janata Party enabled the Congress to return to power and dominate Indian politics from 1980 to 1989 under the leadership of a rehabilitated Indira Gandhi and, following her assassination in 1984, her son Rajiv Gandhi. Indira Gandhi's leadership style changed very little following her return to power. She continued to maintain personal control over the Congress party organisation, manipulated its factions, appointed Congress chief ministers and party leaders in the states, selected cabinet ministers personally loyal to her, reshuffled ministerial portfolios to ensure control and centralised power in her hands in an effort to prevent potential challenges to her leadership. This personalised and centralised leadership style, however, created a variety of problems. The repeated reshuffling of cabinet members led to political and administrative chaos. The treatment of states as potential threats to the center resulted in weak, corrupt and ineffective state governments and alienated provincial vernacular elites. Indira Gandhi's unchallenged control of party and government, moreover, made her increasingly intolerant of dissent, made her more and more reliant on manipulation and coercion to maintain control, and created a party of sycophants. As a consequence of this leadership style, the nation grew increasingly divided.

While on the one hand, the Congress party became weakened, factionalised, criminalised and corrupt; on the other hand, ethnic, tribal and religious identities intensified and resulted in increasing unrest in Punjab, Kashmir and the Northeast.[7]

The mode of selection of Rajiv Gandhi as leader of the Congress party and prime minister following his mother's assassination was a reflection of the political decay that had set in as a result of the centralisation and personalisation of power in India. The transition was handled more as a dynastic succession than a democratic selection process. Rajiv was sworn in as prime minister within hours of his mother's death. There was no appointment of an acting prime minister and there were no meetings of the party executive, the cabinet or the Congress Parliamentary Party, as in the past. Instead, Zail Singh, the president of India who had been selected for the position because of his personal loyalty to Indira Gandhi, appointed Rajiv as prime minister after receiving a letter from the Congress Parliamentary Board, an eight-person subcommittee of the party executive, conveying its choice of Rajiv as leader. Only after he was sworn in as prime minister of India, was his selection endorsed by the more broadly-based organs of the party.

Rajiv Gandhi, a former airline pilot and general secretary of the Congress party, had developed his practical political knowledge in the previous three years under the tutelage of his mother. Although he adopted her abrasive and divisive style during the 1984 election campaign, he briefly altered that style upon becoming prime minister. As prime minister, Rajiv adopted a more open, bargaining and consensual leadership approach that was more reminiscent of Jawarharlal Nehru, his grandfather. He moved quickly and decisively to defuse the challenges to Indian unity in Punjab and Assam that had festered during Indira's rule, promised to reform and rebuild the Congress party, and pledged to end corruption. Rajiv's 'Mr. Clean' image and his accommodating leadership style, however, did not last. By mid-term, when his apparent settlement of the Punjab and Assam problems began to unravel and the Congress suffered a series of major defeats in several state assembly elections, Rajiv retreated to a more confrontational style, brought his mother's discredited advisors back into government and again began to centralise power in his hands. Like his mother, he also became increasingly arrogant, showed little respect for India's governing institutions, engaged in frequent reshuffles of his cabinet, undermined the morale of the bureaucracy, engaged in a direct conflict with the president, ignored parliament and retreated from his attempts to reform and restructure the Congress party. Despite the great hope and promise that greeted his election; poor performance, policy failures, erosion of credibility, and the emergence of numerous charges of corruption involving defence contracts combined to bring about a massive defeat for Rajiv and the Congress party in the 1989 elections, as Table 1 shows.

Table 1: **Party Position In Recent Lok Sabha Elections, 1984–98**

Party	1984–89	1989–91	1991–92	1992–96	1996	1998	1999
Congress	413	197	221	232	135	141	112
BJP	2	85	119	120	159	181	182
Janata Dal	10	143	59	59	43	6	–
CPM	22	33	35	35	32	32	32
CPI	6	12	14	14	11	9	4
ADMK	12	11	11	11	–	18	10
DMK	–	–	–	–	17	6	12
TDP	30	2	13	13	16	12	29
Samajwadi Party	–	–	–	–	17	20	26
Shiv Sena	–	–	4	4	15	6	15
Samta Party/Janata Dal(U) 1999	–	–	–	–	–	13	20
RJD	–	–	–	–	–	17	7
Others	46	48	48	49	87	84	88
Total	543	524	524	537	532	545	537

Notes: (a) The results of 1991 do not include the Punjab seats (13 in number) as elections were not held there. Thus a separate column (5) with results from the Punjab elections which were held in 1992 is included here. (b) The 1996 results are of May 1996.

Source: R. L. Hardgrave and S. A. Kochanek, *India: Government and Politics in a Developing Nation* (San Diego: Harcourt Brace Jovanovich, 1993), 314 and 320; *India Abroad*, 31 May 1996, 6; and the Indian Parliament homepage at: www.nic.in.indpar.html. For 1999 results see *Frontline* (Chennai), 5 November 1999, 120–123.

The defeat of the Congress party brought to power a Janata Dal-led National Front government led by V. P. Singh, a former minister in Rajiv Gandhi's cabinet. The Janata Dal/National Front coalition was composed of a group of centrist and regional parties that formed a minority government supported from the outside by the Hindu nationalist Bharatiya Janata Party (BJP) and the communists. It represented India's second major effort to create a centrist alternative to the Congress and, like the Janata Party in 1977–79, quickly succumbed to factionalism, personality clashes and defections. The Janata Dal government collapsed when the party split and the BJP withdrew its support. The ill-fated government of Chandra Shekar which followed lasted only four months and was forced to resign in March 1991. As a result, India had to go to the polls for a second time in less than two years.

The May–June 1991 elections were marred by the assassination of Rajiv Gandhi and the election of another hung parliament. The sad state of the once dominant Congress party was demonstrated by the fact that the party immediately asked Sonia Gandhi, Rajiv's Italian-born widow to become party president. When Sonia Gandhi refused the party's offer, the Congress turned to P.V. Narasimha Rao, a senior Congressman and Rajiv loyalist. As the result of a last-minute sympathy vote for the Congress party, the party was able to win 227 seats – just 29 short of a majority. On 21 June 1991 P.V. Narasimha Rao, the sixty-nine year old former foreign minister, was sworn in as prime minister and given four weeks to cobble together a majority. Since no party was prepared to face new elections, the Congress was able to win a vote of confidence when the National Front and Left Front decided to abstain.

Despite his tenuous hold over the party and the parliament, Rao's first eighteen months in office were remarkably successful. He introduced a series of significant and substantial economic reforms, held assembly elections in the troubled state of Punjab, and conducted the first internal Congress party elections in two decades. Rao's non-assertive political style and willingness to accommodate diverse views seemed to hold out great promise that he would provide effective leadership for a divided country and deliver on his promise to rejuvenate the Congress party.

Like Rajiv, however, Rao soon returned to the leadership style and tactics of his mentor Indira Gandhi. Due to a series of corruption scandals, his poor handling of the Ayodhya crisis and increasing indecisiveness; Rao's authority began to wane. Rao responded by centralising power in his own hands and came to exercise more control over party and government than Indira Gandhi or Rajiv. He began to manipulate party factions, attempted to marginalise his opponents, split the Congress party, and became increasingly dependent on patronage to maintain his precarious control over party and government. Although Rao succeeded in serving a full five year term; poor performance, indecisive leadership, corruption charges, and a series of disastrous tactical alliances with regional parties led to major defections from the Congress and the worst electoral defeat for the party in its history in the May–June 1996 elections.

The 1996 elections, however, produced another hung parliament. Although the BJP won the largest number of seats and was asked by the president to form a government, the BJP government lasted only thirteen days and resigned when it realised it would lose a vote of confidence. In its place, India's fragmented and increasingly regionalised opposition parties were able to cobble together a weak fourteen party United Front coalition supported by the Congress from the outside. The coalition was compelled to change its prime minister due to the insistence of the Congress, and lasted a mere eighteen months before it collapsed and forced India to go to the polls once again in 1998.

The 1998 elections produced one of the most fragmented election results in post-independence Indian history. Although the BJP won the largest number of seats, it again fell far short of a majority. However, unlike its 1996 debacle, the BJP was able to cobble together an eighteen party coalition, the National Front, and lead a government in power for the first time. Atal Bihari Vajpayee, the BJP prime minister, however proved unable to hold his fractious coalition together. The BJP-led government lasted thirteen months before it collapsed in May 1999 and India was forced to go to the polls for the third time in three years.

The October 1999 elections resulted in a victory for the National Democratic Alliance (NDA), a twenty-four party coalition led by the BJP. The NDA won 299 seats and 40.8 percent of the vote and Atal Bihari Vajpayee was elected prime minister. Vajpayee, however, faced a series of daunting political, economic and security challenges. The most difficult challenge will be managing the tensions within his diverse coalition and within his own party.

Over the past fifty years, the prime minister has become the center of power in the Indian political system. Under the leadership of a series of strong personalities, the prime minister has come to play a crucial role in shaping the institutions of governance including the cabinet, the presidency, the parliament, the bureaucracy and the courts. At the same time, however, the office itself has undergone significant change. Indian prime ministers have employed three major styles of leadership and each style has had a significant impact on the development of India's political institutions and governance. The first style of leadership which was employed by Nehru and his successor Lal Bahadur Shastri from 1947 to 1966, was based on accommodation, consensus and institutionalisation. The second style was developed by Indira Gandhi and was also employed by Rajiv Gandhi and Narasimha Rao. This approach centralised, personalized and de-institutionalised the political process. The third style of leadership was weak and indecisive and has been characteristic of consensus prime ministers selected by the coalition governments consisting of the Janata Party, the Janata Dal, the United Front and the National Front.

These diverse leadership styles have been the product of individual personalities and the transformation of the party system from one party dominance to multi-partyism, alliance and coalition politics. Under one party rule India developed a tradition of strong prime ministers. Coalition and alliance politics, in contrast, have given rise to increasingly weak, ineffective and politically insecure prime ministers unable to cope with the increasingly complex problems facing the Indian republic. The problems of weak leadership and a continuing decay of political institutions have made the management of political conflict in India more difficult.

CHANGING ROLE OF THE PRESIDENT

Prime ministerial leadership styles have had a major impact on the other institutions of governance including the Indian cabinet, the president, the parliament, the bureaucracy and the courts. Under Nehru, Shastri and the early years of Indira Gandhi's rule, the individuals selected for the office of president of India were men of stature and distinction. India's first president, Rajendra Prasad, was a very prominent Congress leader and former president of the Constituent Assembly. His successor was Dr. Sarvepalli Radhakrishnan, a distinguished philosopher, who was followed by Zakir Hussain, a senior Muslim Congressman.[8]

Convinced that her opponents in the undivided Congress sought to use the power of the president to challenge her position and remove her from office, Indira Gandhi broke with her party in the 1969 presidential election and supported the candidacy of V.V. Giri, the vice president and former labor leader. Her actions led to a historic split in the Congress party. Despite Giri's desire for a second term, however, Indira Gandhi insisted on selecting Fakhruddin Ali Ahmed, a seventy year old Muslim and veteran Congressman from the small state of Assam, known for his strong personal loyalty to the prime minister. This loyalty proved to be critical in 1975 when Ahmed meekly signed Indira Gandhi's declaration of a national emergency. Upon his death in 1977, the newly elected Janata government selected N. Sanjiva Reddy.

Following Indira Gandhi's return to power in the 1980 elections, Reddy resigned as president and was replaced by Indira loyalist Zail Singh, a Sikh with limited formal education, background or stature. Zail Singh's loyalty to the Nehru dynasty was demonstrated by the speed with which he appointed Rajiv Gandhi as prime minister following the assassination of his mother. Both R. Venkataraman and Shankar Dayal Sharma, successors to Zail Singh, were former vice presidents and loyal Congressmen who presented little threat to Rajiv Gandhi and Narasimha Rao.

The election of vice president K. R. Narayanan, a seventy-seven year old former scholar, diplomat and Congress politician from Kerala, as India's first Dalit president in 1997 appeared to mark an important turning point in the history of the development of the Indian presidency. For the most part, Indian presidents had been prepared to play the role of titular head of state and act without question on the advice of prime minister and cabinet. Narayanan, however, became the first activist president since independence. On 22 October 1997 he became the first president to send back for reconsideration a cabinet recommendation to declare president's rule under Article 356 in the state of Uttar Pradesh. On 25 September 1998 he returned a second BJP cabinet recommendation to declare president's rule in the state of Bihar. The president justified his actions based on his understanding of a Supreme Court decision in 1994 that laid down guidelines for the exercise of president's rule under Article 356 of the constitution. These guidelines included a stipulation that state governments should not be dismissed unless a situation existed in which the government cannot be carried on in an effective manner and that in all cases the support of a government must be tested on the floor of the legislative assembly in the state. The president also used his position to criticize the behavior of state governors and recommend an increase in Scheduled Castes and Scheduled Tribes representation on the Supreme Court. He went as far as to admonish senior judges for overlooking 'eligible' candidates from these groups.

DECLINE OF PARLIAMENT

The emergence of strong prime ministers has been accompanied by a decline in the role of parliament. The erosion of the authority of the Indian parliament, however, has not been solely a function of prime ministerial behavior but has also been due to changes in the composition, roles and methods of the legislature itself. In the early years of the republic under Nehru and Shastri, the Indian parliament was treated with deference and respect by the prime minister, the cabinet, the press and the public. The legislature was staffed by distinguished men and women who were also outstanding parliamentarians. Like the executive branch and other institutions in India, the parliament from 1952 to 1962 was dominated by prominent leaders of the nationalist movement who were largely Western-educated, high caste, urban-based lawyers. Although the opposition was small, it drew from the same social base and was treated with great respect by Nehru and Shastri who made it a point to be present on the floor of the house.[9]

The decline of parliament did not begin until the 1960s. A major change in the composition of the Indian parliament began with the election of the third Lok Sabha in 1962. As a result of the increasing impact of mass franchise, the number of rural-based agriculturists increased sharply and replaced the more urban-based lawyers as the dominant force in parliament. This process of ruralisation was accelerated following the split in the Congress and the rise in the strength of opposition parties. As the composition of the parliament changed, debates came to focus on more intensely local and indigenous issues rather than foreign policy and national issues.

The changes in the composition of parliament were accompanied by increased prime ministerial neglect of the legislature and an alteration in parliamentary style and method. Indira Gandhi all but ignored the parliament and centralised power in the hands of the prime minister. The centralisation and personalisation of power in the hands of the prime minister resulted in executive inroads in the jurisdiction of parliament.

Parliament's law-making role gave way to executive ordinance; budgets were passed with little serious debate or review, and accountability of the executive to the parliament declined. Increasingly the prime minister and the cabinet decided all important matters and parliament simply ratified these decisions with little, if any, serious debate.

With the change in composition, previously developed rules, conventions and traditions of the parliament were also increasingly ignored. Discussions were marked by 'pandemonium and procedural wrangling' which resulted in the suspension of sixty-three members of the opposition and the adjournment of the house eight times in a single day.[10] Finance bills were passed with almost no debate and members increasingly became preoccupied with regional, local and patronage issues. The Ninth Lok Sabha, for example, passed a bill increasing pensions, allowance and facilities for Members of Parliament (MPs), including proportionate pensions for life for all MPs upon completing only one year as a member.[11] The president, however, refused to assent to the bill. The Twelfth Lok Sabha went much further when MPs agitated to retain their quotas for giving out telephones and gas connections following an adverse court decision and a minister asked Coal India, a public sector corporation, to provide private taxis to all MPs who were members of the consultative committee attached to his ministry.[12]

An even more disconcerting development has been the growing criminalisation of politics in India. Although the problem has been much more acute at the state level, especially in states like Bihar and Uttar Pradesh, the problem has now reached the national level as well. According to the Indian Election Commission, some forty members of parliament and almost 700 members of state legislative assemblies faced criminal charges or had been convicted of crimes in the early 1990s.

ERODING POSITION OF THE BUREAUCRACY

Despite initial nationalist hostility toward the Indian Civil Service (ICS), the Congress retained the framework of the British colonial bureaucracy and the ICS tradition of administration.[13] Although Nehru believed that the system needed an overhaul and maintained a distant and unenthusiastic relationship with the bureaucracy, the Indian Administrative Service (IAS), the successor to the ICS, lobbied effectively to defeat threats to its interests. Under the full impact of a highly interventionist state, moreover, the size of the bureaucracy mushroomed from 1.5 million in 1953 to 4.1 million in 1996 and the number of government ministries almost doubled from 17 in 1947 to 33 in 1991. The system became increasingly complex, while superfluous levels slowed down decision-making and coordination became more and more difficult to achieve.[14] The result was excruciating delays and increasing levels of corruption.

The erosion of the Indian bureaucracy began in the early 1970s when Indira Gandhi began to make political loyalty to the prime minister and the party part of the reward structure of the civil service.[15] The process of political interference accelerated under the emergency from 1975 to 1977, and was followed by a new tradition of punitive transfers with each change of government. Rajiv, like his mother, shared Nehru's attitudes toward the bureaucracy and his treatment of civil servants had a significant demoralising effect. Under Rajiv, frequent transfers of bureaucrats became common place, promotion lists were altered, seniority was ignored, and high-level officials were publicly humiliated.

The ICS tradition again came under threat in the 1990s as public confidence in the bureaucracy reached an all-time low. Ministerial incompetence and venality gutted administrative effectiveness and corruption began to reach even the higher echelons. The combined impact of these changes has resulted in a sharp decline in morale, deterioration in standards of efficiency, ineffective policy implementation and decline in overall administrative effectiveness.[16]

SUPREME COURT AND THE JUDICIAL SYSTEM

The Supreme Court of India stands at the apex of a single integrated judicial system. The Supreme Court is responsible for interpreting and guarding the Constitution and ensuring that all legislation is in conformity with it. Since the Parliament can negate court decisions and alter the jurisdiction of the Court by simply passing amending legislation, the scope of the Indian Supreme Court is not as wide as it is in the United States. When the courts challenged important land reform legislation during the Nehru era, for example, the government simply passed a series of constitutional amendments to free land reform legislation from court jurisdiction.

The first serious challenge to the courts, however, came when Indira Gandhi tried to block judicial review of constitutional amendments in the name of social justice, attempted to establish the supremacy of parliament over the courts and reversed the tradition of appointing the senior-most judge as chief justice by superseding three senior judges. Although her actions were seen as politically motivated, Indira Gandhi defended her court reforms as essential to the interest of social justice.

The virtual capitulation of the Supreme Court to political pressure during the 1975–77 emergency played a major role in eroding the credibility of the Court in the eyes of the public, the press and opposition political leaders. In an effort to rehabilitate itself, the Supreme Court began playing a more active and independent role in promoting social and economic justice in the post-emergency period. Led by Justices V. R. Krishna Iyer and P. N. Bhagwati, the Court began hearing petitions from the poor and downtrodden by expanding the protection of fundamental rights and personal liberties and promoting public interest litigation (PIL).[17] The result has been a tremendous expansion and protection of civil, political, economic and social rights against arbitrary encroachments by the state. The courts have intervened on behalf of bonded laborers, tribals, women, the homeless and those awaiting trial. In the early 1990s, the Court became even more activist by becoming involved in combating corruption and promoting good governance.

The new activism of the courts has been one of the most promising institutional developments in India. It represents one of the few examples of institutional resurgence since independence. Given the decline of parliament and the rising power of the executive, the courts have attempted to fill the gap and become a new instrument for the enforcement of accountability. It also offers hope that other institutions of government that have experienced decay can be rehabilitated and become capable of restoring effective and responsive governance in India.

MASS MOBILISATION OF PARTICIPATION

The process of institutional decay in India has been complicated by the rapid rise of mass mobilisation, political consciousness and participation. The Indian Constitution provides for universal adult suffrage, and the Sixty-First Amendment, passed in 1988, lowered the voting age from 21 to 18. The absolute size of the Indian electorate has more than tripled, increasing from 173 million in 1952 to 605 million in 1998. Although voter turnout has averaged 57 percent since 1952, with a low of 45 percent in 1952 to a high of 64 percent in 1984; in absolute terms voter turnout has increased from 79 million in 1952 to 375 million in 1998.[18]

Contrary to electoral behavior in Western democracies, it is the poor in India who are more likely to vote and join political parties than the rich. The poor and especially the lower castes are more likely to believe that their vote will make a difference. Recent studies have shown that in 1972 only 38 percent of the poor voted, but by 1996 51 percent of the poor voted. This growing sense of political efficacy is reflected in the fact that while 42 percent of the lower castes in 1972 felt that their vote made a difference, this increased to 60 percent by 1996. Similarly, while rates of party membership of the Scheduled Castes increased from 13 percent in 1971 to 19 percent in 1996, party membership of the upper castes declined from 36 percent to 28 percent during the same time period.[19] The major factors influencing the rising political consciousness of the poor were a growing realisation that the state can play a vital role in dispensing public goods and an increasing awareness that politics can serve as a route to greater pride, dignity and confidence in protecting their interests.

FRAGMENTATION OF THE PARTY SYSTEM

Increased levels of mobilisation and participation, especially among the lower castes, have had a profound impact on the Indian party system. Over the past fifty years, the party system has been transformed from a stable one party dominant system to an increasingly fragmented, unstable, multi-party system based on alliance and coalition politics. The most important factor responsible for this transformation has been the decline of the Congress party.[20] Electoral support for the Congress has declined from 48 percent in 1957 to an all time low of 26 percent in 1998. Over time, the Congress has been faced with a gradual erosion of its support base in the higher castes, Scheduled Castes, Scheduled Tribes and minorities, as each of these groups has begun to support other parties. The decline of the Congress has been paralleled by the disintegration of other national centrist parties and the relative stagnation of support for the communist parties. This fragmentation of national parties has been accompanied by the rise of the Hindu nationalist Bharatiya Janata Party and the increasing regionalisation of the party system.[21] As seen in Table 2, these changes in India's party system were clearly reflected in the 1998 and 1999 Lok Sabha elections. The erosion of support for national parties was demonstrated by the fact that the combined vote of India's two largest national parties – the Congress and the BJP – was only 52 percent of the total number of votes cast in 1999. The biggest gains were made by various regional parties and parties representing caste and communal identities. The BJP was able to form a government in 1998 by cobbling together an eighteen party coalition representing a number of these new political forces. This diverse coalition, however, was able to last only thirteen months. In September 1999 India was forced to go to the polls for the third time in three years.

In 1999, the pre-election coalition of twenty-four parties that the BJP cobbled together won a comfortable majority. The BJP, however, failed to make any substantial gains. Although the party was able to marginally increase its number of seats from 179 in 1998 to 182 in 1999, its vote total declined from 25.5 percent to 23.7 percent. This decline was primarily due to the fact that the BJP contested 50 fewer seats in 1999 in an effort to accommodate its allies. The electoral success of the BJP's allies reduced the BJP's share of coalition seats from 72 percent in 1998 to 61 percent in 1999 and resulted in the appointment of an unwieldy seventy member council of ministers.

REGIONALISATION OF PARTIES AND FEDERALISM

The increasing regionalisation of the Indian party system has not only contributed to political instability at the center but has also begun to have a profound effect on the development of Indian federalism. The Indian

Stanley A. Kochanek

Table 2: Lok Sabha Elections 1998 and 1999

Party	1998		1999	
	Seats Won	% Votes	Seats Won	% Votes
Bharatiya Janata Party (BJP)	179	25.47	182	23.7
BJP Allies[1]	73	11.94	117	17.1
	252	37.41	299	40.8
Congress(I)	141	25.88	112	28.5
Congress(I) Allies[2]	26	4.06	22	5.3
	167	29.94	134	33.8
United Front	97	21.80		
Other Parties[3]	18	6.03	104	25.4
Independents	5	1.98		
Total	539*	97.16[4]	537*	100.0

Notes: *The balance of 4 seats in 1998 and 6 seats in 1999 were filled later.
1. Major BJP allies and number of seats in 1999: Shiv Sena (15), Janata Dal (U) (20), Telugu Desam (29), DMK (12), Biju Janata Dal (10), Akali Dal (2), Trinamul Congress (8), Pattali Makkal Katchi (5), Marumalarchi DMK (4), Indian National Lok Dal (5), Loktantrik Congress (2), other parties with one seat each (5).
2. Congress (I) allies and number of seats: Rashtriya Janata Dal (7), AIADMK (10), Muslim League (2), Kerala Congress (M) (1), and Rashtriya Lok Dal (2).
3. Other parties and number of seats: CPI (M) (32), CPI (4), Samajwadi Party (26), Forward Bloc (2), Revolutionary Socialist Party (3), Bahujan Samaj Party (14), National Congress Party (7); Jammu & Kashmir National Conference (4), other parties and independents (12).
4. The balance of the votes were cast for parties that did not win any seats.

Source: The results of the 1998 elections were taken from the Indian Election Commission web site http://www.eci.gov.in/elec98/staticrep/1s221.htm, 21 May 1998. The results of the 1999 elections were taken from Frontline (Chennai), 5 November 1999, 120-123.

Constituent Assembly had created a parliamentary federal system which included a series of important unitary features that gave it a highly centralised form. From 1950 to 1967, center–state relations were based on a complex bargaining process that took place within the framework of the dominant Congress party, supplemented in the government by a series of constitutional and extra-constitutional devices. The result was a pattern of center-state relations known as cooperative federalism.

In the early years of the republic, these unitary features of the constitution were increasingly upset by the politics of mass franchise which gradually led to a federalisation of the Congress party and Indian politics. Within the Congress, a group of powerful state leaders or party bosses known as the 'Syndicate' emerged and came to play an increasingly important role. The power of the Syndicate was clearly demonstrated in the early 1960s during the succession process that followed Nehru's death in 1964 and the election of Lal Bahadur Shastri as prime minister. Although electoral defeats of several party bosses in the 1967 elections weakened the power of the Syndicate, the group was still able to play a major role in the selection of Indira Gandhi as prime minister in 1966 following Shastri's sudden death from a heart attack.

Indira Gandhi, however, was not prepared to accept the domination of the Syndicate and, once elected, challenged their position by employing populist rhetoric in an attempt to undermine their power. When the Syndicate attempted to constrain her, she split the party and concentrated power in her hands. Following her triumph over the Syndicate, Indira Gandhi proceeded to undermine all other potential institutional challenges to her power.[22]

As a centraliser who concentrated power in the hands of the prime minister, Indira Gandhi altered the federal character of both party and government. Party elections were abandoned, and all positions in both party and government became subject to the test of personal loyalty. The party president, the party executive, state party leaders, members of the cabinet and state Congress chief ministers served at her sufferance. While this system of centralisation and personalisation of power ensured that no one was in a position to challenge her authority; it also resulted in weak and ineffective leadership, the erosion of institutions, and an over-centralisation of power which exacerbated the structural incompatibility of a centralised party in a federal system. Indira Gandhi's style of leadership undermined Congress party support and fueled regional ethnic antagonism and nationalism. The results were numerous defections from the Congress, a Sikh revolt in the Punjab, a Muslim uprising in Kashmir, and the rise of regional parties that came to challenge Congress dominance. Both Rajiv Gandhi and Narasimha Rao attempted to follow Indira Gandhi's model of centralisation and personalisation of power with increasingly devastating consequences.

The over-centralisation of power by Indira Gandhi and Rajiv was especially demonstrated by the perceived partisan misuse of the power by the central government to declare President's Rule under Article 356 of the Constitution. From 1950 to 1966, President's Rule had been invoked a total of eight times due to the breakdown of government in a state. Under Indira Gandhi, it was invoked a total of forty-two times and this trend continued under Rajiv. President's Rule was invoked to resolve intra-party disputes, to restore political and administrative stability, to respond to mass upsurges against maladministration and to overcome political paralysis. The excessive use of President's Rule has become a major source of center–state friction. While many Indian politicians demand an outright repeal of Article 356, others demand its reform. Proposals for reform of Article 356 include the appointment of state governors only after consulting the chief minister of the state, greater impartiality and security of tenure for state governors, and the testing of legislative majorities on the floor of state assemblies.

By 1989, defection and defeat ended Congress dominance. The proliferation of regional parties, in turn, began to change the entire character of Indian federalism. Regional party leaders became major power-brokers in determining the composition of national governments which increasingly consisted of coalitions of regional parties. The rising political power of regional parties and leaders was reinforced by the impact of the policy of economic liberalisation adopted in 1991. Liberalisation enabled provincial governments to increasingly break free of the dictates of central planning and emerge as powerful independent actors in the economy, competing with each other for not only federal funds but also direct foreign investment. The combined impact of these changes has enabled the states to move away from the centralised federalism of the past toward an increasing regionalisation of India's parliamentary federal system. In the long run, this political transformation in Indian federalism may result in a re-negotiation of the federal compact that was established by the Indian Constituent Assembly in 1950.

BREAKDOWN OF NATIONAL CONSENSUS

Political, social, economic and global changes over the past fifty years have also eroded the once dominant national political consensus of the immediate post-independence period. During the Nehru era, from 1947–1964, Indians came to share a basic consensus supporting parliamentary democracy, socialism, centralized planning, secularism, social justice and non-alignment. Over the years, however, each of the pillars of this national consensus has been challenged by a combination of internal and external forces.

The first pillar of the Indian consensus to be challenged was the institution of parliamentary democracy. The breakdown came in 1975 when Indira Gandhi declared a national emergency and attempted to reshape the polity. Although this effort was reversed by the Janata government, the rise of alliance and coalition politics have led to increasing calls for replacing parliamentary democracy with a presidential system.[23]

The second pillar to fall was the policy of non-alignment. The end of the cold war and the breakup of the Soviet Union combined to totally undermine this guiding principle of Indian foreign policy. Although India has now become a nuclear weapons state, Indian foreign policy is preoccupied with relations with its neighbor Pakistan and has yet to redefine its place in an increasingly shrinking world.[24]

The third pillar of India's national consensus to be challenged was the country's commitment to secularism. By the late 1980s, the rise of Hindu nationalism and the Hindutva politics of the BJP had called into question the nature of Indian identity, secular nationalism and the principles guiding the organisation of the Indian state. The politics of *Mandir* (religion) effectively have replaced the economic ideological debates of the past in defining the left and the right of the political spectrum.[25]

The fourth pillar to be challenged was India's commitment to centralised planning and socialism. Despite almost fifty years of planning and the creation of a hegemonic public sector, 35 to 40 percent of the Indian population remained in abject poverty. Although India adopted a new economic policy in 1991 based on liberalisation, privatisation, greater reliance on markets and globalisation; the policy has encountered stiff resistance from key elements in the bureaucracy, major sectors of the business community, large numbers of intellectuals, the *swadeshi* lobby, trade unions, and politicians from both the left and the right.[26]

The final pillar of the national consensus of the Nehru era that has been brought into question has been the effort to achieve social justice through a policy of affirmative action for untouchables, tribals and 'Other Backward Classes' (OBCs) based on a system of fixed quotas or *reservations* applied to political representation, government jobs, and seats in educational institutions for these downtrodden groups. Although the principle of reservations was generally accepted in the case of Scheduled Castes and Scheduled Tribes, the issue was reopened and became politically explosive when Prime Minister V. P. Singh in August 1990 extended the benefits of reservations to the OBCs by implementing the recommendations of the Mandal Commission Report, made in 1980. The announcement politicised the issue of reservations and touched off a near caste war as India's upper castes saw their future job opportunities being eroded by the extension of this quota system.[27]

As a result of the breakdown of the national consensus of the Nehru era; the politics of Mandir, *Mandal* (code for caste) and markets (liberalisation) have come to dominate Indian political discourse and reshape party politics. While the issues of Mandir and Mandal intensified the struggle among contending groups in Indian society over the control of political power, state patronage and jobs; the shift in economic policy from centralised planning and socialism to open markets, liberalisation and privatisation threatened the distributional benefits of entrenched groups in the society. Liberalisation has also begun to create new opportunities and greater private space for the development of non-governmental sectors in the larger civil society.

In sum, the crisis of governance in India has been a result of the combined forces of institutional decay which has eroded the openness, transparency, effectiveness and accountability of public institutions; increased division and fragmentation of parties which has heightened political instability; the mobilisation of previously passive social groups that has intensified competition for control of state resources; a breakdown of national consensus that has contributed to a near paralysis in decision-making; and intensified conflict among social groups that has increased the level of violence and weakened the political system's ability to effectively manage conflict.

DEVELOPMENT OF CIVIL SOCIETY

To a limited extent some of the negative consequences of the crisis of governance in India have been counterbalanced by a variety of important changes that have been taking place in the larger civil society that offer increased hope for the country's future. Three of the most promising developments in the civil society have been the explosion of interest group activity, the expansion of private space brought about by the gradual retreat of a highly interventionist state and the growing strength of the country's independent media.

The Nehru era had been characterized by a strong national commitment to an interventionist state which was reflected in the overwhelming support for Nehru's socialist pattern of society. This statist bias first came into question as a result of the economic crisis of the 1960s, and accelerated as a result of the J.P. movement, the abuse of state power during the emergency, and the victory of the Janata Party in 1977. Post-emergency India witnessed an explosion of autonomous group activity. A whole new array of associations came into being and older groups attempted to reorganize and reorient their goals and objectives. From the late 1970s to the late 1980s India witnessed the emergence of non-party trade unions, farmers' movements, women's organisations, human rights and civil liberties groups, non-governmental organizations (NGOs) and a variety of other associations designed to help the poor, improve the environment and press for alternative development models. The explosive emergence of these groups was a result of growing dissatisfaction with the existing political order, the rapid growth of the Indian middle class, government and foreign donor support, the weakening of parties, and increased popular responses to specific government policies.[28]

By the late 1980s, however, the solidarity of this new wave of associations became threatened by the politics of Mandir, Mandal and markets which began to undermine the groups' solidarity and cohesion. The politics of Mandir and Mandal had an especially negative impact on the development of groups as members of demand groups such as those of students, women, farmers and trade unions. These groups became divided by the rise of identity politics based on caste and religion. Identity politics overwhelmed other interest based politics as individuals got pulled into the mobilisation for communal and caste competition.[29]

Other groups, however, grew and expanded their impact. One of the most important developments in India in this regard has been the rise of the

NGO sector. By the early 1990s India had an estimated 100,000 NGOs. The growth of the NGO movement came in several waves. The earlier wave of NGOs came in the immediate post-emergency period as groups became increasingly involved in welfare, relief, charity, health, education, appropriate technology and local planning. A second wave of NGOs emerged in the late 1970s to fight for women's rights, human rights, civil liberties, ecology, bonded labor, child labor and legal rights for the poor. A third wave of NGOs emerged in the 1980s to question the developmental benefits and environmental impact of major dam projects, power plants, road and railroad networks, and aquaculture. By the 1990s, however, the NGO movement also began to falter as critics charged them with a lack of coordination, excessive proliferation, politicisation, nepotism and a lack of accountability. The government sought greater control over their organisation and actions. Yet, there is no denying that the explosion of group activity in the post-emergency period has created a new political force and the strengthening of civil society.[30]

The advent of liberalisation and privatisation in the 1990s has also had its impact on Indian society, group development and the economy. Liberalisation and privatisation are designed to curtail the scope of India's over-extended interventionist state and refocus development priorities. Liberalisation has not only vastly increased the role of the private sector in trade and industry but has also extended the sphere of private action in other arenas. Due to liberalisation and severe budgetary restraints, the government has been forced to open up such areas as health, education, roads, airports and infrastructure to private sector development. This rapid increase in the scope of private sector activity has, in turn, fueled an increase in demand for a variety of professionals and private sector support services such as lawyers, doctors, accountants, consultants, computer programmers, and information technology specialists. As these new forces begin to organize, they are bound to begin to have an impact on the political process.

These changes have further expanded opportunities for the new Indian middle class that has emerged from the past fifty years of development. The middle class now numbers some 150 million and has helped fuel an explosion of new associations in virtually all sectors of civil society. Although only 13 percent of India's 980 million people claim to be members of associations, in absolute numbers this represents a constituency of almost 130 million. Most of this population is drawn from the rising middle class which has traditionally provided leadership in Indian society.[31]

RISE OF AN INDEPENDENT MEDIA

The emergence of a large middle class has also been accompanied by the rapid growth and development of both print and electronic media in India.

The rise of an independent media represents one of post-independence India's greatest achievements. Despite its low literacy rates, the number of daily newspapers has increased from 330 in 1954 to 4,558 in 1996 and circulation has exploded from 2,525,500 to 45,225,000 in the same time period. In addition, the number of periodicals has also increased dramatically from 3,203 to 37,830. The growth in newspapers and magazines has taken place both in the English language media and the vernacular languages. India has also developed a highly sophisticated and professional business and financial press that provides comprehensive coverage of both private and public sector economic issues.[32]

Although government censorship during the emergency of 1975 to 1977 marked the darkest period for the media in the post-independence period, the end of the emergency saw an explosion of media activity. A large number of new weekly national magazines came into existence, investigative reporting emerged as a device to enhance governmental accountability, and the media became more professional and independent. The press has increasingly resisted governmental pressures, has come to play an important role in fostering public interest litigation, and has been responsible for uncovering numerous cases of political corruption, police excesses and governmental abuse of power. The press has also become increasingly more vigilant and critical of government actions and some reporters have even gone to jail in their effort to expose abuse of power. While attempts to impose curbs on the freedom of the press have been thwarted, the press has not been totally free of governmental pressures. The problems that continue to plague the freedom of the press include the Official Secrets Act, the Constitution's emergency provisions, and the ability of the government to use its vast powers to harass the press.

At the same time, the growth of the print media has been outpaced by the phenomenal expansion of television and radio. Television now reaches an estimated 250 million viewers and satellite transmission has provided Indian viewers with a wide range of global information including the BBC and CNN. Although radio has expanded less rapidly due to the limited number of transmitters, growth has still been impressive.

CONCLUSIONS

On 15 August 1997 India celebrated the fiftieth anniversary of its 'tryst with destiny' in an atmosphere that was highly subdued. Yet, despite increased concern over India's growing crisis of governance, most observers saw the country's democratic experiment as a notable success. The Constitution and the country's democratic institutions had taken root and gained legitimacy. Despite its origins, the political system seemed to have adapted to the Indian environment. The country had made significant economic progress and, unlike China, had avoided acute famine. While some commentators called for a second republic of a presidential type, most saw the problem not as a crisis of the system but as a crisis of leadership. Those who saw the problem as a crisis of leadership focused on the need for constitutional reform which should include term limits for the president and the prime minister, electoral reform to reduce the number of parties, state funding of political parties to reduce corruption, the strengthening of the judiciary, smaller states, greater decentralisation of power to state and local bodies, and the creation of a new foreign policy and developmental consensus.

The Indian political system has proven to be remarkably resilient but remains fragile. India inherited a narrowly-based imperial regime based on low levels of political participation. The country has now outgrown that institutional legacy. While in the early post-independence period, the newly structured system proved resilient and succeeded in channeling, managing and reconciling conflict; the decay of institutions, increased fragmentation of the party system and heightened religious and caste identities threaten the system's ability to continue to perform this role. India's institutions of governance have been weakened and eroded by the centralisation and personalisation of power, rapidly expanding participation and the proliferating demands of an increasingly mobilised society. Its ability to meet this challenge requires effective leadership and a restoration of stable and effective government capable of managing these increased demands on the system. Given the diversity and pluralism of the country, however, it is clear that the creation of a more centralized and brittle system, as advocated by the BJP and sectors of the urban elite, would be much less likely to succeed and could result in the balkanisation of the country.

NOTES

1 For detailed discussion of the problem of governance in India, see Paul R. Brass, *Politics of India since Independence* (Cambridge: Cambridge University Press, 1994); Atul Kohli, *Democracy and Discontent: India's Growing Crisis of Governability* (Cambridge: Cambridge University Press, 1990); Satish Saberwal, *Roots of Crisis: Interpreting Contemporary Indian Society* (New Delhi: Sage Publications, 1996) and Bhabani Sen Gupta, *India: Problems of Governance* (New Delhi: Konark Publishers, 1996).
2 James Manor, 'How and Why Liberal and Representative Politics Emerged in India', *Political Studies* 38, 1990, 20–38.
3 For an extremely well-written history of the Indian Constituent Assembly, an analysis of the constitution it created, and a review of constitutional change in India since independence, see Granville Austin, *The Indian Constitution* (New York: Oxford University Press, 1966) and *Working a Democratic Constitution: A Window into India* (New Delhi: Oxford University Press, 1999).
4 For an analysis of the role of the prime minister in India, see James Manor, ed., *Nehru to the Nineties: The Changing Office of Prime Minister in India* (Vancouver: University of British Columbia Press, 1994).
5 See Henry C. Hart, ed., *Indira Gandhi's India: A Political System Reappraised* (Boulder, Colorado: Westview Press, 1976).

6. See C.P. Bhambhri, *The Janata Party: A Profile* (New Delhi: National Publishing House, 1980).
7. For a detailed treatment of major political issues in the late 1980s and 1990s, see the annual collection of essays in Marshall M. Bouton and/or Philip Oldenburg, eds., *India Briefing* (Boulder, Colorado: Westview Press).
8. See James Manor, 'The Prime Minister and the President', in Manor, *Nehru to the Nineties*, 115–37.
9. See Subhash Kashyap, *The Ten Lok Sabhas: From the First to the Tenth, 1952–1991* (Delhi: Shipra Publications, 1992).
10. Subhash C. Kashyap, 'Parliament: A Mixed Balance-Sheet', in Hiranmay Karlekar, ed., *Independent India: The First Fifty Years* (Delhi: Oxford University Press, 1998), 39.
11. Ibid., 40.
12. T. N. Ninan, 'A Year in Purgatory', *Seminar*, no.473, January 1999, 25.
13. David C. Potter, *India's Political Administration, 1919–1983* (Oxford: Clarendon Press, 1986).
14. O.P. Dwivedi and R.B. Jain, 'The Administrative State in India', in Yogendra K. Malik and Ashok Kapur, *Fifty Years of Democracy and Development* (New Delhi: A.P.H. Publishing Corporation, 1998), 18.
15. David Potter, 'The Prime Minister and The Bureaucracy', in Manor, *Nehru to the Nineties*, 74–93.
16. P.C. Alexander, 'Civil Service: Continuity and Change', in Karlekar, *Independent India*, 60–72.
17. Poornima Advani, *Indian Judiciary: A Tribute* (Delhi: HarperCollins, 1997).
18. David Butler, Ashok Lahiri, and Prannoy Roy, *India Decides: Elections 1952–1995* (Delhi: Books and Things, 1995).
19. *New York Times*, 25 April 1999.
20. For the decline of the Congress Party, see Stanley A. Kochanek, *The Congress Party of India* (Princeton, N.J.: Princeton University Press, 1968).
21. For the rise of the BJP, see Thomas Blom Hansen and Christophe Jaffrelot, eds., *The BJP and the Compulsions of Politics in India* (Delhi: Oxford University Press, 1998); and Christophe Jaffrelot, *The Hindu Nationalist Movement and Indian Politics, 1925 to the 1990s* (Delhi: Viking, Penguin India, 1993).
22. Kochanek, *Congress Party*, 84–102.
23. For a review of the factors leading to Indira's political challenge, see Hart, *Indira Gandhi's India*.
24. For a brief overview of Indian foreign policy, see J.N. Dixit, 'Foreign Policy: A Critical Introspection', in Karlekar, *Independent India*, 73–91; and Selig S. Harrison, Paul H. Kreisberg, and Dennis Kux, eds., *India and Pakistan: The First Fifty Years* (New York: Cambridge University Press, 1999), 155–69.
25. See Romila Thapar 'Secularism: The Importance of Democracy', in Karlekar, ibid., 16–23.
26. For an excellent review of the major debates that have shaped India's economic policies since independence, see Terence J. Byres, ed., *The Indian Economy: Major Debates Since Independence* (Delhi: Oxford University Press, 1998).
27. Eleanor Zelliot, 'Fifty Years of Dalit Politics', in Malik and Kapur, *Fifty Years of Democracy*, 285–311.
28. For a review of social movements, see Tom Brass, ed., *New Farmers' Movements in India* (Newbury Park, UK: Frank Cass, 1995); Gail Omvedt, *Reinventing Revolution: New Social Movements and the Socialist Tradition in India* (Armonk, New York: M.E. Sharpe, 1993); Ghanshyam Shah, *Social Movements in India: A Review of the Literature* (New Delhi: Sage, 1990).

29 John McGuire, Peter Reeves, and Howard Brasted, eds., *Politics of Violence: From Ayodhya to Behrampada* (New Delhi: Sage Publications, 1996).
30 Noorjahan Bava, ed., *Non-Governmental Organisations in Development: Theory and Practice* (New Delhi: Kanishka Publishers, 1997); D.L. Sheth and Harsh Sheth, 'The NGO Sector in India: Historical Context and Current Disclosure', in Kuldeep Mathur, ed., *Development Policy and Administration* (New Delhi: Sage Publications, 1996).
31 Pradeep K. Chhibber, *Democracy Without Associations: The Transformation of the Party System and Social Cleavages in India* (Ann Arbor: University of Michigan Press, 1999), 16.
32 Hiranmay Karlekar, 'Media: The Mirror and the Market', in Karlekar, *Independent India*, 504–34.

Chapter 2

The Fragile Base of Democracy in Pakistan

Samina Ahmed

On 12 October 1999, Chief of Army Staff General Pervez Musharraf overthrew the elected government of Prime Minister Nawaz Sharif, suspended the national and provincial legislatures, placed the constitution in abeyance, and arrested Sharif and his key associates in a bloodless coup. The military was given both a motive and an excuse to reimpose direct military rule for the fourth time in Pakistan's history by the political leadership's failure to successfully oversee the transformation of the political system from authoritarianism to participatory democracy. From the restoration of democracy in 1988 to the military coup of 1999, despite the presence of elected governments, the constitutional framework remained weak and ineffective, and democratic norms failed to take root. Regrettably, little progress was made towards accommodating internal pressures and demands for socio-economic equality and a pluralistic, participatory system. As a result, Sharif's declining domestic legitimacy gave a disgruntled and ambitious military leadership an opportunity to assume direct control of the state.

The military's success in derailing the democratic process and the failure of the political leadership to create and to sustain a viable democratic order has its roots in Pakistan's political history. Ever since Pakistan's inception as an independent state, unrepresentative and authoritarian leaders have repeatedly intervened and captured state power. Despite this, authoritarian intervention has failed to gain popular legitimacy and support. To retain and expand their control over the state, authoritarian regimes have created centralised mechanisms of control which have been violently opposed by the country's multi-ethnic population. When popular pressures and ethnoregional divisions threaten regime stability, authoritarian rulers have reluctantly conceded to popular demands for representative rule and political pluralism. However, the willingness of political leaders to accept constraints on their functioning in return for a transfer of power; and when in power, their failure to respect democratic norms and democratic institutions make them vulnerable once again to authoritarian manipulation and intervention.

At the dawn of the twenty-first century, once again under military rule, Pakistan stands at a crossroads. The outcome of the struggle between supporters of the centralised, autocratic status quo and proponents of federal, democratic functioning could either lead to the perpetuation of authoritarian control or to the institutionalisation of democratic governance. Ultimately, the ability of the state's managers to withstand or to meet popular demands for a federal democracy will determine the extent to which Pakistan's citizens will accept the state's legitimacy.

This chapter examines political developments in Pakistan in a historical context, analysing the nature of direct or covert authoritarian interventions with the intention of understanding the imperatives that have shaped its present political order. Particular emphasis is placed on identifying the mechanisms, both constitutional and extra-constitutional, that have been utilised by successive rulers to acquire domestic legitimacy or ensure regime survival. The post-1998 period will be examined in detail to identify the structural weaknesses of Pakistan's democratic order that ultimately led to the return of the man on horseback. Finally, the character of the current military dispensation will be critically examined so as to assess its impact on the future of democracy in Pakistan.

MILITARY–BUREAUCRATIC RULE AND THE EX-COLONIAL STATE

The weakness of democratic institutions and the frequency of authoritarian interventions in Pakistan can be traced back to its colonial past as well as the political imperatives of its post-independence political, social and economic elite.[1] The Westminster model of parliamentary democracy was familiar to the Pakistani political leadership due to the British colonial experience.[2] The Muslim League leadership was equally familiar with the British viceregal structure of hierarchical, centralised control.[3] Having gained independence less than a decade after they launched their movement for Pakistan, the Muslim League leadership, composed mainly of *muhajirs* (migrants) from north and west India, lacked a support-base in the areas that constituted Pakistan.

The ruling party therefore opted to perpetuate colonial practices and mechanisms of centralised control over the new multi-ethnic state, aware that representative institutions and a devolution of authority would weaken its hold over political power. For instance, Pakistan's founder, Mohammad Ali Jinnah preferred the post of head of state, namely the governor general, to that of prime minister – in effect opting to inherit the viceroy's powers of centralised control and absolute authority. After Jinnah's death in 1948, his prime minister, Liaquat Ali Khan, followed Jinnah's example of centralised decision-making, relying on the inherited administrative institutions to govern the state.

The constitutional framework devised by the Muslim League reflected its internal preferences. Under the terms of the Indian Independence Act of 1947, Pakistan's interim constitution was the amended Government of India Act of 1935 in the form of the Pakistan Provincial Constitution Order of 1947. It provided for a federal parliamentary state structure but one with highly centralised features and minimum autonomy for the federating units.[4]

The Muslim League also failed to abide by its pre-partition promises of social and economic equity. Instead, its policies were motivated by a desire to consolidate and expand its limited support-base. To reward its main constituency, the muhajirs, the state adopted preferential policies that helped muhajir merchants in urban Sindh to dominate Pakistan's fledgling industrial economy. By the early 1950s, the Muslim League had also aligned itself with the indigenous Punjabi and Sindhi landowning elite in West Pakistan.

Lacking popular support, especially in the numerically dominant East wing; Muslim League governments held no general elections and instead relied on the coercive apparatus of the state to curb political dissent. As a result, the ruling party's domestic legitimacy was adversely affected, on the one hand.[5] On the other hand, centralised rule and coercive mechanisms of control resulted in enhanced demands by excluded ethno-regional actors for a devolution of power and introduction of representative rule. For instance, as early as 1948, when Bengali students challenged the Centre's intention to adopt Urdu as the sole national language, the government's attempt to forcibly suppress the movement contributed to Bengali perceptions of alienation and support for federalism and representative government.[6] In the West wing also, opposition grew against centralised control and unrepresentative rule, especially in Sindh and the Northwest Frontier Province where provincial governments had become hostages to the dictates of the centre. As the Muslim League's legitimacy eroded, it was forced to depend even more on the state bureaucracy to retain power.

Pakistan had inherited a military and civil bureaucracy whose primary task had been to suppress dissent in the colonial state. Socialised into mistrusting politicians under colonial rule, both the military and civil bureaucracy were contemptuous of the Pakistani political leadership. As the Muslim League's dependence on the state apparatus grew, the predominantly West Pakistan-based bureaucracy sidelined the political leadership with the support of the military high command.[7] The two bureaucracies then devised Pakistan's governing institutions in accordance with their institutional preferences.

MECHANISMS OF CENTRALISED CONTROL

After Liaquat's assassination in 1951, the internal balance of power shifted back from the prime minister to the head of state after a former bureaucrat, Ghulam Mohammad, became governor-general. Heading the federal government, the governor-general exercised complete control over the provinces as well as over the central legislature cum constituent assembly, whose deputies had been elected to the pre-partition provincial assemblies in the areas that now constituted Pakistan. There were no checks on the governor-general's authority, as he was also responsible for appointing the central judiciary. In the following period, prime ministers and cabinets were appointed and dismissed by the governor general, centralised rule became the norm, and federalism became non-existent.

The central legislature, functioning also as a constituent assembly, failed to perform its function of constitution-making due to disagreements between legislators based in West and East Pakistan on issues such as the quantum of provincial autonomy that was to be devolved and acceptance of the numerical majority of the East wing. In 1954, a pliable superior judiciary supported the dismissal of the constituent assembly by Governor-General Mohammad.

Mohammad's successor, Iskander Mirza, a former defence secretary merged all of West Pakistan's provinces into one unit. Subsequently, under Mirza's guidance, a second constituent assembly prepared Pakistan's first constitution in 1956 and Mirza became Pakistan's first president. Although Pakistan was declared a federal republic, the 1956 constitution was closely modelled on the Government of India Act, 1935, giving the centre comprehensive control over provincial affairs. The concept of parity of representation between the two wings of the country, that is, equal seats in a unicameral national legislature, was given constitutional sanction to offset East Pakistan's numerical majority.

The 1956 constitution, moreover, violated the very essence of parliamentary democracy in that an unelected president was given the power to appoint and dismiss prime ministers, to summon and dissolve the national assembly, and to appoint and remove members of the superior judiciary.[8] Mirza created and dismissed governments at will, and postponed elections that were to be held on the basis of adult franchise. When general elections were finally scheduled for February 1959, even this facade of parliamentary democracy was dismantled by the military high command.

MILITARY INTERVENTION AND DOMESTIC DISSENT

The West Pakistan-based military had shared power with the civil bureaucracy since the mid-1950s. However, in October 1958 the military decided to assume direct control, unwilling to risk a possible turnover of power to the East Pakistani majority. Dismissing Mirza, army chief General Mohammad Ayub Khan took over first as chief martial law administrator and then as president. In a reversal of roles, the civil bureaucracy was delegated to being the junior partner, while a compliant judiciary upheld the imposition of martial law under the doctrine of necessity.[9]

The military regime was mistrustful of the political leadership, averse to democratic institutions, and supportive of centralised control over the multi-ethnic polity. Soon after its assumption of power, the Ayub regime imposed restrictions on political activity and used force to curb dissent. However, the imperatives of regime survival propelled efforts to gain internal legitimacy for its rule. The military regime proceeded to adopt democratic trappings, with Ayub claiming that socio-economic justice and the restoration of democracy were the primary objectives of the military take-over.[10] He abrogated the 1956 constitution, and in 1962 devised a new constitutional framework which created a facade of representative rule, even while it reinforced the institutional mechanisms for centralised control.

Under the 1962 constitution, the president was both head of state and government and there were no checks on his powers. The unicameral federal legislature, or the National Assembly, was composed of indirectly elected members. It was subordinate to the president who could veto legislation and summon or dismiss the legislature.[11] The judiciary was deprived of the authority to interpret the constitution or to enforce fundamental rights. While the 1962 constitution formally accepted the principles of federalism, all-important political and economic powers were vested in the centre. The concept of legislative parity was retained and the western 'One Unit' was kept intact. The regime also devised an electoral system under quasi-elected representatives, the Basic Democrats, who elected Ayub as president in 1965. However, the military's support-base remained limited to the West wing where its domestic constituencies included the industrial elite, the beneficiaries of the military's economic policies, and the landowning class, who had also benefited from state patronage. Large sections of West Pakistani society, including students, journalists, lawyers and industrial labour rejected the regime.

After restrictions were removed on the functioning of political parties, resistance to the Ayub regime took a more organised shape, particularly in the East wing. Under-represented in the military, the Bengalis had been excluded from policymaking and the spoils of office. At the same time, the exploitation of the East wing's resources for the development of the West had led to widespread alienation and the growth of support for the East Pakistan-based Awami League's demands for maximum provincial autonomy.[12] By the late 1960s, the opposition in both wings joined hands and launched a movement for the restoration of democracy. As the movement gained momentum, the military ousted Ayub in March 1969, replacing him with army chief Yahya Khan who took over as both chief martial law administrator and president.

Once again, the military faced the dilemma of maintaining its political dominance in the face of popular demands for representative government and provincial autonomy. Yahya claimed that the sole aim of his administration was to ensure a 'smooth transfer of power to the representatives of the people'.[13] The 1962 constitution was abrogated and replaced by the Legal Framework Order of 30 March 1970. The latter outlined the principles for a future constitution, including maximum provincial autonomy and a system of checks and balances. One Unit was dissolved and Pakistan's first general elections were held in December 1970.

The elections were held on the assumption that no political party would emerge with a clear parliamentary majority.[14] The regime had also assumed that elections would restore the military's legitimacy and mollify domestic dissent. The Awami League, however, won an overwhelming victory in the East wing, gaining a two-thirds majority in both the provincial and federal parliaments. The Punjabi-dominated military's refusal to honour the election verdict, its institution of treason cases against the Awami League leadership, and its subsequent use of force to quell widespread East Bengali protests led to a civil war in which Indian intervention spelled an end to Pakistani control over the East wing and led to the independence of Bangladesh.

SEARCH FOR STATE LEGITIMACY

The military's humiliating defeat in the India–Pakistan war in 1971 and its awareness that continued authoritarian rule would be strongly resisted resulted in a transfer of power to civilian hands. Opting against new elections, the military decided to appoint Ayub's estranged foreign minister, Zulfikar Ali Bhutto, as chief martial law administrator and president. Bhutto's party, the Pakistan People's Party (PPP) had won a majority of seats in the West wing in the 1970 elections on a platform of socio-economic equity. Facing the dual challenges of preventing yet another military intervention and re-establishing state legitimacy, Bhutto's response was dictated by internal constraints on his government's functioning as well as by his preference for the 'centralisation of authority in his person'.[15]

To re-establish state legitimacy, the new government opted for the creation of constitutional mechanisms for democratic functioning and the devolution of power. The 1973 constitution was framed with the collective consensus of all political parties in the national assembly. All provinces gained equal representation in the upper house, or Senate, in a bicameral legislature. The prime minister was elected by and accountable to the lower house making the legislature sovereign for the first time in

Pakistan's political history. The 1973 constitution also provided for the separation of the judiciary from the executive within three years of the constitution coming into force and the judiciary was given the authority to review executive actions.[16] Fundamental rights were also provided for citizens.

Although the checks and balances and the devolution of power contained in the 1973 constitution went further than any previous framework for governance, its provisions also reflected both Bhutto's and the military's preference for centralised control. Considerable power was vested in the executive. Judges of the Supreme and High Court were appointed by the executive, albeit in consultation with the chief justices of the superior courts, and the executive could overrule judicial authority if a state of emergency was declared.[17] The centre's administrative and fiscal authority over the provinces offset the decentralisation of legislative power. Continued federal control over provincial financial resources was particularly significant since it pre-empted any future provincial attempt to reallocate expenditure from defence to development.[18]

Having formally restored democracy, Prime Minister Bhutto ignored the task of institution-building and honoured democratic norms in their breach. The ruling party itself was not organised along democratic lines since Bhutto was unwilling to tolerate dissent. The coercive apparatus of the state was used to quell political opposition as the PPP government went back on its electoral pledges of socio-economic justice. For example, Bhutto's pledge to restructure land ownership remained unfulfilled, while alliances of expediency were reached with the large landowners who were included in the cabinet. Although the government nationalised a number of key industries with the declared goal of redressing economic inequalities, the state used force against workers agitating for improved terms of employment in the private sector.[19]

As his domestic legitimacy declined and facing a resurgent political opposition, Bhutto attempted to retain control through a series of constitutional amendments that violated democratic principles and undermined representative institutions. The First Amendment, for instance, gave the executive the power to ban political parties on grounds of national security. The Third Amendment extended the period of preventive detention and the duration of a state of emergency, eroding fundamental rights. The Fourth and Fifth Amendments undermined the judiciary's autonomy, making it vulnerable to executive manipulation.[20]

Bhutto was partially successful in asserting his authority over the civil bureaucracy through the withdrawal of constitutional guarantees of employment. However, he refrained from asserting civilian control over the military for fear of a backlash. Despite its defeat in the 1971 war, the military had basically remained intact since the conflict had not extended to the West wing. Bhutto's policy of consistently increasing defence expenditure to retain the military's support resulted in a rapid expansion of the size of the armed forces. At the same time, Bhutto's neglect of democratic institutions and preference for coercion over democratic bargaining further empowered the military.

In Baluchistan and NWFP, where opposition Baluch and Pakhtun coalitions had come to power, Bhutto dismissed the provincial governments and banned the main opposition party, the National Awami Party. When Baluch dissidents resisted the centre's intervention, military operations were launched in 1973 that lasted until the end of the PPP government, increasing the government's dependence on the military. In Sindh, Bhutto's attempts to reward his Sindhi constituency through affirmative action policies were opposed by the muhajirs, who had long benefited from military-bureaucratic patronage. In the Punjab, right-wing parties opposed the PPP. When the Pakistan National Alliance, an alliance of muhajir-based religious parties, bazaar merchants and industrialists launched an agitation against alleged rigging in divided Pakistan's first general election of 1977, tacit support was provided by an ambitious military leadership. As the agitation intensified, on 5 July 1977 Chief of Army Staff General Mohammed Ziaul Haq overthrew the government and imposed martial law.

MILITARY RULE AND REGIME SURVIVAL

The Zia regime faced the same challenge as its authoritarian and undemocratic predecessors – an inability to acquire domestic legitimacy despite a preponderance of state power. Soon after the 1977 coup, the military tried to gain legitimacy and to contain domestic dissent by pledging a return to democratic rule.[21] When the general election was repeatedly postponed, there was a reassertion of political opposition, particularly after Bhutto's execution in April 1979. Forcibly suppressing dissent, the regime now claimed that the enforcement of Islam had to take priority over elections and the restoration of democracy.

To retain power, the Zia regime depended primarily on its own constituency, the armed forces, which were inducted into every civilian institution. The bureaucracy was also coopted, albeit in the role of a junior partner. The Zia regime forged alliances with sections of the socio-political elite, including the *ulema* (religious scholars), religious parties and groups that stood to gain the most from the islamisation process. Right-wing parties such as the Pakistan Muslim League (PML) entered into alliances of convenience with the military regime against the liberal and left opposition, which was led by the PPP.

The regime was also supported by small and medium-scale industrialists and merchants, who benefited from state patronage as well as from a flourishing informal economy fed by the cross-border trade in arms and drugs, a by-product of Pakistan's involvement in the Afghan civil war. Large landowners formed another domestic constituency for the regime, serving alongside industrialists and merchants in nominated bodies such as the Majlis-e-Shoora (the Federal Consultative Assembly). With the support of selected political partners, the military also created nominated bodies at the local and regional levels.

Political parties became progressively weaker due to the curbs on their functioning and as a result of the military's establishment of patron-client relations through nominated local bodies and within a nominated parliament. These divide-and-rule strategies were used by the military against the political opposition that had joined hands in alliances such as the Movement for the Restoration of Democracy. However, legitimacy continued to evade the military regime while political and ethno-regional polarisation threatened the stability of a weak state. Sectarian conflict became endemic as a result of Zia's policies, which included the extension of patronage to selected Sunni fundamentalist allies against the Shia minority which opposed Zia's attempts to enforce an extremist Sunni version of Islam.

Internal divisions along political, ethnic and sectarian lines were inevitable in the absence of constitutional governance and the absence of representative mediating institutions. Rule of law also became a casualty due to the judiciary's inability to provide a check against arbitrary authority. The Supreme Court, for instance, dismissed Bhutto's widow Nusrat Bhutto's case against General Ziaul Haq under Article 6 of the 1973 constitution which stated that any attempt to subvert the constitution would amount to 'high treason'.[22]

The strongest challenge to the centralised unitary rule of the Punjabi-dominated military came from Bhutto's home province of Sindh where support for federal pluralism and the restoration of democracy was widespread. Adopting a policy mix of coercion and co-optation, the Zia regime launched military operations against the Sindhi opposition while tacit support was provided to the Muhajir Quami Movement (MQM), a party that emerged in 1986 out of the All-Pakistan Muhajir Students Organisation.

Zia also attempted to gain constitutional sanction for his regime by distorting the 1973 constitution that had been suspended, and not abrogated, following the military takeover. In 1984, in a referendum conducted by the military administration, Zia laid claim to the status of elected president. The following year, the Zia regime held partyless elections for a bicameral central legislature as well as for all four provincial assemblies in which the military determined the eligibility of candidates. Under a nominated prime minister, Mohammad Khan Junejo, the parliament passed the Eighth Amendment to the 1973 constitution, the Revival of the 1973 Constitution Order of 1985, fundamentally weakening parliamentary democracy by removing all checks on an unelected president, who was given the authority to dismiss an elected prime minister and legislatures.[23] The president could also appoint the chief justices of the superior courts as well as provincial governors who, in turn, appointed provincial chief ministers with the president's approval. As a result of the Order, Zia's Islamic legislation was given constitutional sanction, all martial law orders and regulations were provided constitutional cover, and Zia was allowed to retain the position of president and the Chief of Army Staff.

Even within the nominal democratic system set up by the military, there soon emerged a conflict between Zia and his nominated prime minister who was under pressure from his political constituents to restore democratic governance. Zia responded by dissolving the national assembly and dismissing Junejo. The military regime once again pledged to hold elections and restore democratic institutions. On 17 August 1988, however, Zia was killed in a mid-air explosion, bringing to an end the longest continuous military rule in Pakistan.

DEMOCRACY RESTORED: CONTINUITY OR CHANGE?

Zia's death marked a major turning point in Pakistan's political history since it led to the formal transfer of power from military to civilian authority. However, the manner in which power was transferred to an elected leadership and the ways in which that power was exercised, created a political system that was marked more by continuity than change. From 1988 until the re-imposition of military rule in 1999, three elected governments were dismissed by the military, distorting the political process by undermining democratic institutions and hampering democratic functioning. The civilian leadership, on its part, proved incapable of resisting military intervention for a number of reasons. This failure ultimately resulted in the military high command supplanting civilian authority in October 1999.

The political polarization of the Zia years continued to mar relations between elected governments and their opposition. Governments were dismissive of the need for democratic bargaining and consensus in parliament. Moreover, successive elected governments accorded priority to survival in power over democratic rule, ignoring constitutional governance and norms. In fact, constitutional checks and balances on the three organs of the state – the executive, the legislature and the judiciary – were constantly eroded, thereby weakening the efficacy as well as the domestic legitimacy of parliamentary democracy. Democratic norms were also ignored by the opposition, which used all means at its disposal to dismiss ruling governments against their political opposition. It also followed past practices of condoning authoritarian intervention.

Democratic institutions remained fragile since the civilian leadership failed to revive the political party system, a major casualty of military rule. On the contrary, the perpetuation of patron-client relations and the personality-based politics of the Zia years, as well as an aversion to internal dissent, all contributed to weakening the support-base and organisational capacity of the political parties. As a result, a major barrier to military intervention – a strong and vibrant popular opposition – has failed to materialise.

Heightened regional, ethnic and sectarian tensions, yet another inheritance of the Zia years, continued to threaten the political stability of every elected government. Elected governments are as predisposed to coercive strategies over mediatory strategies as their authoritarian predecessors. As a result, internal divisions widened and sub-state violence intensified, forcing elected governments to depend on the armed forces to restore internal order. This dependence in turn repeatedly provided the military high command the pretext and opportunity to intervene.

The military, however, refrained from taking over direct control of the state since it was perceived that overt authoritarian intervention would adversely affect its corporate interests. The external environment was no longer supportive of military dictatorships in the third world. In the domestic context, the military high command assessed that direct military intervention would be strongly resisted, especially by assertive ethno-regional forces. The military high command devised a political system to control the functioning and the autonomy of elected governments. Even when the high command, with its mistrust and contempt for politicians, reluctantly handed over power to elected governments, it removed them when the latter were perceived as a threat to the military's interests. Thus, in structural terms, the 1988–1999 period was marked more by continuity than change since the military continued to determine the parameters within which elected leaders could perform, and the civilian leadership remained dependent on the military's tacit or overt support to form a government and/or to remain in power. In October 1999, when the high command perceived that the system they had themselves put in place no longer served their interests, they reimposed direct military rule.

RELUCTANT TRANSFER OF POWER

A transformed political order was put into place after Zia's death in August 1988. The military had reluctantly agreed to transfer power to civilian hands, conscious that continued authoritarian rule would be strongly resisted. However, the military was determined to retain its political dominance. Hence, in the run-up to elections in 1988, the military high command actively supported the formation of a nine-party alliance of right-wing and religious parties, the Islami Jamhoori Ittehad (IJI or Islamic

Democratic Alliance), spearheaded by Pakistan Muslim League's (PML) Nawaz Sharif who had served General Ziaul Haq as finance minister and chief minister of the Punjab.[24] In the elections, however, Benazir Bhutto's PPP, the party that had most strongly opposed the Zia regime, won a slim majority in parliament.

Deeply suspicious of the PPP, army chief General Aslam Beg, with the support of President Ghulam Ishaq Khan (a former bureaucrat and chairman of General Zia's senate) delayed the transfer of power until Benazir Bhutto agreed to work within the confines of a political arrangement acceptable to the military. A compromise was reached when Bhutto accepted a power-sharing arrangement that included non-intervention in the military's internal affairs as well as its guidance in sensitive policy areas such as defence, foreign policy and the economy.[25]

Benazir Bhutto accepted the military's dictates, unwilling to give up the opportunity to form a government. The resultant restrictions on her government's autonomy, however, undermined the PPP's domestic legitimacy as it failed, for example, to meet the demands of its constituents for socio-economic equity and development. On the contrary, in the hope of retaining the military's support, the government continued to allocate federal revenues for defence at the cost of development. Bhutto also failed to pay sufficient attention to the pressing task of reorganising her party and expanding its support base. Instead, alliances of expediency were reached with the landed and industrial elite who were given key party and parliamentary positions, tarnishing the PPP's popular image.[26]

Despite the PPP's willingness to accept its dictates, the military remained hostile to Bhutto and suspicious of her populist rhetoric. Even before the PPP government was midway through its term of office, the military high command decided to dismiss Benazir Bhutto. The IJI, a majority in the senate elected during the Zia regime, headed by Sharif's Muslim League, formed the Punjab provincial government. Impatient to acquire power, Sharif was more than willing to defy the government's authority with the military's encouragement and tacit support.

With its slim parliamentary majority, the PPP government became increasingly vulnerable to the military's divide-and-rule strategies, especially as its internal alliances unravelled. In the Northwest Frontier Province, the PPP's alliance with the Awami National Party (ANP) dissolved since the Pakhtun-dominated ANP favoured an end to Pakistani intervention in the Afghan civil war, while Bhutto was unwilling to oppose the military's preference for a continued interventionist role. In Sindh, the MQM was chosen by the military as its instrument to destabilise the PPP government.

The PPP had formed the government in Sindh in alliance with the MQM, which had obtained a majority of urban seats in the 1988 elections. The alliance came apart since Bhutto was hesitant to meet Muhajir demands that would have alienated her Sindhi support base. However, the military also played a direct role in breaking up the alliance, encouraging the MQM to withdraw its support to the PPP provincial government and to enter into an alliance with the IJI opposition. Following the break-up of the coalition government, the MQM violently challenged the PPP's authority in urban Sindh. Instead of enforcing the rule of law through judicial institutions to contain Muhajir militancy, the PPP chose to depend on the military to reassert its control over urban Sindh. As the government's dependence on the military increased, so did its vulnerability to military intervention.

Benazir Bhutto had inherited Zia's distorted constitutional framework by which a nominated president had the power to dismiss elected governments. Lacking a two-thirds majority in parliament, the government had failed to remove the Eighth Amendment, which became the instrument used by the military to dismiss Bhutto. At the high command's urging, President Ishaq Khan used his powers under the amendment and Article 58 (2) (b) to dissolve parliament and to dismiss the PPP government in August 1990, justifying the dismissal on grounds ranging from corruption to Bhutto's failure to restore law and order in Sindh.[27] The judiciary approved the ouster of the elected government as the Lahore High Court ruled that the president's action was constitutional in view of the atmosphere of political polarisation.[28]

SHAKY ALLIANCES

Nawaz Sharif, heading the IJI alliance, won the October 1990 general election held under the aegis of a shadow military administration and amidst opposition allegations of rigging. It won a two-thirds majority in the Punjab provincial assembly and also formed coalition governments in the NWFP and in Baluchistan. An industrialist himself, Sharif's domestic constituency included industrialists, traders and merchants. To reward its constituency, the IJI government adopted policies to deregulate the economy and to privatise government-owned economic assets.[29] The Punjabi-dominated Muslim League was also supported by the large landowners of the Punjab.

Having served the Zia regime in several senior capacities, Sharif was as convinced as his military mentor of the utility of religion as a means for gaining political legitimacy and mass support. Sharif reinforced Zia's Islamic legislation with a Shariah bill, thereby gaining the support of segments of the Sunni religious elite. As a consequence, sectarian violence once again increased between resurgent Sunni extremist organisations and their Shia opposition.

Ethnic divisions and tensions also remained high, especially in Sindh where the PML allied itself with the Muhajir population and was perceived to represent Punjabi interests by the Sindhis. In the general election, the PPP had won a majority of the Sindhi vote. In Sindh's urban centres, the MQM had emerged with its vote bank intact. Choosing to ignore democratic norms and resorting to divide-and-rule tactics, the Muslim League exploited the atmosphere of ethnic polarisation in the province and forged an alliance with the MQM to prevent the PPP from forming the Sindh provincial government. The subsequent use of force by Chief Minister Jam Sadiq Ali's government against the PPP's Sindhi support base resulted in widespread alienation against the Punjabi-dominated centre.[30]

The Muslim League's alliance with the MQM, however, proved short-lived as Sharif failed to meet MQM demands. This resulted in a resurgence of violence in the MQM-dominated urban centres of Sindh. Following the break-up of its alliance with the MQM in Sindh and facing a resurgent PPP opposition, the government resorted to force against its opponents. Following the example of the Zia dictatorship, the Sharif administration also attempted to strengthen its domestic hold through constitutional manipulation that violated democratic institutions and undermined the rule of law.[31]

Despite Sharif's close ties with the military and civilian bureaucracies, he incurred the high command's wrath since the prime minister attempted to challenge the military's imposed ground rules which included a tacit civilian acceptance of the institutional autonomy of the armed forces. Sharif's attempt to nominate his own candidate for the position of army chief after the sudden death of General Asif Nawaz Janjua in January 1993 was deeply resented by the military. Sharif's action would have influenced the internal power structure of a hierarchical military. President Ishaq, with a bureaucrat's suspicion and contempt for the political leadership, saw the prime minister's ambitions as a threat to his own authority. When the president appointed Abdul Waheed Kakar, the military's chosen candidate as Janjua's successor, the military decided to overthrow the government and was able to do so due to the deteriorating relationship between the prime minister and the president.[32]

Sharif's rift with Ishaq widened after he made public his decision to repeal the Eighth Amendment, which would deprive the president of his powers to dismiss a government. Instead of supporting Sharif's bid to remove Zia's legacy, the leader of the opposition, Bhutto, opted to side with the president in his move to destabilise the elected government. In April 1993, with the military's approval, Ghulam Ishaq Khan dismissed Prime Minister Sharif and dissolved the national assembly, using his powers under the Eighth Amendment. For the very first time in Pakistan's political history, the Supreme Court upheld the central government's appeal against its removal, a judgement that was perceived as partisan by the PPP opposition. Sharif's return, however, proved short-lived as army chief Kakar intervened directly, forcing both the prime minister and the president to resign in mid-1993, demonstrating the military's supremacy over civilian authority and raising doubts about the representative character of the post-1988 dispensation.

GROWING DIVISIONS

Once again, general elections were held under the aegis of a shadow military government. Benazir Bhutto's PPP won only a slim majority in the National Assembly and formed a fragile coalition government. It faced a strong opposition since the Pakistan Muslim League (Nawaz) (PML-N) formed coalition governments in the NWFP and Baluchistan. Although the PML-N won a majority of seats in the Punjab, the PPP succeeded in forming a coalition government in alliance with a breakaway faction of the Muslim League. The PPP's position appeared to strengthen when its candidate, Farooq Khan Leghari, a former bureaucrat, won the presidential polls.

As in her first tenure of office, Bhutto once again underestimated the importance of expanding and strengthening her support base to counter threats to her authority. The PPP's organisational capacity was not built up and the party, in fact, weakened as a result of internal schisms and divisions engineered by the prime minister's brother, Mir Murtaza Bhutto. Democratic institutions remained equally fragile as the prime minister chose to assert personalised control over policymaking, bypassing the party, her cabinet, and her parliamentary representatives. The attention of the government focused instead on ways of neutralising its political rivals. The opposition coalition government in the NWFP, for example, was ousted. When the Muslim League launched a retaliatory campaign to destabilise the central government, accusing the prime minister and her spouse of corruption, the government retaliated by registering cases of corruption against the Muslim League leadership.

In an atmosphere of acute political polarisation, the executive's relations with the judiciary also came under strain as Prime Minister Bhutto decided to appoint selected candidates to the superior judiciary to correct a perceived anti-PPP bias, demonstrated by the judicial decision to restore Sharif's government in 1993 while the PPP government's 1990 dissolution had been upheld.[33] The Supreme Court rejected the PPP-appointed judges, including that of Chief Justice Sajjad Ali Shah, claiming that the superior judiciary had become politicised and inefficient as a result of executive meddling. The rift between the two branches of state widened when the Bhutto government failed to meet Supreme Court demands for a time-bound separation of the executive and the judiciary.

However, it was ethnic violence in Sindh that was to pose the most serious threat to the government's authority. The Sindh provincial assembly elections had resulted in a PPP-majority in Sindhi-speaking constituencies. The MQM, which had boycotted the national assembly elections, swept the polls in the urban Muhajir-dominated areas. A short-lived alliance between the PPP and the MQM unravelled, resulting in a resurgence of violence in urban Sindh. Instead of finding appropriate political solutions for the crisis of governance in urban Sindh, the PPP attempted to forcibly suppress MQM dissent. As the violence escalated, the armed forces were called in to restore law and order. The MQM retaliated by joining forces with Sharif's Muslim League and its allies and the opposition staged nationwide demonstrations and strikes, calling for the government's dismissal. Bhutto managed to withstand the onslaught of the combined opposition, including charges of massive corruption and even accusations of connivance in the death of her estranged brother Murtaza Bhutto in a police encounter in September 1996. Deteriorating relations with the military, however, brought down the government even before it was little more than halfway through its tenure of office.

Bhutto's alliance of expediency with the military which had brought her back to power soon ended due to the prime minister's unsuccessful attempts to assert some civilian control over the institution, which included the effort to appoint her chosen candidate as army chief.[34] However, it was over the issue of Sindh that Bhutto's relations with the military deteriorated to the point that the high command decided, once again, to replace the elected government.

Bhutto's reliance on the military to control the insurgency in Sindh had made her government vulnerable to the military's dictates. Thus, the government acquiesced with the military's divide-and-rule strategies in Sindh, which included the creation of a rival faction of the MQM, the Haqiqis. Although the intensity of violence in urban Sindh increased due to the government's failure to find an acceptable political solution, the military high command demanded expanded powers, including judicial and investigative powers, from the executive. Realising the dangers in accepting the imposition of a partial martial law in the province, Bhutto refused the military's request.

Bhutto's refusal not only resulted in the military's decision to wind up its operations in Sindh, but army chief Jehangir Karamat also opted to side with the Sharif-led opposition. As the opposition campaign gained momentum, the prime minister chose to depend on the civil bureaucracy rather than on her cabinet or party to assert her authority.[35] This dependence proved fatal as her support-base shrunk even further while President Leghari, a former bureaucrat, chose to side with the military against his prime minister. On 5 November 1996 using his powers under the Eighth Amendment, Leghari dissolved the national assembly, dismissing the Bhutto government on charges ranging from extra-judicial killings in Sindh to corruption and interference in judicial appointments. Once again, the Supreme Court rejected the PPP's challenge of the national assembly's dissolution, claiming that the president had the constitutional right to dismiss a corrupt and inept government.[36]

RETURN TO VICEREGAL RULE

In the February 1997 elections, which were once again held under the military's supervision by interim prime minister and PPP-dissident Mehraj Khalid, Sharif's Muslim League won a majority in the national assembly and three-fourths of all Punjab assembly seats, once again amidst opposition allegations of rigging. Prime Minister Sharif's position was consolidated by the senate elections, following which the government acquired a two-thirds majority in parliament with the support of its allied parties, the MQM which had formed a coalition government with the Muslim League in Sindh and with the ANP, Sharif's partner in a coalition government in the NWFP. The PPP was virtually eliminated in the Punjab, the NWFP and Baluchistan, winning only 17 national assembly seats, although in Sindh the PPP managed to retain its support base.

Taking advantage of a weak opposition, in the tradition of Pakistani politics Sharif reverted to viceregal practices: ruling by decree, exercising centralised control over the provinces, overlooking the need for consensus with the opposition in parliament, and forcibly curbing political dissent. In fact, a special bureau, the *Ehtesab* (accountability) cell was set up, with the intention of disqualifying and thereby eliminating the PPP from the political process. Any number of corruption cases were registered against the PPP leadership including Bhutto and her husband Asif Zardari, who was also accused of conspiracy to assassinate Bhutto's brother.

Despite the political acrimony between the government and the opposition, the PPP co-operated with Sharif in passing the Thirteenth Amendment to the constitution in April 1997, repealing the provisions of the Eighth Amendment relating to the president's powers to dismiss the prime minister and to dissolve the national assembly. The president was also deprived of his authority to appoint the service chiefs and the governors of the provinces. Although a major distortion in the parliamentary system had been removed by restoring an elected prime minister's authority over a nominated president, Sharif failed to use his newly gained powers to strengthen democratic institutions and norms.

More concerned about consolidating and centralising power and authority than in reinforcing constitutional governance and norms, the government used its overwhelming parliamentary majority to push through a constitutional amendment that distorted the distribution of power between the executive and the legislature. In July 1997, the Fourteenth Amendment, an anti-defection bill, was passed which gave the political leadership the authority to expel parliamentary representatives who voted against party directives or breached party discipline. The amendment also deprived legislators of recourse to judicial appeal against such disqualification.[37] Parliamentarians were therefore deprived of the right to dissent and to vote according to their conscience.

Although a weak parliamentary opposition and an emasculated legislature posed no challenge to the prime minister's authority, the superior judiciary's role in upholding democratic norms took on a new significance when the assertive Supreme Court chief justice, Sajjad Ali Shah, rejected the government's attempt to establish a parallel system of justice through terrorist courts.[38] The PML-N government retorted by enacting a number of policies to curtail judicial autonomy. These included Sharif's rejection of the chief justice's nominees for vacant seats in the Supreme Court and attempts to reduce the size of the Supreme Court. When Chief Justice Sajjad retaliated by suspending the operation of the Fourteenth Amendment, the government successfully engineered a rift within the ranks of the superior judiciary. The chief justice was forced to resign and his successor was nominated by the prime minister. Soon after Sharif also removed President Leghari replacing him by a Muslim League loyalist, Rafiq Tarar.

Sharif's propensity to concentrate all power within his own person and in his party bore a number of consequences for democratic governance and political stability. In the past, concentration of power in the centre at the expense of the units had led to the disintegration of the state. Under Sharif, the concentration of power in the hands of a Punjabi prime minister who had little regard for provincial autonomy and who headed a Punjabi-dominated party increased alienation within the minority provinces. For instance, Sharif's support for the construction of a controversial hydro-electric project – the Kalabagh Dam which is opposed by the NWFP, Sindh and Baluchistan – is seen as evidence of his desire to develop the Punjab at the cost of the other provinces.[39] Resentment with the centre's perceived disregard for the constitutional distribution of power between the federal government and the provinces led to the formation of a new political alliance of key regional parties in all four provinces, the Pakistan Oppressed Nations Movement (PONAM). Advocating maximum provincial autonomy, PONAM launched a campaign for constitutional reform, proposing a constitutional amendment that would leave only foreign affairs, finance and defence with the centre.

Averse to the devolution of power, Sharif's government continued to pursue policies for more centralised power and authority. One of the most controversial measures proposed by the government was the Fifteenth Amendment to the constitution, or the Shariah Bill. Through this bill, which is ostensibly aimed at enforcing the supremacy of Islam in the state, Sharif hoped to gain the support of the right-wing and religious parties. The more significant aspects of the proposed amendment however centred on the concentration of absolute power in the federal government. The legislature, the judiciary, the provinces and even the constitution would become subordinate to the central executive authority. According to the chairperson of the Human Rights Commission of Pakistan, Asma Jehangir, the amendment 'virtually repeals the constitution. It strikes at the roots of the federal principles'.[40]

Alienated by Sharif's authoritarian policies, all major opposition parties adopted a unified stand in the senate against the Shariah Bill, forcing the government to postpone the passage of the amendment since it no longer commanded the requisite two-thirds majority in both houses of parliament after the dissolution of its parliamentary alliances with the ANP and the MQM. The break-up of these alliances was the result of Sharif's disregard for parliamentary consensus and for democratic norms. Sharif's refusal to accept a consensus resolution in the NWFP provincial assembly against the proposed Kalabagh dam was one of the factors that contributed to the break-up of the alliance with the ANP. The MQM withdrew its support in Sindh when the PML failed to abide by the terms of an alliance agreement.[41] Even during the PML–MQM coalition government, intra-Muhajir infighting had continued, resulting in scores of deaths, which had been overlooked by the government in the hopes of keeping the alliance intact. After the withdrawal of the MQM's support, Sharif's main objective was to prevent the PPP, the majority party in the province, from forming the government. Unrest in the province was used as the justification for him to impose Governor's rule.

The indefinite extension of central rule over Sindh removed any semblance of democratic governance in the province and called into question the prime minister's democratic credentials and domestic legitimacy. The government's subsequent policies in Sindh included the creation of military courts, ostensibly to quell urban terrorism. This attempt to bypass the regular courts resulted, once again, in estranged relations between the central government and the judiciary. Ruling against the establishment of military courts in Karachi, the Supreme Court unanimously concluded that the trial of civilians by military courts is 'unconstitutional' and without 'lawful authority'.[42] Forced to accept the verdict, the Sharif government, none the less, launched a campaign to undermine the judiciary's credibility through the officially-controlled electronic media.[43]

The judiciary's supremacy and internal legitimacy received an impetus from the Supreme Court's ruling which reinforced constitutional norms and upheld constitutionally-guaranteed fundamental rights. However, the opposition expressed doubts about the impartiality and independence of certain sections of the superior judiciary, in particular the judges serving on the Ehtesab branches of the superior courts. Facing charges of corruption, the leader of the opposition, Benazir Bhutto, accused the judges of the Rawalpindi Ehtesab Bench of conniving with the PML government, and declared that the trial 'is a mockery'.[44] Since the accountability process was primarily used by the government against its PPP adversaries, the judicial process against Bhutto eroded the judiciary's legitimacy.[45]

Prime Minister Sharif, however, seemed more concerned about retaining the military's goodwill than in reaching political accommodation with the opposition. The government, for instance, consistently promoted the military's institutional interests through increased salaries and defence expenditure and the extension of patronage to military personnel. The armed forces were closely involved in civil administration. They were given the task of overseeing the fifth national census. Serving and retired military personnel were employed in most branches of the civil administration and in the management of major public sector enterprises such as water, power and the educational sector. While Sharif saw his policy of engaging the military within government as a means of preventing another military intervention, it was perceived by his opponents as a public admission by the prime minister of his inability to govern the country.[46]

Sharif had sufficient grounds for concern about potential military intervention. Tensions between the military and Sharif had increased in direct proportion to the government's dependence on the military to retain its authority, especially in Sindh. The military's impatience with the elected government was amply demonstrated in October 1998 when the then Chief of Army Staff, Jehangir Karamat, publicly demanded a policy providing an enhanced role for the armed forces. Although Sharif succeeded in forcing Karamat to resign, the episode created resentment within the armed forces. When the military opted once again for direct intervention, dismantling the entire edifice of democracy they had themselves put in place, Sharif's ability to resist was minimal in the absence of domestic legitimacy and functioning vibrant democratic institutions.

RETURN OF THE MAN ON HORSEBACK

The final confrontation occurred when the high command perceived the prime minister as a threat to the corporate interests of the armed forces. Following the nuclear tests in India in May 1998, relations between India and Pakistan plummeted to a new low. Under pressure from the military, Sharif's government opted for retaliatory nuclear tests, resulting in the imposition of a US-led multilateral sanctions regime that brought Pakistan's ailing economy to the brink of collapse. Hoping to persuade the United States to remove economic and military sanctions, Sharif initiated a dialogue with India. The Indian nuclear tests had, however, reinforced the Pakistani military's distrust of India. Having demonstrated Pakistan's nuclear weapons capability, the Pakistani military high command was also convinced that a low-level conflict in Kashmir would not result in an all-out war but would serve to increase the military and economic costs for India. Having persuaded Sharif of the merits of intervening in Indian-held Kashmir, the high command escalated its military campaign within the Kargil and Drass sectors of Indian-administered Kashmir.

Contrary to the Pakistani military's expectations, India resisted strongly from its side of the border and the conflict threatened to spiral across the Line of Control (LoC) in Kashmir and the international border. Concerned about an escalation of the conflict between the two nuclear-capable states, the US demanded an immediate withdrawal of the Pakistani-supported infiltrators. With its European allies, the US also threatened to re-impose sanctions on lending from international financial institutions on Pakistan. Recognizing the central role of the Pakistani military in the Kargil crisis, General Anthony Zinni of the US Central Command met his Pakistani counterpart General Pervez Musharraf in Islamabad and demanded the withdrawal of the Pakistan-backed forces from Indian-administered Kashmir.

In a bid to avert an all-out war, Prime Minister Sharif made an unsuccessful bid to elicit Chinese support. Diplomatically isolated and dependent on international goodwill to prop up an almost bankrupt economy, Pakistan could ill-afford to take on a militarily superior foe. When an outbreak of open hostilities appeared imminent, Sharif rushed to the US. At Pakistan's request, President Clinton played the role of mediator. The threat of a fourth war was narrowly averted only after Pakistan accepted India's precondition of a unilateral and unconditional military withdrawal from the Indian side of the LoC. Pakistan's sudden acceptance of India's demands, however, provoked a political backlash against the Sharif government since the fighting in Kargil had been depicted as a major military victory by Pakistan's officially controlled broadcast media.

Under attack from its political opposition, the Sharif government attempted to shift the responsibility for the Kargil debacle on the military high command by implying that the prime minister had not been fully briefed about the operation. As a result, relations became strained between the prime minister and his army chief since the military's internal legitimacy and institutional cohesion was at stake.[47] Fearing that the military would, as in the past, dismiss his government; in a pre-emptive move Sharif dismissed Musharraf on October 11, 1999, attempting to replace him with a chosen nominee when he was abroad on an official trip. Closing ranks, the military mounted a successful coup on October 12, preventing Sharif from arresting Musharraf on his return. Proclaiming himself Chief Executive, Musharraf formally dismissed the Sharif government, imposed military rule, proclaimed a state of emergency, placed the constitution in abeyance, suspended parliament, and placed Sharif and his close associates under arrest.

As his justification for ousting an elected government, Musharraf claimed that the army had intervened reluctantly to prevent an unscrupulous and corrupt political leadership from destabilizing the armed forces – the last viable institution remaining after Sharif had undermined the authority of the parliament and the judiciary. Refusing to give a definite timetable for the restoration of a civilian representative government, Musharraf claimed that the military would withdraw to the barracks once it had prepared the grounds for a 'true democracy'. The military junta's self-proclaimed mission of 'good governance' included reviving the economy, ensuring financial and political accountability, depoliticizing state institutions, providing justice, rebuilding national cohesion and strengthening the federation through the devolution of power.[48]

When the coup occurred, the situation of economic stagnation, underdevelopment, corruption and ineptitude had created widespread popular discontent with Sharif's government. Sharif's attempts to retain power at the cost of democratic governance had also undermined his domestic legitimacy at a time when the political opposition had joined hands in demanding his ouster. As a result, there was no demonstration of public support for the ousted government. Popular disillusionment with the military regime, however, increased in direct proportion to the military's inability to meet any of its stated goals, including the provision of good governance and the revival of the economy. Since public acceptance of the military takeover had not, as in past instances of military intervention, translated into popular support and legitimacy for authoritarian rule, General Musharraf faced the same imperatives of regime survival as his military predecessors. Following the blueprints of past military rulers, the Musharraf regime therefore attempted to gain domestic legitimacy and to prevent and contain internal dissent through coercive means as well as through a democratic facade.

In its first year of office, Musharraf's regime focused its attention on eliminating its political opposition, asserting its authority over all other institutions of the state and perpetuating its rule through the creation of mechanisms for centralized control. Through the Oath of Offices (Judges) Order of 26 January 2000, members of the superior judiciary were forced to take a fresh oath of allegiance to the regime, taking away their right to question any order issued by the military rulers.[49] The national and provincial legislatures were no longer active and the fundamental rights contained in the 1973 constitution were made subservient to military ordinances and acts. The ousted prime minister was imprisoned for an indefinite period following his conviction by an anti-terrorist tribunal on charges of attempting to kidnap and murder Musharraf during his flight to Pakistan on October 12.[50] Using divide-and-rule tactics and an Ehtesab (accountability) process to counter political dissent, the regime imprisoned a number of political leaders on charges of corruption or other criminal offenses and forced others, including former Prime Minister Benazir Bhutto, into political exile.[51]

Depending primarily on its own constituency, the armed forces, the Musharraf regime inducted the military into every branch of government. Military personnel held all sensitive policymaking posts at the centre and in the provinces. To ensure the bureaucracy's continued cooperation in running the civil administration, a number of key bureaucrats were co-opted and others suspended or dismissed on charges of corruption. Efforts were also made to create a civilian constituency for the regime. Under the guise of a devolution of power, an elaborate scheme of local government was announced that resembled the Ayub regime's basic democracies scheme and the local bodies of the Zia era. According to the proposed scheme, non-party elections would be completed by mid-2000 for union, district and tehsil councils, to be followed by a transfer of power to district governments by mid-2001. Since the military would determine the criteria for participation in the local elections, it was expected that successful candidates would, on the one hand, serve as its surrogates at the local level, dependent for their very survival on the military's support. On the other hand, the intended scheme would distort the constitutional distribution of power between the provinces and local governments, undermine the autonomy of provincial governments and provide the centre with a mechanism to extend its authority to the lowest levels of governance. The proposed 'devolution' scheme was, however, rejected by all major political parties, particularly by ethno-regional actors resentful of the reimposition of centralized control by a Punjabi-dominated military establishment.[52]

The continuation of military rule was also opposed by all major political parties and several segments of civil society, including lawyers, human rights activists and the independent print media.[53] Conscious that direct military rule would in the long run erode the regime and hence the military's legitimacy, the Musharraf regime faced the challenge of appearing to ostensibly withdraw but in actuality retaining political power. To do this, the regime had the option of following Zia's example, of ensuring that the ostensible transfer of power to chosen civilian partners was accompanied by a constitutional cover for the military's political order.[54] However, while the regime might have succeeded in determining the parameters within which elected leaders operated, it was likely that centralized unrepresentative rule would engender popular resistance and demands for representative rule and political pluralism, further destabilizing a fragile polity.

MILITARY RULE AND THE FRAGILITY OF PAKISTANI DEMOCRACY

The ease with which military rule was reimposed after over a decade of democratic rule clearly demonstrated the weakness of democratic institutions in Pakistan. The inability of the post-1988 democratic order to withstand military intervention could be partly attributed to its internal contradictions since elected governments operated within the confines of a political system devised by the military itself. When successive elected leaders chose to defy the parameters of the system, their governments were dismissed. This dismissal of elected governments by the military-bureaucratic combine not only weakened democratic institutions and hampered democratic functioning but also eroded the legitimacy of the controlled democracy the military had set in place when it transferred power to civilian hands. Since change was dictated from above, in each election since 1988 voter turnout declined.[55]

The performance of the political leadership, particularly the PPP and the PML leaders in government and in opposition, played an equally important role in undermining democratic institutions, thereby providing the military with repeated opportunities to intervene and to ultimately supplant civilian rule in October 1999. In government, PPP and PML leaders failed to uphold the rule of law or to provide good governance. In an atmosphere of acute political polarization, the result of long years of authoritarian rule, the political leadership refused to work collectively to institutionalize democratic functioning. Instead, elected governments weakened the democratic process by violating democratic norms and opting for centralized control and coercion to consolidate and to expand their authority. Political parties were also weakened as the political leadership neglected institutional development, including that of party organizational structures. Rather than building, sustaining and expanding a popular support base, the attention of the major parties focused on gaining or retaining the support of the politically dominant armed forces for their survival. As a result, a major barrier to military intervention failed to materialize.

While elected governments wilfully distorted the constitution to their own ends, the judiciary and the legislature proved unequal to the task of withstanding executive pressure. The legislature failed to legislate, governments ruled by ordinance, and the need for consensus and bargaining was ignored in parliament. Since the judiciary was internally divided and unable to withstand executive interference, it also gradually lost its credibility as it failed to provide a check on arbitrary executive actions, reflecting its past practice when the judiciary not only gave 'legal sanction to military intervention' but was 'largely responsible for making the space for the acceptability of these interventions'.[56]

When the military did intervene in October 1999, there was little popular resistance due to the declining legitimacy of the elected government. Despite the successful military takeover, there remained overwhelming support for electoral democracy in Pakistan. Hence the Musharraf regime's continued efforts to create a democratic facade, such as its proposed scheme for the devolution of power. Yet the military remains opposed to a participatory system in which democratic freedoms would prevail and is equally averse to an actual decentralisation of power. Should the military decide to retain power indefinitely, depriving a multi-ethnic population of democratic avenues of bargaining, participation and dissent; political instability and internal divisions will threaten the very fabric of the state. If the military opts to contain dissent and to perpetuate its rule through coercive means, the citizens of Pakistan could respond by rejecting the state's authority and legitimacy.

NOTES

1 Hassan N. Gardezi, *Understanding Pakistan: The Colonial Factor in Societal Development* (Lahore: Maktaba Fikr-o-Danish, 1991), 4–5.
2 Richard Symonds, *The Making of Pakistan*, 2nd edn (Lahore: Islamic Book Service, 1987), 38–39.
3 Marvin G. Weinbaum, 'Civic Culture and Democracy in Pakistan', *Asian Survey* 36(7), July 1996, 640–41.
4 Introduced by the colonial administration as a part of the process of self-governance, the Government of India Act 1935 was based on the principles of federalism and provincial autonomy, but contained a number of clauses that ensured continued centralised control over the British Indian Empire.
5 Richard Symonds, *Making of Pakistan*, 91.
6 Talukdar Maniruzzaman, *Group Interests and Political Changes: Studies of Pakistan and Bangladesh* (New Delhi: South Asian Publishers, 1982), 7–8.
7 In the years following independence, the bureaucracy was mainly composed of Muhajirs and Punjabis. Punjabis, followed by Pakthuns, dominated the military's rank and file and the officer corps since traditional patterns of recruitment to the British Indian army were retained.
8 Ibid, 32–33.
9 According to Chief Justice Mohammad Munir, the doctrine of necessity was based on the principle that a 'victorious revolution or a successful coup d'etat is an internationally recognised method of changing a constitution'. Cited in Keith Callard, *Pakistan's Foreign Policy: An Interpretation* (New York: Institute of Pacific Relations), 35.
10 On 8 October 1958 General Ayub Khan declared, 'Our ultimate aim is to restore democracy but of the type that people can understand and work'. Cited in Lawrence Ziring, *The Ayub Khan Era: Politics in Pakistan 1958–1969* (Syracuse, New York: Syracuse University Press, 1971), 10.
11 Y.V. Gankovsky and V.N. Moskalenko, *The Three Constitutions of Pakistan*, 76.
12 By 1967, there was a disparity of 24 percent in the per capita income of both wings: Maniruzzaman, *Group Interests and Political Changes*, 85.
13 Hasan Askari-Rizvi, *The Military and Politics in Pakistan 1947–86*, 3rd edn (Lahore: Progressive Publishers, 1986), 170.
14 Shahid Javed Burki, *State and Society in Pakistan 1971–1977* (London: Macmillan, 1980), 55.
15 Lawrence Ziring, *Pakistan in the Twentieth Century: A Political History* (Karachi: Oxford University Press, 1997), 375.

16 Hina Jilani, *Human Rights and Democratic Development in Pakistan* (Lahore: Human Rights Commission of Pakistan, 1998), 72.
17 Louis D. Hayes, *Politics in Pakistan: The Struggle for Legitimacy* (Boulder, Colorado: Westview, 1984), 76.
18 Only the National Assembly, in which the Punjab (the military's main recruitment ground) had a majority of seats could exercise financial powers: Rafi Raza, ed., *Pakistan in Perspective 1947–1997* (Karachi: Oxford University Press, 1997), 26.
19 Gardezi, *Understanding Pakistan*, 96.
20 Rafi Raza, 'Constitutional Developments and Political Consequences', 32.
21 Pledging free and fair elections in ninety days, General Zia stated, 'I give a solemn assurance that I will not deviate from this schedule ...' Cited in Askari-Rizvi, *Military and Politics in Pakistan*, 226.
22 Gankovsky and Moskalenko, *Three Constitutions of Pakistan*, 127.
23 The president's powers to dissolve the National Assembly were contained in Article 58 (2) (a), and Article 58 (2) (b). For details Makdoom Ali Khan, ed., *The Constitution of the Islamic Republic of Pakistan, 1973* (Karachi: Pakistan Law House, 1986), 40; and Gholam G. Choudhury, *Pakistan: Transition from Military to Civilian Rule* (Essex: Scorpion Publishing Ltd., 1988), 166.
24 Saeed Shafqat, 'Pakistan under Benazir Bhutto', *Asian Survey* 36(7), July 1996, 659–60.
25 Mushahid Hussain and Akmal Hussain, *Pakistan: Problems of Governance* (New Delhi: Konark Publishers, 1993), 101–2.
26 Gardezi, *Understanding Pakistan*, 123.
27 William L. Richter, 'The 1990 General Elections in Pakistan', in Charles H. Kennedy, ed., *Pakistan: 1992* (Boulder, Colorado: Westview Press, 1993), 24.
28 Ziring, *Pakistan in the Twentieth Century*, 529.
29 Shahid Javed Burki, 'Economic Policy After Ziaul Haq', in Charles H. Kennedy, ed., *Pakistan: 1992*, 52.
30 Zahid Hussain, 'Jam's Sindh', *Newsline*, March 1991, 21.
31 The Twelfth Amendment, for example, created a parallel system of justice through summary trial courts.
32 Ziring, *Pakistan in the Twentieth Century*, 540.
33 Mohammad Waseem, 'Pakistan Elections 1997: One Step Forward', in Craig Baxter and Charles H. Kennedy, ed., *Pakistan: 1997* (Boulder, Colorado: Westview Press, 1997), 5.
34 Robert LaPorte, Jr., 'Pakistan in 1996: Starting Once Again', *Asian Survey* 37(2), February 1997, 118.
35 Ziring, *Pakistan in the Twentieth Century*, 563.
36 Waseem, 'Pakistan Elections 1997', 7–8.
37 Anwar H. Syed, 'Pakistan in 1997: Nawaz Sharif's Second Chance to Govern', *Asian Survey* 38(2), February 1998, 119.
38 The Anti-Terrorist Act of August 1997 gave civilian and military law-enforcing agents powers of investigation and arrest and to set up special courts to try alleged perpetrators, with no recourse to judicial appeal except through specially constituted tribunals: Samina Ahmed, 'Pakistan at Fifty: A Tenuous Democracy', *Current History* 96(614), December 1997, 424.
39 Ismail Khan, 'Up in Arms', *Newsline*, July 1998, 46–48.
40 Quoted in Zahid Husain, 'Sharif's Last Refuge', *Newsline*, September 1998, 17.
41 The agreement's provisions included the withdrawal of criminal charges against MQM activists and the provision of compensation to Muhajirs who had been

the targets of past military action in urban Sindh. The text of the PML–MQM alliance agreement was released by the MQM in January 1999: 'Text of PML–MQM agreement', *Dawn*, 19 January 1999.
42 Rafaqat Ali, 'Supreme Court declares Military Courts Illegal', *Dawn*, 18 February 1999.
43 According to a former federal law minister, 'The on-going prime-time PTV campaign against the judiciary is absolutely unprecedented':. Kamran Khan, 'Government's Friction with Judiciary is shaping Another Crisis', *News*, 19 March 1999.
44 'Closure of SGS Case: Bhutto files Appeal', *Dawn*, 18 March 1999.
45 In its report of 1998, the influential independent Human Rights Commission of Pakistan accused the PML-N government of attempting to isolate the main opposition party, the PPP, through a deeply flawed process of accountability. 'Government accused of HR Violations', *News*, 10 March 1999.
46 According to a political observer, 'It is like a quasi-military rule with an increasing army role in civilian affairs': Zahid Hussain and Amir Mir, 'Army to the Rescue', *Newsline*, May 1998, 21.
47 Zahid Hussain, 'Beating a Hasty Retreat', *Newsline*, July 1999, 23.
48 Text of Musharraf's takeover speech in *Dawn*, 13 October 1999. See also 'Musharraf Spells out 7 Point Agenda: Security Council to Run State Affairs', *Dawn*, 18 October 1999.
49 Rafaqat Ali, 'Irshad New Chief Justice: Five Others Refuse to Take Oath', *Dawn*, 27 January 2000.
50 Sharif intended to appeal the verdict of two consecutive life sentences before the High Court of Sindh and, if the sentence was upheld, then before the Supreme Court of Pakistan.
51 Headed by a serving army general, the National Accountability Bureau (NAB) had complete authority to deal with cases of corruption and willful default through especially constituted accountability courts. Armed forces personnel and the judiciary were excluded from the NAB's jurisdiction.
52 The PPP, the Awami National Party and PONAM rejected the scheme as contrary to federal structure of the constitution, claiming that it negated the concept of provincial autonomy and imposed a unitary form of government in the name of decentralization. Human rights organization were also critical with the Human Rights Commission of Pakistan, for example, stating that the 'purpose (of the proposal) seems to be to depoliticise governance and to earn a lease of life for the military regime behind a sort of democratic facade.' Cited in Amir Mir, 'Power to the People?' *Newsline*, April 2000, 54-55. See also Staff Reporter, 'Devolution of Power Scheme in Conflict with Federal System', *Dawn*, 4 December 1999; Staff Reporter, 'PONAM Opposes District Government Plan', *Dawn*, 29 March 2000; and M.B. Kalhoro, 'Devolution Plan Under Fire', *Dawn*, 30 March 2000.
53 The council of PONAM, comprised of twelve ethno-regional parties from Sindh, Baluchistan and the Punjab, for instance, rejected the military takeover as an act of 'naked usurpation', and calls on the military to hand over power to the Supreme Court and to return to the barracks. Correspondent, 'PONAM wants army to hand over power to Supreme Court', *Dawn*, 8 December 1999.
54 According to a former law minister and constitutional expert, before the military formally withdraws from power, 'the new constitution will contain provisions validating all actions taken by them and giving them immunity.' Interview of Abdul Hafeez Pirzada by Taimur Siddiqui, *Newsline*, October 1999, 28.

55 Voter turnout in Pakistan's first general elections in 1970 was 54 percent. In the 1988 election, voter turnout was 43 percent, declining to approximately 40 percent in the 1993 and 1996 elections, and 34 percent in the 1997 elections. Waseem, 'Pakistan Elections 1997', 10.
56 Jilani, *Human Rights and Democratic Development*, 35.

Chapter 3

Bangladesh: An Unsteady Democracy

D. Hugh Evans*

The creation of Bangladesh in December 1971 was as much a struggle for constitutional justice as it was a movement of ethno-linguistic nationalism. Yet, the country's experience as a multi-party democracy could be said to have only properly begun in the 1990s. For most of its first two decades of independence, Bangladesh was dominated by regimes that had a hard time reconciling the pressing development priorities of one of the world's poorest nations – an international basket case to cite Henry Kissinger's grim metaphor – with the requirements of Western-style democracy. These governments made some progress in improving the country's socio-economic condition, but much more still needs to be done. Its Gross Domestic Product (GDP) has averaged a consistent, if unglamorous, 4–5 percent growth since the late 1970s;[1] the population growth rate has declined from 3.2 percent in the early 1970s to around 2 percent today;[2] average life expectancy has risen from 46 years in the 1970s to an estimated 55 years in the early 1990s;[3] and the male literacy rate has steadily increased to almost 50 percent though the female literacy rate remains an abysmally low 22 percent.[4]

Though two successive military-backed regimes after 1975 initially justified their control on the grounds they were better placed than elected alternatives to provide the state with clear, effective leadership, neither was able to fully ignore the pressures for a return to democracy. Such pressures reflected not least the high degree of political consciousness and ideological diversity among Bangladeshis in the wake of their triumphant liberation struggle. Indeed, both General Ziaur Rahman (1976–81) and General Hussain Muhammad Ershad (1982–90) strove to secure legitimacy for their regimes by appropriating the trappings of democratic 'accountability'.

---

*D. Hugh Evans is a member of the British diplomatic service. However, the views expressed in this chapter are the author's own and should not be taken as an expression of the views of the British Government.

They founded their own political parties, sought to ensure that these parties secured comfortable parliamentary majorities, and ratified their own transitions from army chief to civilian executive president through carefully instigated national referenda.

Nonetheless, the collapse of the Ershad regime in 1990 and the rapid transition to a genuine multi-party democracy finally underscored the limits of these attempts at 'guided democracy'. It is clear that the timing of this transition was influenced to some extent by events elsewhere in the post-cold war environment – placing Bangladesh firmly in the so-called 'third wave' of developing nations, which abandoned their authoritarian models in favor of a process of democratization. However, the key factors that gave impetus to the struggle for democracy in the late 1980s were largely rooted in the domestic political context. After outlining the events leading up to the landmark 1991 elections, this study will focus on both the achievements and weaknesses of the country's ongoing constitutional experiment. It will highlight certain distinctive trends in recent years, notably the unwillingness of rival parties to abide by parliamentary rules and the apparently diminished risk of military intervention, and conclude with some thoughts on the longer-term prospects of democracy in Bangladesh.

DEMOCRACY: WON AND LOST

It was Sheikh Mujibur Rahman (1971–75), Bangladesh's founding father and hero of the liberation war against Pakistani military oppression, who first turned away from the country's democratic foundations. This was despite the fact that the legitimacy of his regime had rested on his party's, the Awami League's (AL), sweeping victory in undivided Pakistan's first and only parliamentary elections in 1970. As the party that had championed East Pakistan's interests in the 1950s and 1960s and later spear-headed the independence movement, the left-of-center and secular nationalist AL initially dominated the new state – a fact reflected in its overwhelming triumph in the 1973 parliamentary elections. Parties associated with the former undivided Pakistan had either disappeared or, as in the case of the Jamaat-i-Islami (JI or Party of Islam) and other Islamic groups, been proscribed because of their active collaboration with the Pakistan army's brutal crackdown on supporters of the independence movement in 1971.

Mujib's government undoubtedly faced formidable challenges arising out of the new state's precarious origins. Bangladesh was the foundling of not one but two partitions in South Asia: that of 1947 between India and Pakistan, as well as that of 1971 between West and East Pakistan. With 10 million refugees in neighboring India, the country inherited a shattered and predominantly agrarian economy that had long been subordinated to the industrial needs of first British-ruled West Bengal, and subsequently West Pakistan. Much of its small professional class was killed in the liberation war and its nascent bureaucracy was severely depleted by the departure of Punjab and Sindhi officials. Moreover, while the Indian army had intervened to help Bangladesh gain independence and initially guaranteed its territorial integrity, the new sovereign state was immediately confronted with the challenge of melding together a national army from elements of the former Pakistani military – some of whom had played no role in the secessionist struggle – and the radicalized civilian ex-freedom fighters.

Faced with these challenges, Mujib claimed that the scale of the problems confronting Bangladesh justified his decision in January 1975 to suspend the country's 1972 democratic constitution – despite it being largely of his own conception – and institute a one-party dictatorship. This was widely criticized as a crude effort to repress growing opposition to his rule. Much of this discontent stemmed from a deepening domestic and world economic crisis, compounded by the failure of his pro-socialist policies of nationalization and import-substitution. Mujib's assassination in the coup of August 1975 cut short his authoritarian experiment but ushered in fifteen years of almost continuous military rule.

With the assassination of Sheikh Mujib in August 1975, the AL was effectively driven underground for the next few years. Leadership of the party passed by default to Mujib's daughter, Sheikh Hasina Wajed, who was with her scientist husband in Germany at the time of the coup and thus escaped the massacre of most of her other relatives in the Dhaka family residence. She was formally elected AL president on 16 February 1981, and in May that year she returned to lead the party in Bangladesh after a five-year exile in India.[5]

REINVENTING A POLITY

Ironically, the authenticity of Bangladesh's eventual return to full civilian democracy, highlighted by the 1991 elections, rested in part on the emergence of a multi-party system during the long years of military rule. After seizing power in late 1975, one of General Ziaur Rahman's early acts was to lift the ban on religious parties, including the Jamaat-i-Islami (JI). The Bangladesh Jamaat is a descendant of the movement founded by Maulana Maududi in New Delhi in 1941, whose headquarters he transferred to Lahore in 1948 following the creation of Pakistan. Formerly the East Pakistan branch of the Pakistani JI, the Bangladesh party had vehemently opposed the breakup of Pakistan as a further division of South Asia's Muslim community (Maududi had originally opposed the 1947 partition for the same reason). Like its Pakistani counterpart, the Bangladesh JI remains committed to the establishment of an Islamic state as espoused by Maududi. With a primarily urban middle and lower middle-class following, the party also places strong emphasis on organizational discipline embodied in a cadre of dedicated activists.

Zia's action in legalizing the JI and other Islamic groups was done in part to offset the continuing influence in domestic politics of the AL and its leftist allies. But his action was also motivated by a new foreign policy orientation in which he turned away from the previous government's close friendship with India. The Zia government instead sought to develop economic and political ties to the West, as well as to the oil-rich Gulf states and other Muslim countries, including Pakistan.

However, contrary to the hopes of the JI and other Islamic parties that they would represent the main right-wing challenge to the AL, Zia opted to establish the Bangladesh Nationalist Party (BNP) in 1976 as a vehicle to promote his own bid for power as a civilian leader. Though the BNP was and remains a moderate right-of-center party, Zia sought to appeal to more devout voters by introducing a number of symbolically important pro-Islamic reforms. These included setting up a ministry of religion, making religious studies a compulsory subject in all school curricula, and replacing the AL's stress on secularism as a guiding principle of the constitution with a reference to the country's 'absolute faith and trust in the almighty Allah'. His policies and reputation for personal honesty, as well as the opportunities to dispense the patronage that flowed from control of the government apparatus, enabled Zia to build a constituency for his party. By the end of the 1970s, the BNP drew support from three main sources: serving and retired military officers and civil servants loyal to Zia himself, former supporters of the pro-Pakistan parties, and anti-AL leftists who had backed the charismatic Maulana Bhashani before his death in 1975.[6] A year after Zia's largely unchallenged elevation to the presidency in June 1978, the BNP won a decisive victory in parliamentary elections, securing 206 out of 300 seats. This triumph, however, was marred by allegations of widespread ballot rigging.

Like Mujib before him, Zia, Bangladesh's first military ruler, fell victim to a conspiracy among junior army officers. He was assassinated while visiting the port city of Chittagong in February 1981 and was succeeded as executive president by a civilian, Abdus Sattar, who was confirmed in office in an overwhelming election victory later that year. Sattar's brief tenure in power ended when Ershad, Zia's successor as army chief, toppled him in March 1982. Following Zia's assassination in May 1981, his widow, Begum Khaleda Zia, assumed the leadership of his party.

RISING OPPOSITION TO MILITARY RULE

After seizing power, General Ershad moved swiftly to consolidate his control by imposing martial law and banning political parties. In December 1983, he assumed the presidency, while retaining his positions as army chief and chief martial law administrator.

Following much the same approach as Zia, Ershad sought, albeit unsuccessfully, to legitimize and entrench his authority by assuming a civilian role and instituting a highly restricted version of democracy. The president began the process of civilianising his regime by securing public endorsement of his leadership in a controversial national referendum in March 1985. Repeating Zia's strategy, Ershad in late 1985 founded the Jatiya Party (JP or National Party), another conservative pro-Muslim (but not Islamist) group, to institutionalize his own leadership ambitions. On 1 January 1986, he restored a range of civil liberties, including the right of opposition groups to hold outdoor rallies, and announced that new parliamentary elections would be held later that year. Despite the participation of a thirteen party opposition alliance led by the Awami League in the May 1986 elections, Ershad was widely accused of rigging the polls in favor of his own supporters who emerged with a slim majority of seats. Both the AL alliance and a separate seven party opposition grouping led by the Bangladesh Nationalist Party, which had refused to participate in the parliamentary vote, boycotted presidential elections later that year. Ershad was formally elected JP chairman in September 1986 shortly after stepping down as army chief and retiring from military service. He was then elected civilian president in October, defeating eleven largely unknown rival candidates. Though Ershad won over 80 percent of the vote, his election was also marred by allegations of serious irregularities. On 10 November 1986, parliament approved a constitutional amendment ratifying all legislation passed by the previous military regime and indemnifying its members against any subsequent legal action. The move paved the way for Ershad formally to lift martial law the same day.

Ershad's efforts to impose a stable constitutional order on his own terms failed to stem popular pressure for a restoration of full democratic rights. Frustrated by continued extra-parliamentary opposition to his rule, he began openly to question the suitability of Western-style democracy for Bangladesh. In July 1987, his government pushed through a parliamentary bill to provide for military representation on local government bodies. Passage of the bill was widely condemned as a first step towards replacing the sovereignty of an elected parliament with a more divided, and controllable, military-technocratic power structure possibly along the lines of the systems then in place in Indonesia or Turkey. The AL and other opposition parties withdrew from parliament in protest at the measure and joined the BNP-led alliance in confronting the government on the streets. Though the legislation was later shelved, popular outrage at Ershad's move proved a catalyst for a more prolonged anti-government agitation. Despite deep divisions between and within the two main opposition alliances, anti-Ershad forces launched a partially effective campaign of strikes and demonstrations in late 1987 with the sole aim of forcing the president to step down.[7] By November, Ershad was forced to declare a state of emergency and in December he dissolved parliament and called fresh elections for 3 March 1988. Though the polls went ahead on schedule, all main opposition groups refused to participate, and neutral election observers characterized the vote as blatantly unfair.

For the next two and a half years, the political situation remained in stalemate. The opposition was unable to oust the president who retained the allegiance of the country's bureaucratic and military forces, but Ershad's inability to secure the cooperation of the opposition kept the political situation fluid and deprived his rule of constitutional respectability. The impasse was only broken in October 1990 when the opposition parties mounted a further wave of anti-government strikes and demonstrations. The protests this time were inspired by the success of the post-cold war democracy movements elsewhere in the world, not least in nearby Nepal. Within weeks, the key role of opposition activists in fueling the agitation was supplemented and quickly eclipsed by the participation of a much wider range of predominantly urban groups; including students, merchants and factory workers. By late November, the uprising had effectively paralysed Dhaka and other major cities. Spearheading the anti-government push were student groups, affiliated to various parties, who temporarily submerged their differences in an umbrella movement – the All Parties Student Unity.[8] Ershad's fate was finally sealed when his former colleagues in the army refused to order troops to fire on unarmed demonstrators.

The president resigned on 8 December 1990, making way for a caretaker cabinet of 'non-party' technocrats whose main responsibility was to oversee new elections on 28 February 1991. Ershad himself was arrested and later tried and convicted on corruption, arms smuggling and other charges. He was initially sentenced to a twenty-year jail term, though several of his convictions were later overturned on appeal. The 1991 elections were held under a neutral caretaker government, backed by a disinterested military which provided security at many of the over 20,000 polling nations across the nation. The polls were deemed by domestic and international observers to be the first truly free and fair contest in the country's short but checkered history. The caretaker government subsequently oversaw a peaceful transition of power to the newly elected government – again an unprecedented event for Bangladesh.

Like the BNP, the JP initially benefited from government sponsorship and attracted support from largely the same social groups as the BNP: military personnel, ex-officials, urban professionals, and sections of the rural elite. But Ershad never managed to command the degree of popular support enjoyed by the late Zia; and though the JP undercut BNP support in parts of the country, it never came close to displacing its rival as the main opposition to the AL.

WATERSHED EVENT

In the 1991 elections, both the BNP and AL showed they had acquired sizeable constituencies, which could outlast the patronage of their respective regimes. The BNP and AL each garnered about 32 percent of the popular vote. However, under the vagaries of Bangladesh's Westminster-style 'first-past-the-post' voting system,[9] the BNP secured 142 seats in contrast to the AL's 88. The JP came in a respectable third with 35 seats. Ershad, by this time in jail and unable to campaign, nonetheless captured all 5 seats in his home region of Rangamati. Marking its formal rehabilitation after its post-1971 disgrace, the largest religious party, the JI, picked up 18 seats.

Though most observers had expected the AL, as the country's oldest party which could still boast the most extensive national organization, to emerge with the largest number of seats, a combination of factors resulted in a BNP victory. First, the AL was hurt by lingering memories of its excesses in the early 1970s, and by a perception that it had compromised with Ershad's military regime by participating in the discredited 1986 parliamentary election. In contrast, the BNP was perceived by many voters to have remained more committed to reviving democracy. Moreover, the charismatic appeal of the BNP's late founder Zia might also have helped counterbalance the drawing power of Sheikh Mujib's legacy as the country's founding father. A further, and possibly key, electoral determinant was also the BNP's success in casting the AL, on account of its historic friendship with India, as a party that would subordinate Bangladeshi interests to those of its large neighbor.[10] The perception of the AL's close ties to India was reinforced by the strong support which the party traditionally enjoyed among the country's large Hindu minority, estimated at around 12 percent of the total population. Capitalizing on popular anti-India sentiments, the JI won in a number of constituencies bordering India with significant concentrations of Hindus by wooing support among the Muslim majority.

Narrowly lacking a majority of the 300 directly elected parliamentary seats, the BNP swiftly struck a deal with the JI to divide up the 30 indirectly-elected seats reserved for women. With the addition of 28 of these seats, the BNP was able to form a government on its own with a clear majority in the 330-member assembly. By all accounts, Begum Zia's new cabinet began well, especially in its management of the economy. A series of macroeconomic reforms in 1991–92 helped boost tax revenues and domestic savings and encouraged outside investment, while reducing inflation and the overall budget deficit. In the political sphere, the prime minister, though she personally favored retaining the executive presidency bequeathed by her late husband, bowed to the wishes of the opposition as well as many in her own party by supporting a constitutional amendment which re-established parliamentary government.[11] However, this initial spirit of bipartisan cooperation soon evaporated: Begum Zia increasingly became the target of opposition criticism that she ignored parliament and was seeking to impose a personal dictatorship.

DESCENT INTO TURMOIL

Amid a steady decline in inter-party relations, the AL soundly defeated the BNP in local government elections in the main cities of Dhaka and Chittagong in December 1993. But in March 1994, the BNP claimed victory in a controversial by-election in what had been the safe AL seat of Magura. Accusing the government of blatant election-rigging, opposition members withdrew from parliament and called for future general elections, like the 1991 polls, to be conducted by a neutral caretaker authority. Begum Zia's rejection of the demand as unconstitutional set the scene for a prolonged political struggle.

As the situation deteriorated, the two sides agreed in September 1994 that a Commonwealth mission under Sir Ninian Stephen should attempt to mediate a settlement. The government offered to accept a compromise whereby the BNP and opposition parties would form a coalition cabinet to oversee new elections and Begum Zia would step down as prime minister 30 days before the polling date. But the Commonwealth effort foundered on the refusal of Sheikh Hasina to settle for anything less than a neutral caretaker government. Critics attributed Hasina's intransigence to her personal hostility towards Begum Zia – a feeling fully reciprocated – as well as an inability to accept that her party had genuinely lost the 1991 elections. Other considerations, however, probably weighed as heavily with her. Conscious that her party had lost ground in the elections by its earlier, albeit brief, cooperation with Ershad's regime, she may have resolved this time not to be seen to make any compromise on upholding democratic principles.

The crisis deepened in December 1994 when non-BNP members resigned en masse from parliament and opposition parties stepped up extra parliamentary agitation to force the government's resignation. By mid-1995, a frustrating deadlock had developed. The different opposition groups launched a series of strikes and rallies that paralyzed day-to-day government and caused widespread economic disruption, but they were unable to generate sufficient popular momentum to dislodge Begum Zia from power. For its part, BNP efforts to divide and weaken its opponents made little headway. For example, the government was widely suspected of manipulating the prosecution of Taslima Nasrin, a writer facing charges of offending Muslim sentiments, in a vain bid to detach the JI and other religious parties from the opposition alliance.

Attempts by various mediators; including British Labour MP Peter Shore, the US ambassador, the British high commissioner to Bangladesh, and the head of the Bangladesh Chamber of Commerce; failed to break the impasse.[12] The latter's involvement reflected concern within the business community at the worsening economic climate. The country's textile industry which had displaced jute as the main source of export earnings since the late 1980s, was particularly hard-hit by the protracted unrest that closed the main port of Chittagong for months. GNP growth in 1995 fell by over one percent from its 4.2 percent level in 1994. Though the Supreme Court ruled in July 1995 that by-elections should be held to fill the vacant parliamentary seats created by the opposition boycott, Begum Zia stalled taking action until November when parliament was dissolved. New elections were set for 18 January 1996, almost exactly at the end of the government's five-year term. Declaring they would boycott the polls unless the government gave way to a neutral cabinet, opposition parties continued their separate programs of strikes and demonstrations. The elections eventually went ahead on 15 February 1996. Even though the BNP was the only major party that participated, the vote was characterised by serious irregularities and dismissed by poll observers as fraudulent.

Opposition to the government quickly escalated in the wake of the elections. Over 100 people were killed in clashes between opposition activists and the security forces in different parts of the country. A further 200 were injured when the opposition attempted to storm the parliament building on 19 March to disrupt the swearing-in of Begum Zia for a second term as prime minister. From early March, the AL and other opposition groups called an indefinite national strike, business associations abandoned their longstanding neutrality and urged the government to step down, and civil servants for the first time began to join the street protests. The final straw appeared to be the statement made by senior bureaucrats in late March calling for fresh elections under a neutral government.[13]

DEMOCRACY RESURGENT

Sensing the end was near but insisting on legal niceties, Begum Zia instructed the new BNP-dominated parliament on 21 March 1996 to enact a constitutional amendment providing for a neutral interim government. She and her ministers resigned ten days later and were replaced by a cabinet of 'non-party' technocrats under Chief Justice Muhammad Habibur Rahman. The government scheduled new elections for 12 June 1996. A final note of controversy, however, was the decision of the BNP-nominated president Abdur Rahman Biswas to assume control of the defense ministry shortly before power was transferred to the caretaker cabinet. The president's subsequent decision to dismiss the army chief on grounds of insubordination (discussed later) was condemned by the AL as a 'conspiracy' to sabotage the elections.[14]

Notwithstanding these tensions, the election campaign passed off relatively peacefully. In a vote characterised by domestic and international observers as largely free and fair,[15] the AL initially secured 134 seats with 37.5 percent of the popular vote. The BNP slipped to 104 seats on a 33.5 percent share of the vote. With 16 percent of the turnout, the JP again won a respectable 29 seats, while the JI lost significant ground, picking up only three seats and less than 10 percent of the vote. As with the BNP in 1991, the AL lacked an overall majority. But it soon reached agreement with the JP on a 27 to 3 division of the 30 reserved women's seats. Following repolling in 27 seats where serious irregularities had occurred, the final tally for each party was AL 179, BNP 113, JP 33, JI 3, and smaller parties 2.

The BNP's prospects in the election were clearly damaged by its clumsy and superfluous efforts to rig the February polls. Despite the positive verdict of the neutral monitors in the June elections, BNP supporters suggested that election officials might have massaged the vote count in favor of the AL. Though this claim was not substantiated, Begum Zia's demand that civil servants involved in earlier protests against her government should be sacked, articulated in a speech shortly after her resignation as prime minister, probably did much to alienate the bureaucracy from the BNP. In Dhaka and other major cities, government officials are a numerically significant group.

Other developments may also have directly benefited the AL, especially the narrowing of the country's ideological divisions in the post-cold war era. Like other Third World socialist parties that had followed policies of nationalization, import-substitution and non-alignment in the 1970s, the AL claimed to have reinvented itself as a more broad-based centrist movement attuned to the international and economic realities of the 1990s. On the campaign stump, Sheikh Hasina emphasized her newfound commitment to free market, competition, tariff reform and privatization. She further pledged that an AL government would be more assiduous than its rivals in attracting foreign investment and would support greater regional economic cooperation. Party leaders also downplayed the differences between the secular Bengali nationalism traditionally espoused by the AL and the more pro-Islamic, though not Islamist, Bangladeshi nationalism associated with its rivals. In particular, the AL made clear there would be no reversal of the changes since 1975 emphasizing the country's Muslim character, including Ershad's 1988 constitutional amendment declaring Islam to be the state religion.[16] During the election, commentators noticed Hasina had taken to wearing a *hijab* (Muslim headscarf) while addressing campaign rallies.[17]

Perhaps the most significant contrast with the 1991 polls was that this time BNP efforts to tar the AL as India's stooge had much less impact. This change may have been partly attributable to a decline in popular anti-India sentiment as well as to a recognition that the BNP government had made little progress in resolving disputes with India that are crucial to Bangladesh's long-term development. But, for its part, the AL also made a conscious effort to distance itself from its traditional pro-India stance. Shortly before the election, Hasina pledged not to renew the controversial Treaty of Peace and Friendship with India, signed by her father in 1972 and due for renewal in 1997. Other parties had frequently attacked the treaty as a symbol of Bangladesh's subordination to its neighbor.[18] According to some observers, the AL's alignment with the JI and JP, both known as anti-India parties, during the struggle to oust the BNP government, may also have helped dispel perceptions about the party's cross-border links.[19]

Though the 1996 elections further underscored the evolution of a two-party system in Bangladesh, the vote also confirmed the JP as a significant, if declining, third force. The party's performance might have been more impressive if not for evidence of serious internal divisions exposed by the elevation of Begum Ershad to a key leadership role on behalf of her still-jailed husband, a move resented by some senior party figures. Following the elections, factional strains within the party worsened, exacerbated in part by press reports that General Ershad may have had an extra-marital affair with a party activist.

The diminished fortunes of the JI in the 1996 polls reflected the party's continuing failure to generate much popular enthusiasm for its goal of an Islamic state, as well as a residual bitterness among many Bangladeshis at the party's role in 1971. These emotions were rekindled by the Supreme Court's decision in 1993 to grant Bangladeshi citizenship to the party's long-time leader, Golam Azam, prompting anti-JI activists to condemn him as a 'war criminal' in a mock-trial staged in Dhaka. The JI's loss of seats over its 1991 performance may also have been the result of an unprecedented mobilization of women voters against the party, including those in rural areas. On 1 January 1996, approximately 100,000 women reportedly marched in Dhaka to denounce the religious parties' opposition to the spread of female education and employment opportunities facilitated by the activities of non-governmental organizations, such as the Grameen Bank and Bangladesh Rural Advancement Committee (BRAC).[20]

AWAMI LEAGUE IN POWER: BACK TO THE FUTURE?

The return to office of a freely elected Awami League government after twenty-one years appeared to offer a fresh start to Bangladesh's troubled democracy. The new cabinet sworn in on 23 June 1996 promised to pursue policies of national consensus that emphasized economic reform and political liberalisation.[21] Promising 'to make parliament a focal point of activity,' the new prime minister made a point of participating in most parliamentary debates. She also pledged to follow a neutral merit-based approach towards the appointment and promotion of officials. Moreover, unlike the previous government, Hasina nominated a non-partisan figure, former Chief Justice Shahabuddin Ahmed, who headed the 1991 caretaker government, to succeed Biswas as president in October 1996. One of Ahmed's first actions in office was to appeal to both the AL and BNP to dissociate themselves from their respective student bodies who have long conducted a violent struggle for control of the country's university campuses.[22] The new AL government's first budget underscored its commitment to continuity by drawing heavily on the previous government's proposals.[23] However, though Hasina in opposition repeatedly stressed her support for economic liberalization, her government has so far taken only modest steps to advance the process.

Nonetheless, the Awami League government has pursued some bold, if controversial, policy initiatives. On 12 December 1996, Hasina and Indian prime minister Deve Gowda signed a thirty-year agreement in New Delhi on the sharing of the Ganges River waters. The issue had bedeviled bilateral relations since India constructed the Farakka barrage in 1974, putting India in a position to control water flows from the Ganges into Bangladesh. An earlier agreement expired in the 1980s. Under the provisions of the new accord, Bangladesh was guaranteed a minimum of 35,000 cubic feet of water per second (cusecs) during the lean winter months and an equal share of water at other times. India's willingness to make concessions to the new Bangladeshi government appears to have reflected pressure from West Bengal, especially from its business community, to put cross-border relations on a better footing. The water-sharing agreement was also the first fruit of the so-called 'Gujral doctrine,' named for I.K. Gujral then Indian foreign minister, who sought to build stronger ties to neighboring states.

With both countries hailing the deal as a breakthrough in resolving their most contentious dispute, Deve Gowda was warmly received when he visited Dhaka in January 1997 – his first bilateral foreign trip. Though the Bangladesh opposition accused the AL of promising a secret quid pro quo to New Delhi to secure such favorable terms, the government was careful to delink the agreement from India's request for transit rights through Bangladesh to its northeastern states. BNP and other opposition leaders contended that India would exploit these rights to transport arms and troops to quell insurgencies in its remote hill territories. The government has also taken a cautious line on the question of expanding cross-border trade, with press editorials expressing disquiet at the prospect of Bangladesh being swamped by goods from its larger neighbor.[24] Equally politically sensitive has been the issue of whether Bangladesh should export some of the gas from its substantial natural reserves to India.

Even so, the generally positive initial reaction of Bangladeshis, including the business community, to the water-sharing deal seemed to indicate a growing acceptance that their long-term prosperity would depend on forging closer political and commercial links with India. The two countries, together with Nepal and Bhutan, also agreed to form a sub-regional economic cooperation grouping as part of the South Asian Association for Regional Cooperation (SAARC), despite Pakistani objections. But popular disenchantment with the AL's approach to India increased sharply when the much-vaunted water accord failed to deliver the expected share of river water for northwestern Bangladesh during the 1997 dry season. Opposition parties have subsequently sought to capitalize on this perceived policy failure to stir up nationalist resentment against the government.

Another notable government initiative was the December 1997 peace deal in the Chittagong Hill Tracts (CHT), which ended more than two decades of separatist unrest by tribal rebels. Improved Bangladesh/India relations also seems to have been a key factor in this development, with each country assuring the other that it would refrain from supporting local cross-border insurgencies. The agreement has provided for limited self-government in the CHT and the return of tribal refugees from camps in India. Although the international community welcomed the accord as a major gain for human rights, domestic opposition parties accused the Hasina government of failing to protect the interests of ethnic-Bengali settlers in the CHT. More recent opposition protests against the government have included a demand for a 'review' of the deal. Nonetheless, implementation of the agreement — for which Sheikh Hasina was awarded the UNESCO Peace Prize — has generally proceeded smoothly.

Yet, in contrast to these efforts to project a forward-looking approach, the prime minister has also devoted considerable attention to reopening the unresolved issues surrounding the 1975 assassination of her father, Sheikh Mujib, and other family members. Many observers believe her desire to see justice done after more than twenty years is understandable. Protected by an indemnity provision inserted into the constitution in 1976, two of Mujib's self-confessed killers felt brazen enough to set up their own political party to contest recent elections. One of Hasina's first acts in office was to declare August 15, the date of the assassination, a public holiday dedicated to 'national mourning'.[25] She also ordered the arrest of individuals suspected of involvement in the 1975 killings. Several of them were serving in diplomatic missions overseas, and reportedly sought political asylum in North America, Asia and Europe.[26]

With the indemnity law still in force, the government initially justified the detentions by claiming some of the individuals were plotting to overthrow the present AL leadership. Though the AL election manifesto had ruled out any attempt to overturn the indemnity provision, Hasina's government acted quickly to table a motion to repeal it. The repeal was passed by parliament in late 1996 in the absence of BNP members and amid fierce public debate about whether the provision could be revoked on the basis of a simple parliamentary majority or whether, as a constitutional provision, its repeal required the support of two thirds of MPs. Following its abolition by a simple majority, several key figures accused of participating in the 1975 conspiracy were charged and put on trial in March 1997.

Despite the government's insistence that its only motive in repealing the indemnity provision was to secure justice, critics complained the move was intended as a political snub to the BNP since it was President Zia who originally enacted it. Other government actions also antagonized the BNP in late 1996. BNP MPs accused the AL-elected speaker of limiting their participation time in parliamentary debates and expressed discontent at their exclusion from several parliamentary committees. In addition, BNP leaders alleged that the government was using local police and other official agencies to harass their party workers in Dhaka and other cities. Despite earlier government assurances that it would handle official appointments in a neutral manner, the nomination of Dr. Mohiuddin Khan Alamgir as secretary to the prime minister and Professor A.Z. Azad Chaudhury as Dhaka University's vice chancellor, both perceived to be anti-BNP, also provoked opposition complaints. Relations between the government and opposition reached a breaking point in November 1996 when the son and father-in-law of Begum Zia were arrested on corruption charges arising from the tenure of the previous BNP government.

Within days, the BNP announced its withdrawal from parliament and insisted its members would not return until the government met a list of ten demands, including the dismissal of the chief election commissioner whom the BNP accused of bias in the conduct of recent by-elections.[27] The party also began to mount street demonstrations against what it described as government repression. Amid fears that Bangladesh would again descend into political turmoil, the government and opposition eventually negotiated an agreement enabling BNP MPs to resume their seats in mid-January 1997.

Though the deal probably reflected a genuine desire on both sides to avoid an all-out confrontation so soon in the new parliament, the compromise also betrayed the weakness of the BNP's position. Unlike Begum Zia who had hesitated as prime minister to fill the seats vacated by an opposition walk-out, Hasina had threatened to call immediate by-elections if the BNP did not rejoin parliament.[28] Even if the BNP had opted to maintain a strategy of defiance, Hasina had deftly ensured there would be no united opposition front against her. By agreeing to release former President Ershad from jail on 20 January, she cemented the AL's alliance with his party. In any case the BNP's ability to reproduce the kind of agitation previously mounted by the AL had been partly undercut by Begum Zia's public pledge to her supporters in the business community that she would not inflict further disruption on an already beleaguered economy.[29]

Notwithstanding these constraints, a daylong national strike called by the BNP on 23 March 1997, which particularly affected the main cities, was a timely reminder that underlying tensions remained unresolved. Indeed, periods of unrest punctuated by tactical 'truces' between the government and its opponents have characterized much of the period since. A further strike in May 1997 brought public transport to a halt and provoked violent clashes between BNP and AL supporters. In August, the opposition staged a walkout from parliament to protest the government's allegation that Begum Zia had sought to undermine the day of 'national mourning' for Mujib on August 15 by claiming that her birthday fell on the same day, a charge rejected by the BNP as a 'big government mischief'[30]. In an effort to stem a worsening law and order situation, the two sides brokered an agreement in March 1998. In return for the opposition resuming their seats in parliament, the government promised to ease restrictions on street rallies, drop charges against detained BNP supporters and accord 'equal rights' to the opposition in parliament.

Government-opposition relations, however, soon relapsed into confrontation. Opposition moves to exploit public concern about escalating violent crime and rising food prices, exacerbated by the impact of widespread flooding, resulted in renewed clashes between opposition activists and security forces in the summer of 1998. Tensions peaked in November when the BNP organized a sixty hour national strike. The action followed a court ruling sentencing several former army officers to death for involvement in the 1975 assassination of Mujib. In early January 1999, the BNP and other opposition parties united behind a set of demands calling, inter alia, for immediate mid-term elections under a neutral caretaker government (ironically, the same demand pursued earlier by the AL in opposition).

Though its campaign of strikes and demonstrations has caused serious disruption, the opposition campaign has largely failed to match the intensity of the AL-led agitation between 1994–96. In part, this may reflect the BNP's continued sensitivity to the concerns of the hard-pressed business community, as well as to criticism from external aid donors of the likely impact of the campaign on Bangladesh's long term economic prospects. But it may also reflect the BNP's ongoing difficulties in forging a unified opposition challenge to the government. In December 1998, Ershad broke with the government and announced that his Jatiya Party would join a BNP-led alliance. But the one JP minister, Anwar Manju, refused to resign his post and Ershad's move caused a split in the parliamentary party.[31] Moreover, despite an anti-government boycott of local elections called for February 1999, opposition party members reportedly were among over 9,000 candidates who participated in the poll.[32]

With the opposition unable to generate sufficient pressure to unseat Hasina and the government showing no sign of bowing to a demand for early elections, the depressing cycle of confrontation and short-lived reconciliation at the heart of the Bangladeshi political system looks set to continue. The adverse effects of this impasse have become increasingly apparent. Government preoccupation with containing the opposition seems largely to have deflected its attention from the country's deep-rooted problems, including the need to tackle a deteriorating law-and-order situation, curb corruption and institute long overdue reforms in the civil service, police and legal system.

ARMY ON THE SIDELINES

In view of the problems besetting successive civilian governments, the absence of military involvement has been a major enigma in Bangladesh's tumultuous recent history. Its restraint appears all the more surprising when one considers that many Bangladeshis would have been relieved, though perhaps not happy, to see the army step in to end the prolonged standoff between the previous BNP government and opposition parties. But not only did the military refrain from direct intervention, it also apparently refused to undertake any 'behind the scenes' mediation to defuse the crisis. Instead the army continued to follow official orders, even when these threatened to provoke confrontation with opposition groups – as when the BNP government in early 1996 directed the troops to confiscate 'illegal' arms from anti-government activists. Later, the army was a crucial element in ensuring that the June 1996 elections were held in a relatively peaceful and well-ordered manner.[33] Though a full accounting of the army's unwillingness to be drawn back into politics will have to await more detailed studies, some of the relevant factors may be rooted in changes both within the military as well as in the wider national and international political context.

Elements within the army staged three successful coups and numerous unsuccessful ones in the 1970s and the early 1980s. Both Mujib's overthrow in 1975 and Zia's assassination in 1981 were the result of plots hatched by groups of junior officers acting independently of the top military brass. Instability within the army during this period was partly driven by mundane concerns over pay and conditions, but also mirrored the political fissures and ideological struggles afflicting wider Bangladeshi society. The most acute division was between the 'freedom fighters' and 'repatriates'. The former comprised Bengali deserters from the Pakistan army and ex-civilians who fought in the liberation war and were influenced by the secular and pro-leftist strains of Bengali nationalism. The latter consisted of other Bengali military professionals who were stranded in West Pakistan during the events of 1971 and only later returned to Bangladesh; they tended to be more conservative and pro-Islamic.

Tensions within the military have subsided considerably since the mid-1980s, though a residual 'freedom fighter'/'repatriate' split remains. Reforms introduced by Zia in the late 1970s served to improve troop morale and discipline, and facilitated the emergence of a more cohesive professional army. Ershad, his successor as army chief, who was the main beneficiary of these changes, continued this policy: he never faced a serious mutiny in the ranks while in power. However, the institutional unity and strength attained by the armed forces also ultimately proved Ershad's undoing when his successor as army chief, General Nooruddin Khan, withdrew support for his regime in 1990 amid rising popular discontent. Nooruddin and his successors have since maintained a strictly apolitical stance motivated partly by concern that political entanglements distract the military from its core professional responsibilities.

The army's reluctance to intervene may also reflect other pressures. The public mood in Bangladesh seems to have hardened against a political role for the army; and a new military regime, unlike its predecessors, might not be able to count on a broad measure of popular indifference to sustain its control. Moreover, lacking democratic credentials, such a regime would have to contend with a hostile international climate. As a country that is still largely dependent on external assistance, Bangladesh in such circumstances could be vulnerable to an aid cut-off by its main western donors. The country might also be subject to UN-imposed penalties, not least its exclusion from participation in worldwide peacekeeping operations – a lucrative source of revenue for the Bangladeshi military.

Events in 1996 underscored the army's break with its past. In an unprecedented development, the army acquiesced to the dismissal of its leader, General Nasim, on 20 May by a civilian president. Biswas sacked Nasim for refusing to obey a defense ministry order to retire two senior officers.[34] He was replaced by General Muhammad Mahbubur Rahman. There were early indications that the move would prompt pro-Nasim units to march on Dhaka, but they eventually backed down in the face of a stronger show of force by troops loyal to the civilian government. Though the incident threatened to provoke a split in military ranks and could have led to a coup, its bloodless resolution may have served to reinforce civilian control over the army. In a meeting with journalists in late July 1996, General Rahman ruled out any further coups in Bangladesh, declaring, 'Everyone in the army wants peace and for the politicians to run the country.'[35] Only a month earlier, the army leadership accepted the election of an AL government, despite the military's past aversion to the party. This animosity was mainly a legacy of the 1971–75 period when Sheikh Mujib was widely seen to have downgraded the role of the conventional military, about whose loyalty he had suspicions, in favor of his elite Indian-trained protection force, the Rakhi Bahini.

PROSPECTS

Bangladesh's struggle to establish a working democracy, which finally came to fruition in the 1990s, was no less a triumph against overwhelming odds than its earlier fight for political independence. The stability of the present parliamentary system may be far from assured, but from all current evidence it enjoys the mantle of popular legitimacy. Though most Bangladeshis are preoccupied with the daily struggle to make ends meet, and are often disillusioned with the squabbles of their elected leaders, they appear to support, albeit subconsciously, the Churchillian maxim that democracy is the least desirable form of government except for all the rest.

Popular backing for representative government was reflected in the relatively high turnouts for both the 1991 and 1996 elections and derives, at least in part, from a perception that Bangladesh's earlier authoritarian regimes failed to provide either political stability or faster socio-economic development. It is a perception apparently shared by many in the armed forces, especially its senior leadership, and acts as an important psychological barrier to renewed military intervention in government.

If past dictatorships fell because of their inherent deficiencies, the current democratic experiment will also be judged by how far it delivers the goods in two key areas: improving living standards for the impoverished majority of the population and ensuring that a mix of social groups, including peasants, factory workers, the business community, urban professionals and students, feel they have a political stake in the survival of the system.

It may be that the level of popular enthusiasm for democracy in Bangladesh will depend, to some extent, on the performance of the present government, especially its capacity to boost economic growth and implement significant public sector reform. But the longer-term viability of the system probably will hinge crucially on whether its participants can overcome certain operational weaknesses. Among the most serious failings are the continuing lack of executive accountability to the legislature, the centralization of power within the rival political parties, and the unwillingness of the party leaders to play by accepted parliamentary rules, whether in government or opposition.[36] It is perhaps the last of these, the acrimonious relationship between the 'two ladies,' Prime Minister Hasina and BNP leader Begum Zia, that continues to pose the most acute danger to political stability.

NOTES

1   1993 estimate, cited in Barbara Leitch LePoer, 'Bangladesh: Background and US Policy Interests', Congressional Research Service Report for Congress, August 1994.
2   Ibid.
3   Ibid.
4   Ibid.
5   For a fuller account of this period, see Craig Baxter, 'Bangladesh: A Parliamentary Democracy If They Can Keep It', *Current History*, March 1992.
6   Baxter, ibid.
7   Marcus Franda, *Bangladesh: The First Decade* (New Delhi: South Asian Publishers, 1982), 325–6.
8   Franda, ibid., 223.
9   Bangladesh uses the plurality electoral system with single member territorial constituencies.
10 For an excellent analysis of the outcome of the 1991 elections, see Gowher Rizvi, 'Bangladesh: Towards Civil Society', *Current History*, September 1991.
11 Baxter, ibid.

12 The business community's role in the crisis is well documented in Stanley A. Kochanek, 'Bangladesh at Twenty-Five: The Growing Commercialization of Power', unpublished paper presented at the 'International Conference on Bangladesh at Twenty-five', Columbia University, 5–7 December 1996.
13 Agence France Presse (AFP, Hong Kong), 28 March 1996.
14 AFP (Hong Kong), 21 May 1996.
15 See the 'Preliminary Statement of the NDI (National Democratic Institute) Observer Delegation to the June 12, 1996 Parliamentary Elections in Bangladesh,' 14 June 1996.
16 For an elaboration of the differences between Bengali and Bangladeshi nationalism, see Ghulam Murshid, 'Vacillating Muslim Identity in Bengal', unpublished paper presented at the international conference on 'Bangladesh 1971–96: Past, Present and Future', London, 13–15 December 1996.
17 Author's interviews with journalists, Dhaka, September 1996.
18 A comprehensive examination of the treaty is contained in Syed Mahmud Ali, 'The Centre-Periphery Paradigm In South Asia: Elite Insecurity Perceptions in Bangladesh vis-a-vis India', unpublished paper presented at International Conference on 'Bangladesh 1971–96: Past Present and Future', London, 13–15 December 1996.
19 *Dhaka Dainik Inqilab*, 13 November 1996 (FBIS).
20 Associated Press (AP), 1 January 1996.
21 AFP (Hong Kong), 23 June 1996.
22 *Dhaka Janakantha*, 16 October 1996 (FBIS).
23 See text of finance minister's budget speech: *Daily Star* (Dhaka), 29 July 1996.
24 AFP (Hong Kong), 13 August 1996.
25 Reuters, 15 August 1996.
26 AFP (Hong Kong), 4 September 1996.
27 United News of Bangladesh, 1 January 1997.
28 Reuters, 10 January 1997.
29 United News of Bangladesh, 6 October 1996.
30 *Economist*, 27 September 1997.
31 Economist Intelligence Unit, *Country Report: Bangladesh*, 15 March 1999.
32 Ibid.
33 United News of Bangladesh, 1 October 1996.
34 Dhaka radio, 20 May 1996.
35 United News of Bangladesh, 16 October 1996.
36 For a useful survey of the problems still facing Bangladeshi democracy, see Mohammad Mohabbat Khan and Syed Anwar Hussain, 'Process of democratization in Bangladesh', *Contemporary South Asia* 1996, 328–332.

Chapter 4
Nation-Building in a Demotic State: The Failure of Political Leadership in Sri Lanka
A. Jeyaratnam Wilson

Britain transferred power in 1948 to a chosen collaborator, Don Stephen Senanayake, a Sinhala Buddhist statesman who commanded the confidence of most of the Sinhala middle classes and large sections of the peasantry (the rest backed the left wing) but with little support from the most articulate of the other co-indigenous group, the Sri Lankan Tamils. Senanayake also did not have the trust of the Indian Tamils. The Muslims acquiesced, as did a minority of the Sri Lankan Tamils. To forge a unity of these diverse groups, Senanayake and his leading supporters organised the United National Party (UNP) in 1946. Its name indicated its goal: essentially it was to become an amalgam of the Westernised and conservative Sinhala Buddhist bourgeoisie with cooptionists from the other communities.

Neither Senanayake nor any of his successors had, unlike Jawaharlal Nehru or Tunku Abdul Rahman, a wider vision on how a newly independent multi-ethnic polity should have political institutions, as in India, and ways and means of accommodating ethnic minorities, as with the Alliance Party in Malaysia, to ensure for some length of time a peaceful polity. There was in Sri Lanka's case an absence of consensus or any serious attempts to forge inter-ethnic agreements based on an understanding of the problems of the different groups in the polyethnic state. A constituent assembly, as in India, or an all-representative political grouping, as in Malaya, could have helped to bridge gaps. Tragically, as this essay will demonstrate, this failure of political leadership was characteristic of each of Sri Lanka's seven heads of government after independence. There were no long-term goals projected for either a new society or an inclusive deal for the minorities or for the vast majority of poor people. The alternative model which Sri Lanka's political leaders chose was that of a *demotic state* in which appeals by competing parties to the ethnic majority at the expense of the principal ethnic minority gave rise in the end to armed insurrection by the latter. The majority's leadership followed the crowd instead of observing the basic rules of the democratic process which consists of more than merely respecting the will of the ethnic majority.

On the first question, that of creating consensus, rather than affect compromises agreeable to the various ethnic groups on lines similar to Arend Lijphart's consociationalism, the Sinhalese leadership unwisely principally cultivated the ethnic majority of the Sinhala Buddhists. Thereafter, the national question became one of which major party was more favourable to providing benefits to the ethnic majority, so that politics became a veritable auctioning game between the two main competing Sinhala-dominated parties, the United National Party which governed during 1947–1956, 1965–1970, 1977–1994 and the Sri Lanka Freedom Party (SLFP) which with its allies held the government in 1956–1959, 1960–1965, 1970–1977. Both parties promoted Sinhala Buddhist political claims at the expense of the Ceylon and Indian Tamils and to some extent of the Muslims on such issues as the national flag, state-aided Sinhala colonisation of the traditional Tamil homeland, the decitizenisation and disfranchisement of the Indian Tamils, Sinhala as the only state language, the nationalisation of the Christian denominational schools, standardisation of marks for admission to the universities to give an advantage to the Sinhala students, and the unilateral framing of two constitutions (in 1972 and 1978) without the cooperation of the major Ceylon Tamil grouping in parliament. Table 1 provides a demographic picture of the multi-ethnic composition of the island's population.

Ceylon (renamed Sri Lanka in 1972) is a unique and unfortunate example of the perversion of power by an ethnic majority as soon as the moderating apparatus of Britain's suzerainty was withdrawn.

Table 1: **Sri Lanka: Ethnic Composition of Population** (*in percent*)

Ethnic Group	1946	1981
Sinhalese	69.6	74.0
Sri Lankan Tamils	11.0	12.6
Indian Tamils	12.2	5.6
Muslims	6.0	7.3
Burghers and others	1.2	0.5

Source: Department of Census and Statistics.

Note: (1) the majority of Indian Tamils live outside the Tamil-majority Northern and Eastern provinces.
(2) some 30 percent of Muslims live in the Northern and Eastern Provinces while the rest are scattered in the Sinhala districts; there is a strong concentration of Muslims in the Colombo district.

DON STEPHEN SENANAYAKE, PRIME MINISTER 1947-1952

D.S. Senanayake, as the last visiting reforms commission to the island (1945-1946) headed by Viscount Soulbury opined, would have been able to weld the communities together and share with the ethnic minorities the power transferred to him in a way as to win their confidence. Instead Senanayake followed a two track policy – one that was utterly pro-British in external affairs but designed to reduce and break up Tamil solidarity whilst maintaining the illusion of national mindedness in internal affairs. His unexpressed ultimate goal was to achieve a Sinhala dominant polity. Ideally, Senanayake would have preferred a gradualist approach to a unilingual state in which the Ceylon Tamils would have meekly accepted a secondary place and agreed to have the Sinhala language as the common medium of communication.

An assessment of D.S. Senanayake is essential for understanding the path that political events took in Ceylon. Endowed with an uncommon degree of common sense, Senanayake understood that in politics, ruthlessness, amorality and purchaseability of rival politicians was the highroad to success. Fortune placed him where he arrived. The true leader, his elder brother, Francis Richard Senanayake, died in the mid-1920s leaving the throne to his rustic brother, a politician no doubt but one who spent much of his time managing the family estate and plumbago mines.

D.S. Senanayake was at first a rebel against the British but soon learned that cooperation and collaboration would pay richer dividends. He had his school of supporters. Foremost among them was the press monopolist, D.R. Wijewardene, owner of the Lake House Press, which published all the newspapers in English, Sinhala and Tamil. Senanayake also had the skilful support of a clever strategist in Oliver Ernest Goonetileke who acted his role well but made his motives too obvious. In the second phase of his pre-independence career, Senanayake also had available to him the expertise of Sir Ivor Jennings, the principal of the island's University College which was later elevated to university status, and became its first vice-chancellor. Jennings was the senior-most acknowledged constitutional authority in the Commonwealth. He proved adept at steering the negotiations in respect of formulating a constitution, which obtained minimalist acceptance from the leaders of the minority communities.

D.S. Senanayake committed serious errors in policy, perhaps because of his limited high school education (he did not go beyond the final grade) which in turn limited his vision and narrowed his worldview. He was successful in eliminating rivals who could deny him the exalted office. Sir Claude Corea was briskly despatched as an ambassador as was Sir Baron Jayatilaka in an earlier phase. S.W.R.D. Bandaranaike was virtually edged out and provided enough rope to hang himself with while serving as a senior minister in the Senanayake cabinet. No doubt the Senanayakes were known for their loyalty to their supporters, but nothing was permitted to stand in their way. This was accompanied by a cold cynicism, even in times of grave danger. The unflappable Senanayake could play a waiting game, and if the waiting period was too long a minion was despatched to offer a price to the source of the disturbance. There were some who spurned, but many succumbed. In Senanayake's worldview, as long as Ceylon was in the Commonwealth, Sri Lanka had nothing to fear from imagined Indian expansionism.

In internal matters, however, he thought that as long as the Tamil minority was left undisturbed in its vantage position in the public sector, and as long as its access to education was assured, accompanied by a reasonable freedom to trade and move around the country, the grand design of converting the traditional Tamil-speaking Eastern Province into a Sinhala majority one could be attained.

Senanayake was a practising Buddhist, but he was a cut above the rest. He steadfastly refused to countenance Buddhism as a political force or a major religious symbol for political purposes. Therefore the question of the nationalisation of denominational schools, a demand of militant Buddhists was brushed aside. Similarly, he was not forthcoming on the Sinhala language. It is probable that he favoured the continuance of English and a shade or two of bilingualism (Sinhala and Tamil) in the schools and lower levels of administration. On state control of the means of production, he was committed to the minimum of government interference in private enterprise. So he dismissed proposals for the nationalisation of plantations, a favourite response of his being that he did not wish to kill the goose that laid the golden eggs.

Given this philosophy, the elitist leaders of the minority communities were at ease with Senanayake. What is more, despite his years (he was sixty-four when he became prime minister) and his debilitating diabetes, Senanayake proved a strong leader whom neither ministers nor bureaucrats could trifle with. In contrast, the failure to implement policy or to distort it in its implementation, especially in vital areas, was not an infrequent phenomenon in the case of all Senanayake's successors with the single exception of Premadasa.

Despite his exceptional skills, Senanayake failed in a calculated gamble to win the *unconditional* support of the principal Sri Lankan Tamil political organisation, the All Ceylon Tamil Congress (TC). Formed by G.G. Ponnambalam in 1944, the TC was heir to the problems and frustrations of the Sri Lankan Tamils under British colonialism. During all of the one hundred and fifty years of British rule, the Sri Lankan Tamils had retained a separate identity and a majority of them lived in their traditional homeland in the Northern and Eastern provinces. They readily took to English education provided by Christian missionary schools, and quite a few converted to Christianity in the process. Knowledge of the English language gave English-educated Tamils ready access to low and middle level jobs in the colonial administration as well as in the professions. Yet, Ponnambalam's agitation for fifty-fifty in legislative and executive representation in the late 1930s and early 1940s failed, despite his determined efforts. A different leader may have been willing to compromise and accept other rigid constitutional instruments such as a comprehensive bill of rights and an independent judiciary, or even switched to a demand for a federal structure. But Ponnambalam also had a limited vision, and his entry into the Senanayake cabinet in 1948 marked the beginning of his fall from grace with the Tamil electors.

The Tamil public were not certain that his meek-mannered lieutenant, S.J.V. Chelvanayakam, could fit the bill even when he broke with Ponnambalam and his TC in 1948 and formed a new Tamil party in 1949, the Federal Party (FP). Chelvanayakam infused a sense of nationalism in the Tamil people and taught them that language and territory are one. That if territory is taken away, there will be no language to defend. He united the Tamil-speaking people of the north and the east and forged a new alliance with the leadership of the disfranchised Indian Tamil leadership. The FP was ideologically a more solid organisation than the TC and became from 1956 the rallying point and the bulwark of a new defensive Tamil nationalism.

The parting of ways between Ponnambalam and Chelvanayakam is significant for the insights it provided with regard to Sinhala–Tamil relationships. For Senanayake, cabinet portfolios were adequate to paper the cracks between the two communities. But differences began to surface from the very start. Shortly after independence (on 4 February 1948), a decision had to be made on the new state's national flag. Sinhala opinion favoured the adoption of the 'lion flag' of the last king of the interior kingdom of Kandy, which was conquered by the British in 1815. The Ceylon Tamils were opposed to it because the lion signified the origins of the Sinhala people, the 'people of the lion'. In the end, Senanayake had a parliamentary committee which included Ceylon Tamil representatives to come up with a design. The committee recommended in February 1950 the retention of the lion with two stripes, one for the Tamils and the other for the Muslims. The decision was acceptable to Ponnambalam who served as a member of the committee, but was opposed by Chelvanayakam and others of the FP. Senanayake obtained parliament's support notwithstanding the opposition.

Far more devastating for the Tamil minority was Senanayake's enactment in 1948 and 1949 of citizenship legislation for the new state, a move which resulted in over 95 percent of the resident Indian Tamil plantation workers being rendered stateless and disfranchised. This community had exercised their franchise in the pre-independence phase, elected seven Indian Tamils to parliament at the general election of 1947 and influenced the outcome in favour of candidates opposed to Senanayake's UNP in twenty other constituencies. In fact, the provision for seven Indian Tamils as part of the total contingent of MPs from the minority communities had been Senanayake's response to the Ceylon Tamil demand for fifty-fifty representation – a compromise which satisfied the British. Shortly after gaining state power, Senanayake reneged on his undertaking.

As disconcerting was Senanayake's colonisation policy, which disturbed the demographic composition of the Tamil-majority Eastern Province. The settlement of Sinhala peasants in new colonies in areas opened up by the restoration of irrigation tanks served two purposes. One, it helped elevate the restorer of the great ruined tanks to the glorious status of the Sinhala kings who first built them. Two, the policy aided the encroachment of the majority community to the traditional homelands of the Tamil-speaking peoples of the province, that is the Ceylon Tamils and Muslims. The changes affected the voting strength of the Tamil-speaking people in the constituencies demarcated and recognised as theirs. The FP agitated against these state-aided colonisation schemes, but successive Sinhala-oriented governments remained insensitive. However, inter-ethnic agreements, the Bandaranaike-Chelvanayakam Pact of 1957 and the Dudley Senanayake-Chelvanayakam Pact of 1965, though not implemented because of strong Sinhala opposition, recognised the existence of the problem as well as the fact that the Eastern Province was part of the traditional Tamil homeland in the Northern and Eastern provinces.

Coupled with these major policies of the so-called 'government of national unity' of D.S. Senanayake, there were other minor irritants which brought home to the Tamil people that all was not well in the new state. Increasingly qualified and meritorious Ceylon Tamil applicants for positions in the public and private sectors found that less qualified members of the Sinhala majority being given preference. Though the government had not given any written directions, the duly-constituted boards of selection in the private and public sectors seemed to know what was expected of them. The safeguard instituted in the pre-independence Soulbury constitution for ensuring impartiality in public appointments, in the form of a politically-insulated Public Services Commission, did not live up to expectations. Where under the colonial dispensation the three members of the commission would have been the nominees of a disinterested colonial governor; in the post-independence set up, the commissioners were aware that the wishes of the prime minister and the more assertive members of his cabinet must be satisfied. Under the new system of cabinet government, the prime minister and his ministers had to be certain that they had senior officials whom they approved of, not merely persons selected on grounds of merit. The frustrated candidates of the educated Tamil community were left aggrieved. This applied as well to matters of promotion within the services, especially when proficiency in Sinhala as the official language was required as a prerequisite for promotion after 1956.

Thus, in the four years that the ship of state was steered by D.S. Senanayake, the navigator failed to inspire confidence in sections of his complement of passengers. This dissatisfaction provided fertile ground for the growth of support for the Tamil FP after 1956, with an armed Tamil insurrection taking over leadership from the moderate Tamil parliamentary leaders after 1983. It could be said with some degree of conviction that the seeds for the disintegration of the island polity were laid during the five-year tenure of D.S. Senanayake.

DUDLEY SENANAYAKE, PRIME MINISTER 1952–1953, MARCH–JULY 1960, 1965–1970

The new prime minister had hardly any experience in government other than serving a five-year term as minister of agriculture in his father's cabinet. D.S. Senanayake had indirectly expressed the wish to the governor-general, Lord Soulbury, that his son should succeed him, and the governor-general acceded to the wishes of the dead prime minister in a manner which is not beyond reproach. Dudley dissolved parliament within weeks of his succeeding to the premiership, claiming that he sought a mandate of confirmation from the electors. In reality, he and his UNP hoped to harvest the groundswell of support created by the Lake House newspapers to the memory of 'the Father of the Nation'. In the three periods that the junior Senanayake served as prime minister, though there were differences in regard to the ethnic question, Dudley was basically a copy of his father.

Dudley was inexperienced, moody and therefore unpredictable and dependent on an inner circle of women whose advice may or may not have had an impact on him. They were, however, supportive of him emotionally, and their perseverance provided the prime minister with a degree of staying power. The latter was excessively sensitive on certain issues of state. The deaths by military and police action of nine demonstrators during the great *hartal* (strike) of August 1953 sent him into a tailspin. Thereafter, it was only a question of time till he resigned in October without even designating a successor. The source of much of his troubles was the frustration and anger at his cousin, Sir John Kotelawala, a senior minister since 1931 and government Leader of the House from 1951, who had looked on himself as the heir presumptive to D.S. Senanayake.

On the Tamil question, Dudley retained his father's policies during his first and second premierships (the latter all too short but sufficiently indicative of his train of thought). He maintained ties with Ponnambalam and the TC, which had succeeded in winning in the Tamil areas at the general election of 1952. The main thrust of Dudley's election campaign was directed against the Marxist parties for their support of citizenship rights and the franchise to the now stateless Indian Tamil population. There is no evidence that as prime minister he sought an accommodation on the disputed issue. He also avoided references to colonisation policies and communal selections in public and private sector appointments. Nor did he touch the question of an official language for the new state despite the opposition, especially S.W.R.D. Bandaranaike, clamouring for the declaration of Sinhala and Tamil as state languages. In effect, Dudley had nothing new to offer but his approach won the enthusiastic support of the Colombo establishment, the Sinhala middle class and major sections of the elite among the Ceylon Tamils and the Muslims. Only the Indian Tamils were left out in the cold.

Dudley's government, however, came a cropper when it tried to implement the report of a World Bank mission which recommended cuts in welfare subsidies and greater rigour in the state's public works programmes. The sum effect was felt most adversely by the majority of poor people. The left parties seized on the opportunity to organise a countrywide hartal. Clashes resulted and police firing causing the death of nine civilians had a numbing effect on the prime minister. Not having effected any significant changes in policy for the betterment of the island state, his resignation in October 1953 did not make much of a difference.

In his tenure of office during March–July 1960, he first headed a minority government which was defeated at the division on the Address of Thanks to the Throne Speech in April 1960. He continued as head of a caretaker government after securing a controversial dissolution of Parliament, Dudley's conduct of the general election campaign again evidenced the taint of anti-Ceylon Tamil communalism. He appealed to voters to not permit the FP to hold the balance of power in the new parliament and thus dictate policy to one or other of the major Sinhala parties. In other words, the Sinhala electorate should, he appealed, give a clear majority to the UNP or the SLFP. Ironically, it was the SLFP that obtained the majority.

Dudley had endeavoured to secure the support of Chelvanayakam and his FP in March 1960 when, as leader of the largest single party with a plurality in Parliament, he was commissioned by the governor-general to form a government. Dudley spent weeks of negotiation with Chelvanayakam in the hope that the latter would, at a minimum, support the government he would head as long as it did not act against the interests of the Ceylon Tamils. Chelvanayakam responded that that was how he expected any democratic government to function. His position was that Dudley should agree to his 'four points' for the amelioration of the position of the Tamils: namely, one, the creation of a single regional council comprising the Northern and Eastern provinces with sufficiently devolved powers; two, Tamil be made an official language; three, re-enfranchisement of the Indian

Tamils be accomplished by appropriate amendments to the citizenship legislation of 1948; and four, till the citizenship legislation of 1948 and 1949 was amended, four of the six appointed MPs provided for in the constitution should be from the Indian Tamil community and be nominated by the main organisation representing the Indian Tamils at the time, the Ceylon Workers' Congress (CWC). Dudley stated he could not concede or compromise on any of these demands because his election campaign had been conducted on a platform that rejected them. Despite much pressure on Chelvanayakam from prominent Colombo Tamils and Ceylon Tamil associations in various parts of the seven Sinhala provinces, Chelvanayakam remained as inflexible as Dudley. Thus, at the division, the FP supported the opposition and the government was defeated.

Dudley conducted a fiercely anti-FP campaign in the general election that followed. The ordinary Sinhala voter could not make a distinction between a Ceylon Tamil and the FP: they were stereotyped as one and the same. This was similar to the heyday of the Tamil Congress; and it is not uncommon in present times for uninformed Sinhala people to stigmatise all Ceylon Tamils as *Eelamkarayas* (Eelam people/supporters) or *kotiyas* (Tigers).

Dudley's third government, between 1965–70, was a coalition with the FP as the main ally. The UNP obtained a plurality again at the general election of July 1965. To some extent, such an outcome had been anticipated. J.R. Jayewardene had done much of the groundwork prior to the election. Meetings were held between Jayewardene and the FP leaders; and it seemed as if the UNP leadership had accepted the FP's insistence on preserving the Tamil-majority complexion of the traditional Tamil homeland, the Northern and Eastern provinces. The UNP leader also realised the need to amend the citizenship legislation of 1948 and 1949 to enable a larger number of Indian Tamils to enter the electoral registers. The unwritten understanding was that the CWC, led by S. Thondaman, would deliver the Indian vote to the UNP.

Before forming his government, Dudley entered into an agreement with Chelvanayakam under which he agreed that (a) Tamil be made a language of administration in the Northern and Eastern provinces; (b) legal proceedings in the two Tamil-speaking provinces be conducted and recorded in Tamil; (c) district councils be set up, with powers to be agreed upon between the two leaders, with the proviso that the central government should have power 'to give directions to such councils in the national interest'; and (d) in respect of land allocation, preference be given in the Northern and Eastern provinces to 'landless persons in the district', and next to Tamil-speaking citizens in the rest of the island. The agreement was signed on 24 March 1965, the day before Dudley Senanayake was commissioned to form the government. An agreement touching on the issues of the Indian Tamils was also concluded at about the same time by the prime minister-designate.

The 'national government', as it came to be called, was one of national reconciliation over the short term. The FP had a representative in the cabinet (M. Tiruchelvam), a member of the Senate and not of the popular House, because all FP MPs had pledged that they would not accept any cabinet appointments till their party's basic demands were met. M. Tiruchelvam had an exceedingly difficult responsibility to discharge, which he nevertheless did effectively. He framed the Tamil Regulations under S.W.R.D. Bandaranaike's Tamil Language (Special Provisions) Act of 1958, which parliament enacted in January 1966. These regulations recognised Tamil as a language of administration along with Sinhala in the Tamil provinces.

The District Councils Bill, also framed by Tiruchelvam in close consultation with the prime minister, Chelvanayakam and Ponnambalam was, in the end, abandoned by the prime minister in 1968 due to threats of a Sinhalese backbench revolt. This was a severe blow to the FP. Though the prime minister explained his difficulties to the FP leaders and offered to resign, they demurred. The relationship, however, cooled shortly afterwards. Tiruchelvam resigned over a dispute with the prime minister when the latter disbanded a committee that the minister had appointed to recommend to him the steps he might take to declare the precincts of the Koneswaran temple in Trincomalee, sacred to the Hindus, a protected area. On this occasion, the prime minister acceded to the protests of an influential Buddhist monk in the neighbouring vicinity of Seruwila. The FP realised that even in a government whose formation had depended almost wholly on its participation, the government's leader could not resist the importunings of a member of the Sinhala Buddhist clergy.

The Indian Tamils and the CWC, on their part, secured the necessary enactment of the amending legislation that ameliorated the existing situation. The Indo–Ceylon Agreement Act of 1968 removed the element of compulsion as well as the principle of relating the grant of Sri Lanka citizenship to the physical repatriation of Indian Tamil persons opting for Indian nationality. These provisions had been included under the Indo–Ceylon Agreement of 1964, also referred to as the Sirima–Shastri Pact. Under the amendment, Indians Tamils granted Indian citizenship were allowed to remain in the island till their retiring age. These changes were accepted by all the Tamil parties in parliament. In addition, Dudley Senanayake had two Indian Tamils appointed as members of parliament. These acts of reconciliation, taken as a whole, augured well for a greater degree of ethnic harmony and a healing of the serious rifts caused during the prime ministerships of S.W.R.D. Bandaranaike (1956–59) and Mrs. Sirima Bandaranaike (1960–65). However, they were not part of an overall strategy of a prime minister infused with new national goals, but were concessions extracted from him in return for electoral support and parliamentary backing for his National Government. As such, they were defined by necessity. Consequently, the Tamil regulations were not implemented in the proper spirit by Sinhala bureaucrats. As for the District Councils Bill, the prime minister from the very beginning of the consultations had stated that he hoped that after the experience of working with his government, the Federalists would realise that the device of district councils was not necessary to defend their interests. Thus, the spirit of the UNP of 1946-47 still prevailed and the answer of the UNP leadership to the anxieties of the ethnic minorities was still the same, namely to coopt into their ranks one or two leaders of the community concerned as show pieces.

In addition, Dudley was a weak man. Besides his moods, he was incapacitated by the diabetic illness like his father which in the end took his life in 1973 at the relatively young age of sixty-four. His government was riddled with factional squabbles, so that there was no unity at the top. The prime minister tried veering away from the themes of Sinhala Buddhism and the Sinhala language because of his alliance with the two Tamil parties, the FP and CWC. But instead, his speeches concentrated on other aspects of the ancient Sinhala heritage, in particular the close affinity between the Buddhist priesthood and the tank irrigation system that had once prevailed.

JOHN KOTELAWALA, PRIME MINISTER 1953-1956

When Dudley resigned after his illness in his first term in October 1953, Sir John Kotelawala was appointed in his place. Kotelawala was also a member of the Senanayake family, being the nephew of the first prime minister. His handling of the ethnic problem was as inept as his handling of all other matters.

Kotelawala had scarcely any understanding of the Ceylon Tamil question when he decided, within weeks of his taking office, to dispense with the services of his principal pillar of Tamil support, G.G. Ponnambalam. The latter had made the serious blunder of throwing his forces into the Dudley camp at the time of the latter's appointment. In politics however this could have been overlooked because Ponnambalam would have supported any prime minister on whom he was dependent for office. Sir John's mistake, however, lay in that he thought that Ponnambalam's place could be taken by any other Ceylon Tamil of standing. In this case, it happened to be Sir Kantiah Vaithianathan, a senior civil servant of excellent credentials and widely respected but only for his reputation as a bureaucrat. Sir Kantiah's appointment was symbolic of another line of Sinhalese thinking – that the Ceylon Tamils would accept any nominee of a Sinhala prime minister, not necessarily one of their own acclaimed political leaders. In this respect, Vaithianathan was not representative of any Tamil constituency except a very narrow base in Colombo.

The prime minister was not well advised with regard to the Sinhala language storm which was about to break over him at a time when he could have acted circumspectly. Instead, on his visit to the island of Delft in Tamil-dominated north Ceylon, he was persuaded by antediluvian Ceylon Tamils living in frustrated retirement to announce to the country that he would amend the constitution to grant parity of status to the Sinhala and Tamil languages. This was tantamount to lighting a match under a powder keg. Even as the prime minister made his pledge, the Sinhala language movement had been gaining unprecedented momentum with supporters from all sectors of Sinhala society; especially the poor and the dissatisfied non-English speaking lower middle class.

The Sinhala language movement responded by demanding that Sinhala be made the one and only state language on various grounds: one, it had suffered centuries of neglect owing to foreign occupation and stood in danger of atrophying; two, the Sinhala language was spoken nowhere else on the planet but on the island of Ceylon and therefore needed special protection; and three, the Tamil language was a force in neighbouring Tamilnadu and being a more advanced language, would, if given parity of status with Sinhala swamp the latter. Four, it was alleged that the Sinhala people had been deprived of opportunities under foreign occupation, and the Ceylon Tamils had obtained a disproportionate share of positions in the public and private sectors. This situation had to be ended.

The UNP leadership generally favoured the continuance of English because its middle and upper echelons came from the English-speaking elite. It was reluctant to widen the base of political participation for fear of endangering elite dominance and encouraging the protagonists of the two national languages. The unforgivable aspect of this whole unfortunate affair was that the State Council in the Donoughmore period had resolved in 1944, on a motion moved by J.R. Jayewardene, to accept both Sinhala and Tamil as official languages when a change in the official language was undertaken. Instead, Sir John's ill-advised pronouncement gave a fillip to the Sinhala language movement, and by the end of 1955 S.W.R.D. Bandaranaike and his SLFP, sensing the direction of the political winds, changed from support for both Sinhala and Tamil as official languages to 'Sinhala Only'. In February 1956, Sir John was forced to agree to his party's decision to also adopt Sinhala to the exclusion of Tamil.

This casual and reckless pattern of decision-making, in which neither of the two major parties seriously consulted or responded to their Tamil constituents, reinforces our thesis of the promotion of the demotic state by the Sinhala political leadership which was indifferent to nation-building and universalistic values. In fact, the constitution was such that the sensitivities of the Tamils could be ignored. Kotelawala called a general election in November 1956 to enable the voters to resolve which of the two parties should be entrusted with the mandate to legislate for Sinhala as the only official language.

Kotelawala also tried his hand at resolving the Indian Tamil problem. Again, this was a naive effort at tinkering with a serious ethnic problem. However good-intentioned he may have been, there was no consensus between the two Sinhala parties and the Tamils on the question. Consequently, each prime minister after the first prime minister tried his/her hand at sorting through the ethnic debris created by the citizenship policy through what in the end came to be a game of one upmanship. There was, nevertheless, a difference between the UNP's willingness to settle for half measures versus the SLFP's inflexibility on the issue.

An Indo-Ceylon agreement was signed on January 1954 between the Indian prime minister, Jawaharlal Nehru, and Sir John. The latter obtained some gains. The Indian prime minister reluctantly agreed to a separate electoral register for the Indian Tamils who were granted Ceylon citizenship for a limited period of ten years before they were absorbed into the general electorate. They would elect a certain number to parliament. This satisfied the Kandyan Sinhalese, who feared the Indian Tamil presence in their constituencies, but it created a domestic furore on the score that this was a reversion to separate communal electorates considered anathema after the Donoughmore Commission's abolition of separate electorates in 1931. Provisions were agreed to expedite registration by the Indian authorities of persons of Indian origin seeking Indian citizenship, with the latter being provided financial incentives by the Ceylon government. Indian Tamils admitted to local citizenship should acquire 'a knowledge of the language of the area'. This again caused great controversy with S.W.R.D. Bandaranaike, as Leader of the Opposition, alleging that the prime minister had by this formula agreed to Sinhala or Tamil as the language of the area, thus dealing another deathblow to the Sinhala language. The prime minister insisted that it was meant only to be Sinhala.

The prime minister expected that there would, as a result of this agreement, be only two categories of Indian nationals, those who registered as Indian citizens and those recognised as Ceylon citizens. The Indian government, however, envisaged a third category, the stateless, consisting of those who failed to qualify for either citizenship. Thus, the Indian Tamil problem was no nearer solution, much to Sir John's disappointment.

S.W.R.D. BANDARANAIKE, PRIME MINISTER 1956–1959

The general election of April 1956 resulted in a landslide victory for S.W.R.D. Bandaranaike and the broad coalition front he led (the People's United Front, the MEP) with his SLFP as the main component. Language had been the over-riding issue in the election and though both parties pledged to make Sinhala the only state language, the voters accepted the bona fides of S.W.R.D. Bandaranaike.

More important was the effect on the Tamils. Until 1956, there had been vestiges of hope among some Tamils that the UNP was genuine in its professions of being multi-racial and multi-religious, guaranteeing equal rights to all members of the polity. The changes in 1956 became a pointer to them that both the major political parties would dispense with their interests if that were a means to gain power. The majority of the Tamil electorate confirmed through the overwhelming victory of the FP that they saw the defensive Tamil nationalism propounded by the latter as the only way to counter the creeping Sinhala demotic state. From the general election of 1956 to that of 1977, the Ceylon Tamil voters of the Northeast reposed their confidence in the FP, and regarded it as the vanguard of Tamil nationalism.

In June 1956, legislation was enacted providing for Sinhala as the only official language in an island where some 27 percent of the population was Tamil-speaking. The prime minister tried to mitigate the rigours of the act with a number of provisions for the 'reasonable use of the Tamil language' as he had pledged in his Front's election manifesto. Expectations had, however, been raised in the minds of members of the government parliamentary group, but the hysterical mob outside parliament was not in any mood to make concessions to the Tamils.

The demotic state had emerged *par excellence*. Bandaranaike had unleashed the forces of Sinhala chauvinism and he was not able to rein them in. The Sinhala crowds that poured into the chambers of parliament (the House of Representatives) on its opening day held the Speaker's sceptre and cheered wildly '*apay anduwa*' (our government). This was equated to a Sinhala government and the question of a Sri Lankan/Ceylonese government in which the Tamil and Muslim components mattered did not arise. Heretofore, the 'apay anduwa' mentality dominated, judged by the criteria of how far Sinhala governments distributed largesse to the Sinhala people.

Bandaranaike, already known for his weak leadership qualities and notoriously lacking conviction in his beliefs, gave in to the demands of his parliamentary group. In June 1956, parliament enacted Sinhala as the only official language, without any provisions for Tamil as sought in the original draft. The prime minister was also notoriously volatile. He had promised that Sinhala would become the state language in twenty-four hours, if not in twenty-four minutes. The gullible electorate had taken him at his word that the new official language would replace English overnight. Instead Bandaranaike, realising the difficulties and dislocation in administration that such a change would cause, had the full implementation of the act postponed by five years to January 1961. This was not intended as a sop to the Tamil people or Tamil public servants but arose from the impracticalities of implementing a speedy change.

Led by the FP, the Ceylon Tamils were unwilling to submit themselves to the absolute elevation of Sinhala. The typical Sinhala argument was that if the Tamils had accepted English, why could they not accept Sinhala; and that the Tamil people would gripe over the new legislation but would accept it with the passage of time. The principal reason for the Tamil objection to Sinhala, of its being used as an instrument of discrimination against Tamils seeking admission to the public and private sectors, was ignored. The latter became the motivating force in the Tamil resistance against the unilateral imposition of Sinhala.

The FP realised that it could not register its protest only in parliament, and adopted the route of extra-constitutional protest causing acute embarrassment to the Bandaranaike government. On the day of the passing of the Sinhala Only Act, the FP staged a sit-down protest on the Galle Face Green, a stone's throw from parliament. The peaceful demonstration attracted hoodlums from fringe groups within the governing party along with elements from the opposition UNP. In the end, what was expected to be a non-violent expression of lack of faith in a Sinhala-dominated government generated a chain reaction in parts of the island, leaving loot, destruction and death in its wake, Ceylon experienced its first bout of inter-ethnic violence after independence. The FP leader commented that his party's action had achieved a cent percent success. The fact however was that the basis and foundations of a consensual bi-ethnic state had been shaken.

In the following month, the FP pursued its path of extra-constitutional remedy seeking. A peaceful pilgrimage to Trincomalee was organised, processions commencing from every leading town in the two Tamil provinces. The Trincomalee Convention of the FP held in August 1956 presented the prime minister with an ultimatum demanding satisfaction on four demands, namely, (a) a federal constitution, (b) parity of status for the Sinhala and Tamil languages, (c) repeal of the existing citizenship laws, and (d) an end to colonisation of the traditional Tamil homelands. The party pledged to launch 'direct action by non-violent means' if satisfaction was not obtained in one year.

In the interim period, a sustained campaign against a confrontation was carried on by the evening daily *Ceylon Observer* and its humane and intelligent editor, Denzil Peiris. Two intermediaries close to Bandaranaike and Chelvanayakam, the eminent lawyer P. Navaratnarajah, Q.C., and the former chief justice, Sir Edward Jayatilleke, urged that both leaders should meet and resolve their differences. Their intervention had the desired effect.

S.W.R.D. Bandaranaike had no blueprint to offer the Tamil FP. He was willing to negotiate and to effect a compromise on the specific demands but had no overall plan to contain minority ethnic discontent. Negotiations took place intermittently whenever the prime minister was free and after a couple of months, on 26 July 1957, what came to be known as the

Bandaranaike-Chelvanayakam Pact was signed. The prime minister agreed to: (a) regional councils with sufficient powers of devolution to be negotiated as a substitute for federalism; it was agreed that the Northern Province would have one regional council and the multi-ethnic Eastern Province two or more councils; (b) Tamil would be made a national language and, without infringement to the national official language, it would be granted official status in the two Tamil provinces; (c) colonisation would not be used to disturb the demographic complexion of the Tamil areas; and (d) the citizenship issue would be negotiated with the two principal Indian Tamil organisations, the Ceylon Workers' Congress, led by the influential S. Thondaman, and the Democratic Workers' Congress (DWC) under A. Aziz.

Bandaranaike sought to implement this agreement in the best way he could. He was wise enough to realise that it would not be a panacea to the communal ills of the island's body politic. He had not expected the Sinhala language movement to gather such momentum. In private conversation he expressed the view that the switchover would take place only at the administrative levels, and not expand into the professions and the universities. In a sense, he was the instrument of a movement which failed to examine the repercussions of its activities on the other communities, especially the Ceylon Tamils. In addition, there was no ignoring the fact that the Ceylon Tamils and Indian Tamils had forged closer links and launched a united campaign against the government.

Bandaranaike was more at ease dealing with the honourable men of the FP. His sworn adversaries were in the UNP who gave him no quarter and to whom he was also not sparing. Bandaranaike alleged that the UNP stoked the communal flames and the prime minister was hard put to fight a fire of unmanageable proportions. He had, therefore, to rely heavily on the highly effective, though crafty, governor-general. Had Bandaranaike lived, it is possible that he would have lost the next general election. He was however, as he told this writer, keen on accomplishing two goals before going to the polls. First, he wanted to revise the constitution and revert to the Donoughmore Constitution's executive committee-type of government. This would clip the wings of full-fledged cabinet ministers who tended to ride roughshod over their parliamentary supporters. The Donoughmore system was more democratic, but the prime minister failed to realise that it only functioned well in a semi-colonial society – one which was fairly prosperous and in which the state did not have onerous responsibilities. Secondly, Bandaranaike felt that his party would certainly be returned as the largest single party but with a plurality of seats. He told this writer: 'I may not be the prime minister in the way I am at present but I could be prime minister as head of a different but like-minded combination of parliamentary groups.' He certainly had in mind the fact that different left wing groups would have accepted his leadership. If he was still short of a majority, he would have presumably negotiated with Chelvanayakam and formed a broad anti-UNP front.

Bandaranaike, however, had vicious enemies in the right wing UNP. The latter could never forgive him for deserting their ranks. They expected him to recognise his own deficiencies of not being suitable for the succession to the prime ministership when D.S. Senanayake died or retired, and to have remained loyal to the propertied class. Instead, he had broken ranks and allied himself with class enemies, the electorally powerful Marxist elements. To the UNP higher echelons, Bandaranaike appeared to be a weakling who could be manipulated by 'the scheming Marxists' who the UNP cogitated, would make Bandaranaike their Alexander Kerensky.

The UNP leadership did not challenge Bandaranaike on his alliance with the Marxists. Instead, they saw opportunity beckon when in July 1957, a year after his victory, Bandaranaike entered into the Bandaranaike-Chelvanayakam Pact (the B–C Pact). That pact, though it left much room for future negotiations, could very well have been the panacea for all the communal ills that overtook the body politic in the years to come. Hard as the prime minister tried to persuade the Sinhala electorate that his compromise agreement was 'a triumph for sanity', he found himself balked by the cynical machinations of his principal political rival, the UNP. The latter launched a 'March to Kandy' to seek the blessings of the chief prelates of the two leading Buddhist orders. The 'march' collapsed after a couple of miles but had the effect of rousing hostile Sinhala opinion.

An ill-advised despatch of the Sinhala '*sri*'-lettered buses to the Tamil areas resulted in a hugely successful 'anti-sri campaign' by the FP. The sending of these buses was said to be the work of Sinhala saboteurs in the public service. The consequences were disastrous: Bandaranaike faced Buddhist monks in the lawn of his private residence demanding the abrogation of the pact, and was compelled to submit to their wishes.

The FP responded with a civil disobedience campaign, which forced the prime minister to proclaim an island-wide state of emergency. In the midst of this emergency, Bandaranaike had parliament enact the Tamil Language (Special Provisions) Act of 1958, which laid the groundwork for the reasonable use of the Tamil language. The act was given teeth only after a different regime under Dudley Senanayake took office in 1965. Even so, in 1966 when the Tamil regulations were passed by parliament, they were met with disturbances and mass protests organised by the UNP's rivals, the SLFP led by Mrs. Bandaranaike and her Marxist allies.

In sober reflective moods, Bandaranaike was keenly aware of the hornets' nest that he stirred by having won the general election, among other things, on the singular slogan of 'Sinhala Only'. Tucked away in the inner recesses of his manifesto had been the pledge for the 'reasonable use' of the Tamil language. The prime minister probably did not expect the clear majority he obtained in which event his formula for the reasonable use of Tamil would have ensured the latter the status of a second official language. Indeed, he may well have expected to enter into a coalition with Chelvanayakam's FP.

SIRIMA BANDARANAIKE, PRIME MINISTER 1960–1965, 1970–1977

The demotic state reached its acme during the two terms Mrs. Bandaranaike served as prime minister. The conjunction was appropriate though accidental. Sri Lanka could not have had a prime minister more ill-prepared for the position. She was convent-educated, but not beyond high school. This might not have mattered if she had participated in politics alongside Bandaranaike and taken an active role in his inner court. But S.W.R.D. Bandaranaike was the traditional South Asian husband who preferred his wife to play her traditional part and not discuss political or non-domestic problems with him. There were some discussions certainly on subjects which touched on Mrs. Bandaranaike's personal interests, such as the Paddy Lands Bill of 1958, but other than such occasional coincidences of interests, the role assigned to her was that of the charming hostess. It was therefore no surprise that in July 1960, Ceylon had a prime minister who hardly knew its political alphabet.

What was more distressing was that the prime minister claimed 'to follow her late husband's policies'. Mr. Bandaranaike broadly had been a middle-of-the-road, somewhat eclectic and intensely pragmatic person, to the point that he was accused of being opportunistic in incorporating programs and policies from rival parties which he thought would have a better audience if voiced by him or his spokespeople. In this manner, important aspects of the left platform had become part of his policies, even though Bandaranaike was careful not to be personally grouped with the left leadership. He knew his strength lay in his SLFP being looked upon as a democratic alternative to the UNP.

Mrs. Bandaranaike's sins were in a way greater than her husband's. We are sharply confronted with the problem of the failure of leadership in that during her time there was no blueprint or even the outlines of a program of action that could bring the Tamils back to the mainstream of politics. In order to defeat Dudley Senanayake's minority government in April 1960, she and her principal advisors pledged to Chelvanayakam and the FP leaders that, in keeping with her late husband's policies, her party would implement the B–C Pact. Dudley Senanayake's government was defeated with the FP's parliamentary votes. In the election campaign that followed the SLFP leadership sought the FP's support to garner the Tamil vote in the seven Sinhala provinces. Mrs. Bandaranaike won a clear majority in July 1960, but thereafter kept the FP at arm's length, not even caring to reply to the letters of Chelvanayakam and his fellow MPs.

Worse was to follow. Mrs. Bandaranaike's government functioned in a most politically immature and stupid manner. She had able ministers but quite a few of them were manipulated by Sinhala Buddhist lobbies and pressure groups and were communal-minded. The Language of the Courts Act of 1961 was the first of several acts aimed at establishing Sinhala dominance in the Tamil areas. In January 1961 the government proceeded to implement the postponed provisions of the Sinhala Only act in all their rigour. This placed large numbers of Tamil public servants at risk as they had no proficiency in the official language. Added to this was the nationalisation of the majority of denominational schools in 1960–61. The FP objected to this measure not merely in support of the Christian missionaries but also because the Tamil middle-class depended very much on education. The government's majority held the day and one more bastion of Tamil safeguards fell to the demotic illiberal Sinhala-Buddhist oriented state.

Nor was Mrs. Bandaranaike's government conciliatory or slow to proceed on the colonisation question. The minister in charge, C.P. de Silva, openly expressed his plans for breaking up the contiguity of Tamil territories in the Eastern Province by launching new irrigation schemes in strategic areas such as Padaviya and Kantalai. The FP, being a parliamentary party and middle class in orientation, merely recorded its protest. It was only the civil war engaged in later by Tamil militants that served to decisively interrupt the West Bank-type colonisation of the traditional Tamil areas.

The period of Mrs. Bandaranaike's first government was one of increasing suffering for the Tamil people. In April 1961, the government declared a state of emergency in the Tamil provinces to control the massive civil disobedience campaign organised by the FP. Due to her narrow worldview, Mrs. Bandaranaike could not provide wise leadership to her government.

In her second period as prime minister, Mrs. Bandaranaike was even more disastrous. She headed a United Front government and had as her partners some of the most sophisticated left wing thinkers, Trotskyist and Communist (Moscow-oriented), in her cabinet. It was in this period, in 1976, that the Ceylon Tamils resolved in their Vaddukoddai Resolution to demand the right of self-determination and the creation of a separate Tamil state named *Tamil Eelam*.

A Trotskyist who was her minister of Constitutional Affairs was the draftsman of a republican constitution, a unilateral construction without the participation of a majority of the Tamil MPs. The Tamil Regulations of 1966 were assigned the role of subordinate legislation to be changed at will by the Sinhala-dominated legislature and Buddhism, the religion of the Sinhala ethnic majority, was marked out for state patronage. Apart from one or two minor concessions to the Indian Tamil plantation workers, the constitution was solely designed for the benefit of the majority Sinhalese.

To cap these efforts at nation breaking, Mrs. Bandaranaike's officials in the ministry of education in cooperation with some of the ministers in her government (including Marxist ones) devised the scheme of 'the standardisation of marks' for admission of students to the universities of the island, especially the professional-oriented faculties such as of medicine, engineering, law, and the sciences. Students with lower marks from designated backward areas were admitted while students with higher marks were excluded. The merit of such a scheme, it was claimed, was that it would benefit students from the backward and rural areas. Its practical effect was that it fell heavily on all Tamil students, especially those from schools in the Jaffna peninsula. This was the last nail in the coffin of a united Ceylon for which the Sinhala Buddhists professed to stand. In actual practice, they had been assiduously dismantling the state by these unilateral acts of callous discrimination.

By the end of Mrs. Bandaranaike's term of office, the Westminster type of government with the parliamentary executive headed by a prime minister accountable to parliament came to an end. The seeds of the presidentialism that followed Mrs. Bandaranaike were sown in this period. The emphasis was on the concentration of power in parliament, not its distribution and division in three separate branches. Parliament during 1947–1978 had been utilised to emphasise and accentuate the will of the ethnic majority. It was shorn of the trappings of liberal democracies the world over which had evolved over time through convention and usage that the wishes of the ethnic minority also ought to be respected. The Sinhala majority leadership from the prime minister downward had developed an insensitivity to the problems of the Tamils. The inadequacy of Tamil representation in parliament was a major factor. More importantly, there was absent a spirit of accommodation, a belief that the island was not the haven only of the Sinhalas but a multi-ethnic mosaic of communities. The task of politically educating the Sinhala Buddhist electorate in the ways of democracy was the responsibility of the Sinhala political leaders. A bolder leadership could have, without losing the support of its ethnic majority base, effected the changes that would have contained the discontent of the Tamil community. There were several such opportunities during 1947–77 but these were let go by the Sinhala leadership which attempted to outbid each other in political gamesmanship, and in the process marginalised the Tamils to the political periphery.

J.R. JAYEWARDENE, EXECUTIVE PRESIDENT 1978–1989

Jayewardene was prime minister for the brief period of 23 July 1977 to 4 February 1978. In February, parliament constitutionally deemed that

Jayewardene be declared the executive president, presaging the new constitution of 1978. For the better part of his two terms in office, I functioned as his constitutional advisor. I was also the intermediary between him and the moderate Tamil parliamentary leadership, the Tamil United Liberation Front (TULF), from 1978 to 1984.

President Jayewardene had a greater historical awareness than any of his predecessors. He had intellectual sense and rare political insights underpinned by good political instincts. His unfailing weakness was a lack of a sense of timing where the Ceylon Tamil question was concerned. Consequently, whilst conscious of the dangers, he was overly concerned about the erosion of his Sinhala Buddhist political base and permitted the solutions that could have delayed the Sinhala-Tamil war to slide. No amount of persuasion would compel him to act swiftly. When the calamitous overtook him, he was not prepared for the shock and its disastrous consequences.

In its manifesto for the 1977 general election, the UNP made pointed reference to 'the problems of the Tamil-speaking people' in the most critical areas: 'education, colonisation, use of the Tamil language and employment in the public and semi-public corporations'. But no sooner had the party received its overwhelming mandate of a five-sixths majority than it pushed the Tamil problem to the back burner. Apparently, the UNP had learned nothing from the past. Instead of moving with a sense of urgency, President Jayewardene sought to paper the cracks by appointing Tamil ministers to his government, coopting Tamils to other positions, and rendering other token concessions at the altar of rising Tamil tempestuousness.

President Jayewardene did very little or nothing to enlist the cooperation of the TULF till I appealed to him to act in the interests of the future. 'What would history have to say should he permit the gulf between the two communities to widen beyond hope of building any bridge?' I asked him. The 1978 constitution was, like that of 1972, a unilateral act with the parliamentary representatives of the TULF boycotting the proceedings. The president concentrated on his open economy and accelerated the Mahaveli river valley scheme. The latter worsened inter-ethnic relations because it opened up the Eastern Province for further state-aided Sinhala colonisation. The TULF registered their protests in parliament. Tamil militant groups meanwhile trained and equipped themselves for an armed struggle. Once again, complacency and lack of vision towards the most serious problem, the possible break-up of the country, characterised the behaviour of the Sinhala political elites. I persuaded President Jayewardene that the parliamentary select committee that was examining Tamil grievances was unrepresentative and would not inspire confidence or achieve tangible results. A round table conference would be counter-productive and merely provide opportunities for every splintered shade of political opinion to stymie the proceedings. A commission that was as representative as possible could work to devise a scheme for the devolution of powers to autonomous councils in the existing administrative districts, and this might arrest the decline to civil war. The president accepted my proposal, though he met with some opposition from his most senior bureaucrat, G.V.P. Samarasinghe, and the top administrator of his party, N.G.P. Panditharatne.

Even the commission was not sympathetic to finding a solution to the demand for autonomy. In the end, President Jayawardene and I drew up a scheme for devolving powers to autonomous districts. The TULF leadership was persuaded to accept the proposed district development councils which they agreed to as an advance on local self-government but not in exchange for their goal of a separate Tamil state. President Jayewardene's hope was that these councils would be given as much assistance as possible for economic development and that in time the question of statehood could be laid aside or even become superfluous. Legislation was enacted in 1980 and despite opposition from Tamil militant groups, elections to the councils were held in 1981. However President Jayewardene and his ministers failed to breathe life into the councils by delegating and devolving powers and by providing them with the much needed financial wherewithal. This failure, despite my constant requests to the president, confirmed the Tamil militant view that the government had no honesty of purpose. Senior bureaucrats were actively involved in sabotaging the work of the councils.

The inevitable consequence was that the Tamil militant groups took to arms. The insurrection that followed pushed out the Tamil parliamentarians from their moderating role. India was drawn into the controversy. The Tamil problem was internationalised. President Jayewardene (and Premadasa also) utilised consultative apparatus other than parliament to seek agreement on a solution after 1984. He convened an All Parties Conference in 1984 to discuss the proposals of G. Parthasarathy, Mrs. Gandhi's special emissary, which were referred to as Annexure 'C'. By the end of 1984, President Jayewardene announced what he thought the consensus was and this statement fairly approximated the terms of the Indo-Sri Lanka Accord of July 1987. Although President Jayewardene subsequently signed the Indo-Sri Lanka Accord of July 1987 with the Indian prime minister, Rajiv Gandhi, on pressure from India, the Tamil militants no longer trusted the Jayawardene government.

Since the Indo-Sri Lanka Accord of July 1987, Sinhala opinion has endeavoured to view the island as a multi-ethnic polity and not as the proprietorial asset of the Sinhala Buddhist majority. The concept of provincial autonomy as a compromise to statehood was finally given serious consideration. Yet, the degree of autonomy conceded was limited by the overarching powers retained by the Centre. It was rejected by the Liberation Tigers of Tamil Eelam (LTTE) and their armed struggle against the Sri Lanka government continued unabated.

RANASINGHE PREMADASA, EXECUTIVE PRESIDENT 1988-1994

President Jayawardene's successor, President Ranasinghe Premadasa made efforts to engage in dialogue with the LTTE but there was a lack of faith and a serious credibility gap between the two sides. Foreign governments, such as Australia and Norway offered to mediate between the two parties but there was a lack of positive response from both sides. The LTTE refused to go for bilateral talks with the Sri Lanka government on the grounds that, unless there was a third party present, the government could not be trusted in regard to what its negotiators stated and what was actually done to transcend the crisis.

Like Jayewardene, Premadasa also utilised consultative bodies other than the parliament. He declared his objectives as consisting of 'consultation, compromise and consensus' ('the three Cs'). With this in view, an All Parties Conference deliberated on possible ways out of the impasse after 1990. President Premadasa expressed a willingness to arrive at an understanding short of a separate independent state. The problem had, meanwhile, become more convoluted because the Muslims of the Eastern Province had emerged to express a separate identity, provoked by the LTTE attacks on the Muslim population. The LTTE, in turn, denied responsibility and accused the Muslims of acting as informers and agents for the Center. Both presidents were to some extent sandbagged by political interventions from the Buddhist *sangha* (clergy). It proved very difficult, indeed impossible, for either president to find a way out of this maze.

A further and more serious complication was the emergence of the Sri Lanka army (by now nearly hundred percent Sinhala) and the military complex as a third force in Sri Lankan politics. The army began to insist that it must secure the upper hand in military operations against the LTTE before negotiations could commence with the latter.

Though Premadasa commenced his term with considerable promise, he soon fell a cropper to the plots and plans of his opponents both in the cabinet and among the Sinhalese middle and upper class elites. Premadasa made a fundamental mistake of attempting to eliminate the latter as a political force thus mobilising them as an antagonistic impediment to his rule. Leading members of his cabinet had nothing but contempt for him. He tried holding them on leash but a strong group resisted his attempts at domination.

Ultimately, not even the schemes energetically initiated and implemented by Premadasa to win over the poor in the rural areas bore political results in favour of the UNP. Most of the schemes became instruments of the rich people in their midst and in the end, the poor found themselves worse off despite the massive efforts by the president to alleviate their situation. Premadasa had little to his credit and his passing had little effect on the core classes he had antagonised.

Premadasa sought to be conciliatory with the Tamils, but soon earned their suspicion. In the end, the Tigers allegedly succeeded in having the president assassinated. He was followed in power by his handpicked loyalist, D.B. Wijetunga, who served as a stop gap president for some six months or so till the next elections. Wijetunga did not have the time or opportunity to launch any substantial project which would give him enduring fame.

CHANDRIKA KUMARATUNGA BANDARANAIKE, EXECUTIVE PRESIDENT 1994–

Kumaratunga started her presidency with a great deal of good will and engendered hope amongst the rural poor who expected her to improve their lot and provide employment to the youth. Even sections of the Tamil minority expected a great deal from her promises of amity and statesmanship. But her term has been plagued by scandals, jobbery and various forms of bribery and corruption. It is likely that she will not be successful in obtaining as large a share of the popular vote as she had been in the previous presidential election.

The irony of Sri Lanka's dismal record is that many of the political participants in this demotic state at present continue to seek to dismantle the few weak multiethnic foundations and pillars which have been erected within it despite everything: the amalgamated Northeast Province, which, even though temporary until confirmed by a referendum, pledges not to distort the demographic complexion of this area; the formal recognition accorded to the Tamil language as one of the state's official languages; some remedial steps taken to reverse the iniquitous provisions giving advantages to Sinhala students seeking admission to institutions of higher education, and the creation of a degree of provincial autonomy. These were all attempts to bring the horse back to the stable after it had bolted. A clear lack of vision, an inability to see the problem in all its complexity, the dangers posed by a highly motivated Tamil minority driven to the wall are some of the cardinal errors of this grim history. The question is whether a *status de novo* should be instituted.

Sri Lanka is today a broken-backed state and the solutions proffered by the current government constitute concessions, which are uncertain of implementation and have been delayed until they have lost their grace. A demotic state cannot expect to prevail if it meets with determined opposition from an ethnic minority that becomes convinced that its future lies only in obtaining its rights by the use of force and through an armed confrontation.

CONCLUSION

The above analysis highlights that the process of state-building in a multi-ethnic society is much more complex than that of a political party seeking electoral approval from the ethnically most numerous group. This can be identified as the principal error in Sri Lanka's political development. A system modelled on Arend Lijphart's principles of consociational inter-elite accommodation may have carried the state over a transitional phase in the post-independence period during which the electorate could have been educated on the virtues of democratic tolerance. The converse argument is often made that the majority would have taken to insurrection had its grievances not been redressed. Our view is that there were other alternatives available to remedying the situation than the easy chauvinistic choices that were made by the Sinhala leadership.

The Indian Tamil problem was capable of resolution in the way it was eventually resolved by the Indo-Ceylon Agreement of 1964 and subsequent agreements. There was no danger of a Sinhala upheaval if the Tamil language had been given its due place, as ultimately happened through the Tamil Language (Special Provisions) Act of 1958, the Tamil Regulations of 1966, the Indo-Ceylon Accord of 1987 and the Thirteenth Amendment (1988) to the Sri Lanka constitution of 1978. The whole exercise in state-aided colonisation was capable of being amicably settled by an agreement between the political elites to avoid disturbing the demographic patterns in the two Tamil provinces. Employment in the public and private sectors would have in time adjusted to population proportions instead of the stringent measures that were adopted. University admissions required more universities, a solution which would have cost less than a continuing war. Consociational understandings at the inter-elite levels would have arrested the downward slide to civil war. In short, the vulgar adoption of the demotic model was unnecessary. Sri Lanka would have gained much by maintaining and strengthening its standards of constitutional government and of a welfare system in a Third World context.

The *status quo ante*, such as prevailed in the immediate postcolonial years, cannot be restored. But a *status de novo*, which provides for the constitutional changes the Tamil minority demands to feel assured they are integrated as political equals in a single island polity, may achieve a new equilibrium which could re-establish near normalcy. For this to happen, a change in attitudes of the elites of the ethnic majority is necessary.

REFERENCES

Austin, Dennis and Gupta, Anirudha, *Lions and Tigers: The Sri Lanka Crisis* (London, 1988).

Austin, Dennis and Gupta, Anirudha, *The Politics of Violence in India and South Asia: Is Democracy an Endangered Species?* (London, 1990).

De Silva, C.R., 'The Sinhalese-Tamil Rift in Sri Lanka', 155–74, in A. Jeyaratnam Wilson and Dennis Dalton, eds, *The States of South Asia: Problems of National Integration* (London, 1982).

De Silva, H.L., *An Appraisal of the Federal Alternative For Sri Lanka* (Dehiwela, Sri Lanka, 1991).
De Silva, K.M., *A History of Sri Lanka* (London, 1981).
——, *Managing Ethnic Tensions in Multi-Ethnic Societies: Sri Lanka 1880–1985* (London, 1986).
——, 'University Admissions and Ethnic Tension in Sri Lanka: 1977–82', 97–110, in Robert Goldmann and A. Jeyaratnam Wilson, eds, *From Independence to Statehood: Managing Ethnic Conflict in Five African and Asian States* (London, 1984).
Jayaweera, Neville, *Sri Lanka: Towards a Multi-Ethnic Democracy, Report of a Fact-Finding Mission* (Oslo: International Peace Research Institute, 1991).
Jeffries, Charles, *Ceylon: The Path to Independence* (London, 1962).
Kodikara, Shelton U., 'Internationalization of Sri Lanka's Ethnic Conflict: The Tamil Nadu Factor', 107–14, in K.M. de Silva and R.J. May, eds, *Internationalization of Ethnic Conflict* (London, 1991).
Lijphart, Arend, *Democracy in Plural Societies* (Yale, 1977).
Malalasekera, G.P., 'The Language Problem, I, II and III', *Ceylon Daily News*, 10, 11 and 12 October 1955.
Manogaran, C., *Ethnic Conflict and Reconciliation in Sri Lanka* (Honolulu, 1987).
Marasinghe, M.L., 'Ethnic Politics and Constitutional Reform: The Indo-Sri Lanka Accord', *International Comparative and Law Quarterly* 37, July 1988.
Nadesan, S., *Ceylon's Language Problem* (Colombo, 1956).
Russell, Jane, *Communal Politics under the Donoughmore Constitution 1931–1947* (Dehiwala, Sri Lanka, 1982).
Smith, Donald E., 'The Sinhalese Buddhist Revolution', 453–88, in Donald E. Smith, ed., *South Asian Politics and Religion* (Princeton, 1966).
Tamil Times 11(3), 15 February 1992.
Weerawardena, I.D.S., *Ceylon General Election* (Colombo, 1960).
Weerawardena, I.D.S., 'The General Elections in Ceylon 1952', in *Ceylon Historical Journal* 2 (1 and 2), 1952.
Wilson, A. Jeyaratnam, 'Buddhism in Ceylon Politics, 1960-1965', in Smith, Donald E., ed., *South Asian Politics and Religion* (Princeton, 1966).
——, *Electoral Politics in an Emergent State: The Ceylon General Election of May 1970* (London, 1976).
——, *Politics in Sri Lanka, 1947–1979* (London, 1979).
——, *The Break-Up of Sri Lanka: The Sinhalese-Tamil Conflict* (London, 1988).
——, *The Gaullist System in Asia: The Constitution of Sri Lanka* (London, 1980).
——, 'The Tamil Federal Party in Ceylon Politics', *Journal of Commonwealth Political Studies* 4, July 1966.
Woodward, Calvin A., *The Growth of a Party System in Ceylon* (Providence, 1969).

Chapter 5
The National Political Culture and Institutions in Nepal
Leo E. Rose

Diversity is the norm in the political cultures of the South Asian states. They all must contend with a wide variety of political, social, religious, and ethnic traditions and values in their efforts to construct coherent and integrated national societies. India was the only state in the subcontinent that formally adopted 'unity in diversity' as its operating principle for national integration tasks at independence, but the others have had to pursue similar strategies in fact, if not in form. While the results have not always been particularly impressive, the latter have had some success in integrating a *national* political culture that is usually identified as *modern*, with subnational cultures based on religion, ethnicity, language, local customs and values, or a combination of some or all of these. The subnational cultures are commonly classified as *traditional* and seen as potentially fissiparous forces. Full integration has certainly not been achieved, but there has been substantial progress.

In critical respects, Nepal used to be an exception to this rule but has now begun to conform to it. The Himalayan kingdom has only quite recently begun to make progress toward the integration of a highly traditional national political culture, that goes back at least two centuries, with a wide variety of equally highly traditional but distinctive local political cultures of diverse origins. The gap in terms of political values, styles, and goals between the national elite, whose focus is almost exclusively centred on Kathmandu, and various local cultures did not lead to confrontation because over the years a well-developed sense of tolerance and accommodation, based on the acceptance of divisions of responsibility and authority rather than integration, had been inculcated in the political cultures at both levels. However, as the central elite became more assertive in its insistence upon integration on its terms, substantially expanding the powers and functions of the national political system in the process, the traditions of mutual accommodation were undermined and the potential for inter-elite conflict heightened by the late 1980s.

It is interesting therefore to analyse the Nepalese process of political development. I will first examine the traditional political system. This will be followed with an exploration of the 1950–1990 period. Finally, I will discuss the period following the 1990 'revolution'.

SOCIAL BACKGROUND

The traditional political system in Nepal had a bifurcated culture with clear lines of distinction between the national and local elite cultures as the general rule. The national political culture emerged in the aftermath of the unification of the country by the Shah dynasty in 1770, but in terms of its conceptual foundations it had been implanted much earlier in certain levels of the society throughout the central Himalayas.[1] It was high caste Hindu (Brahman and Kshatriya) in origin and the product for the most part, of descendants of elite Hindu families who had fled to Nepal in the twelfth to fifteenth centuries to escape subordination to Muslim conquerors. These families, strongly orthodox Hindu due to both their Indian heritage and experiences, attained a dominant status in most of the fifty or more principalities into which Nepal was divided prior to unification in the eighteenth century. While they were not particularly ardent advocates of a unified political system before the event, they were products of a fairly homogenous orthodox Hindu political, social and religious culture – as was the ruling Shah dynasty – and thus were well situated both socially and psychologically to assume responsible positions in the national political system which was established, centred in Kathmandu. Not all these Brahman and Chhettri families – *bahuns,* as they are called in Nepal – transferred their home bases to Kathmandu after 1770; the large majority stayed where they were, usually as the dominant element in the local and regional elite. This provided the central government with a useful and reliable instrument for exercising some degree of control over areas of the country in which most of the population had their own traditional and often non-Hindu elite.[2]

After 1770, the national elite in Kathmandu expanded over time to include several other social groups whose support was critical to the central government but who were products of somewhat different political and social traditions from the dominant bahun group. Probably the most important of these were from the Newar community, the dominant indigenous community in the Kathmandu valley prior to unification. The Newars are non-Indo Aryan in origin, but had been ruled for more than a millennium by high caste Hindu dynasties from India. A vigorous and dynamic Newar socio-political and intellectual culture developed in the Kathmandu valley that was a synthesis of both Hindu and Buddhist principles and concepts but was dissimilar in some key respects from that of the hill-area bahun system that accompanied the Shah dynasty to its new capital in Kathmandu. Social interaction between these two very assertive elite groups was never extensive: intermarriage between the hill elite and Newar families of nominally equivalent caste status for instance, was very rare. Despite this, eventually they learned to work together on certain aspects of Nepal's political and economic system rather effectively.

This relationship took some time to develop, however, as in the immediate post-1770 period the Newar elite was suspect in the eyes of the new rulers in the valley and were carefully excluded from the Shah's governmental system. But the Newars had talents, both bureaucratic and commercial, that were badly needed by the Shah's courtiers. A pattern of accommodation of the Newars into the administration emerged in the early nineteenth century and lasted virtually unchanged until about 1960. With few exceptions, under its operating rules, Newars did not hold the highest posts and only a couple of Newar families eventually achieved *bharadar* (nobility) status. But the Chhettri officials who held such posts in the government invariably had Newars as their principal administrative assistants as well as Newar economic 'consultants' who managed their family's financial affairs. Thus, while rarely prominent in the central elite in status terms, Newars were critical to the effective functioning of government institutions on all but military and judicial matters – both of which were the preserve of the bahuns.

The Chhettri families that dominated the Nepali national political culture in formal terms usually claimed high caste Indian origin and some had wonderfully contrived family *vamshavalis* (histories) as documentary evidence. In actual fact, however, some of these families belong to the Chhettri *jatis* (subgroups in the caste system) that were descended in part from the old local ruling families of non-Hindu origin that had been conceded high caste Hindu status either through intermarriage with Brahmans or Chhettris or through proclamation by pragmatic Chhettri rulers in the hill areas. One of the most notable examples was the Rana (Kunwar) family that controlled Nepal's government from 1846 to 1951 through a hereditary prime ministership. Such families invariably adopted the high caste Hindu social and political culture of the 'purer' Kshatriya families with the usual fervour of converts, but also with remnant adaptations of their old local culture (as of marriage and inheritance practices, for instance) that never completely disappeared. Because of this, they were assigned a slightly lower position in the Chhettri caste hierarchy (Khatri Chhettri) which could be raised only over several generations of intensive endeavour. Once the Ranas were in power, for instance, they virtually forced marriage relations on the royal and other Kshatriya families in Nepal and later married into some prestigious Kshatriya families in India. The differences within the Kshatriya/Chhettri caste structure in Nepal, thus, were subtle but not unimportant in social and political terms, and were at times critical factors in the power struggles at the centre as well as in the relationship between the central and local elites.

Another high caste Hindu group in Nepal that, until recently at least, was kept on the periphery of the national political system are the families of relatively recent Indian origin that dominate the politics and economy in most parts of the Tarai – the plains area in southern Nepal between the hills and the Indian border. These families share the basic Hindu values, customs and rituals of the hill Brahmans and Chhettris, but again with some differences. In contrast to the high caste Hindu families in the hills, most of whom migrated to Nepal before 1400, the Tarai high caste families came in the nineteenth and twentieth centuries after long exposures to Muslim and British political cultures as well as reformist and revivalist Hindu movements in India. Again the distinctions are subtle and almost indistinguishable to the outsider, but are important enough to both elite groups to deter intermarriage between what would appear equivalent caste families. This may also help explain the hypersensitivity of the hill elite to the integration – or lack thereof – of the Tarai into Nepal's dominant hill political culture, for the hill and Tarai high caste elites were indeed products of quite different political and social experiences.

Despite these divisions within the political elite system, between 1770 and 1950 a reasonably coherent national political culture was evident about which there was a broad consensus within the elite. This provided the foundation for a reasonably effective government system at the centre and in the districts for what were considered to be essential objectives: one, maintenance of national unity and the exclusion of excessive foreign influence; two, an indirect but still rather efficient capacity for the implementation of policies on the two principal tasks of government at that time – namely, the maintenance of law and order and the collection of revenue; and three, the gradual inculcation, both through legal codes and 'good example', of certain basic high caste Hindu social and political principles among the non-Hindu general populace as part of the process of establishing a broader legitimacy. The pre-Muslim Hindu orthodoxy of India was asserted as the norm, and the insidious 'foreign' influences that had crept into Hinduism in India under the Muslims and British were vigorously rejected. While a number of 'deviant' Hindu sects gained small followings in the Kathmandu valley and the Tarai, the hard-line orthodoxy prevalent in India in the fourteenth century remained the dominant influence in Hinduism in the hill areas of Nepal.

The role of the monarchy in the political system has always been a bit equivocal in Nepal as classic Hindu political philosophy does not concern itself with theories of sovereignty or the source of sovereignty in a political system. The focus, rather, is on the interrelationship of social groups in a political hierarchy. While the powers and status of a ruling monarch are not defined in theory, in practice they are restricted by the injunction that rulers must respect the status and rights of all social groups defined under Hindu principles – such as the total ban on the execution of a Brahman even for high treason to state and/or royal family. Thus, despite the broad powers exercised by the Hindu rulers in Nepal, the concept of an absolute monarch is not congruent with Hindu orthodoxy.

THE TRADITIONAL NATIONAL POLITICAL CULTURE: STRUCTURE AND PROCESS

Having discussed the social and ideological underpinnings of the traditional national political culture, let us turn to an analysis of the system in operation. While there was a national political system in Nepal in operation after the late eighteenth century, till 1950 it was dominated by an elite that was motivated almost exclusively by familial interests rather than monarchical loyalties or nationalist sentiments. An amoral narrowly-defined familism provided the basis for political activity in Nepal. The family was the critical political as well as social unit: temporary alliances based on expediency were often made with other elite families at the central or local levels, but inevitably these were short-lived and subject to constant realignments, with politics essentially seen as a zero-sum game. A family could hope to achieve or maintain a dominant position in politics only through the systematic elimination, by force if necessary, of other competing elite families. As a result, few high officials died natural deaths in those troubled years.

The structure of government also reflected the authoritarian organisational principles intrinsic to the elite families, and an individual attained position and power in the government hierarchy – as in the family – more on ascriptive than achievement factors. The heads of contending elite families participated in the government, professed eternal loyalty to the ruler but primarily acted in the spirit of amoral familism with the primary objective being the maximisation of gains at the expense of other rival families. At the same time, the elite families, were, in almost all cases dedicated to preserving the political, religious, economic and social status quo. Thus, political changes constituted little more than shifts of power from one family to another and involved no radical changes in the operating principles of the political system.[3]

There were some modifications in this system after 1850 when the Rana family established a dominant position within the government, a position which it managed to maintain for over a century. The difference, however, related more to the length of time for which individual Ranas managed to stay in power than in the objectives of government which remained focussed on: one, maintenance of a monopoly control over key government and military positions; two, the suppression of other elite families that refused to accept a subordinate position within the Rana system; and three, political neutralisation of the royal family. Intrigues, conspiracies, coups and countercoups, accompanied by bloody intra-family and inter-family confrontations were as much a part of the history of the Rana period as they had been of pre-1850 Nepal. And amoral familism, with sub-units of the Rana family now playing the critical competitive role within the political system, still remained the basis of politics.

However, during the Rana period there was a gradual institutionalisation of governmental and administrative functions on a more 'rational' and even, in the latter part of their period of dominance, increasingly non-ascriptive basis. This was evident in various aspects of Nepal's political, social and economic life: the introduction and periodic revision of a national legal code; reforms in the land tenure and taxation system; and the gradual extension of the authority of the Centre over the former principalities and ethnic communities that had enjoyed broad internal autonomy since their incorporation into the Shah dynasty's kingdom.[4]

Probably the most important development in the Rana period was the establishment of a novel form of inter-familial relations that proved to be much more enduring than anything along these lines before. This was termed the *chakari* system, under which a number of 'client' families from diverse backgrounds – Brahmans, Newars, Chhettris, and occasionally even families outside the national elite culture – were affiliated with a patron family, usually one of the Rana sub-branch families. The client families would serve various functions for the patron: priest and educator of the children for the Brahmans; economic advisor and manipulator of investments in Nepal and abroad for the Newars; land agent for the patron family's large landholdings and administrators in the patron's civil and military posts for Chhettris. A number of these chakari relationships lasted for several generations and were an integral basis of the administrative and political system in the Rana period. While loyalty to the immediate family was still the predominant force in Nepali politics, identification with and even loyalty to a trans-familial institution, the chakari, it substantially improved the political structure's operational efficiency.[5]

The Bureaucracy

The expansion of the small principality of Gorkha into a large nation-state in the central Himalayas with its capital at Kathmandu required the establishment of a national bureaucracy to assist the court in the governance of this complex amalgam of unruly ethnocentric social groups. The new national bureaucracy gradually acquired certain characteristics – a bureaucratic culture – that became well defined and persisted into the post-Rana 'modern' phase.

In the immediate post-unification period, the national bureaucracy was drawn almost exclusively from the high caste Hindu elite families of

Gorkha that had assisted the Shah dynasty in establishing its rule over Nepal. A few Newar elite families that had served the Malla rulers of the Kathmandu Valley prior to 1769 quickly transferred their allegiance to the Shahs and were gradually brought into the palace-centred administrative system. A little later, high caste Hindu elite families from some of the hill principalities that had been absorbed into the Shah's kingdom were also brought into the national bureaucracy. The most important of these – the Thapas, Basnyats, and Pandes – transferred their familial centres of operation to Kathmandu and became identified as part of the national elite. Other families of similar background, including the ruling families in forty or more former principalities, remained in their home area and provided the local elite from which the government usually selected regional and local officials. Occasionally, members of these families were promoted to official posts in the Centre. Sub-branches of these families became Kathmandu-based, but their principal centre of operation would still be the local area. By the early nineteenth century the central government was dominated by the hill elite families that were non-Gorkha in origin and who provided the Shah dynasty with a truly national – in regional if not in social terms – bureaucratic structure.

A number of practices, such as the assignment of a particular office to one family, was introduced as a common – but not exclusive – principle of the bureaucratic structure. At different periods of time, the post of *mukhtiar* (prime ministership) was the exclusive monopoly of the Chautaria family (a sub-branch of the royal family), the Thapas, and then after 1850 the Ranas. The post of *raj guru* (or royal priest) was held by one Brahman family of Gorkha origin until 1850, and then transferred to another Brahman family by the Ranas. Relations with foreign powers were entrusted to the Pandey family, and then to the Ranas after 1850. The concept of hereditary office, thus, extended beyond the royal family and provided an element of stability and continuity in the otherwise chaotic political environment prior to 1850.

Thus the concept of the family as the 'working unit' with which one was identified was intrinsic to the Shah system from the very beginning. For the national bureaucracy, nepotism in an explicit form was the standard operating procedure. Indeed, it constituted a social obligation rather than a form of corruption, and the confusion still evident in contemporary Nepal on this issue is a natural derivation from the traditions and practices of the Shah and Rana periods. Today, young educated Nepalese from elite families verbally espouse 'Western' concepts of merit and competition, but in practice, often tend to function on more traditional principles in this matter. Indeed, the failure to do so would probably be the best guarantee of a short, inglorious career in the 'public service'.

The Rana family structure solidified, rather than modified, the existing hierarchical bureaucratic system in most respects. The association of family and office was made the rule by law through the 1856 Sanad that gave royal sanction to the Rana system and also provided the legal basis for the Rana 'rule of succession' to all top civil and military posts. Through the chakari client family system, the monopolisation of offices at slightly lower levels was also extended to other dependent elite families – for instance, one Newari family inherited the title and post of *kazi*, while another Newari family headed the important Tibet/China Relations Office for several generations. The Ranas also reinforced and expanded the 'classic' Hindu political and social concepts by the periodic revision of the 'national' legal code (*Muluki Ain*) first introduced in 1884. Later revisions extended the Hindu ban on cow slaughter, pollution through social contacts, and so on to the partially Hinduised and even non-Hindu communities in the realm. Eventually this began to have an impact on the functioning of the bureaucratic and judicial systems, as well as social customs, particularly at the local level.[6]

The Rana regime, thus, introduced some changes that were radical for their time and that significantly modified the political and bureaucratic system by the time that the Ranas were 'overthrown' in 1951. A process of centralisation was evident throughout the Rana period in such matters as standardisation of the land tenure and legal system. There was also a degree of 'modernisation' of the bureaucracy, particularly at the middle and lower levels – that is, below the Rana officials who held the highest positions on the basis of their order of rank in the family. Formal rules for procedure (*sawals*) were introduced and enforced and the bureaucracy was not the haphazard, whimsical institution as it has sometimes been described as being. The sawals included rules for appointment and promotion based, in theory at least, on merit. There was also an annual review (*panjani*) procedure under which all officials except the Ranas were subject to dismissal for poor performance of their duties. There were, of course, serious deficiencies in the implementation of the principles embodied in the sawals, but then probably no more than in 'modern' bureaucratic systems in which merit is supposed to be the criteria used for personnel evaluation purposes.[7]

The Rana system lasted for more than a century, seemingly unchallenged by serious domestic political forces. Yet, the process of internal disintegration within the Rana family was evident in the second generation of Rana rulers and proved to be increasingly divisive, as the family became characterised by greater heterogeneity and decreasing cohesion. By the early twentieth century, subordinate branches of the family had become permanent cliques engaged in conspiracies directed at the dominant Rana groupings. Eventually the more 'underprivileged' of the Rana sub-branches joined political movements that ended in the overthrow of the Rana system itself.

THE NATIONAL POLITICAL CULTURE: CONTEMPORARY SETTING

The traditional national political culture in Nepal was analysed in some detail for several reasons. First, in contrast to the rest of the South Asian states other than Bhutan and Maldives, there has been a broad degree of continuity in the fundamental characteristics and functioning of the central political system in Nepal in the post-colonial (that is, after 1947) period. While Nepal had its own 'revolution' in 1950–51, this was comparable to the earlier political convulsions in the country that brought changes in rulers rather than in ruling systems. Despite four decades of political experimentation and development, a skilled practitioner of politics reincarnated from the Rana period in the nineteenth century would have had to learn some new tricks of the trade and some new jargon, but he would nevertheless be familiar with most aspects of the structure and modus operandi of elite politics at the central level in Kathmandu in the 1980s.

Second, while there have been substantial changes and expansion of opportunities (for instance, in access to education) for local and ethnic elites and even non-elites since 1950, the dominant status of the national political elite, and its basic familial composition, has remained reasonably constant. There have been serious challenges to this largely Kathmandu-based elite from a variety of sources after 1950 including challengers with strong political support bases both inside and outside the capital. But until 1990, the national political elite demonstrated an impressive capacity to counter, accommodate, absorb, and eventually defeat the attempted intrusions by 'outsiders' into their playing field. There was, thus, a significant degree of political activity and participation by the 'politically conscious' public in Nepal but with only a limited effect upon the governmental process. To use a popular Nepali phrase, the 'source and force' (social and familial connections) of decision-making authority at the critical national level did not change very much.

Third, Nepali political culture retained many of its traditional characteristics under extreme pressure from a wide diversity of external influences and ideologies. The isolation policy that effectively immunised most of Nepal from outside cultural and political influences during the Rana period collapsed completely after 1951. By the 1980s, most Nepalis had been exposed to a broad gamut of foreign values, life styles and political and social concepts through education abroad, work experience in India, recruitment and service in the Indian or British armies, and the ubiquitous transistor radios within the country that could pick up a wide array of Indian, British, American, Chinese, Soviet and Pakistani broadcasts. Censorship of the domestic press and radio, practised widely by the Nepal government until 1990, was an exercise in futility under such circumstances for it could not prevent the rapid spread of information on developments inside and outside Nepal.

Moreover, Nepal's geographical location between Asia's two largest and most dynamic powers that loudly trumpet abroad the virtues of their very different political values and systems was a major complication for the authorities in Kathmandu who were determined to maintain and develop a political culture based on Nepali values, traditions, and needs. While many young Nepali students went abroad and acquired a high level of competence in both Western and Marxist theories of organisation and governance, most of them adjusted with seeming ease into a Nepali bureaucratic system that functioned on very different principles. The broad degree of continuity in Nepal's political culture into the 1980s, thus, was not due to a lack of exposure to the outside world as had been the case until 1950, but rather to some intrinsic strengths and capacities within the traditional system itself. We turn now to examine these and the challenges faced, through an analysis of the principal national governmental and political institutions and their interactions over the 1950–1990 period.

The Palace

The fortunes of the monarchy in Nepal have varied widely since the unification of the country in 1769 from an absolute monarchy (1767–1799, 1956–1959, 1981–1990) to a weak monarchy (1800–1846, 1951–1955, 1990–1995) and a powerless monarchy in which the king was only the token head of state (1846–1950). Obviously, there has been no steady unilinear evolution in the definition of the powers and status of the monarch or other royal institutions, but rather extreme fluctuations over relatively short periods of time. The sense of insecurity that pervades the royal households even in periods when the monarchy is a dominant force, as well as the awareness among 'competing' elite groups and institutions (for example, other bharadar families, prime ministers and their cabinets, political parties, and so on) that it is possible to reduce the royal family to a subordinate position in the political system, thus, has a substantial basis in historical fact.

The history of the monarchy, particularly during the Rana regime when it virtually disappeared as an active participant in the governing process, is still vivid in the memory of the royal family. The period after the overthrow of the Ranas in 1951 was marked by a steady growth in the powers and authority wielded by the palace. King Tribhuvan, the ruler at the time of the 1950–1951 revolution, was disinclined by temperament and to some extent by the politics of the immediate post-Rana period from asserting a leading role for the palace, but evident incapacities of the party-led governments to provide the leadership required gradually forced him to participate more actively in politics. His successor, King Mahendra (1956–1972) was much less inhibited in this respect and, except for the brief experiment in parliamentary government in 1959–1960, moved inexorably and successfully to make the monarchy the fulcrum of the decision-making and administrative processes. King Birendra (1972–) has devised a different set of strategies from those of his father, but initially with similar objectives in mind. By 1980 Nepal had something approximating an absolute monarchy, in operational terms if not in formal constitutional principles. King Mahendra's bitter memories of the degradation of the royal family under the Ranas made him intensely suspicious of any governmental or political institution that might seek to reinstitute another political system in which the monarchy would be relegated to the sidelines – or even discarded entirely. The *panchayat* political system that he devised after the dismissal of an elected government and his assumption of full powers in December 1960 was complex in organisational design but relatively simple operationally. All other administrative and political institutions were, in effect, prevented from carrying out the functions and responsibilities nominally assigned to them except under the direct supervision of the palace. The critical channels of communication within the government were carefully constructed to run directly to and through the palace rather than in any orderly hierarchical devolution of authority. A diagram of the system as it actually operated would appear unworkable to students of organisational theory and public administration. In fact it functioned rather effectively because of the king's skill in providing the active and direct leadership required as well as because of the reluctant acceptance of the 'system' by most of the key governmental and political institutions.

King Birendra was the product of a very different political socialisation and education from that of his father. He made the reorganisation of the government along more orderly and structured lines a major objective of his regime. This was not easily accomplished given the messy (in organisational terms) system he inherited. A series of experiments based upon different political principles from those of the Mahendra period were introduced in order to 'rationalise' the decision-making and governing processes. From 1972–1978, efforts were made to improve the capacity of the system to implement economic and social development programs through technocrat-dominated centres of authority operating directly in the palace. The results, by and large, were disappointing. Birendra therefore initiated a new series of experiments in 1979 under which first a referendum on the panchayat political system was held in 1980, and then in 1981 the first popular election of a national assembly since 1959 was held.

The immediate consequence was to strengthen the position of the king, but in the process potentially rival institutions to the monarchy were also created. In formal terms, the trend appeared to be toward a strong constitutional monarchy in which powers and responsibilities would be shared by the king and the other main national political institutions – the cabinet and the national assembly. However, there were doubts in Nepal that the component parts of the palace system – the king, the royal family, and various 'client' families, and the palace secretariat – would accept a significant diminution in their authority and dominance. Another reenactment of an intrinsic aspect of the Nepali political culture, involving definitions of the power relationship between the monarchy and competing political forces and institutions, became inevitable.

The Cabinet

The history of prime ministers and their cabinets in Nepal has usually been a mirror image of that of the monarchy. Only rarely has a cooperative relationship based upon a sharing of power between these two institutions come about. The norm has been the subordination of one to the other. In the Rana period, it was the Rana prime minister who governed and the king who acted on his instructions. From 1961 to 1990, the trend was in the opposite direction with the prime minister and his colleagues becoming virtual ciphers responsive to royal commands. Yet, the dominance of one or the other institution has never been easily effected or accepted as legitimate. In the 1961–1968 period, for instance, at a time that the power of the throne seemed unchallengeable, King Mahendra still had to contend with a number of cabinet ministers who, despite the lack of any substantial political base of their own, sought to exercise a degree of independent authority in the conduct of their office. Thereafter, the prime ministers and other ministers were generally more docile, to the point that the cabinet (with the important exception of the finance minister at times) became of incidental importance to the administration in the formulation of programs.

Another aspect of the cabinet system that was established after 1951 which gained importance in the national political culture was the effort to make it into a broadly representative institution in regional and ethnic terms. On some occasions – for example under the elected Nepali Congress government in 1959–1960 – the objective was to achieve truly national representation. This was so much the case that the dominance of the central government by the Kathmandu-based political elite was seriously threatened for the first time – an important factor in their endorsement of King Mahendra's dismissal of B.P. Koirala's elected government and the abolition of parliamentary democracy in December 1960. After 1961 the cabinet continued to be selected by the King with regional and ethnic factors in mind, but the ministers appointed in these capacities tended to be token representatives, selected precisely because they lacked any broad support base within their own communities and, thus, could be easily manipulated and exploited by the palace at no great expense to the existing national elite families.

Representative and Legislative Institutions

Since 1769, Nepal has had a variety of representative institutions that wielded some influence in decision-making functions, but the composition and powers of these 'legislative' bodies has differed greatly. The *Bharadari* (Council of Nobles) that served in this capacity till 1951 under both the Shah rulers and the Rana prime ministers had an important voice in crisis situations but rarely met as an institution under normal conditions. It was composed almost exclusively of the leading members of the Kathmandu-based national political elite and was, thus, unrepresentative of the regional and ethnic elite, not to mention the general public.

The several advisory assemblies that were appointed to serve as representative institutions after the 1951 revolution never really operated in that or any other capacity. It was only with the first general election in 1959 that a House of Representatives (*Pratinidhi Sabha*) was established under the 1959 constitution and was unlike any institution Nepal had known before. The powers and functions of this representative and legislative body as defined in the constitution were similar to those of the parliament in the Indian and British political systems – that is, the executive branch (or cabinet) was elected by and was directly responsible to the House and all legislation required its approval. While a majority of the members of the House were from the three national caste groups – Brahman, Chhettri, and Newari – there were also a number of members, including Prime Minister B.P. Koirala, who were from regional rather than Kathmandu elite families. The representatives, moreover, were responsible to the national electorate that had placed them in office and were expected to serve as spokesmen for regional and ethnic group interests. The House membership, thus, was a 'national elite' in a very different sense from the Kathmandu-based 'national elite' as identified in this study. For the first time since the unification of the country, the predominance of Kathmandu in the governance process was seriously threatened. Before a confrontation could take shape, however, King Mahendra dissolved the parliament, abandoned the 1959 constitution, and embarked on a new experiment in system-building that was intrinsically centrist in character.

Under the 1962 constitution introduced by King Mahendra, the National Assembly (*Rastriya Panchayat*) was a very different institution from the 1959 parliament in that the National Assembly was elected indirectly by a small number of district level panchayat officials under a system that exposed them to pressures – rewards, threats, bribes, and the like – from palace and central government officials. Under this system, a large proportion of the Assembly members 'elected' were, as one would expect, Brahmans, Chhettris, and Newars. There was a substantial number of members from regional and ethnic communities as well, but they operated in an institution which had very limited powers and influence over government policies and the distribution of resources. They were rarely able to serve as effective representatives of the interests of their areas or ethnic and social communities. Over the years, there was a growing frustration with the operation of the 1962 constitution, even among some active participants in the panchayat system. This was greatly enhanced in the mid-1970s by the efforts of King Birendra's palace secretariat to establish even broader controls over the panchayat system through the appointment of a central committee that was given a virtual veto over the selection of members to the National Assembly, thus further limiting the influence of regional and ethnic elites in the political process at the Centre. The political changes introduced by King Birendra in the 1979–1981 period, thus, were as much a response to the intense dissatisfaction prevailing among a large proportion of participants in the panchayat system as it was to the oppositional politics of the 'illegal' political parties and their supporters among the students and public. The impact of the decision to revert to popular election of the National Assembly was tempered initially by the fact that most of the political parties boycotted the 1981 'partyless' elections. Politics in Nepal, nevertheless, underwent another period of adjustment in the way power was exercised and distributed. The effect of the 1981 election in terms of the representation of broad social groups did not appear to be too significant as once again a majority of the elected members (63 out of 112) were from the three dominant caste groups – about the same as in the 1959 elections. What was different, however, was that a number of the successful candidates from *both* the national and the regional and ethnic elites defeated candidates in their constituencies who had been endorsed by the palace and/or the prime minister's political group.[8]

The Bureaucracy

Perhaps the most important source of continuity and stability in the various political systems that have been imposed on Nepal over the past century has been the bureaucracy, both civil and military. Indeed, for most of this period Nepal has been a bureaucratic polity under which, in most instances, the dominant force in the decision-making process has been the bureaucratic leadership. Moreover, there was an impressive degree of continuity within the bureaucracy at the top administrative (that is, gazetted officer) level, both in terms of operating principles and in the social and familial background of a large proportion of new recruits into the bureaucratic channels that led up to high status positions. In 1968, it was estimated that 80–90 percent of the gazetted officers came from the national political elite. Another survey a decade later indicated that this situation had not changed appreciably despite the large number of students from other social groups who had earned degrees that qualified them for bureaucratic posts. It was a common perception in Nepal that selection for such posts still depended on 'source and force' factors despite the formal adoption of public service regulations that in theory based recruitment upon merit and personal qualifications.

The comparative homogeneity of the upper stratum of the bureaucracy in social terms, however, did not result in an integrated, smoothly functioning bureaucratic structure. Rather, the central bureaucracy was subdivided into several well-defined factions that competed vigorously for the key posts in the economic and development ministries which had the most resources to distribute. These factions remained organised along the lines of the pre-1951 chakari patron-client family system, though with less cohesiveness and sense of identity with the unit than under the Ranas. There was also open rivalry between the dominant social groups in the national political elite, directed primarily at the Chhettris because of their increasingly pre-eminent position in both the central and palace secretariats (the latter had previously been a Newar monopoly except for the military aides), the military (as had been the norm since 1769), the cabinet, and even the 1981 National Assembly (43 of 112 elected members). The Chhettris, Newars, and Brahmans still managed to cooperate in maintaining the bureaucracy as their preserve through their control of the recruitment system.

While the bureaucracy generally played a critical role in the governing process, this was challenged by several sources of political authority in the post-1951 period. Curiously, the 1951 revolution had relatively little effect on the existing bureaucracy other than to remove the Ranas from the highest political posts. A fairly large number of new appointments were made to the central secretariat, but virtually all of these came from the same families that had provided bureaucrats for the Ranas and there were few conflicts between those appointed before and after 1951.

The first post-Rana purge of the bureaucracy was carried out by King Mahendra in 1956, and then again more extensively in 1961 after his dismissal of the elected Nepali Congress government. Mahendra's strong suspicions about the reliability of the bureaucrats, because of their alleged ties to political parties, was evident in his political strategy in the 1961–1967 period when he used the cabinet rather than the central secretariat as the primary institution for the formulation of policies. But by 1968 Mahendra had reversed the order of priority within the government. The cabinet and his small private secretariat were relegated to the background and a core group from the central secretariat assumed the role of principal consultants and advisors to the King on policy matters.

The pre-eminence of the bureaucracy, however, lasted only until King Birendra succeeded to the throne in 1972. One of the new ruler's first political moves was directed at the powerful secretaries who had formed the core group around his father. Once again there was a major shift in the locus of decision-making authority – this time from the central secretariat to an ad hoc group of young well-educated Nepalis, some of whom had served Birendra while he was crown prince and who were now brought into the palace secretariat as his closest advisors. This was more than a change in influential personalities, as the institutional relationship between the palace secretariat and the cabinet and central secretariat was modified. The palace secretariat, through its newly established planning unit (*Janch Bhuj Kendra*) replaced the central secretariat as the primary institution in the formulation of programs and it was even assigned supervisory powers over the bureaucracy in the implementation process. The secretaries in the palace secretariat were also assigned 'portfolios' for the various ministries often superseding, in fact if not in form, the cabinet ministers who nominally headed these departments.

Within the bureaucracy there was a strong sense of dissatisfaction with its reduced role in policy and decision-making. This led to a propensity for 'sabotaging' programs by doing as little as possible in their implementation. It also further reinforced the tendency prevalent among Nepali bureaucrats to work the system in such ways as to avoid responsibility for a program – for example, through the assignment of responsibility for a program to a committee in which no one bureaucrat could be blamed if things went wrong, as they usually did. The palace could initiate programs, but it lacked effective instruments to compel the central secretariat to fulfil its duties in the implementation of the programs. There was, perhaps, more noise and less substance in governmental policies in the 1972–1990 period than any time in the past, with an increasingly negative reaction from the public as it raised questions about the capacity of the political system to carry out badly needed economic and social development.[9]

The military is usually ignored in discussions of government and politics in Nepal as it has maintained a very low profile since 1951. It has consistently acted on instructions from the responsible civil officials when ever it has intervened in political affairs. The reorganisation of the army after the 1951 revolution left the command positions in the hands of the Chhettri military officers, but denied them the linkages with the civil government that had been an integral aspect of the Rana system. King Mahendra used the military in asserting his control in December 1960, but used them sparingly and only for a limited period of time. Once the political opposition had been handled, the military returned to the barracks. Mahendra was careful to avoid making the military an institutional base for his regime. Indeed, he depoliticised the officer corps effectively through his policies on promotion. To get ahead in the army, it was essential for young officers to avoid any public involvement or even demonstration of interest in politics. Several officers were close to Mahendra in their personal capacities as aides in the palace, but not on an institutional basis. It is ironic that a country which prides itself on its great martial tradition has managed far better than most other developing states to confine the military to its professional responsibilities.

Political Organisations

While political parties were illegal after 1961, political organisations espousing a broad spectrum of ideologies have played a critical role in Nepali politics since the founding of the first party in 1948. The ban on parties was quite explicit in the 1962 constitutional provisions and supplementary ordinances, but in fact parties continued to operate relatively openly throughout this period. The parties functioned underground only marginally and even published party-affiliated newspapers. King Birendra's decision in 1979 to hold a referendum on the political system ended most of the restrictions that had been imposed on parties and their supporting institutions in practice, if not in law.

While some party leaders and workers, mostly belonging to the Nepali Congress or factions of the communist movement, were arrested and detained for varying periods of time; their colleagues and supporters continued to function fairly openly even though their activities were well-known to the authorities. There was, it would appear, a set of informal rules and tacit agreements that set imprecisely-defined but mutually understood boundaries between permissible and forbidden political activities. A pragmatic approach to the parties was considered necessary for two good reasons. First, virtually all of the party leaders (including the communists) were from the same elite social groups and families as most of the high government officials, and it would have been destructive of the elitist social and political fabric in Nepal to apply the law against party leaders and workers too strictly. Second, the two principal political parties/movements, the Nepali Congress and the various factions of the Communist Party, had party bases and organisations in India from which they could launch movements in Nepal against the regime. The government, therefore, usually preferred to have the party leaders operating on a somewhat restricted basis but under its supervision within Nepal rather than in India where they were less susceptible to control and had easier access to financial support from external political sources – Indian, Chinese, and Soviet.

Another factor in the comparatively tolerant attitude of the government toward political parties after 1979 was the character of the organisations in both their legal and illegal manifestations. Political parties were first formed in the late 1940s by a number of Nepalis in India who had been socialised into politics through the Indian nationalist movement. The manifestos issued by these new parties in Nepal invariably reflected the secular, democratic and in some cases, socialist ideologies of their Indian gurus; but in organisational and operative terms the parties were classic traditional

Nepali. The chakari patron-client relationships typical of the Rana regime were duplicated in the parties and most of the numerous small parties formed after the 1951 revolution were, in fact, one-person dominant parties in which a prominent leader would have a tightly-knit core of followers which would expand dramatically if the patron was in a position to distribute rewards and offices but contract back to the original group when he was not.

The Nepali Congress and the Communists were the only parties that had any success in expanding beyond the one leader syndrome, but even they were composed of factions that were in most instances centred around a single leader as the focus of loyalty. Over the years, the Nepali Congress, with its moderate centrist political philosophy, survived the divisive pressures reasonably well even though the party's component factions often took different positions on specific political issues and events. The Communists fared less well, in part because ideological controversies and the Sino-Soviet dispute were added to the existing social-based divisions within the party – for example the Newar factions versus Brahman factions versus regional ethnic factions, and so on. One gets the impression that the social factors are more important than the ideological among the Communists, but the financial support from competing Soviet, Chinese, and Indian communist sources had also proved divisive.

Nepal's political party system, thus, was marked by factional and personality conflicts that severely limited effective collaboration between the parties even on basic political issues, affecting their role in government and politics.[10] In December 1960, for instance, many opposition party leaders supported King Mahendra's dismissal of the elected Nepali Congress government, imprisonment of its political leaders, and suspension of the 1959 constitution and parliamentary democratic system – even though political parties were banned in the process! Again, two decades later in the 1980 referendum election that presented the public with the option of a multiparty or non-party governmental system, a number of party leaders actively opposed the change that would have legalised parties. Many others who nominally supported the multiparty side actually undermined the efforts to build a strong coalition of parties on this issue. The evident disdain of the public for the egocentric behaviour of these party leaders was a significant factor in the narrow victory of the panchayat group in the referendum.

Moreover, however different their public political postures may have been, some party leaders – including most extreme leftists – found the panchayat system more rewarding and protective of their interests than a highly competitive party system in which survival depended upon success in elections. As a further complication, there was a substantial body of panchayat politicians who supported the legalisation of political parties, but on special terms: either a one-party panchayat system or a multi-party system functioning within the panchayat framework on terms advantageous to themselves. Again, leaders of several communist factions found collaboration with this 'progressive' panchayat group more attractive than the restoration of a more standard party governmental system.

While divisiveness, pettiness, and proclivity for self-destructive behaviour by the parties was more than evident, it did not mean that these organisations were unimportant to political and governmental processes in Nepal. On the contrary, the parties, and particularly the Nepali Congress, were viewed by most of the public as the only viable alternative to the panchayat political system. Even more important perhaps, the parties remained the best channel for political participation by much of the regional and ethnic elites as well as some elements of the national political elite in both local and national politics. To have a government based upon a broad public consensus it was essential for the government (notably the palace) and the parties (especially the Nepali Congress and Communists) to work out arrangements that would enable them to cooperate in social, political, and economic development tasks.

THE 1990 'REVOLUTION': A NEW POLITICAL CULTURE?

For the first time since 1960, a broadly-based national political movement erupted in early 1990 led by the Nepali Congress (NC) and the Nepal Communist Party (NCP) who agreed, temporarily as it turned out, to stop the infighting within the opposition forces in Nepal in order to pressure King Birendra into accepting a systematic change in Nepal's political system. Even more surprising, however, was the broad public support extended to the movement throughout Nepal by some normally cautious and conservative caste, economic, professional and social organisations that had previously carefully avoided participation in dissident political movements. The reasons for this impressive response to the NC/NCP led movement were evident: the failure of most of the Panchayat's economic development programs and the declining standards of living for an already-impoverished public; the clearly farcical nature of local and regional panchayat institutions that remained totally submissive to the 'boys in the palace' in Kathmandu; and the incredible decision by the palace secretariat in early 1989 to push policies that lead to a confrontation with New Delhi over the Indo-Nepal Trade and Transit Treaty which had disastrous consequences on the economy outside Kathmandu and even for some critical economic groups in the highly subsidised capital city.

By April 1990, King Birendra had correctly appraised the political and economic crisis that his government faced and agreed to basic changes in the political system. A coalition NC/NCP interim government, headed by the NC president K. P. Bhattarai, was appointed which then suspended the panchayat constitution and appointed, with Birendra's approval, a committee to formulate a new constitution. On 9 November 1990, the King promulgated the constitution which transformed him into a constitutional monarch, proclaimed the people as the sovereign, granted universal suffrage in elections, protected the fundamental rights of the people and organisations, allowed a multi-party political system, and provided for an independent judiciary with broad powers on constitutional issues. The first democratic multi-party elections since 1959 were held in May 1991 in which the NC, the largest NCP group (the United Marxist-Leninists or UML), and the National Democratic Party (NDP) composed mostly of former panchayat officials, were the principal contestants. The results were clearly indicative of the public's support for the political changes as less than 15 percent of the voters cast their ballots for candidates identified with the panchayat system, and most of those that won had been moderate reformers. The NC won an absolute majority of seats and a NC government, headed by G. P. Koirala (the brother of B. P. Koirala), was formed.

Establishing a broadly participatory and open democratic political system in a country in which power had been highly centralised for virtually the entire twentieth century has not been an easy task. The political parties had no experience in operating as legal entities or as ruling and opposition parties within a sovereign parliament. The bureaucracy at both the central and regional levels had to adjust to new politics on both the decision-making process and policy implementation, so there was bound to be confusion in identifying the real source of authority. The police had to adjust to a new political environment in which their powers to suppress and oppress the public were greatly restricted, so that for the first year or so the police were reluctant to use their legal authority even in cases where criminal acts were committed. The public in rural areas and small towns had to learn how to use their increasingly critical role in local political and development issues. Finally, King Birendra and his palace secretariat had to identify their proper role in a democratic constitutional monarchy.

None of these were easy but, all things considered, the new political system functioned much more efficiently than any one had expected and without any serious crises that posed a challenge to parliamentary institutions. The major political parties initially focused their attention on establishing party organisations on a national basis, in the process creating local party units that began to demand a voice in the running of the party at the central level. A gradual democratisation of party organisations was the result for all but a few small communist factions that retained their adherence to Marxist-Leninist principles – that is of elitist democratic centralisation. In the Nepali Congress, Prime Minister Koirala was accepted as the leader in virtually all NC party organisations except in the Kathmandu Valley where Bhattarai and Ganeshman Singh's supporters ran the show. But Bhattarai's defeat in the 1991 parliamentary election and in a 1994 by-election in a Kathmandu constituency deprived him of any basis for a claim to be the party's leader, even though he continued to serve as the party president. This resulted in a major crisis in the party due to Bhattarai and Ganeshman Singh's refusal to accept Koirala as the head of the party, and eventually led to parliamentary elections in the fall of 1994, more than a year ahead of schedule.

Within the NCP, the comparatively moderate (some even say conservative) UML faction had clearly demonstrated its primary status in the badly fractionalised communist movement in the 1991 elections in which it won the second largest number of seats. Since then, the UML has usually operated as a proper democratic party in the parliament, though one might not get that impression from the extremist language that is occasionally used by UML leaders, presumably to maintain the allegiance of the numerically small but important young party cadres, mostly students, who still support classic Marxist-Leninist rhetoric. UML-sponsored demonstrations, usually confined to the Kathmandu valley, were occasionally reminiscent of the violent tactics used in the NCP's carefully-managed protests during the Panchayat period that were turned on-and-off as seemed appropriate. This is still the case as the UML has avoided organising directed at the overthrow of the new constitutional system, just as it did through the pre-1990 period. It would appear that the UML leader's involvement in the interim coalition government in 1990-91 had a positive impact on the kind of politics the UML played when it was the main opposition party in parliament in 1991-94.

Nepali politics became even more complex in the summer of 1994 when Prime Minister Koirala felt compelled to advise King Birendra to dissolve parliament and hold new parliamentary elections. King Birendra did as advised and in the elections held in October 1994 the UML emerged as the winner of a plurality of seats, with the NC a close second. As neither the UML nor the NC could work out an agreement with the other parties to form a coalition government that would have a majority in parliament, the king asked the UML to form a government. The UML agreed and the new government was approved by a majority vote in parliament, with even the NC voting for the new cabinet.

It should be noted that Koirala had not been forced to take these actions by the tactics of the opposition parties inside parliament or out on the street but rather because of infighting within the Nepali Congress leadership. Approximately 30 NC MPs, encouraged by Bhattarai and Ganeshman Singh, threatened to vote against the Koirala government in a projected no-confidence motion in parliament. And as all the opposition parties had indicated their intention to support the motion, the Koirala government would have been forced out of office. It was in these circumstances that Koirala went to the king and requested new parliamentary elections. In the 1994 elections, again it was the division within the NC organisation that led to the loss of about 20 seats, thus relegating the NC to the status of the primary opposition party in parliament to the UML government.

The UML cabinet lasted for nearly one year, which was better than most people expected, due primarily to the failure of the opposition parties to reach a consensus on the passage of a no-confidence motion until September 1995. One factor in the division of the opposition was the moderate position taken by the UML on most key policy issues that differed little from those of the Koirala government. This was perhaps most evident in the vigorous efforts made by the UML, in competition with the NC, to persuade the conservative NDP's 20 MPs to form a coalition government. Finally, however, it was the NC and the NDP that agreed to support a no-confidence motion against the UML government which would have got majority support in parliament. In these circumstances, the UML Prime Minister Man Mohan Adhikari did what Koirala had done in 1994: ask King Birendra to dissolve parliament and call for new elections.

The king accepted Adhikari's 'advice' as he had Koirala's, but the circumstances in the two cases differed in one key respect. In 1994, Birendra consulted with the opposition parties and ascertained that there was no alternative government to the NC that could gain a majority support in parliament. If he had done this in 1995 he would have found that there was a majority coalition that should have been allowed to at least make an attempt to form a government. The king's action was questioned in a case brought before the Supreme Court which, in a novel expression of its power in the new Nepali legal system, declared that the king had acted illegally and ordered the old parliament to be reinstituted. This was done, a no-confidence motion against the UML government was passed, and the cabinet resigned. Subsequently, a three-party coalition government took office and won a vote of confidence in parliament.

A coalition government, headed by Surya Bahadur, the leader of the National Democratic Party (NDP), was formed in October 1997 with the support of the NC and the NSP (Nepal Sadbhavana Party), but with only a bare majority in parliament. In April 1998, the coalition collapsed because of a split in the NDP. The king then asked G. P. Koirala to form another NC government. Koirala commenced negotiations with several other parties in search of majority support in parliament. Finally, the NC formed a coalition with the most unlikely opposition party, the ideologically leftist Marxist-Leninist party (ML) that had split off from the more conservative UML in mid-1998. This coalition, however, lasted only until December 1998 when the ML ministers submitted their resignations. G. P. Koirala headed a minority NC government until parliamentary elections were held in May 1999 in which the NC emerged with a majority of seats (109 of 205) and formed a one-party government in late May headed by the number two NC leader, K. P. Bhattarai. The UML became the largest opposition party (69 seats), and something like a two-party system may be in the process of emerging in the complex politics of Nepal. In any case, there emerged a government in Kathmandu that would be in a position to make some of the critical decisions on key political, economic and foreign issues that the weak coalition governments had all carefully avoided.

The first years of the new political system in Nepal, thus, were a bit traumatic but overall they were similar to the experience of several democratic parliamentary regimes in Europe and Asia. The lack of stability in the composition of cabinets was lamented by some critics, particularly in Kathmandu, who looked back somewhat nostalgically to the panchayat days during which officials came and went but there was a basic continuity in policy matters due to the palace's dominant role. What has been ignored is the fact that the various governments that have held office since mid-1990 have all adopted similar policy positions and considered similar policy options on the principal economic, political and social issues for the very good reason that there were no real alternatives that made more sense on such vital issues as the economic relationship with India, key development projects (for example, the Arun dam), or the need to encourage the private sector of the economy if Nepal is ever to rise above its current status at the bottom of the international GNP scale. On balance, the first eight years of the new politics compare favourably with the panchayat system which was good at introducing impressive new programs but failed badly in their implementation.

There are, of course, numerous questions raised about the political changes that have occurred. One question that is frequently voiced concerns the role of the palace in the new politics and the suspicion that King Birendra has as his ultimate objective the restoration of the old palace-centred system in some form or another. One can speculate about this endlessly, but it seems clear that so far King Birendra has acted like a proper constitutional monarch. To date whenever he has become involved in politics, it has invariably been at the request of the sitting prime minister. His decision in 1995, for instance, to accept Adhikari's advice on the dissolution of parliament, later declared illegal by the Supreme Court, cannot be reasonably interpreted as part of a broad palace conspiracy to change the system.

There have also been some doubts that the post-1990 politics have had a real impact on the old Brahman–Chhettri–Newari elite structure that has long controlled the decision-making process in Nepal. A quick survey of the leadership of the principal parties shows that a high percentage of the party leaders, and especially in the UML, come from high caste elite families. But even here, some changes are underway. Most of the NC leaders are Brahman or Chettris, but many of them are from local elite families from outside Kathmandu, and are supportive of the decentralisation programs that most of the old 'national' elite families in the capital find threatening.

G. P. Koirala's inter-party conflicts with Bhattarai and Ganeshman Singh were, in reality, a confrontation between the regional and Kathmandu party units, and in the new cabinet formed in October 1995, it was the regional units that won the battle. Even in the UML, party units outside Kathmandu now often display an evident disinclination to accept the dictates of the Kathmandu-dominated central committee.

In the national bureaucracy in Kathmandu, there has been some shifting around of the top officials of various departments, but again most of them still come from the old elite families. However, demands by the Tarai and the hill ethnic communities for greater representation in the administrative system and the judiciary cannot be ignored and, according to some reports, there have already been substantial, if little noted, changes in the social composition of the bureaucracy at the regional level. This is bound to have a gradual impact on the national bureaucracy as well.

There have been some potentially important changes in Nepal's national political culture since 1990. The Nepali Congress government (1991-94), for instance, introduced a radical program intended to facilitate the decentralisation of the government system by conceding to elected local bodies the authority to collect some taxes and use the revenues for their own developmental programs. In the past, this revenue was sent to the central government which then distributed some of the money to the districts for programs approved by the Kathmandu authorities. In 1994-95, the centrist-inclined UML government tried to reverse this NC program by once again distributing a set sum to each of the districts for Kathmandu's development programs, but the expectation is that the new NC government formed in May 1999 will go back to the NC policy on this issue. A primary political struggle for power within Nepal, thus, continues to be the age-old confrontation between the old Brahman–Chhettri–Newari elite based in Kathmandu and the regional and local elites that are broadly representative of the ethnic and regional communities in their areas. It should be an interesting struggle to watch.

NOTES

1 While the literature dealing specifically with Nepal's political culture is very limited, there is a substantial body of publications by Nepali, Indian, and Western historians and social scientists that analyse various aspects of this subject in considerable detail. My own interpretation of the evolution of the national political culture in Nepal is heavily dependent upon these sources, although at times in ways that the authors might not recognise.
2 See Ludwig F. Stiller, *The Rise of the House of Gorkha* (New Delhi: Manjusri Publishing House, 1973) for a detailed analysis of the formation and organisation of a national political system in the post-1770 period in Nepal.
3 Rishikesh Shaha, *An Introduction to Nepal* (Kathmandu: Ratna Pustak Bhandar, 1976), 4; Bhuwan Lal Joshi and Leo E. Rose, *Democratic Innovations*

in Nepal (Berkeley: University of California Press, 1966), 1; and Ludwig F. Stiller, *The Silent Cry: The People of Nepal, 1816-39* (Kathmandu: Sahayogi Prakashan, 1976).

4 Prayag Raj Sharma, 'Caste, Social Mobility and Sanskritization: A Study of Nepal's Old Legal Code', *Kailash* 4, 1977, 277-299. I have also discussed this in 'Secularization of Hindu Polity: the Case of Nepal' in Donald E. Smith, ed., *Religion and Political Modernization* (New Haven: Yale University Press, 1974), 31-48.

5 Satish Kumar, *Rana Polity in Nepal* (New Delhi: Asia Publishing House, 1967); and Pramede Shamshere Rana, *Rana Nepal: An Insider's View* (Kathmandu: R. Rana, 1978).

6 Prayag Raj Sharma, op. cit.; Mahesh C. Regmi, 'Preliminary Notes on the Nature of Rana Law and Government', *INAS Journal* 2(2), 1975, 103-115.

7 Daniel Edward, in 'Patrimonial and Bureaucratic Administration in Nepal' (Ph.D. dissertation, University of Chicago, 1977) discusses the extensive 'modernisation' of the administrative system under the Rana regime.

8 Harka Gurung, 'Sociology of the 1981 Election in Nepal', *Asian Survey* 21 (12), December 1981.

9 Pashupati Shumsher J. B. Rana, 'Sociological and Psychological Aspects of the Problem of Administration' (unpublished paper).

10 For a thorough study of the role of parties in the 'non-party' system in Nepal, see Lok Raj Baral, *Opposition Politics in Nepal* (New Delhi: Abhinav Publications, 1977).

PART II

IDENTITY

Chapter 6

The Rise of Hindu Nationalism and the Marginalisation of Muslims in India Today

Christophe Jaffrelot

India, the 'largest democracy of the world' has also been known after 1947 for its attempts at establishing a secular regime and its success – quite exceptional – in maintaining it for decades despite ups and downs. Even though Indira Gandhi had the notion of secularism inserted in the Indian Constitution in 1976, almost twenty years after independence, the political system set up during the reign of her father, Jawaharlal Nehru, was already designed along those lines. Secularism has been understood in India not as a synonym for the French word *laïcité*, which implies separation between church and state; rather, it designates the equidistance of the state vis-à-vis all religions and an equally positive attitude towards them all. For instance, Article 25 of the constitution emphasizes that 'all persons are equally free to profess, practice and propagate religion', and Article 30 states that 'All minorities, whether based on religion or language, shall have the right to establish and administer educational institutions', which can also receive subsidies from the state.

Paradoxically, to provide an added sense of security to the religious minorities, specifically the Muslims (12 percent of the population in the 1991 census) and the Christians (about 2 percent) were also entitled to use their personal law for regulating their community life, whereas the Hindu majority forming 82 percent of the population had to submit to the Hindu Code Bill which, in the 1950s–1960s, reformed the traditional practices regarding divorce, inheritance and adoption in the light of Western law. This is something that most militant Hindus still regard today as unbalanced treatment of the different religious groups.

The relationship between the Hindus and the religious minorities has always been in the form of a dialectic. Authorities such as Paul Brass, Gyanendra Pandey and Sandria Freitag have argued that economic factors and the emergence of a proto-democratic political arena during the British Raj[1] gradually led all the communities to reshape their identity along ethno-nationalist lines to give birth to what is known as *communalism* in India.

While these elements need to be highlighted, I would like to stress the subjective aspects of the Hindu–Muslim relationship by focussing on the largely irrational feeling of vulnerability in certain segments of the Hindu community. The sentiment that Muslims pose a threat to the majority community was the root cause for the crystallisation of a form of Hindu nationalism about one hundred years ago, its reactivation in the 1920s and 1930s, and most recently in the 1980s and 1990s. This last episode unfolded itself while the Muslim community, which was never in a strong position in post-independence India, has been further marginalised.

THE BIRTH AND RISE OF HINDU NATIONALISM: STIGMATISING AND EMULATING 'THREATENING OTHERS'

In the past, the word 'Hindu' primarily designated those who lived to the east beyond the river Sindhu, or Indus, not the followers of a creed. In fact, Hinduism can hardly be considered to be a religion since, although it sanctions a strong orthopraxy as embodied in the caste system, it does not contain real orthodoxy. It has no Book which can serve as a common reference to its adherents; the relevant books have been written by *gurus* for their sects (*sampradayas* or *panths*) which, indeed, represent the basic units of the Hindu world.[2] The only approximate form of 'ecclesiastical structure'[3] was created by Shankara who in the eighth century established monasteries in the four corners of India. Interestingly, he did so as a way of countering the growing influence of Buddhism which threatened to displace the Brahmins as the religious élite. The heads of the four monasteries were ordained to exercise a spiritual authority comparable to that of the Buddhist clergy: a Hindu pattern of reaction to exterior threats was taking shape which consisted, for the brahminical élite, in imitating those who were perceived as posing a threat to them in order to resist them more efficiently.

This modus operandi was again at work, in a way, in the nineteenth century in the context of European colonisation. Upper caste Hindus reacted to the British utilitarian administration and Christian missions which shared an aversion to Hinduism for its idolatrous polytheism and caste system. They invented a Vedic golden age in which God was presented as unique (as propounded by Raja Ram Mohun Roy, the founder of the Brahmo Samaj in 1928 in Calcutta) and in which the Aryans were deemed to occupy positions in the social system according to their merits (as advocated by Swami Dayananda Saraswati, founder of the Arya Samaj in 1875 in Bombay). The nineteenth century socio-religious reform movements tended to modernise Hinduism along Western lines – they protested against child marriage and the *sati*, militated in favor of female literacy etc. – but they also emulated the British in order to fight their influence more effectively. For instance, the Arya Samaj reinterpreted the old notion of *shuddhi*, a ritual which traditionally enabled an upper caste Hindu to purify himself when he has been soiled by some polluting contact, and transformed it into a re-conversion procedure, thereby making Hinduism a proselytising creed, more similar to Christianity and Islam.

The Muslims' attitudes precipitated the next stage in the formation of a Hindu nationalist identity. The peace negotiations following the First World War made Indian followers of Islam apprehend that the Caliphate, hitherto embodied in the person of the Ottoman Sultan, would be suppressed. In 1919, some of their leaders launched a 'Khilafat Movement' against the British who were taking part in the negotiations.[4] This mobilisation degenerated in some instances into Hindu-Muslim riots, especially on the Malabar coast in 1921. It triggered a cycle of violence which lasted till the late 1920s in North India and reinforced a sense of vulnerability among many Hindus. In response, Hindu activists launched the movement Hindu Sangathan (Organisation of the Hindus). Hindu nationalism crystallised in this context into an ideology and a political movement.

THE HINDUTVA MOVEMENT:
AN ETHNO-RELIGIOUS NATIONALISM

The Hindu nationalist ideology was first thoroughly codified in 1923 by Vinayak Damodar Savarkar (1883-1966) in *Hindutva: Who is a Hindu?* In this work, a Hindu is primarily someone who lives in Hindustan, the land beyond the Indus, between the Himalayas and the Indian Ocean. But Savarkar does not believe in territorial nationalism, a notion that implies a universalistic worldview. For him, the historical place of the Hindus is remarkable because of rootedness south of the Himalayas. Due to this, the first Aryans, in Vedic times, were immune from foreign influences and intermarried in such a way that all Hindus 'can claim to have in their veins the blood of the mighty race descended from the Vedic fathers...'[5] In addition to geographical and ethnic unity, Savarkar, paradoxically emphasises India's linguistic unity by arguing that Sanskrit is set up as the referent of all the sub-continental languages. Thereafter, every political program based on the Hindu nationalist ideology – and especially those of the Hindu Mahasabha, the political party headed by Savarkar in 1937-1942 – would call for recognition of Sanskrit or Hindi, the vernacular language closest to Sanskrit, as the national language.

The tenets of Hindu nationalist ideology were subsequently revised by the Rashtriya Swayamsevak Sangh (RSS - Association of National Volunteers), which was founded in 1925 by an admirer of Savarkar, Keshav Baliram Hedgewar (1889-1940) and which soon became the leading organization in the Hindutva movement. Golwalkar, who succeeded Hedgewar as chief of the RSS in 1940, gave the movement its ideological charter in 1938 with his book *We, or Our Nationhood Defined*, in which religious minorities were called upon to pledge allegiance to Hindu symbols of identity as the embodiment of the Indian nation.[6] With Hindu culture embodying the essence of Indian identity, religious minorities were requested to limit expressions of community distinctiveness to the private sphere.

The concept of *chiti* or 'race-spirit' in the writings of Savarkar, and later of Golwalkar, conveys the idea of the soul of the nation rather than biological connotations.[7] This conception allows, in fact insists upon, the integration of minorities by means of acculturation and at a subordinate level, whereas the tenets of biological racism, reasoning in eugenic terms, could well have incorporated an idea of total exclusion. This difference reflects the importance of social categories in Hinduism, a civilisation that has always been characterised by an ability and a determination to assimilate the Other at a subordinate level as part of the organicist, hierarchical rationale of a caste-based society. Golwalkar considered as *mleccha* (barbarian) foreigners 'who do not subscribe to the social laws dictated by the Hindu religion and culture',[8] a definition which closely coincides with the traditional usage of this term. In ancient India, a *mleccha* was someone on the fringe of the orthopraxy specific to the caste society dominated by Brahminical values.[9]

THE HINDU NATIONALIST NETWORK

The Hindu nationalist network first spread among the high castes of northern India and is still largely confined to this area. This geographical situation can be explained in two ways. Firstly, the Sanskrit Great Tradition on which the ideology is based is closely related to the Hindi-speaking north. Secondly, this is a region inhabited by a large proportion of high-caste Hindus who are attracted to the Hindutva movement because, with its emphasis on social organic unity, it seems well equipped to protect them from the increasing demands of the low castes.

The Hindu nationalist movement, especially the RSS that is its backbone, has always regarded itself as destined to encompass the whole of India. This being so, it determined at a very early stage to spread throughout Indian society. First, it developed a network of *shakhas* (local branches) which organised daily physical training and Hindu nationalist propaganda sessions in urban neighborhoods and villages. The RSS's ultimate ambition was to reach all the cities and villages of India in this way. Its membership rose from 10,000 in 1932 to 600,000 in 1951 and today stands at around 2 million, divided among 27,264 branches (*shakhas*) and 39,175 sub-branches (*upshakhas*).[10] The upshakhas are the RSS's real basic units since the number of shakhas simply indicates the places where the movement is present – thus a town may contain several sub-branches.

After independence, this effort to cover the territory of India was supplemented by an effort to develop a network of sectoral affiliates. The aim here was not to penetrate society directly by means of shakhas, but to set up unions or organisations to defend specific social categories. These organisations give the Hindu nationalist movement a foothold in most sectors of society, where they work hand in glove with the shakha network. All these bridgeheads are presented by the mother organisation as the *Sangh parivar*, 'the family of the Sangh' (i.e. the RSS).

In 1948, Delhi-based RSS officials founded the Akhil Bharatiya Vidyarthi Parishad (ABVP – the Association of Students of India), a students' union which was primarily intended to counter communist influence on university campuses. Today it is the student union with the largest membership – about one million students. A few years later, in 1955, the RSS set up a trade union, the Bharatiya Mazdoor Sangh (BMS – the Indian Workers' Association) primarily to oppose the 'Red unions'. In the name of Hindu nationalist ideology and in line with organicist principles, the BMS attaches greater importance to social cohesion than to class struggle, hence its references to Gandhi's political philosophy and economics. By the late 1980s, the BMS had become India's biggest trade union. While the Congress-backed Indian Trade Union Congress (INTUC) came first with 2.2 million members in 1980 against 1.2 million workers affiliated to the BMS, it had only 2.7 million members in 1989 while the BMS stood at 3 million.[11]

Along with these unions, the RSS developed a number of more specialised organisations. In 1952, it founded a tribal welfare movement, the Vanavasi Kalyan Ashram (VKA – Center for Tribals' Welfare)[12] whose purpose was primarily to counter the influence of the Christian missionaries among the tribals of central India where their evangelisation and social work had led to conversions. The VKA imitated the techniques of the missionaries by developing dispensaries and schools to bring about a number of 're-conversions'. The strategy of stigmatisation and emulation of the so-called 'threatening others' was still at work.

THE VHP, A HINDU CONSISTORY?

In 1964, in association with Hindu religious figures, the RSS launched the Vishva Hindu Parishad (VHP – World Hindu Council), a movement designed to bring together the different Hindu sect leaders and provide this loosely organised religion with some kind of centralised structure.[13] The VHP succeeded in gathering together the heads of different Hindu sects on a covertly political platform.

Till the 1960s, few heads of traditional sects had joined the Hindu nationalist movement. Digvijay Nath, the Gorakhpur-based chief of the Naths, had been returned to the Lok Sabha on an Hindu Mahasabha ticket.

The Rise of Hindu Nationalism

Before that, Swami Karpatriji, one of the most influential ascetics of Varanasi had founded the Ram Rajya Parishad (Association for the Kingdom of Ram) in 1948 in order to fight the Hindu Code Bill which, according to him, went against Hindu traditions. He received the support of several maharajahs in Rajasthan and Madhya Pradesh where he maintained pockets of influence till the 1960s. He then played a key part in the 1966 cow protection movement, which aimed at prohibiting cow-slaughter through the constitution itself, something Nehru had refused out of respect for the non-vegetarian communities. Large numbers of sadhus took part in this movement, the biggest that had been held in Delhi till then. At that time, the VHP was instrumental in bringing many more religious figures into the Hindu nationalist movement.

The ground had been prepared for this task by the profound change Hindu ascetics were undergoing. These *sadhus* were generally known as itinerant individuals absorbed in the solitary quest for God, even when they belonged to monk orders. However, even before independence, the urban middle class had been a favorable milieu for the emergence of new kinds of sadhus who, even though they were initiated in traditional orders, preached in English and downplayed their individual relationship with their disciples in comparison to imparting 'mass enlightenment'. In fact, they specialised in the collective healing of the psychological distress of the middle class, which suffered from stress and urban anomie. Even today their teaching aims more at making life a success than at spiritual salvation. The modern sadhus almost ignore their sectarian affiliation and, by contrast, emphasise their 'Hinduness'. They develop so-called philanthropic activities and establish their reputation via lucrative travels in the West. Many of them eventually joined the Hindu nationalist movement. Swami Chinmayananda, a 'modern guru' who established his *ashram*, the Sandypani Academy, in Bombay in 1963 was one of the founders of the Vishva Hindu Parishad.

The VHP was founded in his ashram, but under the auspices of the RSS which seconded one of its *pracharaks*, Shiv Shankar Apte, to become its General Secretary. Since then the objective of the movement has been to strengthen Hinduism by endowing it with a centralised organisation. For the Hindu nationalists, there is an urgent need for federating the sects of their religion which otherwise appears to be at the mercy of the minorities. The circumstances of the founding of the VHP are illuminating in this respect. The movement was launched in Bombay just before the visit of the Pope who, it had been announced, would convert a large number of Hindus to Christianity. Once again, Hindus feeling threatened by a 'semitic' creed, responded by imitating its centralised structure. Indeed, the VHP's organisation drew its inspiration from the Catholic notion of *consistory*, that is a body of religious leaders dealing with the affairs of their community. Moreover, it then tried to evolve a Hindu catechism, to standardise the Hindu rituals, and to deploy its own preachers in the regions where the missionaries were operating. It thus implemented the strategy of stigmatisation and emulation in its own way.

THE AYODHYA MOVEMENT

The Vishva Hindu Parishad became the spearhead of Hindu nationalism in the early 1980s, primarily because the RSS decided to make it the principal means of action after it had distanced itself from the BJP. The BJP, from the RSS' point of view, had shown itself to be too prompt to dilute its Hindu nationalist character, primarily so that it could form electoral alliances with parties of different persuasions, as evident from its aborted Janata phase in 1977–1980.

The Sangh parivar benefited from the reactivation of a Hindu sentiment of vulnerability consequent to the conversions of Meenakshipuram. In that village in Tamil Nadu, several hundred Untouchables had converted to Islam in 1981. These conversions were interpreted by *Hindu Vishva*, the official organ of the VHP, as constituting 'part of a long-term plan intended to transform the [Muslim] minority into a majority'.[14] The VHP sponsored Hindu Solidarity Conferences all over India to awaken solidarity among Hindus, for *jana jagaran*, according to the common expression, which tended to replace the RSS slogan of *Hindu sangathan*.

The VHP also organised the *ekatmata yatra* (literally, 'pilgrimage of unity') from the same perspective in 1983. Three caravans connecting Kathmandu and Rameshwaram (Tamilnadu), Gangasagar (Bengal) and Somnath (Gujarat), and Haridwar (Uttar Pradesh) and Kanyakumari (Tamilnadu), distributed water from the Ganges and provided themselves with sacred water from local temples or from other sacred rivers encountered on the way. This mingling was intended to symbolise Hindu unity and, indeed, all the caravans converged in Nagpur, the headquarters of the RSS and the geographical center of India. The Ganges, the river of salvation, was a shrewd choice since, just like the cow, it represents a symbol venerated by all Hindus.

The manipulation of religious symbols appeared even more distinctly in the Ayodhya movement. In Ayodhya in the sixteenth century, the Mughal emperor Babur had a mosque built on a site which many Hindus believed to be the birthplace of Ram, the most popular god in North India. In 1984, the VHP started a movement claiming the retrocession of the *Ramjanmabhoomi* (birthplace of Ram) to the Hindus. In May – June, the VHP provided itself with an organisation, which assembled young Hindu militants, the Bajrang Dal.[15] Its founder, V. Katiyar, had until then been a pracharak of the RSS. However, the Bajrang Dal proved to be less disciplined than the RSS and its violent utterances as well as actions were to precipitate many communal riots.

In September 1984 the VHP conducted a march beginning in Sitamarhi (Bihar) in the name of the 'liberation' of the Ayodhya temple, the site of which was reached on 7 October. In accordance with its interest in acting as a pressure group, the march set out to convey a petition to the government in Lucknow and then took the route to Delhi, which it should have reached in December, shortly before the elections foreseen for January 1985. However, in the meantime, the assassination of Indira Gandhi completely transformed the political atmosphere and led the VHP to change its plans.

The Ayodhya movement underwent a new stage of development in 1989 when the VHP decided to build a temple at Ram's birthplace. Its *Ramshila pujan* program consisted in taking the bricks with which the temple was supposed to be built to thousands of towns and villages in order to have them consecrated by sadhus and to collect donations. More importantly, this campaign surcharged the atmosphere with communal feelings, which were to influence the results of the late 1989 elections. The BJP joined the Ayodhya movement at that stage, realising its growing popularity among the Hindus of north India. It registered a significant electoral advance, winning 88 seats in the 1989 election as opposed to only two in 1984. This gain was further strengthened in 1991 when it won 119 seats, of which six were won by 'modern *gurus*'. In September 1990, Hindu militants tried to take by storm the Babri Masjid. The mosque's domes were damaged but the militants were successfully repressed by the authorities. A dozen or so of the casualties amongst the militants enhanced the cause of the so-called 'Hindu martyrs'.

The Ayodhya movement which took shape in the context of this new reaction to the perception of 'threatening others' was of far greater magnitude compared to previous ethno-religious mobilisations triggered by Hindu nationalists. Paradoxically at that time the Muslims looked more marginalised than ever.

MUSLIMS AS SECOND CLASS CITIZENS

The constitutional dispositions, which were intended to found a multi-cultural polity after independence, remained largely non-implemented because Hindu traditionalists from the Congress were well-entrenched in the North Indian states. These leaders, exemplified by S. Sampurnanand, the chief minister of Uttar Pradesh in 1954–1960; and R.S. Shukla, the chief minister of Madhya Pradesh in 1947–1956; were known for a staunch attachment to Hindu culture which found expression in the promotion of Hindi, Ayurvedic medicine and protection of the cow.[16] Their prejudice against Muslims was expressed in their bias against Urdu and their low levels of recruitment to the bureaucracy and the police.[17] In 1964, only 7.7 and 5.5 percent of those in the bureaucracy of Uttar Pradesh and Bihar respectively were Muslims, two states where they constituted 15 and

14 percent respectively of the population. Nehru promoted Muslim leaders such as Maulana Azad and Rafi Ahmad Kidwai as his ministers in the national cabinet and Zakir Hussain as vice president in 1962 (who later became president in 1967–1969). But at the state level, Muslims often did not reach such posts of responsibility.

The hiatus between New Delhi's policies and politics at the state level was especially striking in the linguistic domain. In 1963, the Official Languages Act established English as an 'associated official language', to the chagrin of Hindu nationalists who wanted Hindi to be the only official language. In the states of the Hindi belt, where almost half of the Muslims live and where traditionalist Hindu Congressmen were in command, the latter's policy put Urdu, the language recognised by the Muslims as an identity symbol, in jeopardy. Hindi was considered as the official language by the states of this area after 1947. In Uttar Pradesh, the government of G.B. Pant declared that Hindi was the language to be used in courts and by the administration, whereas Urdu had been an official language during the British Raj. The Anjuman-e-Taraqqi-e-Urdu (Academy for the Promotion of Urdu) organised a protest movement in the form of a signature campaign, and in 1958 Nehru demanded that the Urdu-speaking population of the state be allowed to be educated in their language. The reluctance of the state authorities to amend the education policy, which was in the state's domain of competence, was such that Urdu continued to lose ground, so much so that today Muslim institutions have the Koran printed in Devanagari (the script used for writing Hindi) in order to reach their co-religionists. Urdu newspapers are also developing Hindi editions, but this effort does not enable them to resist the general trend very efficiently, as Table 1 shows. The Muslims of Uttar Pradesh had to wait until the 1989 election campaign before the Congress state government declared Urdu as the second official language. This decision was obviously taken with an eye on the Muslim vote.

Such a tactical move was not new. Muslims supported the Congress after independence because, as a secular party, it promised to protect their interests better than any other party. Nehru especially was regarded as a

Table 1: **Hindi and Urdu Media** (*numbers of each*)

	Dailies		Weeklies		Bi-monthlies	
	1958	1990	1958	1990	1958	1990
Hindi	73	1381	233	4669	60	1652
Urdu	44	344	117	903	24	261

Source: M. Hasan, 'Minority Identity and its Discontents: Ayodhya and its Aftermath', *South Asia Bulletin* 14(2), 1994, 32–33.

custodian of Muslims' interests. The Congress maintained this relationship even after his death, but it tended to assume a more and more clientelistic form. The ruling party was eager to co-opt and patronise Muslim leaders who often turned out to exert a conservative influence over their community, especially when they were religious leaders. Gradually, the notion of secularism got perverted because of them and their association with the Congress party.

The conservative leadership of the Muslim community erected the *Shariat* (the Muslim legal code) as a symbol of Muslim identity and of India's multiculturalism, whereas they did not show much tolerance themselves. This complex issue was well illustrated during the Shah Bano affair. Shah Bano, a Muslim woman, had been divorced by her husband according to the Shariat. On appealing to the courts, she was granted some alimony by the High Court of Madhya Pradesh where she lived, but her former husband appealed the decision before the Supreme Court which reconfirmed the judgement in 1985. Immediately, Muslim leaders started an agitation with 'Shariat in danger' as the standard slogan and went to Rajiv Gandhi, the prime minister. Gandhi, who did not want to alienate them, had the Congress party vote an amendment in Parliament in order to exclude the Muslim community from the article of the Code of Criminal Procedure on the basis of which the Supreme Court had pronounced its judgement. This move was strongly disapproved of by the Sangh parivar which saw it as a sign of the 'pseudo-secularism' of the Congress and of its pampering of the most obscurantist Muslims. The Shah Bano affair prepared the ground for the Hindu mobilisation around Ayodhya.

The attitude of Rajiv Gandhi was in tune with the way his mother had tended to communalise politics after her come-back in 1980. On the one hand, she recognised the long-awaited status of autonomy for the Aligarh Muslim University in 1981,[18] and on the other hand, she multiplied her visits to Hindu temples and let one of her lieutenants, C.M. Stephen, declare in 1983 that the Congress culture was on the 'same wave-length' as Hindu culture. Simultaneously, she gave indirect support to the Sikh extremist Sant Bhindranwale in order to destabilize the more moderate factions of the Akali Dal, the main rival of the Congress in Punjab. The second reign of Indira Gandhi was thus marked by an erosion of secularism which had been the dominant ideology of the Congress leadership at the Center.

Similarly, Rajiv Gandhi did not choose one community over another but admitted the legitimacy of communal considerations in the public sphere. In 1986, he tried to balance his decision in the Shah Bano affair by accepting the demand of the VHP concerning the unlocking of the Babri Masjid, so that the Hindus could worship there. This concession, far from defusing the Hindu nationalist agitation re-launched it. Similarly, in 1989, he accepted that the first stone of the temple envisioned by the VHP was laid in front of the mosque, on disputed land. Rajiv Gandhi even started his election campaign from the neighboring town of Faizabad, 'Ram's land' as he called it. He was obviously trying to hijack some of the Hindu mobilisation which were boosting the BJP's electoral prospects. In fact, his tactic was responsible for removing all inhibition regarding the use of communal discourse in politics and prepared the ground for the unleashing of Hindu nationalism in the Ayodhya affair.

The Muslims were the first victims of this mobilisation. As Table 2 shows, the average number of communal riots per annum jumped from 400 in 1980–85 to about 700 in 1986–89 and rose from 1,000 to 2,000 between 1990 and 1993. Rioting was especially intense before the elections, when the Sangh parivar used communal violence as a means for polarising the electorate along religious lines. In 1989, out of the 88 constituencies where the BJP won the seat, 47 had just been affected by communal riots.[19] However, the worst riots took place after Hindu militants destroyed the Babri Masjid on 6 December 1992. At that time, Muslims demonstrated in the streets and attacked symbols of the state to protest against the leniency of the Congress government which, according to them, should have averted the demolition. Police forces and then Hindu activists retaliated. The toll was especially high in Bombay, Surat and Bhopal. The BJP was, in effect, punished for these excesses during the 1993 state elections when it lost Uttar Pradesh, Madhya Pradesh and Himachal Pradesh. The party then shifted from its strategy of ethno-religious mobilisation to a more moderate approach in politics. As Table 2 shows, the number of riots started to decline at that time.

If the number of communal riots have returned to the level of the 1950s and 1960s, it does not mean that India is back to the situation that was prevailing then. The rise of the BJP is accompanied by a banalisation of the Hindu nationalist discourse as testified by the Supreme Court verdict of December 1995. The judges had been asked to decide over the legality of the communal propaganda displayed by BJP and Shiv Sena leaders. Their utterances were obviously at odd with the Representation of the People Act which prohibits all references to religion during election campaigns. Surprisingly, the judges concluded that there was nothing wrong in canvassing on the theme of *hindutva* (hinduness) since this notion, like that of 'Hinduism', referred to 'a way of life', not to a religion.

Similarly, many communal riots have not been investigated seriously, like that of Bhopal in which there were 120 casualties in 1992. Nor have the reports of commissions of investigation been tabled before the assemblies or followed through in any way. The Bhagalpur riot, which resulted in about 1,000 casualties in 1989, the worst toll since 1947, was investigated by a commission but its report was made public almost eight years later and the judicial procedures followed were erratic:

Table 2: Hindu–Muslim Riots

Year	Number of riots	Number of deaths
1954	83	34
1955	72	24
1956	74	35
1957	55	12
1958	41	7
1959	42	41
1960	26	14
1961	92	108
1962	60	43
1963	61	26
1964	1070	1919
1965	173	34
1966	133	45
1967	209	251
1968	346	133
1969	519	674
1970	521	298
1971	321	103
1972	240	70
1973	242	72
1974	248	87
1975	205	33
1976	169	39
1977	188	36
1978	219	108
1979	304	261
1980	427	375
1981	319	196
1982	474	238
1983	500	1143
1984	476	445
1985	525	328
1986	764	418
1987	711	383
1988	611	223
1989	706	1155
1990	1404	1248

(contd.)

Table 2: Hindu–Muslim Riots (*Continued*)

Year	Number of riots	Number of deaths
1991	905	474
1992	1991	1640
1993	2292	952
1994	179	78
1995	Not available	62
1996	728	209
1997	725	264
1998	626	207

Sources: C. Jaffrelot, *The Hindu Nationalist Movement*, op. cit., 552; for 1993–94, 'Ministry of Home Affairs' Note for Consultative Committee Meeting on Communal Situation', *Muslim India*, no.156, December 1995, 558; for 1995, A. A. Engineer, 'Communalism and Communal Violence in 1995', *Economic and Political Weekly*, 23 December 1995, 3267–69; for 1996, 1997 and 1998, Lok Sabha Questions, no.110, 23 February 1999, reproduced in *Muslim India*, no.196, April 1999, 161.

The 142 cases filed in court accused 1,932 people of participating in incidents of violence and looting. Six years later, 87 cases against the 901 accused were still pending. Of the 55 cases decided, 11 have ended in convictions in which 50 people have been punished. Of the 406 people accused in murder cases, the court has decided on 95 people, of whom 94 have been acquitted.[20]

The growing under-representation of the Muslims in elected bodies also bears testimony of their relegation to the status of 'second class citizens'. As my computations show in Table 3, the gap between the percentage of the Muslims in the Indian population and their share of the Lok Sabha has never been so pronounced as in the 1990s. Not only does the BJP, which has become the largest party in Parliament since 1996, not give tickets to many Muslim candidates, but the Congress has been doing the same because the general atmosphere makes their chances of winning very slim.

The under-representation of Muslims in the administration and the police continues to be very pronounced. In 1991 they represented only 4.9 percent of the police force in Uttar Pradesh (where they formed 17.3 percent of the population), 4.2 percent in Maharashtra, 6.2 percent in Gujarat and 2.3 percent in Delhi.[21] At an all-India level, Muslims represent only 5.5 percent of the Central Reserve Police Force and 4.4 percent of the central administration (forming less than 3 percent of its elite group, the Indian Administrative Service).[22] In the private sector, a survey of the eight largest Indian firms in 1984 showed that the share of Muslims among the executives varied between zero and 5.6 percent.[23]

Table 3: **Muslims in the Lok Sabha**

Year	Muslim MPs (No.)	Total MPs (No.)	Muslim MPs (percent)	Muslims in population (percent)
1952	22	489	4.5	9.5
1957	26	494	5.3	9.5
1962	23	494	4.6	10.7
1967	30	520	5.7	10.7
1971	30	518	5.8	11.2
1977	32	542	5.9	11.2
1980	47	529	8.9	11.2
1984	47	542	8.7	11.4
1989	32	544	5.9	11.4
1991	27	544	5.0	12.1
1996	21	544	3.8	12.1
1998	27	544	4.9	12.1

Source: data compiled by author.

In the rural areas also, data collected by the National Sample Survey Organisation has shown that in 1987–1988 Muslims on average owned less land than Hindus, as highlighted in Table 4.

The same survey also highlighted the backwardness of Muslims in terms of education. The illiteracy rates are 42.4 and 59.5 percent for Muslim men and women respectively, and 25.3 and 42.2 for Hindu men and women. In keeping with the pattern, in rural India 58.2 percent of the males and 76.1 percent of the females are illiterate amongst Muslims, as against 51.3 percent and 75 percent respectively for the Hindus.[24] This lack of

Table 4: **Land Ownership Among Hindus and Muslims** (*in percent*)

Size of Plot of Land	Hindus	Muslims
Landless	28.0	34.7
Less than 1 acre	17.3	24.4
1–2.5 acres	18.3	17.5
2.5–5 acres	16.3	12.9
More than 5 acres	20.1	10.5

Source: *Muslim India*, no.140, August 1994, 378.

education is in part due to the anti-Urdu policies of the states but also due to the archaic system of the Koranic schools favored by many Muslims. In turn, it partly explains the under-representation of Muslims in the administration.

CONCLUSION

The secular regime that was enshrined in the Indian constitution half a century ago still remains far short of its expectations. Nehru's dream of multiculturalism has largely turned sour. One might argue that he should be considered responsible for this state of affairs, that he prepared the ground for the Hindu backlash since he failed to impose the same treatment such as a common civil code for instance on people of all creeds. Yet, as this essay argues, communal tensions in post-independence India have much deeper roots.

The interaction between the religions of India has gradually transformed them into something different. The worldly non-spiritual aspect of them has acquired a political and ideological dimension. Hinduism has probably undergone the most profound change of all in recent times after ideologues have attempted to endow what they regarded as an amorphous and quietist collection of sects with a proselytising mission and disciplined organisation. Paradoxically, in this process, they have tended to imitate the 'semitic religions' they professed to stigmatise.

The resulting ideology of Hindu nationalism has been supported by a network of organisations – the Sangh parivar – whose strength has no equivalent. In addition to their deep-rooted implantation in certain segments of the society, Hindu nationalists have now captured the state apparatus and are attempting to use it to propagate their views.

The first casualties of this trend have been the Muslims who already suffered the prejudice of many Congress leaders in the states in north India. Their continuing, and even growing, marginalisation in the administration, in elected bodies and in the economy jeopardise the very multiculturalist aspirations of 'the largest democracy in the world'.

Indian Muslims, however, are beginning to develop alternative strategies. While some of their leaders have adopted defensive postures by asking for quotas in the administration, members of the intelligentsia are trying to emancipate their community from the influence of obscurantist religious leaders. More importantly, Indian Muslims have started to use their main asset – their numbers – so precious at the time of elections to consolidate an alliance with opponents to the Sangh parivar, to be found not only among the religious minorities, such as the Christians who have also suffered atrocities during the Vajpayee governments, but also the lower castes who are fighting the Hindutva movement because it is directed by 'twice-born Hindus'. Muslims, Scheduled Castes and many low caste Hindus are

The Rise of Hindu Nationalism

already making common cause and voting for the same parties, as in Uttar Pradesh and Bihar for instance.

NOTES

1. On these historical developments which cannot be covered in the scope of this chapter, see P. Brass, *Language, Religion and Politics in North India* (Cambridge: Cambridge University Press, 1974); L.S. Freitag, *Collective Action and Community: Public Arenas and the Emergence of Communalism in North India* (Delhi: Oxford University Press, 1990); and G. Pandey, *The Construction of Communalism in Colonial North India* (Delhi: Oxford University Press, 1990).
2. H. von Stienencron, 'Hinduism: On the Proper Use of a Deceptive Term', in G.D. Sontheimer and H. Kulke, eds, *Hinduism Reconsidered* (New Delhi: Manohar, 1989), 20.
3. R. Thapar, 'Syndicated Moksha', *Seminar*, September 1985, 17.
4. G. Minault, *The Khilafat Movment: Religious Symbolism and Political Mobilization in India* (New York: Columbia University Press, 1982).
5. M.S. Golwakar, *We, or Our Nationhood Defined* (Nagpur: Bharat Prakashan, 1939).
6. Ibid.
7. C. Jaffrelot, 'The Idea of the Hindu Race in the Writings of Hindu Nationalist Ideologues in the 1920s and the 1930s: A Concept Between Two Cultures', in P. Robb, ed., *The Concept of Race in South Asia* (Delhi: Oxford University Press, 1995).
8. M.S. Golwalkar, *Bunch of Thoughts* (Bangalore: Jagaran Prakashan, 1966), 62.
9. Romila Thapar explains that this exclusion is not based on a racial criterion; it is social and ritual and hence can be overcome via acculturation and recognition of the superiority of the Brahmin: R. Thapar, *Ancient Indian History* (New Delhi: Orient Longman, 1978), 165, 169 and 179.
10. H. Barthval, *Rashtriya Swayamsevak Sangh: Ek Parichay* (New Delhi: Suruchi Prakashan, 1998), 16.
11. Lok Sabha Debates, third session, col.8, no. 2, (New Delhi: Lok Sabha Secretariat, 1990), 633. For more details, see C. Jaffrelot, 'Note sur un syndicat nationaliste hindou: le travail et les travailleurs dans l'idéologie et les stratégies du Bharatiya Mazdoor Sangh', in G. Heuzé, ed., *Travailler en Inde, Purushartha*, no. 14 (Paris: EHESS, 1992), 251–70. Today, the BMS has about 4.5 million members, *Muslim India*, no. 208, 20 April, 182.
12. The Hindu nationalists translate 'indigenous peoples' by *vanavasi*, literally 'those of the forest' and not, as is generally the case in India, by *adivasi*, i.e. 'those who were there before', because from their point of view, the country's first inhabitants were the 'Aryans' and not the autochthonous populations which were driven back or conquered by the Aryan invaders, from whom today's tribes are descended.
13. For further details, see C. Jaffrelot, 'The Vishva Hindu Parishad: Structures and Strategies', in J. Haynes, ed., *Religion, Globalisation and Political Culture in the Third World* (London: Macmillan, 1999), 191–212.
14. *Hindu Vishva*, March – April 1982, 7.
15. *Hindu Vishva*, 21 March 1986, 30. The term 'Bajrang' is generally attached to the name of Hanuman (the monkey leader and head of the armies of Ram) to characterise his strength.

16 B. Graham, 'The Congress and Hindu Nationalism', in D.A. Low, ed., *The Indian National Congress* (Delhi: Oxford University Press, 1988), 174.
17 M. Hasan, 'Adjustment and Accommodation: Indian Muslims after Partition', *Social Scientist* 18(8–9), August–September, 1990, 52.
18 V. Graff, 'Aligarh's Long Quest for "Minority" Status – AMU (Amendment) Act, 1981', *Economic and Political Weekly*, 11 August 1990, 1771–81.
19 J. Chiriyankandath, 'Tricolour and Saffron: Congress and the New Hindu Challenge', in S.K. Mitra and J. Chiriyankandath, eds, *Electoral Politics in India: A Changing Landscape* (New Delhi: Segment Books, 1992), 69.
20 'Recalling Bhagalpur: Aftermath of 1989 Riots', *Economic and Political Weekly*, 4 May 1996, 1057.
21 M. Hasan, *Legacy of a Divided Nation: India's Muslims since Independence* (London: Hurst, 1997), 294.
22 *India Today*, 31 January 1993, 31–37.
23 M. Hasan, 'In Search of Integration and Identity: Indian Muslims since Independence', *Economic and Political Weekly*, November 1988, 2470.
24 *Muslim India*, no.140, August 1994, 378.

Chapter 7
State, Nation, Identity: The Quest for Legitimacy in Bangladesh
Tazeen M. Murshid *

This paper examines the case of Bangladesh in order to demonstrate the contextual nature of the definitions of states, nations and identities. Nationalists[1] engaged in the quest for legitimacy and power have formulated and reformulated these so that they may exercise political control over power and resources. Specifically, the paper explores how the quest for legitimacy by successive regimes in Bangladesh has led to the rise of the religious right in politics, thus posing a challenge to the secular order visualized by the liberal intelligentsia.

Democracies achieve legitimate authority through the political process in the form of elections to ascertain popular opinion, and through other consensus-building activities aimed at 'homogenising' the population.[2] The latter often involve mobilization around particular conceptions of the social and moral order which appeal to ties of language, culture and religion. Some scholars, like Geertz and Shils, have argued that these ties are primordial and underived; whereas others, like Anderson, Hobsbawm and Ranger, have contested this position in favour of an instrumentalist interpretation which posits identities as constructed, imagined, or even invented.[3] Brass has identified three phases through which an 'ethnic group' can become a nation. In the first phase, people are distinguishable by 'cultural markers' of identity – such as race, religion or language – but do not pursue social and political goals based on these. In the next phase, they emphasize their distinctiveness as an ethnic group in order to lay claim to status, and use distinctive markers to achieve internal cohesion. In the final phase, they may act as an interest group or pursue the politics of

---

*Earlier drafts of this paper were presented at the Thirteenth European Conference of Modern South Asian Studies in Toulouse in September 1994 and in a seminar at the Institute of Commonwealth Studies, London, in October 1995. I would like to thank the participants for their lively contributions, which I found very useful. A fuller version of the paper was published in *South Asia*, 20 (2), 1997, 1-34.

nationalism, they could become a 'nationality', and demand either secession or federation or autonomy.[4] In the process of political and social mobilization, nationalists often seek to project an imaginary homogeneity in order to construct a new national identity or vision of a utopia. But utopias commonly run into conflict when competing nationalisms based on alternative interpretations of history, religion and culture generate demands for alternative state structures.[5]

The history of Bangladesh presents clear examples of diverse bases of mobilisation and ensuing conflicts. The experience of Bangladesh bears out the arguments of the instrumentalists, for it clearly demonstrates that ethnic and national identities are not primordial or 'given'. Such identities have been derived through social and political interaction. 'Elites in competition for political power and economic advantage' have constructed and given form and content to national group identity.[6] While the ruling elite has played a decisive role in ensuring state patronage for the promotion of its particular world-view, counter-elites have risen to challenge its hegemony. Elite conflict in Bangladesh has focussed on ideological differences regarding the nature of the war of liberation in 1971 and the role of Islam in its social and political life subsequently. In this context, death sentences passed by *fatwa* courts on self-confessed atheists in the 1990s were particularly controversial.[7] Religion has periodically played an important role in shaping the nature of politics in South Asia. It is regarded as a marker of identity in the process of political mobilization alongside other markers, such as language, and is often presented as a primordial bond of identity.[8] Certain Islamist political groups and parties claimed to know the ultimate truth in matters pertaining to religion and demand the right to be the sole interpreters of Islamic law as experts in the field. Such groups declared certain principles of the faith to be uncontestable, such as the finality of the prophethood of Muhammad and the Koran as the supreme source of divine law. However, it can be argued that there is no essentialised Islam in a world where its interpretation and practice has varied from place to place: for there exist many sects among Muslims and four major schools of Islamic jurisprudence, all with equal claims to legitimacy.[9] There is, therefore, considerable potential for conflict in formulating the nature of the state.

A study of the rise of the religious right during the political elite's search for legitimacy in Bangladesh serves to illustrate the processes through which the concepts of state, nation and identity were formulated.[10] Competing political elites from among the religious orthodoxy, the liberal intelligentsia and the army who were each engaged in a struggle for power, sought to achieve a consensus in favor of their particular world view in order to gain majority support amongst the electorate. They appealed to distinctive 'cultural markers' of identification based on shared experiences including xenophobia, linguistic specificity and religious affiliation, and subsequently projected these as symbols of group solidarity – a process described by

Brass as 'symbol manipulation'.[11] The religious orthodoxy seeks to forge a nation defined by Islam and a state based on *shariah* laws, notwithstanding the fact that large segments of the diasporic Muslim population belonging to other spatial, cultural and political locales, cannot be included within this construct.[12] This conception of the state and nation is also theoretically discriminatory to religious minorities within the country whose status would suffer under shariah laws, for they could be barred from high office and compelled to pay *jizya* (a protection tax). Hence, the liberal intelligentsia has rejected this view and emphasizes other identity markers such as the Bengali language and the common cultural roots of the Bengali peoples, as discussed later. Their vision of a secular pluralist state acknowledges that population groups may share their nationalities with others beyond their political frontiers. This is as true of the Bengalis in the plains as the Chakmas in the hills. However, there is a third view which argues that the raison d'etre of a juridical state must lie in its distinctiveness as a nation which is at odds with the position of the liberal intelligentsia. The proponents of this view, particularly segments of the army, have engaged themselves in constructing such a distinct nation, described as 'Bangladeshi', after the name of the new state.

Thus, while one can agree with Gellner and Hobsbawm that nationalists aim at a congruence between national and state boundaries, effectively this is illusory.[13] Following the arguments of Hugh Seton-Watson as opposed to that of Anthony Smith, I make a distinction between state and nation. A *state* is territorially bounded and governed by a set of legal and political institutions through which it maintains order.[14] A *nation*, on the contrary, may not have such institutional structures, but may nevertheless share a common history, language or other cultural markers of identity, symbolic or otherwise, while being territorially dispersed.[15] In the conception of neither the religious orthodoxy nor the liberal intelligentsia is there an exact correspondence between state and national boundaries, although some members of the political elite aspire to it in Bangladesh.

ISLAM IN DANGER VS. JAI BANGLA

The history of Bangladesh and its search for a national identity is replete with tensions between perceptions based on religious orthodoxy and secular rationalism.[16] Hence, both national identity and state ideology have remained contested. The national and political boundaries of Bangladesh have been reconstituted several times reflecting the fluid and contextual nature of identity selection. The emergence of Pakistan in 1947 was accompanied by a strong assertion of Muslim nationalism. The emphasis on Islam as the basis of identity and unity bound together disparate groups. Muslims, in pre-independence India, felt deprived as Muslims vis à vis the Hindus and hence the emphasis on their religious and communal identity.

The emergence of Bangladesh in 1971 drew support from the rising Bengali ethnic consciousness in post-independence Pakistan. The Muslims of East Pakistan felt their relative deprivation as Bengalis vis-à-vis the non-Bengalis of West Pakistan who sought to use religion to control Bengali aspirations. In both instances, the basic struggle was for economic emancipation, but the formulation of new identities served to mobilize popular support and provide legitimacy for the struggle through which the new imagined nations were emerging. In both cases, such reformulations merely achieved a fragile unity.

After the creation of the new states, the fragile consensus on ideology and identity broke down in both Pakistan and Bangladesh. Secular politicians had rallied Muslim support for Pakistan with the slogan of 'Islam in danger'.[17] In the new state, created ostensibly to guarantee Muslims the right to live in their own way, there were several contenders for power in East Pakistan challenging the authority (and ideology) of the ruling party, the Muslim League. Among these were the Awami Muslim League, a party which broke away in 1951 and sought to open up its membership to all communities regardless of religion, the Jama'at-e-Islami which demanded an Islamic state ruled by shariah laws, and the underground communist movement which rejected the partition of India. Notably, in the very first provincial elections in East Bengal in 1954, the Muslim League was routed.

The emergence of Bangladesh in 1971, unlike that of Pakistan, was sudden – the inevitable aftermath of genocide perpetrated by the West Pakistan dominated 'junta' in defence of its decision not to share power or resources with East Pakistan. The struggle of the Bengalis in 1971 was one for sheer survival rather than a self-conscious attempt to build a secular polity, even though inspiration was sought in slogans like '*Jai Bangla*' (Victory to Bengal) which had no religious connotations. Yet, Bangladesh came to be associated with secular symbols and ideologies, until the state-led reversal after the assassination of the first prime minister of Bangladesh, Sheikh Mujibur Rahman, in 1975.

The history of the region demonstrates that the process of identity selection was not constant and the cultural markers adopted were not fixed. Ethnic, cultural and national identities were in a state of flux, with their boundaries constantly changing. Here, statehood has been defined and re-defined three times within a quarter of a century. However, shifts in political identity did not necessarily imply a change in cultural identity. While the citizenship status of the people changed from Indian to Pakistani in 1947 and to Bangladeshi in 1971, they continued to share their Bengali 'nationality' and other social and cultural affinities with people in West Bengal across their political frontier. Subsequently, however, competing political elites continued to engage in efforts to reformulate national identities so as to drive a wedge between the shared linguistic and cultural identities of all Bengalis, by opposing Bengali with Bangladeshi nationalism.[18]

STATE INTERVENTION AND IDENTITY CONSTRUCTION

Bangladesh has inherited a tradition of state intervention in the process of identity construction from Pakistan, where the state subscribed to Islamic ideology, albeit superficially. In an effort to contain the political opposition, the ruling party of Pakistan, the Muslim League, had claimed for itself the sole right to interpret 'what Islam is'.[19] It had equated itself with the state, Pakistan, and with the state religion, Islam. Henceforth, any criticism of the party was interpreted as an attempt to divide Pakistan and attack Islam. In effect, the state introduced religion into politics. Even its anti-Indian stance was projected as Islamic. A great deal of effort went into drawing a distinction between the cultures of East and West Bengal. In fact, any stress on cultural similarities between these two regions was interpreted as a desire for unification of the two Bengals. As a result, the struggle to establish Bengali as one of the state languages of Pakistan was perceived to be a major threat to the ideology of Pakistan as a whole, because Bengali was one of the cultural links between the two parts of Bengal. However, the state took no steps to build an Islamic society or polity.

In such a context, discussions about the identity of Bengali Muslims was fraught with controversy as 'Bengali' and 'Muslim' were presented as incompatible in state parlance, following a tradition from colonial times. This was deeply problematic for many. *Madrasahs* (Muslim schools) taught Urdu rather than Bengali. Because it was written in the Arabic script, Urdu enjoyed greater status and was considered an Islamic language by the dominant section of the elite. The non-Bengali upper classes, who dominated politics and the economy, as well as sections of the upwardly mobile Bengalis tended to look down upon the Bengali language as inferior. Experiments were even made to write Bengali in the Arabic script.[20] This attitude to Bengali, the mother tongue of the majority, was resented by the middle classes. Not surprisingly, a tension developed between the religious and the secular basis of identity.

The religious basis of identity acquired a special importance because religion was politicised in Pakistan. The pull towards a secular definition was, however, inevitable in East Pakistan not only because of the Bengali Muslims' rejection of state hegemony, which historically predate their conversion to Islam, but also because of their heritage of eclectic cultural patterns, which arguably carry a secular connotation.[21] Local cultural patterns such as the use of *alpana* (floor decoration with rice paint) at weddings, or wearing colourful *bindi* (cosmetic dots) on the forehead, or making offerings at the shrines of holy persons (regardless of community), as well as various forms of celebrations were insidiously projected by the ruling elite as being essentially Hindu and, as such, opposed to Islamic culture.[22]

Another important factor, which contributed to the religious–secular tension, was related to the culturally ambivalent self-image of the intelligentsia in the erstwhile East Pakistan – its basic inability to come to terms with the evident facts of its identity. While the intelligentsia idealized *ashraf*[23] ethics and values supposedly derived from the Middle East; the harsh reality was that the majority of them were descended from converts, were of peasant stock, spoke Bengali, and shared nothing with the ashraf except religion. Hence their fear that Bengali Islam was contaminated by local and un-Islamic practices.

The tradition of distinguishing between a Bengali and a Muslim provided grounds for some of the problems of self-perception, which confronted Bengali Muslims later on.[24] In Pakistan, this issue appeared to have lost its significance initially. Until the mid-1960s, there was no perceived conflict in identities in East Bengal as to whether one was a Bengali, a Pakistani or a Muslim.[25] However, the movement leading to the emergence of Bangladesh in 1971 induced the need to once again define one's identity: being 'Bengali' seemed to connote a secular definition which emphasised the ethnic and cultural dimension; whereas identifying oneself as 'Pakistani' implied a continuing belief in the two-nation theory and an emphasis on Islam as an overall guiding principle. In fact, the distinction was not as clear-cut as this. Some Bengalis such as Abul Mansur Ahmed, a politician and writer, saw the emergence of Bangladesh as the 'restoration of the Lahore Resolution'.[26] Thus, his basic faith in the two-nation theory remained intact.

THE SECULAR PHASE AND THE RISE OF THE MUSLIM BENGAL MOVEMENT

Independent Bangladesh came to be associated with a secular ideology because of a number of factors. The autonomy movement of the 1960s, which was a sequel to the language movement of the 1950s, addressed itself mainly to economic and political issues. The language movement had already created a secular cult and carried the message that culture be allotted a neutral, non-religious and to that extent, a secular zone. The non-communal, eclectic cultural ethos of East Bengal supported this secular orientation.[27] The 1972 constitution formally enshrined secularism as one of the four pillars of state ideology. In the 1973 election, which was regarded by the ruling party as a referendum on the four principles of state policy; nationalism, socialism, democracy and secularism; the Awami League won a massive victory. It secured 73.2 percent of the votes cast and 292 of the 300 seats contested.[28]

Despite this, there was no national consensus about what secularism meant. Sheikh Mujib took pains to explain, 'Secularism does not mean the absence of religion... No communal politics will be allowed in the country'.[29] But this distinction was not clearly appreciated at large. Some continued to believe that secularism was a form of atheism or absence of religion. They could not comprehend the concept of religious tolerance in public life along with religiosity in personal life as a practicable possibility.[30]

Mujib faced strong opposition from two fronts: the fragmented left and the Islamic right. Neither recognized the basis of the new state. While political parties from the Islamic right such as the Jama'at-i-Islami and the Nizam-i-Islam had been banned, most of the pro-Chinese factions of the Communist Party had gone underground. The Islamic right had already challenged the foundation of Bangladesh at the very inception of the new state by the assassination of intellectuals, like Munier Chowdhury on 14 December 1971, two days before the Pakistan army surrendered to the Combined Forces.[31] It may be assumed that the 'Islamic' parties still had some following despite their support to Pakistan's war effort against the liberation of Bangladesh. The 'Islam-*pasand*' parties, which included the Jama'at-i-Islami, Pakistan Muslim League (Council), Pakistan Muslim League (Convention), the Pakistan Democratic Party and the Jamiyat-ul-Ulama-i-Islam and Nizam-i-Islam parties, had altogether polled 12.7 percent of the votes cast in the 1970 elections in East Bengal.[32] It may be assumed that some of the following of these groups persisted after liberation. In addition, the Awami League too had some non-secular elements in its membership.

It is, thus, not surprising that a 'Muslim Bengal' movement emerged shortly after liberation. The idea of Muslim Bangla came from a Radio Pakistan Broadcast on 17 December 1971, in which Pakistan welcomed the formation of Muslim Bangla and the restoration of the original spirit of the 1940 Lahore Resolution which envisaged Pakistan as a federation of independent states.[33] Interestingly, this movement received support from some of the underground communist groups because of shared anti-Indian and anti-Awami League feelings. The East Pakistan Communist Party (Marxist-Leninist) claimed 'Muslim Bengal' as its ally in their underground paper *Janayuddha*.[34] Several factions of the pro-Chinese Communist Party, which either did not support the liberation war or fought a dual war against both the Pakistan army and the Mukti Bahini, insisted that colonialism and exploitation persisted in Bangladesh, which they alleged was a client state of India, and therefore there was continued need for struggle. They refused to recognize Bangladesh and continued to refer to it as 'East Bengal' or 'East Pakistan'.[35]

The relative success of the movement to alter the identity of the new state is evident in the policies adopted since the assassination of the father of the nation, Mujibur Rahman. That act was part of a series of events, which led to the adoption of Islam as an instrument of state policy and even made possible a return to the theocratic folds of Pakistan.

Some scholars have argued that Mujib himself contributed to the process by invoking Islam in state affairs, adopting 'ill-defined secularist goals', and pursuing recognition by Muslim countries that had favoured Pakistan in 1971.[36] For instance, he replaced a television and radio programme called 'Speaking the Truth' based on secular ethics with one based on citations from the scriptures of Islam, Hinduism, Christianity and Buddhism – allowing equal opportunity to all faiths.[37] This was more in keeping with the Indian perception of secularism as equivalent to *sarba dharma sama bhaba*, or religious tolerance, rather than that inscribed in the 1972 constitution of Bangladesh as *dharmanirapekshata*, or religious neutrality. Mujib's actions, thus, brought religion to the public domain instead of keeping it in the private sphere.

BENGALI NATIONALISM CHALLENGED

The assassination of Mujib brought the military into politics. The new power elite actively engaged in forging new identities to gain new allies and legitimacy. The outcome, however, was nationally divisive. Nationality, which had been defined in terms of the Bengali ethnic, linguistic and cultural identity since independence, was redefined after the 1975 coup on the basis of political calculations. Although there was no popular demand for such a reformulation, the measure was expected to win new support bases for the regime. The new definition of national identity required that a distinction be made between the languages of East and West Bengal, where the former was said to be distinct from the Sanskritic Bengali of West Bengal. The basis for such an argument had been provided by Abul Mansur Ahmed in the period after Partition when he chose to describe the language of East Bengal as Pak Bangla, though there was little support for this proposition at the time.[38]

In 1978, under President Ziaur Rahman's military regime, citizens of Bangladesh were designated as 'Bangladeshi' instead of 'Bangalee', as had been stated in the constitution of 1972. This was a strategic move to specifically demarcate the area and population of the new juridical state. Zia seems to have also been motivated by an underlying xenophobia which plagued sections of the population, particularly segments of the religious right, the pro-Chinese left, and factions within the army which had inherited the anti-Indian traditions of the Pakistan army.[39] At one level, it was an assertion of sovereignty in relation to India which not only dominated the region geo-politically but also had a sizeable Bengali population. At another level, he was discarding the pro-India sympathies of the previous regime, unpopular among his new following. Instead, he began to woo the Pakistan–USA–Saudi Arabia axis which, incidentally, had resisted the emergence of independent Bangladesh. Zia went further in implying that Bangladeshis were a culturally distinct entity and a nation in their own right. He suggested in a speech that Bangladeshis were different from the Bengalis of India, as was their culture and their language: the latter had to be moulded 'in our own way', he argued.[40] His message recalled Jinnah's famous statement which distinguished the cultures and religions of Hindus and Muslims as two different social orders. Zia, thus, not only asserted the precedence of the religio-political identity over the ethno-cultural but also, as his subsequent policies indicate, attempted to redefine that ethno-cultural identity as well. In ideological terms, this also connoted a rejection of Mujib's secular stance: 'secularism' was explicitly discarded as a principle of state policy through a constitutional amendment in 1977.[41] Aware that a non-secular stance would be regarded as communal, or anti-Hindu, he asserted through the manifesto of his political party, the Bangladesh Nationalist Party (BNP), that Bangladeshis had freed themselves from 'the evils of communalism' because of the 'great teachings of Islam'. The desecration of Hindu temples that occurred in Bangladesh in retaliation for the demolition of the Babri Masjid in Ayodhya (India) in 1992 indicates that the statement is untrue. Zia's actions, nevertheless, acknowledged once again the concept of two nations on which Pakistan had been founded and which had been rejected by the war of liberation in 1971. The basic complexities in culture and identity which had existed during Pakistani rule, thus, continued to persist in Bangladesh.

Ziaur Rahman came to power after a series of military coups, the first of which overthrew the civilian government of Sheikh Mujibur Rahman.[42] In the following period, he failed to win over Mujib's following or sympathisers of the ousted Awami League. In his search for legitimacy, he turned to the opponents of the Awami League for support, which included the extreme left and the extreme right, neither of which believed in the creation of Bangladesh.[43] Though Zia's primary motive was to stabilise his rule rather than promote an Islamic upsurge, the long-term result of his strategies was the latter.

Zia's policies aimed at giving an Islamic gloss to the state. Among his 'Islamisation' policies were the enactment of the Islamic Universities Act 1980 and Islamic Education and Research Act 1980.[44] He also expected to obtain approval from the Arab bloc which had great sympathy for Pakistan and held promise of economic gains. Although the amounts he obtained were not large in global terms, it was politically advantageous because it signified a degree of acceptance by the community of Islamic nations. Of particular interest to Bangladesh were crude oil imports and the export of manpower to the Gulf states. He failed to procure the former at a concessionary rate; but earnings from labour exports, though small in comparison to India and Pakistan, became a lucrative source of remittances.[45]

The Zia period ushered in a new ruling ideology determined by pragmatic concerns for its own legitimacy rather than any ideological convictions. The new ideology was reflected in the use of a new political and cultural vocabulary. The slogan of *Jai Bangla,* which is linguistically of

Bengali origin, was replaced by *Bangladesh Zindabad* where zindabad is of Urdu and Persian derivation. The de-emphasising of the Bengali language was carried further by referring to 'Bangladesh Betar' as 'Radio Bangladesh' and to the Bengali language as the 'Bangladeshi' language.[46]

The rise of the military in politics provoked a legitimacy crisis. The search for new support bases by the leadership led to the adoption of new policies of inclusion and exclusion. Islamists and the forces opposed to the Bengali language and the liberation of the Bengali people from the control of Pakistan were included; but Zia, the freedom fighter, excluded the major force behind the liberation of the new nation, the Awami League, which had also been a champion of secularism and inclined favourably towards India. By the same token, he excluded Hindus and those who drew their inspiration from the common cultural heritage of Bengal, such as people from literary circles, musicians, artists, dancers and painters.

Zia implicitly rejected Bengali nationalism without ever acknowledging the implications for national politics and international relations. Nationally, the previously marginalised groups of the right and left interpreted his policies as signals inviting them to re-enter the political scene. This move was facilitated by the 1976 Political Parties Resolution that lifted the ban on religion-based politics.[47] At the international level, a deteriorating relationship with India corresponded with growing overtures of friendship to Pakistan. For example, Pakistani industrialists like the Dawoods and the Ispahanis who had lost their factories in the former East Pakistan as a result of the war, were invited back to run them, after being paid compensation.

THE RISE OF THE RELIGIOUS RIGHT

Although Zia's primary objective was to maintain himself in power, he effectively laid the foundations for the rise of the Islamic right and the forces favourable to closer ties with Pakistan. By the 1990s it appeared that the Bengali nationalists had lost the initiative while the Islamists were setting the political agenda and the tempo. The latter penetrated influential positions in the government, and emerged with a blueprint for the creation of an Islamic state, along with an armed cadre to enforce that vision.

How did the Islamists orchestrate such a comeback? Ershad's succession to the presidency, following the assassination of Zia in 1981, signaled the end of the influence of freedom fighters in politics and ushered in the political dominance of repatriated officers from Pakistan. Ershad, a repatriated officer, was himself a usurper of power like Zia, but lacked the legitimacy enjoyed by Zia as a freedom fighter. It has been argued that 'the Islamic quantum of state orientation increased with decreasing legitimacy of the ruling elite'.[48] Not surprisingly, he also pursued Zia's Islamising policies, but did so with less restraint. Like Zia, he also identified the Islamic right as a potential ally. To win them over, Ershad emphasised the Islamic character of the state, led Friday prayers, made periodic attempts to control the norms of social behaviour, dress, and manners and, more importantly, initiated policy changes which replicated constitutional measures adopted in Pakistan. Through the Eighth Amendment of the constitution, Islam was given the status of a state religion in 1988. Even the wording was similar to the relevant provision in the 1973 constitution of Pakistan. Notably, no lessons were learned from Bhutto's predicament in Pakistan: the man who gave the country its first Islamic constitution to appease the orthodoxy, was nevertheless ousted and hung by one of its members, a Jama'at supporter.[49] The moral of the tale – that the forces of 'fundamentalism' will not be placated until they have control over political power – was lost to Ershad, whose downfall in 1990 was assisted by the religious right including the Jama'at.

Ershad's strategies of rule, particularly the Eighth Amendment, were controversial and it was deemed that his parliament had no authority to make such changes. Women's groups contested it as an infringement of human rights, and secularists feared that the country was sliding towards becoming an Islamic state.[50] The example of Pakistan stood clearly before them: constitutional change under military rule had cleared the path for the introduction of shariah laws in 1979. Even the Jama'at-i-Islami and the Muslim League protested on the grounds that it was a ploy to prevent the establishment of an Islamic Republic based on the principles of the Koran and *sunnah* (traditions of the Prophet). However, various other Islamic organisations and individuals; such as the Jamiat-i-Ulama, Jamiat-ul-Mudarresin, Sirat Mission, and the *pir* of Sarsina; were pleased with the developments.[51]

Overall, it may be argued that the Eighth Amendment was a major gain for the Islamists who were now closer to achieving a state modelled after Pakistan. They also made gains elsewhere. Their increasing influence in the sphere of education was manifest in the number of madrasahs and recruitment of teachers and students. While there has generally been a steady increase in the number of madrasahs, student enrollments, and in the expenditure for such education; periodically there were dramatic fluctuations. Table 1 indicates that under the Mujib government, between 1972–73 and 1974–75, there was a slight decline in the total number of madrasahs of all types accompanied by a small increase in student numbers by 17,072 although both had experienced better growth in the previous year. Under Zia, steady growth continued, though more rapidly as regards student enrollment. For example, in the case of government and affiliated madrasahs, secondary level and above, the numbers increased from 1,976 in 1977–78 to 2,259 in 1978–79 for institutions and from 375,200 to 543,579 for student enrollment during the same period.[52] However, Table 2 demonstrates a drop again in enrollment by 1981–82 indicating either an ambivalence, or perhaps some uncertainty about the future of madrasah

Table 1: Student Enrolment in Madrasahs: 1970/71 to 1975/76

Year	Number of Madrasahs[#]	Number of Students
1970/71	6,260	716,202
1972/73	6,565	739,163
1973/74	6,807	844,479
1974/75[#]	6,471	756,235
1975/76[##]	7,971	808,000

Notes: [#] Includes all types of madrasahs: reformed, old scheme senior and junior, recognized and unrecognized.
[##] Includes *forquania* madrasahs as well.

Sources: *Statistical Digest of Bangladesh*, no.8, 1972, table 13.1, pp. 252–53; *Statistical Year Book of Bangladesh*, 1975, table 7.1, p. 177; *Statistical Year Book of Bangladesh*, 1978, pp. 252–53.

Table 2: Students and Teachers in Government and Affiliated Madrasahs: 1977/78 to 1991/92

Year	Number of Madrasahs[###]	Number of Students	Number of Teachers
1977/78	1,976	375,200	21,579
1981/82	2,864	388,000	29,608
1990/91	5,959	1,028,000	83,761
1991/92	6,025	1,735,000	94,961

Notes: [###] From secondary level and above – government and affiliated only

Sources: Bureau of Statistics, *Statistical Pocketbook of Bangladesh*, various issues, based on information obtained from the Madrasah Board.

education. A very different picture emerges during the period of Ershad's rule. As Table 2 shows, there was more than a hundred-fold increase in the number of government and affiliated madrasahs and nearly 300 percent increase in the number of staff and enrollment of students. Increased allocation from the education budget and financial assistance from Saudi Arabia, Kuwait, Libya and Pakistan have contributed to these developments. The curriculum of these institutions, kept secret until recently, contains a distorted history of the liberation of Bangladesh.[53] The graduates of these institutions along with those of the newly established Islamic universities began to receive specialised training and enter the professions. They have become doctors, lawyers, engineers, theologians of seminaries, *imams* of mosques, teachers of educational establishments and directors of Islamic missions and foundations. Inevitably, Bangladesh has witnessed the emergence of two nations once again.

Another significant gain made by the Jama'at and its supporters occurred in 1991. During the elections none of the major parties achieved an absolute majority: the Bangladesh Nationalist Party (BNP) won 140 seats, the Awami League-led eight party alliance got 100, the Jatiya Party of Ershad won 35, while the Jama'at-i-Islami bagged 18 seats.[54] Unable to form a government with an alliance with the deposed Ershad's Jatiya Party, or with the Awami League whose ideological position was diametrically opposed to their own, the BNP achieved a majority in parliament with the support of the Jama'at. Thus, for the first time in the history of the new state the Jama'at gained a formal role in government.

While its position in government was a recognition of its rehabilitation at the state level, the matter was far from resolved in the streets. The secular forces represented by the arty/intellectual circles – the musicians, dramatists, litterateurs – and bereaved families of martyred freedom fighters who had so far been in relative hibernation, or perhaps were neutralised by the fear of military rule, sprang into action under the freedom and tolerance permitted by the relatively democratic atmosphere of the post-election phase. Their concern was to counter the influence of the religious right and keep alive the threatened memory of the liberation war. Of the latter there was ample evidence, including the omission from school text books of even the name of Sheikh Mujibur Rahman, the founder of the nation.[55] In particular, the selection of Golam Azam, as the *amir* of the Jama'at-i-Islami provoked a massive protest organised by the newly established Ekatturer Ghatok Dalal Nirmul Committee (Committee to Eliminate the Killers and Collaborators of 1971) which demanded his trial for war crimes. It was widely believed that Golam Azam was guilty of incitement to murder intellectuals in 1971, as a result of which he had lost the right to Bangladeshi nationality in 1973. In 1978, he was allowed to return from exile in Pakistan by Zia. As a Pakistani citizen, he continued to advise the Jama'at behind the scenes until the 1990s when he was emboldened by electoral gains to seek a higher public profile. His election as amir was considered by many to be not only a blatant contravention of Article 38 of the constitution, but also added insult to injury as far as the bereaved families were concerned.[56]

The movement was spearheaded by the founder-president of the Nirmul Committee, a woman called Jahanara Imam, who had lost her son in the liberation war. It achieved a wide following among otherwise non-political common people and subsequently drew the support of the Awami League. The BNP government, dependent as it was on Jama'at support to establish its rule, was reluctant to investigate the charges. The organisers of the committee were intimidated in various ways. Some, including Jahanara

Imam, were manhandled by the police. They were refused permission to hold rallies and observe the Bengali New Year in the agreed venue. Frustrated, they eventually set up a *gana adalat,* or people's court, which was convened on 26 March 1992. This court found Golam guilty as charged and recommended the death penalty and demanded that the state take action to mete out justice to the people of Bangladesh.[57] The state, however, declared the court unconstitutional, arguing that the law of the land should follow its course. Golam had already been taken into protective custody on the 24th; and warrants were issued for the arrest of the 24 people involved with the *gana adalat*.[58] Subsequently, in order to divert attention, a trial was staged to determine the citizenship status of Golam Azam, rather than ascertain his role in 1971. In April 1993, the high court declared his previous loss of citizenship under the Mujib government to have been unconstitutional; and he was deemed a citizen by birth under Article 2 of the President's Order No.149 of 1972. The court therefore concluded that his election as amir did not contravene the constitution, but it made no comment on Azam's failure to apply for the citizenship of Bangladesh before the onset of this controversy.[59] The subject of trial for war crimes under a special tribunal was totally fudged. Nor did it resurface after the formation of the Awami League government in 1996.

SECULAR-RATIONALISTS CHALLENGED

The Jama'at-i-Islami thus enjoyed considerable political space and found a new lease of life. It began a violent counter-offensive against secular groups. Their objective was to divert attention away from Golam Azam and increase the momentum of their campaign for the establishment of an Islamic state based on shariah laws. The feminist writer Taslima Nasreen offered them a timely pretext. As a lone woman perceived to have stepped out of acceptable social bounds, she was an easy prey. A barrage of propaganda was directed at her from the pulpit and in public platforms. Taslima was accused of subverting the cultural and religious values of the state and hence was depicted as a traitor to the state and religion, *rashtradrohi* and *dharmadrohi.*

The Jama'at and its various front organizations took full advantage of the fact that Taslima's provocative message, language and style had alienated large segments of Bengali society. Women accused her of 'derailing the feminist movement'.[60] Politicians held her responsible for the bad press Bangladesh was receiving abroad. Religious bigots insinuated she was pandering to the West, India and the religious rightwing party, the Bharatiya Janata Party (BJP). Intellectuals implied that she was after cheap publicity. Literary competitors considered her work shallow. Others envied her success, while most men were annoyed at her audacity: in one of her poems, *Dour Dour,* she advises women to flee from men in the same way that one runs from dogs that have rabies, because men carry syphilis.[61] Taslima was all too painfully aware that she had no champion, as she says in one of her columns: 'Like a dot I am alone in this universe.' Taslima was socially and politically isolated.

The Awami League, ostensibly a proponent of a secular democratic state, gave her no backing, not even when fatwas were declared thrice by mullahs for her death on the ground that she had insulted Islam.[62] The Awami League was loath to jeopardize its 'undeclared alliance with the Jama'at in its struggle to force the BNP government to amend the constitution to concede to its demand to establish a caretaker government which would be entrusted to conduct future elections in a free and fair manner.[63]

The BNP government too was hostile. The police protection, which she had obtained through a court injunction after the announcement of the first fatwa, was withdrawn. Then on 4 June, the home ministry obtained a warrant for her arrest on the grounds of hurting the feelings of Muslims, but it took no action against those who violated the law through incitement to murder – a sharp contrast to its handling of the people's court. This provoked an outcry from foreign governments including some members of the European Union, Sweden, Norway and the United States. Some of these countries threatened to withdraw aid, while others thought it prudent to negotiate.

Nationally, however, the state had played into the hands of mullahs. Interpreting government and opposition roles as tacit support for their stand, they believed that victory was within reach and intensified their campaign for Islamic rule at various fronts. There were demands for the introduction of blasphemy laws as in Pakistan, for the execution of all atheists and apostates (*nastik* and *murtad*), for the ban on all publications by such people, for Ahmadiyas to be decreed non-Muslims etc. These were accompanied by massive demonstrations, meetings and the setting up of organisations such as the Sanmilita Sangram Parishad and branch committees with names such as Islami Chhatra Sena (Student Soldiers of Islam) to spread the message into villages.[64] Through the repeated publication of lies the 'psychological manipulation' of a large segment of the population was effected. Taslima was even condemned by those who had not read her work. A mass hysteria was effectively created. Taslima had been transformed into a monster in the popular imagination and many 'were prepared to destroy that monster'.[65] The immediate background to this hysteria was a much-publicized interview of Taslima in the *Statesman* (Calcutta) on 9 May 1994. In it she is quoted to have advocated a revision of the Koran. Her disclaimer to the effect that she referred only to shariah laws fell on deaf ears.

The controversy surrounding Taslima Nasreen makes sense only if it is seen in the context of a struggle between the forces of religious extremism and secular liberalism, which are both vying for the hearts and minds of the people in Bangladesh. These forces are engaged in symbol manipulation to secure the social and political order they desire. The main difference is that the former are now well organised, armed and carrying out a plan of action much of which had already been tried out in Pakistan.[66] The latter are disorganised, unarmed and believe, perhaps complacently, that Bengalis will not turn into religious fanatics.

But Taslima is only one of the many victims of the vengeance of fanatical forces. She survived because of the publicity, foreign interest, and the support of a few who rose to defend the rule of law.[67] Several intellectuals and writers, like the poet Shamsur Rahman and the scholar Ahmad Sharif, also faced death threats because they subscribe to secular, rationalist, non-communal and democratic values.[68] Religious extremists have described them as *deshdrohi*, *rashtradrohi* and *dharmadrohi*: traitors to the nation, state and religion.[69]

A series of such provocative actions have virtually led to the establishment of a parallel structure of authority in remote areas far from the reaches of officialdom. Various front organisations of the Jama'at, supported by their own armed cadre, have begun to impart Islamic justice. They derive their authority from fatwas given by local mullahs and not from any court. Not only have thieves lost their limbs and 'adulterers' been stoned, but also opposition newspapers have lost access to various distributors and their clients.[70] Women have been targeted for particularly vicious attacks.[71] Many rural women have been divorced by fatwa for practicing birth control. Such a situation is novel in the history of the region. Women are also losing their marital status for taking bank loans for their small businesses. It is argued that economic independence for women is undesirable because it can give them a status superior to men, which was not part of God's plan.[72] Economic competition under conditions of unemployment and poverty cannot be ruled out as a more mundane explanation for such political behaviour. Non-government organisations like BRAC and their workers have been attacked by madrasah students for allegedly spreading Christianity. BRAC schools for girls have been burnt in protest against 'westernised' female education. Coercion is a method of neutralising the sources of alternative ideologies. Various women's groups and legal bodies have gathered evidence and successfully convicted some of the *fatwabaj mullahs*.[73] But the trend persists unabated while the police find themselves inadequately armed to face the challenge.[74]

The strategy of the religious right has been to pursue all means at its disposal, both constitutional and unconstitutional, to achieve its goal of establishing an Islamic state-whether it be through persuasion, intimidation or coercion. One of the constitutional methods resorted to has relied on its successful infiltration into the lower courts in small towns like Rangpur and Maulavibazaar. Its modus operandi followed a particular pattern, which took advantage of the existing legal system. First, a mullah decreed a fatwa.

Subsequently, one of the faithful filed a case in a lower court where the magistrate was a sympathizer or supporter of the Jama'at-Shibir. The magistrate immediately issued a warrant for the arrest of the accused without hearing his defence. Such warrants were issued against the editors of *Janakantha, Bhorer Kagaj, Ajker Kagaj* and *Jai Jai Din* who were accused of hurting the sentiments of Muslims.[75] For example, an issue of *Jai Jai Din* contained a cartoon involving the letter *alif* of the Arabic alphabet. The editor was compelled to obtain bail from three different courts for the same offence.[76] Such persistent harassment could hope to achieve conformity if not consensus.

These developments have been accompanied by provocative statements by some members of the religious right in key positions which raise serious questions about their commitment to democracy and the nature of the state, nation and religion they envisage. The Pir of Charmonai declared at a meeting on 29 July 1994 that 'all non-fundamentalists were of illegitimate birth'. At the same meeting, the *khatib* of the Baitul Mukarram Mosque, Maulana Ubaidul Huq, noted that Pakistan was divided in 1971 as a result of the *gaddari* (treachery) of certain Western educated individuals who were currently involved in similarly deceiving the people.[77] Later, in an interview on 4 August, he announced that 'the state should be run by a fatwa committee consisting of the ulama' thus voicing the thoughts of Maulana Maududi for which Ayub Khan kept him behind bars for many years.[78] The statements provoked an outraged protest from teachers, students, freedom fighters, political groups and a large section of the ulama numbering 227 of them, indicating that there were divisions in the ranks of the ulama. The khatib lost his lucrative job and a case was filed against him and the pir on the grounds of hurting the religious sentiments of crores of Muslims. Just when it seemed that religious extremists could no longer be contained these measures acted as a check on their activism albeit temporarily.

An important source of strength for the Jama'at-i-Islami has been its ability to forge alliances with various groups depending on the issues. It built strategic links with the BNP and the Awami League in turn, thus neutralising them sufficiently to open a greater political space for itself. It also established a broad front with various parties and organisations, which had a similar objective, i.e. the establishment of an Islamic state based on shariah laws. It successfully brought the Wahabis within its fold and developed a modus operandi with the Nizam-i-Islam, Jamiyat-ul-Ulama-i-Islam and Freedom Party and other like-minded bodies.[79] Politically, however, the Jama'at remained the most powerful of the Islamist groups, as evident from the election results.

This may be attributed to some extent to its methods of mobilisation, which has been most successful among the lower middle classes. It follows a strict method of recruitment based on a lengthy initiation process for its cadres, like communist parties. To maximise gains, it worked in various arenas, similar to other parties. It had youth and student organisations, such as the Islami Chatra Shibir which tended to be militant and aimed at gaining control over university campuses.[80] There were women's branches whose members made door-to-door contact with sympathisers. Unlike other parties, however, it set up trust funds to support charitable causes such as schools, clinics and hospitals; and opened Islamic banks aimed to support income-generating activities.[81]

Notably, Jama'at membership and resources received a boost in recent years, despite the setback in the immediate post-liberation period. Based on interviews with unidentified important party members, U.A.B. Razia Akter Banu states that between 1981 and 1987 the number of the Jama'at's full members rose from 650 to 2,000; associate membership rose from 100,000 to 2 million.[82] The Jama'at admits to receiving indirect assistance from Saudi Arabia, although others have charged it with receiving direct monetary assistance. In May 1984, Golam Azam apparently was sent a cheque for US $327,000 from Saudi Arabia which went astray in the mail.[83] The Jama'at has certainly demonstrated its capacity for survival and potential as a significant political force, even while its methods of dealing with opponents holding alternative ideologies gives rise to profound misgivings.

IMPLICATIONS FOR DEMOCRACY AND THE ROLE OF THE STATE

The developments identified so far bode ill for the future of a pluralist secular liberal democracy. A democratic system is essential for a country that has religious, ethnic and ideological diversity, which must be accommodated if fratricidal tendencies and ethno-religious conflicts are to be avoided. Clearly, the state can play a role in determining the outcome of the tussle between the Islamists and the secular rationalists and in restoring a semblance of order in civil society. The history of Bangladesh shows that in the interest of legitimacy the state has been instrumental in defining ideologies, identities, states and nations, and that it can enforce the rule of law. Whatever its ideological predisposition, the state must guarantee minimum human rights – to life, to property, and to persuasion. It needs to challenge public violations of the legal system, including the authority of fatwas; and contain street violence in the interest of public order. It must recognize diversity, help build a non-communal democratic ethos, and propagate the values of civil society.

These have been difficult tasks, not only because of the frequent crises besetting the government, but also because the relative autonomy of the state to carry them out has been weak.[84] As the government is headed by a centrist party which does not represent any ideological monolith, its options for manoeuver are limited. The BNP's support comes from both the right and the left-Islamists and secularists; pro-liberation and anti-liberation forces; Bangladeshi nationalists who are anti-Indian but not pro-Pakistani and those who are pro-Pakistani; those for whom the language 'martyrs' day' is meaningful and those for whom it is not. Naturally, these various opinions are reflected in key official appointments. Particularly controversial were the appointments to the ministries of information, home and education, of Najmul Huda, Abdul Matin Chowdhury and Zamiruddin respectively, who have been identified as belonging to a strong pro-Pakistan lobby.[85] The manipulation of history in school text books and the unchecked rampage by gun-toting members of the Jama'at-Shibir have been attributed to these appointments.[86]

The relative weakness of the state to pursue ideologically neutral policies is demonstrated by the action or inaction of these ministries. The information minister under the BNP government was charged in the press with spreading misinformation by attempting to rewrite the history of the liberation of Bangladesh and in particular denigrating the role of Sheikh Mujib and the Awami League, while building up the image of the Jama'at-i-Islami.[87] The home minister was held responsible for the unchecked growth of training camps for the armed cadre of the Shibir. No public investigations were carried out despite armed attacks on the BNP student wing in Chittagong, even though they protested alongside other student groups against Golam Azam holding a mass rally.[88] State inaction under the circumstances may be interpreted as an inability to meet the basic criteria outlined above, that is, a failure to govern. Alternatively, it may be regarded either as tacit approval, or a failure to exercise its autonomy in the greater interest of the common good.

The state of Bangladesh is caught in an ideology trap. While secularists accused the BNP government of pandering to the Jama'at, the latter charged it with not doing enough for Islam. Sections within the BNP wish to maintain Jama'at support because the main objective of political parties today appears to be access to and the maintenance of power irrespective of the costs involved. The Awami League entered the same game by forging alliances with the Jama'at and the Jatiya Party, thus obfuscating their ideological differences to some extent.[89] However, unlike the other parties, the Jama'at and the religious right have a very clear objective: the establishment of an Islamic state based on their interpretation of shariah laws – something which has been attempted in Pakistan. If successful, it would lead to the emergence of a one-party theocratic state wherein all power would be vested in the men of religion and not in any representative body. If Maududi's dictum were followed to the letter, as some aspire to, then general elections would be dispensed with. This would pose a threat to the democratic aspirations of the majority, endanger minority rights, and render the state 'irrelevant' to the needs of the people.[90]

The Awami League government which succeeded the BNP in office in 1996 has trodden a cautious path, but was nonetheless beleaguered by rather similar concerns of legitimacy and good government. It took up the task of setting straight the ideological record, restoring the image of Sheikh Mujib and acknowledging his role in the history of Bangladesh. It concentrated on resolving outstanding issues of economic regeneration and disaster preparedness; settling the ethnic conflict in the Chittagong Hill Tracts through a political compromise; and resolving a long-standing dispute with India over water sharing. While these acts have been lauded abroad, the political opposition at home has been violent and aggressive, and official retaliation provocative.

What is needed is a vigilant state that can rise above ideological differences, create alternative national interests based for example on economic considerations, accommodate pluralistic structures, and generate a climate where democracy would have a chance to mature. Such a state cannot afford to pamper the forces of coercion, communalism or sectarian conflict. But there are only a limited number of options available to the state if it is to achieve these objectives. It can choose to exclude communal and fascist parties from the political process by banning them through constitutional measures as Mujib did after liberation. Alternatively, it can render such bodies ineffective by delineating the terms of reference within which these may operate, such as prohibiting the use of religion in politics, which too was once constitutionally provided for in 1972 but reversed under Zia. It can also offer alternative ideologies and value structures based on humanist thought to maintain a climate favourable to democratic dialogue. Importantly, it can enforce the existing laws of the land to ensure that fundamental human rights are not violated. However, such measures would be possible only if the power elite itself is not compromised. Herein lies the problem with the state in Bangladesh which is threatened with becoming irrelevant even as the country becomes increasingly ungovernable. The state is unable to mediate between the various 'demand groups' in the streets and outside these because the interests of the ruling elite are identified with specific segments of society and its actions have yet to rise above partisan interests.

Given the massive poverty and economic hardship facing the country, the state could attempt to separate the ideological from the economic problems, and steer the country towards resolving the latter issues. This would help reformulate a national agenda based on an understanding of the general good, rather than in purely sectarian terms. It would be one way of re-establishing the relative autonomy of the state so that it could mediate impartially between various interest groups.

NOTES

1 The term nationalist is used loosely here to include all those who are engaged in conceptualizing homogenous nations based on their particular worldview; such as elites, intellectuals, political parties, decision-makers, and officers of state.

State, Nation, Identity

2 For the usage of the term homogenise, see Urmila Phadnis, *Ethnicity and Nation-Building in South Asia* (New Delhi: Sage, 1989), 80–81.
3 Clifford Geertz, 'The Integrative Revolution: Primordial Sentiments and Civil Politics in the New States', in C. Geertz, ed., *Old Societies and New States: The Quest for Modernity in Asia and Africa* (New York: Free Press, 1963), 105–57; Benedict Anderson, *Imagined Communities: Reflections on the Origin and Spread of Nationalism* (London: Verso, 1991), 5–7; Eric Hobsbawm and Terence Ranger, eds, *The Invention of Tradition* (Cambridge: Cambridge University Press, 1983). Ranger has since modified his position to argue like Anderson that identities are imagined rather than invented. See Terence Ranger, 'The Invention of Tradition Revisited: The Case of Colonial Africa', in Terence Ranger and Olufemi Vaughan, eds, *Legitimacy and the State in Twentieth Century Africa* (Houndmills: Macmillan, 1993), 62–111.
4 Paul R. Brass, 'Ethnicity and Nationality Formation', *Ethnicity* 3(3), September 1976, 225–40. See also J. D. Eller and R. M. Coughlan, 'The Poverty of Primordialism: The Demystification of Ethnic Attachments', *Ethnic and Racial Studies* 16 (2), April 1993, 195–96.
5 For a discussion of the idea of utopias in conflict, see Ainslie T. Embree, *Utopias in Conflict: Religion and Nationalism in Modern India* (Delhi: Oxford University Press, 1992), 1–18.
6 Paul R. Brass, *Ethnicity and Nationalism: Theory and Comparison* (New Delhi: Sage, 1991), 15.
7 *Fatwa* refers to a religious decree which may be pronounced by a *shariah* court. In Bangladesh, the authority of such courts are of doubtful legitimacy as these have been set up on an ad hoc basis, defying existing legal structures.
8 Such as by Shils, Geertz and Robinson, op. cit.
9 Speech by Suhrawardy, in Constituent Assembly of Pakistan, *Debates* 6, March 1948, 262.
10 The term power elite is used to refer to decision-makers in the same sense as C. Wright Mills, *The Power Elite* (London, 1966), 3.
11 For a discussion of the term 'symbol manipulation', see Paul Brass, 'Elite Groups, Symbol Manipulation and Ethnic Identity Among the Muslims of South Asia', in David Taylor and Malcolm Yapp, eds, *Political Identity in South Asia* (London & Dublin: Curzon Press, 1979), 35–76.
12 The orthodoxy seeks to generate political unity among the faithful at home by applying the tools of modern democracy; the Jama'at appears to have lost its previous scruples regarding territorial nationalism.
13 Ernest Gellner, *Nations and Nationalism* (Oxford: Blackwell, 1983), 1–6; E. J. Hobsbawm, *Nations and Nationalism since 1780: Programme, Myth, Reality* (Cambridge: Cambridge University Press, 1992), 9.
14 Hugh Seton-Watson, *Nations and States: an Enquiry into the Origins of Nations and the Politics of Nationalism* (London: Methuen, 1977), 1; Anthony D. Smith, 'The Problem of National Identity: Ancient, Medieval and Modern?' *Ethnic and Racial Studies* 18, 1995, 375–83.
15 On this line of argument, see Gellner, Hobsbawm and Seton-West as indicated above. The idea of 'cultural markers' of identity refers to symbols such as language, religion, mythical past, or shared experiences which are drawn upon by elites engaged in political mobilization. The term has been used by various scholars including Paul Brass, *Ethnicity and Nationalism,* ch.1. For a discussion of the notion of symbolic ethnicity, see, Herbert J. Gans, 'Symbolic Ethnicity and Symbolic Religiosity: Towards a Comparison of Ethnic and Religious Acculturation', *Ethnicity and Racial Studies* 17, 4 October 1994, 577–92.

16 For a detailed study of the theme, see Tazeen M. Murshid, *The Sacred and the Secular: Bengal Muslim Discourses, 1871-1977* (Calcutta, New Delhi: Oxford University Press, 1995).
17 Sir Stafford Cripps to Butler, under-secretary of State for India, Letter dd. 24 August 1936, in 'Elections in India in 1937: Interference by Public Servants, Bengal', *India Office Records: L/P&J/7/1126*.
18 Tazeen M. Murshid, 'Bangladesh: The Challenge of Democracy: Language, Culture and Political Identity', *Contemporary South Asia* 2(1), 1993.
19 Speech by Liaqat Ali Khan, prime minister of Pakistan, at the first session of the Pakistan Muslim League Council held on 20 February 1949 in Khaliqdina Hall, Karachi (Government of Pakistan Publication, English translation of Urdu speech).
20 Government of East Pakistan, *Report of the East Bengal Language Committee, 1949-50* (Dacca, 1958), 6–26; Badruddin, Umar, *Bhasa andolan prasanga: katipay dalil*, vol 1, (Dacca, 1984), 139.
21 For a discussion of this theme, see Murshid, *Sacred and the Secular*, introduction.
22 Examples of shared customs are: attendance at and participation at *tazia* processions, *janmashtimi* processions and Saraswati *puja*, observance of the *pir* cult (also common in the Middle East); recital of Gorakher Laru, Padma Purana and Mangal Chandijai; occasionally a girl was married to a tree; some wore the sacred thread like Brahmins; observance of caste practices whereby occupational groups are given a lower status (viz. weavers, potters, washermen). See Rafiuddin Ahmed, *The Bengal Muslims, 1871–1906: A Quest for Identity* (Delhi: Oxford University Press, 1981); S. M. Nazmul Karim, *Changing Society in India and Pakistan* (Dacca: Oxford University Press, 1956).
23 Bengal Muslim society was traditionally divided into *ashraf* or noble born and *atrap* or lowly born. The former was largely of foreign origin, the latter local.
24 For an analysis of the consequent culture conflict, see B. Umar, *Samskritir samkat* (Dacca, 1967).
25 Howard Schuman, 'A Note on the Rapid Rise of Mass Bengali Nationalism', *American Journal of Sociology* 78(2), September 1972.
26 Abul Mansur Ahmed, *End of a Betrayal and Restoration of Lahore Resolution* (Dacca, 1978). The resolution had envisaged Pakistan as a confederation of states.
27 See Murshid, *Sacred and the Secular*, 5–9.
28 *Bangladesh Observer*, 8–10 March 1973.
29 Bangladesh, Ministry of Foreign Affairs, External Publicity Division, Dacca 1972, English translation of speech, 16–17.
30 Ali Anwar, ed., *Dharmanirapekshata (Secularism)*(Dacca, 1973), 86–87.
31 *New York Times*, 26 December 1972, 12, column 3. The Al-Badr, an action front of the Jama'at-e-Islami, was responsible for a mass murder in Muhammadpur. The only survivor, D. Hossain, recounted the events. More recently, the British media has uncovered war criminals belonging to the militant Al-Badr and Al-Shams, currently living in exile in Britain: 'Despatches', Channel 4 Television, United Kingdom, 1995.
32 See Election Commission, *Report on General Elections, Pakistan, 1970–71*, vol. 1, (Karachi: Manager of Publications, 1972), 216–17.
33 Author's interview with Kamal Hossain, 27 August 1994, Oxford.
34 *Janayuddha*, May–June 1973, 33, cited by Abul Fazl Huq, 'The Problem of National Identity in Bangladesh', *Journal of Social Studies*, no. 24, April 1984, 52.

35 For a detailed discussion of the role of the left in the Liberation war and in Bangladesh, see T. Maniruzzaman, *The Bangladesh Revolution and its Aftermath* (Dacca, 1980), pp. 141–53, 169–75, 175–79; Fazl Huq, ibid., 49–55.
36 Syed Anwar Hussain, 'Islamic Fundamentalism in Bangladesh: Internal Variables and External Inputs', in Rafiuddin Ahmed, ed., *Religion, Nationalism and Politics in Bangladesh* (New Delhi: South Asian Publishers, 1990), 141–42, 150.
37 He has therefore been ridiculed for adopting a 'multi-theocracy' model of secularism: Talukder Maniruzzaman, 'Bangladesh Politics: Secular and Islamic Trends', in Rafiuddin Ahmed, ed., *Islam in Bangladesh: Society, Culture and Politics*, (Dhaka: Bangladesh Itihas Samiti, 1983), 193.
38 Murshid, 'Bangladesh: the Challenge of Democracy', op. cit., 70.
39 Several authors have commented on the strong xenophobia in Bangladesh particularly in relation to India, and fears about national sovereignty against the designs of a big and powerful neighbour. See B. M. Monoar Kabir, 'The Politics of Religion: the Jama'at-i-Islami in Bangladesh', in Ahmed, ed., *Religion, Nationalism and Politics in Bangladesh*, 123; Husain, 'Islamic Fundamentalism in Bangladesh', in Ahmed, ibid., 141–42; Tajul Islam Hashmi, 'Islam in Bangladesh Politics', in Hussain Mutalib and Tajul Islam Hashmi, eds, *Islam, Muslims and the Modern State: Case Studies of Muslims in Thirteen Countries* (London, Basingstoke: St. Martin's Press, 1994), 105–107.
40 Zia's speech in 1978, cited by Huq, 'The Problem of National Identity in Bangladesh', op. cit., 58.
41 Husain argues that Zia theoretically Islamized the constitution with this amendment known as the Fifth Amendment. See his 'Islamic Fundamentalism in Bangladesh', op.cit., 150.
42 There were seven coups in quick succession. These were either anti-Indian or pro-Indian; some were led by officers, others by the rank and file; ideologically leftist and rightist, etc. For a discussion of these military coups and the rise of the military in Bangladesh politics, see Laurence Lifschultz, *Bangladesh: the Unfinished Revolution* (London: Zed Press, 1979), part 2.
43 In April 1979, Shah Azizur Rahman was made prime minister of Bangladesh. He was a member of the counter vernacular intelligentsia who resisted the movement to establish Bengali as one of the state languages of Pakistan. See *Eclipse of Secular Bangladesh* (London: Radical Asia Publication, 1981), 17.
44 On his Islamization policies, see Bangladesh, Ministry of Law and Parliamentary Affairs, A *Collection of Acts and Ordinances* (Dacca, 1980), Acts No. 31 and 37.
45 See Hussain, 'Islamic Fundamentalism in Bangladesh', op. cit., 144–149; Murshid, *Sacred and the Secular*, 369.
46 *Eclipse of Secular Bangladesh*, 13.
47 Most of these parties formally entered politics in 1979.
48 Other scholars have come to a similar conclusion. See Hussain, 'Islamic Fundamentalism in Bangladesh', op. cit., 149.
49 Afzal Iqbal, *Islamization in Pakistan* (Lahore: Vanguard, 1986), 106. In the years after partition, the political leadership took no chances and kept Maududi at arms length. While religious forces were allowed a social and educational role, they were barred from all political roles until the fall of Ayub Khan. In his statement before the Supreme Court Bhutto said, 'I appointed a chief of army belonging to the Jama'at and the result is before all of us.'
50 *Sangbad* (Bengali Daily, Dhaka), 17 April 1988.
51 Hashmi, 'Islam in Bangladesh Politics', op. cit., 115–117.

52 See Bangladesh, Bangladesh Bureau of Statistics, Ministry of Planning, *Statistical Pocket Book of Bangladesh* (Dacca: Bangladesh Secretariat, 1979), table 8.16, 424.
53 Interview with Kamal Hossain, Oxford, 27 August 1994.
54 BAMNA (Bangladesh Mukto Nirbachan Andolan), ed., *A Report on the Elections to the Fifth National Parliament, 27 February* 1991 (Dhaka: 1991), 62–63. The Jama'at obtained 12 percent of the votes cast.
55 Interview with Syed Hassan Imam, Secretary to the Nirmul Committee, at London, 25 August 1994.
56 *Eastern Eye* (London), no.124, 28 April 1992; *Surma* (Bengali weekly, London), 17–23 April 1992.
57 *Bangladesh Observer*, 27 March 1992.
58 The cases were eventually withdrawn on the 29 June 1992.
59 *Bangladesh Observer*, 23 April 1993; also see Tazeen M. Murshid, 'Democracy in Bangladesh: Illusion or Reality', *Contemporary South Asia* 4(2), 1995, 207.
60 View of Mahila Parishad and various other women's organisations.
61 Taslima Nasreen, '*Dour, dour*' in her *Nirbachita Kabita* (Calcutta: Ananda, 1993), 12.
62 Fatwas were given in Sylhet in October 1993 and twice in June 1994 in Bogra and Khulna, Bangladesh. In Sylhet a price of Tk. 50,000 (approximately US $1,500) was put on her head.
63 Barrister Sarah Hossain, interviewed for Newsnight, BBC 2, London, 4 August 1994.
64 *Inquilab*, Dhaka, 12 August 1994.
65 Interview with her defence lawyer, Kamal Hossain, Oxford, 27 August 1994.
66 Ibid. Kamal Hossain, ex-Awami Leaguer and ex-foreign minister of Bangladesh until 1975, who also heads the newly founded party, Gano Forum, believes that the Jama'at-Shibir Jubo Command have training camps in the border areas of northeast Bangladesh. He has requested the home ministry to set up a Committee to investigate this, but to no avail. Also see Leaflet, Elimination Committee (Dhaka, 6 June 1992). There is also ample newspaper coverage of the clandestine trafficking in arms in which members of the Jama'at have been involved, not to mention the fact that the police have at times considered themselves inadequately equipped to deal with them. Newspapers have also covered campus violence in Rajshahi, Chittagong, Dhaka and elsewhere extensively where the Shibir has been more successful in inflicting severe casualties on their opponents. See *Bangladesh Observer*, 7 February and 12 May 1993; *Sangbad*, various issues, March 1991, December 1992, 12 August 1994, 6.
67 Taslima went into hiding because she could not even present herself at court in safety. She emerged from hiding on 4 August 1994 after assurances and armed protection was secured.
68 Statement of a close friend and associate of Shamsur Rahman.
69 Leaflet, *Dharmadrohi o deshdrohi nastikder rukhe darao,* (Dhaka: Oitijhya Sangsad, , 26 June 1994).
70 Anis Alamgir, 'Shafiq Rahman ebong bichar', *Janomat* (Bengali weekly), 1–7 July 1994.
71 Ain-o-Shalish Kendra, 'Threats of Violence and Violation of Human Rights by Imams of Mosques and the Religious Right in Bangladesh', a collection of cases compiled for the period 1992–94 (Dhaka: unpublished, 1994).
72 *Inquilab*, 12 and 19 August 1994.
73 Ain-o-Shalish Kendra, 'Threats of violence and violations of human rights', op. cit.

74 In Chittagong, the police confessed their inability to control the Shibir-Yuva Command because their own weapons were inferior. There was evidence to suggest that arms were coming to specific Shibir members from Pakistan by post. See *Dainik Sangbad* (Dhaka), 12 August 1994, 6.
75 Alamgir, 'Shafiq Rahman ebong bichaar', op. cit., 22. Apart from the editor of *Janakantha,* the others were released on bail.
76 Comment of the co-editor, Taleya Rahman, London, 17 August 1994.
77 Janomot (London), 19–25 August 1994; *Saptahik Bichitra,* (Dhaka), year 23, no.12, 12 August 1994, 27.
78 *Saptahik Bichitra,* ibid., 27–33.
79 This party was founded by Colonel Rafiq and Colonel Farouq, two of the four killers of Sheikh Mujibur Rahman.
80 Politicians tend to regard the control of campus student politics to be indicative of political strength nationally. As a result the extent of campus violence has multiplied in the 1990s tremendously. As against 7 deaths a year in the 1980s there were about 25 such cases annually in the 1990s. Ganoforum, *Eto Laash Rakhbo Kothai?* (Dhaka, 1994), 30.
81 For a further discussion of the Jama'at's ideology, programme and method of recruitment see, U.A.B. Razia Akter Banu, 'Jama'at-i-Islami in Bangladesh: Challenges and Prospects', in Mutalib and Hashmi, eds., *Islam, Muslims and the Modern State,* op. cit., 83–94.
82 Ibid., 86.
83 See *Bichitra* (Bengali weekly, Dhaka), 1 June 1984; also see Hussain, 'Islamic Fundamentalism in Bangladesh', op. cit., 146.
84 One major crisis was the lengthy boycott of Parliament by the opposition Members in support of their demand that a constitutional amendment be introduced in order to make provisions for the establishment of a caretaker government which would have the responsibility of holding elections. It was argued that ruling parties used the instruments of power under their control to obtain favourable election results. A deeper constitutional crisis arose out of the mass resignation of these MPs on 28 December 1994.
85 Though not officially acknowledged, it is widely speculated that this was the compromise struck with the Jama'at-i-Islami for its support to the BNP in 1991 which enabled it to form a government. View of Syed Hasan Imam, Secretary, Nirmul Committee, London, 25 August 1994.
86 *Khabarer Kagaj,* 28 June 1994; Yasif Akbar, 'Shiksha Pratisthane Santras: rajnitite ashani sanket', *Purnima,* yr.7, no.6, 29 September 1993, 23.
87 *Janomot,* 19–25 August 1994.
88 *Sangbad,* 12 August 1994, 6.
89 While the Jama'at was held responsible for collaborating with the Pakistan army and killing Bengali nationalists, the Jatiya Party was accused of having links with the killers of Sheikh Mujib.
90 For a discussion of the idea of the irrelevant state, see Julius O. Ihonvbere, 'The Irrelevant State, Ethnicity, and the Quest for Nationhood in Africa', *Ethnic and Racial Studies* 17(1), January 1994, 44–50.

Chapter 8

State Support for Religion in Contemporary Sri Lanka: Some Ideological and Policy Issues

Chandra R. de Silva

Recent writers on the subject of the state and religion in contemporary Sri Lanka have taken one of two ends in a continuum. Some of them have argued that Sri Lanka is essentially a sectarian state. Others have taken the position that active state support for all religions in Sri Lanka marks a unique experiment in an effort to create a multi-religious society. This paper seeks to examine these two arguments in the light of concrete measures taken by the state to support the four major religions in Sri Lanka. It will, therefore, analyse the specific ways in which this state support is operationalised. It will also argue that these concrete policies mask a contestation within the state apparatus itself regarding the very nature of the relationship between the state and religion.

Let us first outline the main elements of the two contrasting views. The contention that Sri Lanka is a sectarian state has been made in many different places. For instance, David Rapoport, in an essay published in 1993 in one of the series of volumes on fundamentalism, makes the assertion that one could distinguish between what he called 'sectarian' states and 'secular' nation-states. For him 'Iran, Sri Lanka, Afghanistan, Lebanon, Saudi Arabia, Bahrain, Qatar, Kuwait and the United Arab Emirates are sectarian states...'[1] Such a stance is often taken on the ground that the Sri Lankan constitution since 1972 gives Buddhism, the religion of the majority of the population, a special place. A contrast is often drawn with the Independence constitution of 1946–48, in which Section 29(1) specifically forbade all legislation which discriminated on grounds of religion.[2] This clause was not incorporated in the 1972 constitution. Instead, Section 6 of that constitution stated, 'The Republic of Sri Lanka shall give to Buddhism the foremost place and accordingly it shall be the duty of the State to protect and foster Buddhism while assuring to all other religions the rights granted by Section 18(1)(d).' Section 18(1)(d) laid down that 'Every person is entitled to freedom of thought, conscience and religion.' Critics pointed out that this section was subject to 'such restrictions as the law prescribes in the interests of national unity and integrity, public safety, public order, and the protection of public health or morals, or the protection of the rights and freedoms of others, or giving effect to the Principles of State Policy set out in Section 16,' and thus provided virtually no safeguards. Those who argue that Sri Lanka was becoming increasingly sectarian also argued that the special position given to Buddhism was further strengthened in the constitution of 1978. Article 9 of that constitution states that 'The Republic of Sri Lanka shall give to Buddhism the foremost place and accordingly it shall be the duty of the State to protect and foster the Buddha Sasana, while assuring to all religions the rights granted by Articles 10 and 14(1).'[3] These articles are listed in a chapter on fundamental rights. Article 10 reads as follows: 'Every person is entitled to freedom of thought, conscience and religion, including the freedom to have or to adopt a religion or belief of his choice.'[4] Article 14(1)(e) guarantees every citizen 'the freedom, either by himself or in association with others, and either in public or in private, to manifest his religion or belief or worship, observance, practice and teaching.'[5] However, according to Article 15(7), all provisions in Article 14 are 'subject to such restrictions as may be prescribed by law in the interests of national security, public order, and the protection of public health or morality, or for the purpose of securing the due recognition and respect for the rights of others, or of meeting the just requirements of the general welfare of a democratic society.'[6] Critics have argued that Article 9 ensures unequal treatment for religious minorities. Peter Schalk in a recent article stated that Article 9 was a major impediment to ethnic peace in Sri Lanka.[7]

Those who disagree with this view point out that not only is there no evidence of religious persecution in Sri Lanka but the state is known to actively support all four of the major religions in the country: Buddhism, Hinduism, Islam and Christianity. In the case of Buddhism, the Ministry of Buddha Sasana was established on 18 February 1989. The Ministry includes the existing Department of Buddhist Affairs, the *Buddha Sravaka Dhammapitaya*, and the Buddhist and Pali University.[8] Hinduism is fostered through the Department of Hindu Religious and Cultural Affairs first created in 1986. Its major functions include fostering Hinduism, research on Hindu and Tamil culture, Tamil language, and education in Carnatic music and dance. To achieve these objectives the department administers the Hindu Cultural Fund, a research library, the Swami Vipulananda College of Music and Dance, Kataragama Hindu Pilgrims' Rest and the Hindu Cultural Hall in Batticaloa.[9] A Department of Muslim Religious and Cultural Affairs has also been in existence since 1986. Currently both these departments are part of the Ministry of Cultural and Religious Affairs. Finally, in 1995 a separate director was appointed in the same ministry to look after Christian affairs. Those who argue that Sri Lanka is not a sectarian state also point to the constitutional protection afforded to all religions. Any person can apply to the Supreme Court in respect of the infringement or imminent infringement by executive or administrative action of a fundamental right and freedom to have or to adopt a religion or belief of one's choice, this being a fundamental right listed in the constitution.[10]

The main thrust of this paper is to argue that an understanding of the situation in Sri Lanka needs some research into the actual modalities and extent of state support for the various religions rather than a mere analysis of the constitutional provisions and bureaucratic apparatus. Nevertheless, since much of the debate on the state's relationship to religion is connected with the issue of the 'secular state', it seems appropriate to deal with this question at the outset. Over thirty years ago, in a book titled *India as a Secular State*, Donald Smith pointed out that the theory of the secular state envisaged three distinct but interconnected sets of relations involving the state, religion and the individual or groups of individuals.[11] First of all, there is the assumption that religion should not be a factor in determining citizenship or membership of a state. Secondly, there is the idea that the state should not interfere with religious freedom – which includes the freedom to worship, to organise, to foster and to promote a religion, and indeed, if an individual opts to do so, the freedom not to have a religion at all. Thirdly, the concept of the secular state is based on the assumption that religion and the state function in two basically different areas of human activity, each with its own objectives and methods. The distinction between politics and religion is often equated to the distinction between the public and private spheres of activity. It is this third aspect of the secular state – the doctrine of separation of state and religion – that has been most under assault recently in Sri Lanka, in India and, indeed, in other parts of the world. The issue has become volatile because those who advocate the separation of the state and religion are seen, sometimes with good reason yet often unfairly, as being anti-religious.

However, the application of Western theoretical constructs in non-Western contexts can become less than meaningful unless they are contextualised within local understandings of reality and tradition. We thus need to start with Sri Lankan historical traditions about relationships between the state and religion, not with the objective of reconstructing a historical 'reality' of the past but to understand current perceptions of the past. It is important to remember that perceptions of history are multiple, changing and malleable. Nevertheless, in the short run, existing historical perceptions, even those which are hotly contested, are a reality which affect policy formulation and policy implementation.

It is well known that the first two aspects of secularism – religious freedom and the grant of citizenship irrespective of religious affiliation – have had long acceptance in Sri Lanka. The Sri Lankan, as part of the larger Indian tradition, did not make religious conformity a prerequisite for political loyalty and it is known that Sri Lankan rulers; whether Sinhala or Tamil, Buddhist or Hindu; accepted persons of varying religious faiths as members of their polity and, indeed, appointed them to important positions in royal service.[12] While temples were plundered during times of war and there is evidence of occasional religious discord, there is no memory of any of the traditional rulers ever pursuing a policy of religious intolerance. Indeed, the only 'memory' of religious persecution and of religious exclusivity comes with European colonial rule, particularly under the Portuguese. The colonial model is one which the majority Buddhists[13] and the minority Hindus and Muslims have condemned and which even modern Sri Lankan Christians, particularly Catholics, are uncomfortable with.[14]

On the other hand, there is a strong tradition of the intermeshing of the state and religion. As Ven. Bellanwila Wimalarathana claimed, 'There was a close relationship between Buddhism and the state from the time of Asoka and Devenampiyatissa. There was the tradition that the person who had the Tooth Relic was the legitimate ruler.'[15] The state and the order of Buddhist monks certainly did have a relationship which was mutually reinforcing. The state patronised the monks and supported the *sangha* (order of monks) with extensive endowments of land and income, while the monks strengthened the legitimacy of the state apparatus and provided spiritual solace to individual rulers. Conflicts between individual monarchs and sections of Buddhist monks were seen as aberrations of the normal order. In the period from the thirteenth to the seventeenth centuries, a similar symbiotic relationship seems to have existed between the rulers of the predominantly Hindu kingdom of Jaffna and the Hindu priests in the region. Memories of the introduction of Roman Catholicism, Calvinism and Anglicanism also cannot be divorced from their sponsorship by successive European colonial powers in Sri Lanka.

The tendency to accept the connection between state and religion is furthered by the fact that state sponsorship of religion, while it conferred most benefits on the religion of the dominant group, did not exclude those who followed other faiths. The state provided them, not only with religious freedom but also with some measure of state patronage. The major exception to this was the period from the sixteenth to the nineteenth century when European colonial powers restricted the rights of those of other faiths. However, for much of this period, the traditional kingdom of Kandy which exercised authority over most of the country continued to provide an alternative paradigm.

Thus, for a Buddhist or a Hindu to sever the relations between state and religion is to positively deny the very support which has enabled these religions to survive. This is key to understanding the absence of popular support for the separation of state and religion in South Asia. Yet the issue is even more critical than that. Secular philosophy is an import from the West. In South Asia, religion is a source of values. Politics and social life without religion would be understood as activities stripped of ethical values. As Mahatma Gandhi said, 'Those who say that religion has nothing to do with politics do not know what religion means.'[16]

Finally, one needs to take into account the adoption of an adapted version of Western-style democracy in South Asia. While the working of democratic politics in South Asia has its own dynamics, it is certainly a system of adversarial politics. Given the political imperative of maximising votes in a given area, appeals to religious loyalties through promises of state support to particular religions become inevitable in the context of widespread popular support for state patronage. Politicians are especially sensitive to this need particularly because in post-colonial South Asia, they are or at least they are seen to be more Westernised and less religious than the majority of their followers. They are therefore compelled to demonstrate their religious commitment in very public ways, and would find it very difficult to campaign for a separation of state and religion. For the same reasons, politicians seek to enlist the support of particular religious dignitaries in their party and political campaigns, and to obtain this support they are compelled to promise state patronage to individuals or groups. These factors go a long way in explaining why the 'wall of separation' is not practicable in South Asia. As Partha Chatterjee has argued, the very search for a new meaning for the word 'secularism' in the Indian context denotes the failure to transplant the Western concept to the South Asian context.[17]

Given this context, one way to analyse the state's relationship with various religions is to examine the ways through which it seeks to foster each religion.[18] Let us begin with Buddhism and the Ministry of Buddha Sasana. What does the Ministry of Buddha Sasana really do? One of its important responsibilities is to provide some measure of direct financial support to Buddhist monks and temples. For example, it administers a fund established under Act No. 35 of 1990 which is run by a state-appointed board that meets thrice a year and oversees the *Samanera Kapakaru Dayaka* scheme. This scheme involves granting 2,300 bhikkus a monthly allowance of Rs 150 a month till they reach twenty-one years of age or leave the order.[19] It also assists over twenty-five Samanera Institutes. These institutes, located in temples, provide young initiates with a basic introduction to the nature and responsibilities of monkhood.[20] In 1997, the ministry also allocated Rs 1,800,000 to provide alms to Buddhist monks and Rs 700,000 to provide training for *dasa sil mathas*.[21] The ministry provides further grants to selected Buddhist institutions. Thus, for example, the 1997 budget provided Rs 1.8 million for foreign Buddhist institutions like the Buddhist Vihara in Washington, DC. The Buddhist Publication Society in Kandy was scheduled to receive Rs 100,000 and the Sasana Sevaka Society at Maharagama was to get Rs 120,000.[22] In that year, a sum of Rs 2 million was set aside for the fostering of religious activities in selected temples, while Rs 500,000 was kept for the education of mentally and physically handicapped Buddhist children. *Sasanaraksha mandalas*, set up within each administrative division in Sri Lanka to co-ordinate the work of Buddhist groups within each area are advised and encouraged by the ministry.[23] The ministry also maintains registers of *samanera* and *upasampada* monks, appoints trustees of temples, and supervises the administration of temple lands under the laws governing Buddhist temporalities.

A major concern of the ministry has been support of the *daham pasal*, the Buddhist Sunday schools. A major portion of the expenditure goes for the printing of *dhamma* (religious) school books. After numerous complaints about the shortage of books, in 1997 Rs 30 million were allocated for that purpose.[24] Seminars are held for teachers of the *daham pasal* and public exams are organised. The 1997 allocation for the conduct of exams in the *daham pasal* was Rs. 1.6 million.

Finally, the Ministry of Buddha Sasana promotes research on Buddhism and the dissemination of Buddhist ideas. Projects financed by it include the translation and publication of the *Tripitaka*, and the Buddhist Encyclopaedia. In 1996 for the first time, Rs 500,000 was allocated for the dissemination of Buddhist ethical concepts by the publication of popular books on Buddhism.[25]

In many ways the activities sponsored by the Department of Hindu Religion and Tamil Culture are similar. It makes small grants to Hindu religious organisations.[26] *Saiva siddhantha* classes in Colombo, Kandy and Vavuniya were allotted Rs 50,000 in 1977. The department organises festivals for the celebration of the four major Hindu festivals (Thaipongal, Maha Sivarathri, Adivel and Deepavali).[27] The Hindu Cultural Fund receives an annual grant of Rs 150,000 from the state.[28] The subsidy for the running of the Kataragama Hindu Pilgrims' Rest in 1997 was Rs 575,000.[29] The maintenance of the Hindu Cultural Hall was expected to cost the government Rs 300,000 in 1997.[30]

Additionally, it supervises a network of Sunday religious (*araneri*) schools. In 1993 there were a total of 358 such schools with a student enrolment of some 55,000. By 1997 there were over 400 such schools.[31] The department provides all textbooks as well as registers and record books free of charge for these schools and finances the cost of the Year 11 examination.[32] It conducts seminars and refresher courses for teachers.[33] About a third of the schools also receive small cash grants and the state sponsors student competitions, both district-wide and nationally. For example, Rs 200,000 were allocated for religious knowledge contests in 1997. Ten scholarships for Hindu orphans who attend regular schools were expected to cost the government Rs 100,000 in 1997.

Finally, the department sponsors Hindu publications. It has prepared and published a three volume *Encyclopaedia of Hinduism*.[34] In 1997

Rs 100,000 were allotted for this.[35] The Department publishes a quarterly journal entitled *Gopuram*. It also sponsors public lectures on Hinduism.[36]

The Department of Muslim Religious and Cultural Affairs, in turn, operates a network of over 100 Muslim religious schools (*madrasahs*).[37] In 1995, seven Muslim students were given scholarships to Al Azara University in Cairo, and five were sent to Koran contests in Egypt and Malaysia.[38] Muslim pre-school teachers are offered a basic training. The department also facilitates the *hajj* pilgrimage.[39] Subsidies are provided to encourage various activities on Islamic holy days.[40] It examines the accounts of mosques, and appoints trustees and makes grants to them.[41] It administers *wakf* boards under Act No. 51 of 1956 as amended by Acts No. 21 and 33 of 1982. In 1997, the department budgeted Rs 550,000 for the National Milad un Nabi Festival where awards are presented annually to Muslim artists and writers. The state's Department of Education also maintains a special category of Muslim schools with school vacations scheduled differently so that Muslim school children would be able to fast at Ramadan.

The director for Christian Affairs had not developed a program by 1996 but there was little doubt that there would soon be state funding for similar types of activity. Indeed, looking at the various types of activities sponsored by the state it seems reasonable to argue that the Sri Lankan state is supportive of all four of the major religions and that it is not a 'sectarian' state.

However, a slightly but not entirely different picture emerges if we analyse the amounts of funding involved. In 1996, the total estimated expenditure for the ministry (including the Department of Buddhist Affairs) was Rs 63,406,300.[42] If we add the expenditures of the Department of Education for *pirivena* schools which provide an education for Buddhist monks (and leave aside activities of the Departments of Archaeology and of Cultural Affairs), we have annual expenditures by the state in support of Buddhism coming to over Rs 100 million.[43]

In terms of the scale of expenditure, state support for Hinduism is more modest. In 1997, for example, the total recurrent expenditure under the department was estimated to be Rs 16,155,000.[44] The capital budget has varied between Rs 7 million and Rs 2.6 million in the last few years the latter figure representing the 1997 capital allocation. In some years, the support was minimal. For instance, in the year 1992 alone the department estimated that 796 Hindu temples had been damaged in the fighting in the north and east. The estimate of the funds needed to repair this damage alone came to Rs 98.6 million. In 1995 the total aid provided for 'neglected' Hindu temples was Rs 80,000; and in 1997, it was Rs. 120,000.[45] Regular grants for statues, *kumbhabishekams*, and the like to 30 to 35 institutions in 1997 was estimated to cost only Rs 250,000; a somewhat larger sum than Rs 150,000 in 1995.

The 1997 allotment to the Department of Muslim Affairs was even more modest. The total allocation was Rs 11,567,000 of which Rs 8,987,000 was the estimate for recurrent expenses.[46] The director of Christian Affairs was allotted a token Rs 350,000 but there is considerable state aid given to Christian 'assisted schools' and the state expended a considerable sum on the occasion of the visit of Pope John Paul II in January 1995.[47] All in all, therefore, although the Buddhists as a group might be seen to receive proportionately more assistance, the picture of Sri Lanka as a state supporting all religions has considerable evidence to back it.

On the other hand, this multi-religious patronage provided by the state masks a real contest within the polity regarding the extent to which the state should be concerned with religion. One of the problems related to this issue is that there is a belief among some Buddhist leaders that the state has a special relationship and a special duty towards Buddhism. As Rambukwelle Sri Dharmarakshitha, the chief monk of the Malwatta Chapter of the *Siyam nikaya* explained, 'One of the most important features of the history of the Buddha Sasana in Sri Lanka has been the connection between the *sasana*, the state and the people. A key duty of the rulers was the protection and fostering of the Buddha *sasana*. Our historical documents well illustrate the ways in which our rulers successfully executed this responsibility during the long period of many centuries from the time that Buddhism became the state religion in the third century B.C.'[48] The Buddhists who take this view point out that when the British took possession of the last independent kingdom in Sri Lanka, they agreed in writing to protect Buddhism. The modern state, in their view, ought to do no less. Some of this thinking has entered official government documents. For instance, one of the functions of the Department of Buddhist Affairs is listed as fostering and promoting Buddhist culture and safeguarding it against alien influences.[49]

State involvement with religion has led to calls by some Buddhists for the use of the state administrative apparatus to promote Buddhism and the use of legislation to prevent 'disrespect' to Buddhism. Some of this is provoked by insensitive behaviour by non-Buddhists, largely foreigners. For example, in January 1995, George Arney, the BBC correspondent in South Asia, was arrested for seating himself on the lap of a Buddha image while his companion photographed him.[50] Eventually, all charges against him were dropped after an apology. Nevertheless, the same concern for 'respect' has led to more questionable steps. The same argument was used to ban a scholarly book on Buddhism by Stanley Tambiah in 1997.[51] A conference in 1990 which was attended by major Buddhist leaders proposed laws to punish disrespect shown to the Buddhist flag.[52]

The danger with state involvement with religion is that the borderline between protecting a religion and restricting the rights of an individual are not always clear. For example, one of the constant complaints of Buddhist leaders has been that a number of foreign organisations have begun activities in Sri Lanka under the guise of social service and have begun converting Buddhists and Hindus to Christianity. In May 1995 this issue was brought up before the Supreme Advisory Council of the Ministry of Buddha Sasana. This Supreme Council of 31 religious leaders had been set up in 1991 to advise the president of Sri Lanka on issues relating to Buddhism. A sub-committee to which this matter was referred decided on 11 August 1995 to recommend legislation which would prohibit conversion of all those under eighteen years of age. It also recommended that those who seek to convert persons under the age of eighteen to another religion through material incentives and other means should be liable to five years' imprisonment and a fine after trial. Foreigners who violated this law would also be liable to expulsion. The committee also recommended that the establishment of new places of worship should require the approval of the Secretary of Cultural Affairs and the assent of the people through a referendum in the area. Such applications should also be referred to the Supreme Council. Conduct of religious ceremonies without this approval would make such persons liable to five years in prison and/or a fine of one million rupees.[53] The proposals were discussed but no action was decided on in the subsequent meetings of the Supreme Council because several Buddhists within the council had reservations about the wisdom of these proposals. They had come to the point where they felt that state intervention in support of religion might conflict with another broadly accepted principle – that of religious freedom.

We might add another concern arising from state intervention in religion to the two we have already discussed (namely, the differential conferment of advantages and the possible danger to religious freedom by the use of state power by the adherents of one religion). This third danger is in some ways the reverse of the second: that religion would become subservient to the state and perhaps even to partisan party and political interests. As Venerable Bellanwila Wimalarathana, the chief incumbent of the Bellanwila temple located near Colombo, explained, 'My personal opinion is that Buddhist monks should not participate in the party politics which prevail today in any way. [Such participation] means the distancing of the Buddhist monk from the people because people look at Buddhist monks as persons belonging to our political party [or theirs].'[54] Ananda Guruge, a well known Buddhist scholar and Sri Lanka's former ambassador to Washington, while advocating state intervention in support of Buddhism, cautioned in 1990 that Buddhist temples and organisations should retain their independence and resist being converted into a government department. Therein lies the dilemma for us in South Asia. A strict separation of state and religion is not practical. As T. N. Madan put it '... in the prevailing circumstances, secularism in South Asia as a generally shared credo of life, is impossible, as a basis for state action, impracticable, and as a blueprint for the foreseeable future, impotent.'[55] Yet, state intervention in religion leads us through pathways full of land mines. In the context of what Amrita

Basu and Atul Kohli termed the 'normative and organisational vacuum' caused by the declining support for secularism, the erosion of traditional hierarchies and increased competition for state controlled resources, is likely to bring us into more conflicts.[56]

NOTES

1. David C. Rapoport, 'Comparing Militant Fundamentalist Movements and Groups', in *Fundamentalism and the State: Remaking Polities, Economies, and Militance*, edited by Martin E. Marty and R. Scott Appleby (Chicago: University of Chicago Press, 1993), 432.
2. Section 29(2) read: 'No law shall (a) prohibit or restrict the free exercise of any religion; or (b) make persons of any community or religion liable to disabilities or restrictions to which persons of other communities or religions are not liable; or (c) confer on persons of any community or religion any privilege or advantage which is not conferred on persons of other communities or religions, or (d) alter the constitution of any religious body except with the consent of the governing authority of that body, Provided that, in any case where a religious body is incorporated by law, no such alteration shall be made except at the request of the governing authority of the body.' *The Constitution of Ceylon, February 1948*, (Sessional Papers no. 3, 1948).
3. *The Constitution of the Democratic Socialist Republic of Sri Lanka, 1978* (Colombo: Department of Government Printing, 1978), 5.
4. Ibid., 6.
5. Ibid., 8.
6. Ibid., 9–10. Moreover, this clause further states that 'For the purpose of this paragraph, 'law' includes regulations made under the law for the time being relating to public security'.
7. Peter Schalk, 'Articles 9 and 18 of the Constitution of Lanka as Obstacles to Peace', *Lanka*, 5, December 1990, 276–295.
8. Its functions were defined as follows: To propose and execute measures to implement Article 9 of the Constitution, to publicise Buddhist moral principles, to administer Buddhist temple lands, to develop the Buddhist and Pali University, to encourage Buddhist activities, to prepare and publish the Buddhist Encyclopaedia, to translate the *Tripitaka*, to register *bhikkus* (Buddhist monks) to register *dasa sil mathas* and to [foster] higher learning for bhikkus. *Buddha Sasana Amatyansaya*: 1990 *Agosthu 20 Sita 22 Dakvaa Kolamba Bandaranaike Anusmarana lathyanthara Saalawedi Pavathwanalada Buddha Sasana Amathyansaye Karyabharaya Pilibanda Samantranaye Varththva*, (Colombo: Department of Government Printing, 1990), vi.
9. *Varshika Veda Satahana '97* (Battaramulla: Ministry of Cultural and Religious Affairs, 1997), 44.
10. See Article 17 in *The Constitution of the Democratic Socialist Republic of Sri Lanka*, 10.
11. Donald E. Smith, *India as a Secular State* (Princeton: Princeton University Press, 1968), 5–9.
12. For instance, in the sixteenth century, Aritta Keevendu Perumal, confidant of Rajasinha I of Sitawaka, and later commanding officer of the Sitawaka army was almost certainly a Saivite Hindu in a largely Buddhist kingdom. See C. R. de Silva, 'The Rise and Fall of Sitawaka', in K. M. de Silva, ed., *History of Sri Lanka* (Peradeniya: University of Peradeniya Press, 1995), 102.

13 Ven. Bellanwila Wimalarathana, chief incumbent of the Bellanwila temple stated as follows in an interview with the author in August 1993, 'During that [colonial] time there were anti-Buddhist activities, for example the Portuguese destroyed many temples including this one. Apart from that they rewarded those who converted to their religion. The English, though they pledged to protect Buddhism, actually did not do so. If you examine the reports they sent to their superiors on Buddhist monks and their actions (*kriyadamayan*) there are clear recommendations on what should be done about them. There should be more research done about the subtle ways in which Buddhism and the culture of our country were undermined in this period of and after the arrival of Western invaders'.

14 As R. L. Stirrat perceptively points out Catholic memories focus more on the period of Dutch Calvinist rule when they were the targets of persecution, than on the period of Portuguese Catholic ascendancy when their religion was introduced into the country: R.L. Stirrat, *Power and Religiosity in a Post-Colonial Setting: Sinhala Catholics in Contemporary Sri Lanka* (Cambridge: Cambridge University Press, 1992), 14. Contemporary Catholic opposition to extensive state connections with religion also stem from their minority position and their relative Westernisation in the last two centuries.

15 Interview cited above.

16 M. K. Gandhi, *An Autobiography or the Story of My Experiments with Truth* (Ahmedabad: Navjivan, 1940), 383.

17 Partha Chatterjee, 'Religious Minorities and the Secular State: Reflections on an Indian Impasse', *Public Culture* 8, 13–15.

18 For a good survey of post independence relations between the state and religion in Sri Lanka, see K. M. de Silva, 'Religion and the State', in K. M. de Silva, ed., *Sri Lanka: Problems of Governance* (New Delhi: Konark Publishers, 1993), 306–344.

19 The scheme was started with 2,300 samaneras ordained between June 1992 and June 1993. Vacancies are filled by nominations from the Mahanayakas on a proportionate basis.

20 For details see 'Recommendations on Samanera Institutes drafted by Welamitiyawe Kusaladhamma, Chair, Samanera Institute Supervisory Board March 11, 1994.' Unpublished typescript available at the Ministry of Buddha Sasana. An *adeekshana mandalaya* appointed by the Supreme Council (*Uttarithara Mandalaya*) consisting of Ven. Welamitiyawe Kusaladhamma, Ven. Kotugoda Dhammavasa and Ven. Yalegama Dhammapala decides which institutes are to be supported. Institutes are registered with the Department of Buddhist Affairs and have to send monthly reports. Author's interview with Deputy Assistant Secretary, Ministry of Buddha Sasana, 3 July 1997.

21 This includes maintenance for monks displaced from the north and east due to the civil conflict.

22 These figures are from *Estimates of the Revenue and Expenditure of the Government of the Democratic Socialist Republic of Sri Lanka for the Financial Year January 31–December 1997* (Colombo: Department of Government Printing, 1997), vols 1–3.

23 See *Buddha Sasana Amatyansaya: 1990*, 2–3, for the proposal.

24 In 1992 the allocation was Rs 9.5 million. In 1994, it was 16 million.

25 The same sums were maintained in the 1997 budget estimates excepting that the first item was given Rs 2,250,000.

26 Aid to thirty-five to forty Hindu religious institutions was estimated at Rs 175,000 in 1997, and Rs 125,000 in 1995.

27 Ibid., 2.
28 *Varshika Vada Satahana '97*, 54; *1995 Sanvardhana Vada Satahana*, 50.
29 Ibid.
30 Other provisions include Rs 100,000 for furniture and Rs 20,000 for books.
31 The figures are from the *Performance Report 1992* (Ministry of Hindu Religious Affairs and Tamil Culture, 1993), 1: supplemented by an interview with K. Shanmugalingam, Director, Hindu Religion and Cultural Affairs in January 1995. It is important to remember that the only other way in which Hindu students receive organised religious instruction is in state schools. Virtually all schools in Sri Lanka are run by the state and unlike in the United States, all of them are expected to teach all students their own religion, provided there is a minimum of 15 students in the school belonging to a particular religion.
32 Books distributed free included a new course syllabus, *Panniru Thirumurai Thothirathiraddu*; a compendium of devotional hymns, *Saiva Samaya Saram* (The Quintessence of Saivism); and *Indu Samaya Vilakkalum Virathangalum* (Guide to Hindu Festivals and Folklore): *Performance Report 1992*, 2.
33 The approximately 1,500 teachers are volunteers, mostly school teachers: *Performance Report 1992*, 1. Training seminars for teachers were budgeted in 1997 at Rs 100,000. In 1995, the estimated cost was Rs 75,000: *Varshika Vada Satahana '97*, 49; and *1995 Sanvardhana Vada Satahana*, 50.
34 *Performance Report 1992*, 6–7.
35 In 1995 the sum was Rs 90,000: *Varshika Vada Satahana '97*, 51; and *1995 Sanvardhana Vada Satahana*, 50.
36 Rs 80,000 allotted in 1997: *Varshika Vada Satahana '97*, 51.
37 *Muslim Cultural Awards Ceremony 1994* (Colombo: Office of the Minister of Muslim Religious and Cultural Affairs, 1994), 148; and interview with U.L.M. Haldeen, Director, Dept of Muslim Religious and Cultural Affairs, Colombo, 5 January 1995.
38 *1995 Performance Report of Ministry of Cultural and Religious Affairs*, 16.
39 *Monthly Progress Report, April 1996* reported that the special passport counter for Hajj pilgrims from 18 March to 10 April issued 2,810 passports and that the Saudi Embassy arranged for 5,400 visas for the Hajj (p. 1). Air fares to Saudi Arabia were reduced, twelve Air Lanka flights and five Saudi flights were arranged and a team of eleven persons was sent to Saudi Arabia to look after the pilgrims (p. 2). In 1997, Rs 300,000 were budgeted for such activities: *Varshika Veda Satahana '97*, 63.
40 *Varshika Veda Satahana '97*, 63.
41 *Monthly Progress Report*, November 1996, 3. In 1997 aid to mosques was Rs 150,000: *Varshika Veda Satahana '97*, 64.
42 In 1995 it was Rs 52,015,000.
43 The Buddha Sasana Fund, for instance, commenced activities from 30 November 1995 with a donation of Rs 25 million from the state. Further state and private donations have enabled the fund to grow to Rs 85 million by 3 September 1995: Ministry of Buddha Sasana, 1996 Budget. Unpublished Typewritten Brief for Committee Stage Discussions: Progress Report of Development Activities during 1994–1995, 1–2. Philanthropists are invited to give donations of Rs 10,000 each and each unit of Rs 10,000 used to finance a bhikku's education. In 1995 contributions from foreign and local donors totalled 14.4 million rupees. The interest on the donations was Rs 200,000 and the government gave Rs 8.4 million more that year thus increasing the fund by Rs 23 million in all. These funds are kept in a fixed deposit at the National Savings Bank.

44 *Varshika Vada Satahana* '97, 47–48. In 1995 it had been Rs 13,960,000: *1995' Sanvardhana Vada Satahana*, 47–48.
45 *Varshika Vada Satahana* '97, 51; *1995 Sanvardhana Vada Satahana*, 50.
46 *Varshika Vada Satahana* '97, 63. The 1995 estimates were somewhat higher: Rs 6,379,000 for recurrent and Rs 7,879,000, for capital expenses: *1995 Sanvardhana Vada Satahana*, 55.
47 See, Chandra R. de Silva, 'The Monks and the Pontiff: Reflections on Religious Tensions in Contemporary Sri Lanka', *South Asia, Special Issue on Asia and Europe: Commerce, Colonialism and Cultures* 19, 1996, 233–244.
48 *Buddha Sasana Amatyansaya*, 1990, xvi–xviii.
49 *1997 Estimates of Revenue*, vol. 2, 107.
50 Reuters newsreport on SLNet, 23 January 1995.
51 The banned book was S. J. Tambiah, *Buddhism Betrayed? Religion, Politics and Violence in Sri Lanka* (Chicago, University of Chicago Press, 1992).
52 *Buddha Sasana Amatyansaya* 1990, 3 and 10.
53 Minutes of the Supreme Council of 20 June 1995.
54 Interview with author at Bellanwila, January 1993.
55 T. N. Madan, 'Secularism in its Place', *Journal of Asian Studies* 46(4), November 1987, 748.
56 Amrita Basu and Atul Kohli, 'Community Conflicts and the State in India', *Journal of Asian Studies* 56 (2), May 1997, 321.

Chapter 9
The 'Nationalities' Question in South Asia
Raju G.C. Thomas

Many of the problems that afflicted the Soviet Union, Yugoslavia and Czechoslovakia at the end of the cold war, causing them to fall apart, may be found among the states of South Asia. The experience in Europe in the 1990s suggests that South Asian states could meet the same fate. Indeed, Kashmiri separatists pointed to the secessions of the Baltic states from the Soviet Union in 1991 on grounds of wrongful annexation by Stalin in 1939, as not being fundamentally different from their claim of wrongful annexation of Kashmir by Nehru in 1947. Similarly, Sikh separatists seeking to create an independent Khalistan out of the Indian state of Punjab argued in the early 1990s that their objective was no different from the successful secessions and recognition of Slovenia and Croatia from Yugoslavia.

The secession of Muslim Pakistan from Hindu majority India in 1947 following the end of British rule, and then Bengali East Pakistan from the Punjabi–Pashtun dominated Pakistan in 1971, seemed to be the first stages in the 'Balkanization' of the Indian subcontinent. At the time of independence, Indian political leaders, especially Jawaharlal Nehru, expressed doubts as to whether Islam could keep the several linguistic and racial groups of Pakistan together, especially since Islam had failed to do this elsewhere. Those forebodings proved right in 1971 when Muslim Bengalis and Punjabis fought a civil war that led to East Pakistan's secession. Thereafter, political gurus in India have continued to predict that Pakistan could soon prove to be a failed state.

Likewise, Pakistan and other critics have doubted that the myriad linguistic, religious, racial and caste groups of India could be united within a secular and democratic system when only imperial and authoritative rule had brought them together during the past three millenia. Muslim Kashmiris and Sikh Punjabis, converted Christian tribals in the northeast of India and Hindu Assamese have sought to separate their states from India, though without success. Thus, Pakistani expectations of the imminent collapse of India have yet to come about.

Meanwhile, Sri Lanka with only two major ethnic groups, the mainly Buddhist Sinhalese and Hindu Tamils, is locked in a civil war over a separate Tamil homeland.

Herein lies a puzzle. Why has Pakistan, with far fewer ethnic groups and under a more unifying and centralized Islamic faith, failed to remain united; a fate which also sharply threatens Sri Lanka? And why has India with its vastly diverse ethnic 'groups under a free-wheeling and highly decentralized Hindu faith along with other disparate religious beliefs and practices, succeeded?

The perennial crises of too many nations and too few independent states in South Asia have been of two types. The first problem is that of ethnic nations or ethnically-oriented provinces or states that emerged from British India wishing to become independent states. The argument for independence mainly rests on the claim that the creation of only India, Pakistan and Sri Lanka out of the British empire in South Asia, all multiethnic civic nations, would appear to be illogical and inadequate. The precedent set by the secession of Bangladesh from Pakistan based on the Bengali nation more than twenty years after decolonization would seem to suggest that other nations within the existing post-colonial states also have the right and possibility of becoming independent too. The second problem is that of ethnic nations which have been divided by international frontiers wishing to unite into a single nation-state. Thus Pashtuns and Baluchis are divided by the Pakistan–Afghanistan and Pakistan–Iran borders respectively, Kashmiris by the India–Pakistan border, Bengalis by the India–Bangladesh one, Tamils by the India–Sri Lanka distinction, and Gurkhas by the India–Nepal divide. Since most post-colonial boundaries usually carry no ethnic rationality on the ground, the demands by divided ethnic groups for redrawing international frontiers would at first glance appear to be reasonable. Besides, the territorial status of Hindus from Sindh who fled to India and Muslims from Bihar who fled to East Pakistan after the 1947 partition, remain problematic. In the case of the Sindhi Hindus; their language, culture and identity are in danger of being lost along with their territorial roots.

A major problem in South Asia is thus one of the prevailing international boundaries and of unwilling, most often divided, ethnic minorities caught within the structure of existing states. Under these circumstances, should the 'international community' maintain the territorial integrity and sovereignty of existing states, whatever their origins and justification? Or, should it allow the state's various ethnic groups or 'nationalities' the right of self-determination and territorial secession from existing states because of failed domestic inter-ethnic relations or human rights violations? A third alternative to these two options – as contradictory as it may seem – would be to propel historically conflicting states and antagonistic 'nationalities' within a region into a confederation as much of Europe has done.

NATIONS AND STATES

Determining the number of nations and types of nationalisms, or justifying the rationale for existing or new states in South Asia, can be an elusive enterprise. The practitioners of several major religions are found on the subcontinent, 17 official and over 35 major languages and over 180 minor languages and a thousand dialects are spoken, numerous tribal groups with distinct racial differences live in various parts of the region, and there exist many castes and subcastes that include some with strong social and political bonds within the group. Then why only the creations of Pakistan and Bangladesh since independence in 1947? Should not the Indian subcontinent be divided into at least a 100 separate states, if not more? Recall that at the time of independence there existed over 580 autonomous princely Indian states in addition to the dozen or more large provinces of British India proper. If the existence of a small independent state of Bhutan can be justified, then why should there not exist the independent states of Dravidastan, Assam, Nagaland, Mizoram, Meghalaya, Manipur, Gorkhaland, Bodoland, Jharkhand, Kashmir, Khalistan, Pashtunistan, Baluchistan, Sindhudesh, Tamil Ealam, and many more?

There are parallels between Europe and South Asia: the existence of many religions, languages and cultures is accompanied at the same time by an overarching 'European' or 'Indian' ethos of beliefs, customs and ideals respectively. But except along the fringes of the continent, the characteristics of the peoples of Europe as a whole appear different from those of the peoples of the Indian subcontinent. There is more ambivalence, vagueness and fluidity in the South Asian experience than in Europe reflecting the differing nature of South Asian experience from that of Europeans. Though some Pakistanis believe they have more in common with the Islamic Middle East and Central Asia than with India, the peoples of these regions tend to see the peoples of the Indian subcontinent as mainly of the same race and culture. This Pakistani belief may be more wish than reality, given impetus by Pakistan's perennial security fears of being drawn back into a Hindu-majority Greater India.

Concepts of nations, nationalism and state carry distinctive connotations in the South Asian context. Unlike Europe, 'nation-states' have rarely existed in South Asia. Instead, great multi-ethnic empires have arisen and disintegrated. They were replaced by lesser empires and minor kingdoms that were either multi-ethnic themselves; or, if ethnically pure either with reference to language or religion (or both), they rarely encompassed all members of that ethnic group within their boundaries. Thus, empires such as those of the Mauryas, Guptas, Moghuls, Marathas and Sikhs involved the subjugation of several ethnic groups by a dominant conquering group, while kingdoms such as those of Jaipur, Holkar, Hyderabad, Kashmir and Mysore were either ethnically hybrid or did not include all the members of a particular ethnic group.

As in the case of Europe, religion and language have bred diverse ethnic nationalisms in South Asia. Punjabis, Sindhis and Bengalis – linguistic groups that are found on both sides of the international frontiers of India, Pakistan and Bangladesh – are united by language, race and culture, but separated by religion. The United Bengal movement before Partition in 1947 emphasized Bengali language and culture over religion. At the height of the Sindh nationalist separatist movement in the 1980s, Sindh Muslims talked about recovering the old Sindh where Sindhi-speaking Muslims and Hindus would live together in an independent Sindhudesh.

Several ethnic groups in India; classified by race, language and/or religion, overlap with like ethnic groups in Pakistan, Bangladesh, Sri Lanka, Nepal and Bhutan: e.g., Urdu-speaking Muslims, Muslim and Hindu Sindhis and Bengalis, Tamils, Gurkhas, and Terai Hindus. However, nations and states still do not coincide in South Asia. Even if independent Baluchistan, Pashtunistan, Sindhudesh, Khalistan, Kashmir, Assam and Tamil Ealam were to be recognized, it would still require considerable 'ethnic cleansing' of minorities and/or annexations of land in adjacent sovereign states to create nation-states that are comprehensive and ethnically unified. At present, the Baluchis, Pashtuns, Bengalis, Gurkha and Terai Nepalis, and Tamils, straddle at least two countries. Setting a single precedent of a comprehensive and ethnically cohesive nation-state, the kind that Western policies advertently or inadvertently brought about in the former Yugoslavia, would prove even more dangerous and destabilising when applied to the Indian subcontinent.

NATIONALISMS AND SECESSIONS

Accompanied by both intra- and inter-state violence, two successful territorial secessions have already taken place in South Asia; that of Pakistan and Bangladesh. In 1947, at the time of independence, Pakistan broke away from British India, a then quasi-autonomous state which was in transition towards full independence.[1] The rationalization for the partition of British India was that the Islamic religion endowed nationhood on its practitioners thereby justifying separate statehood for 'Indian' Muslims. The paradox here was that the Muslims of British India who demanded Pakistan the most were mainly from areas that remained part of India. In 1971, East Pakistan broke away from Pakistan to become the independent state of Bangladesh. The rationalization in this case was that the Bengali language and culture constituted nationhood, not Islam, thereby justifying separate statehood for Bengalis for both the majority Muslims and minority Hindus. The paradox here was that this Bengal Nation (Bangladesh) did not include the Bengalis of West Bengal in India the majority of whom are Hindus with a minority of Muslims.

The 'Nationalities' Question in South Asia

The Indian nationalist movement of the Indian National Congress for an independent India, the Muslim nationalist movement of the All-India Muslim League for a separate and independent Pakistan, and the Bengali nationalist movement of the Awami League in East Pakistan for an independent Bangladesh, represented three different and successful forms of nationalism in South Asia. The concepts of nation and state of Jawaharlal Nehru of the Indian National Congress, Mohammed Ali Jinnah of the Muslim League and Sheikh Mujibur Rahman of the Awami League, were significantly different from each other and serve (or served) as models of past, ongoing and future nationalisms and demands for new states in South Asia.

In demanding a separate state for Indian Muslims, Mohammed Ali Jinnah, leader of the All-Indian Muslim League after 1930, argued that there were two nations in India: a nation of Hindus and a nation of Muslims. Religion defined nation. This called for the creation of two states out of British India: Hindustan for the Hindus and Pakistan ('Land of the Pure') for the Muslims. Rejecting Jinnah's famous 'two nation theory'; Jawaharlal Nehru, leader of the Indian National Congress, argued that there was only one nation in India that encompassed all the peoples of the Indian subcontinent whatever their religion, race, language or culture. Geography, history and political experience defined the nation.

Thus the concurrent 'Pakistan' and 'Indian' nationalist movements represented two forms of nationalisms based on differing concepts of nation. Jinnah claimed that Islam defined nationhood because Muslims followed specific religious practices and were expected to obey common laws based on the Koran and the Shariat. While Hindus and Muslims might speak the same language, they lived for the most part separately within those regions. If not by race or language, then Hindus and Muslims could often be distinguished by their dress or way of life. But Jinnah's 'two nation theory' did not explain why only 'Indian' Muslims constituted part of this Islamic nation and not those beyond the subcontinent. Do Muslim Pakistan and Bangladesh have more in common with Muslim Turkey and Indonesia than with Hindu north India? Does Buddhist Sri Lanka have more in common with Buddhist Thailand than with Hindu south India? Pakistanis have repeatedly claimed that their identity is more closely tied with the Middle East and Central Asia than with India. But by focussing on the Islamic link between West and East Pakistan and ignoring the Indian link between the two wings, the old Pakistan undermined its unity and integrity. Indeed, while Islam was the basis for the creation of Pakistan, the real link among all the Muslims of theoretical Pakistan was that they were all Indians in the broadest sense. There is, after all, a sort of transcendental 'curry–cricket–salwar-kamiz' unity in South Asia that distinguishes the region from countries beyond. Even after the creation of Bangladesh, the search for Pakistani roots in the Middle East and Central Asia threaten the cultural identity and security of Sindhis and Mohajirs who are not anxious to become a part of a 'Greater Pakistan' that would swallow them up.

Nehru claimed that there was little or no difference in race, language and culture in the various regions of India of peoples practising different religious faiths. Punjabi Muslims, Hindus and Sikhs had more in common compared to the separate but common bonds among Bengali Muslims, Hindus and Christians. Moreover, the historical experience of the peoples of the subcontinent, beginning with the coming of the Aryans in 1700 B.C. (perhaps even with the Harappan/Dravidian civilization that originated in 3000 B.C.) through the end of British rule, were common. The Harappan/Dravidian, Hindu, Buddhist, Muslim and British phases of Indian history were not only chronological and cumulative, but also interactive. They cannot be separated easily. As a group this historical experience was distinct from that of peoples beyond the subcontinent. History and geography had produced a broader Indian *weltanschauung* and destined the peoples of the subcontinent to live together. As Nehru questioned, why only two nations in India of Hindus and Muslims, why not several nations if religion and/or language were to be the basis of nationhood?

As the clash continued between the exclusive concept of a separate Muslim but multi-linguistic Pakistan and an inclusive concept of a united multi-religious and multi-linguistic India, there were other weaker claims at the time for nations and states based purely on language or linguistic group and culture. The Bengalis of Bengal, mainly under the Muslim leadership of Fazlur Haq and H.S. Suhrawardy, argued that Bengali language and culture constituted the basis of a single nation. Thus, according to the Bengali nationalists, while Jinnah could have his Pakistan and Gandhi and Nehru their Hindustan, there ought to be a separate independent state of Bengal consisting of Muslims and Hindus. Likewise, briefly in the 1920s, and then again briefly after Indian independence, the Tamils of the extreme south argued that the real divide in India was the great linguistic one between the Indo-Aryans of the north, of whatever religion, speaking several languages derived from Sanskrit that included Hindi, Bengali, Assamese, Oriya, Punjabi, Sindhi, Gujerati and Marathi; and the Dravidians of the south, of whatever religion, speaking laguages derived from classical Tamil that included Tamil, Telugu, Kannada and Malayalam. This formed the basis of Tamil claims for the creation of a separate independent Dravidastan.

All of these earlier concepts of nation in South Asia had a multi-something to it of varying degrees. The concept of the Indian nation was multi-religious, multi-linguistic and all-encompassing. The concept of the Pakistani nation was uni-religious but multi-linguistic. The concept of the Bengali nation was uni-linguistic but multi-religious within a specific region. And the concept of a Dravidian nation was a regional and more narrowly multi-linguistic and multi-religious than the broader Indian version. Post-independent concepts of nation and accompanying nationalisms in South

The 'Nationalities' Question in South Asia

Table 1: Separatist and Non-Separatist Ethnic Movements

Ethnicity	Type	Objective	Status
INDIA			
Muslims	religious	Pakistan independence	Achieved
Tamils	linguistic/quasi-racial	Dravidastan independence	Ended in 1967 after DMK gained state power
Kashmiris	religious/linguistic	Kashmir independence	Active, some groups wish to join Pakistan
Sikhs	religious/linguistic	Khalistan independence	Resolved internally, occasional activity
Assamese	linguistic	Assam independence	Resolved internally, occasional activity
Nagas	tribal/religious/racial	Nagaland independence	Resolved through internal statehood, sporadic activity
Mizos	tribal/religious/racial	Mizoram independence	Resolved through internal statehood
Gharos, Khasis, etc.	tribal/religious	Meghalaya	Resolved through internal statehood
Gurkhas	racial/linguistic	Gorkhaland internal statehood	Partly resolved through greater autonomy
Adivasis	tribal/caste	Jharkhand internal statehood	Somewhat active, likely to be granted
Bodos	tribal/religious/racial	Bodoland internal statehood	Active, periodic violence
PAKISTAN			
Bengalis	linguistic	Bangladesh independence	Achieved
Pashtuns	linguistic/quasi-racial	Pashtunistan independence	Ended after Soviet invasion of Afghanistan in 1979
Baluchis	linguistic/quasi-racial	Baluchistan independence	Crushed, now dissipated
Sindhis	linguistic	Sindhudesh independence	Receded or dissipated
Muhajirs	linguistic	No name	Active internal statehood
Siraikis	linguistic	No name internal statehood	Occasional demands
SRI LANKA			
Tamils	linguistic/quasi-racial	Tamil Ealam independence	Active, violence continues

Asia tended to be much more narrow. They were usually uni-linguistic and uni-religious as in the case of the Kashmiris, Sikhs, Assamese, Pashtuns and to a lesser extent, Sindhis. The major exceptions were the demands for identification based on Hindutva by Hindu nationalists that was uni-religious but multi-linguistic, and the demand for a Tamil Ealam by militant Tamils in Sri Lanka that was uni-linguistic but multi-religious.

THE DYNAMICS OF NATIONAL IDENTITIES

An examination of the dynamics of the two successful independence movements in South Asia will show the nature of overlapping identities and the changing emphasis among these identities. When Muslims ruled Hindus in large parts of India for over five centuries between 1300 AD and 1857 AD, there was a great deal of social and political interaction, of communal intermingling through intermarriages or through Hindu conversions to the Islamic faith, so that the two religious groups became racially and culturally similar. Cultural and linguistic differences became more regional rather than religious, though religion still dictated some major differences in social practices within the same regions. For example, while religion may have divided Muslim and Hindu Punjabis or Bengalis; race, language and culture also united them.

It was only towards the end of the nineteenth century, that 'Indian' Muslim political elites began to perceive themselves distinctly as a separate nation of 'Muslim' Indians that could find salvation only in the creation of an Islamic Pakistan. The founding of the Anglo–Mohammedan College in 1877 (later Aligarh Muslim University) by Sir Sayyid Ahmad Khan and then of the All-India Muslim League in 1906 gave impetus to the development of a separate Muslim identity. These Muslim elites, primarily from the Hindi-speaking Hindu heartland of the United and Central Province of British India (the provinces where Muslims were a minority and felt threatened by the Hindu majority), then began to emphasize Muslim religious symbols and identity in order to mobilize support in the 1930s for the two nation theory of Mohammed Ali Jinnah. After Partition, many Muslims were left behind in India as a more insecure and even greater religious minority to face a more hostile and even greater Hindu majority.

Following the breakup of Pakistan in 1971, Indian Muslim identity became fundamentally different from what it was before and after Partition. Bangladesh now represented only Muslim Bengalis, and Pakistan could no longer claim to represent the Muslims of the entire subcontinent. Moreover, the size of the Muslim populations of India, Pakistan and Bangladesh were now each approximately the same. Pakistan had become a territorial state consisting of 'sons-of-the-soil', namely, Punjabis (including Siraikis who claim to be different and have demanded a separate province), Baluchis, Pashtuns, and Sindhis. The Muhajirs, who

The 'Nationalities' Question in South Asia

had migrated from India to Pakistan, found themselves residents of Sindh but in reality 'provinceless'. The Sindhis do not want these Urdu- and Gujarati-speaking immigrant Muslims from Uttar Pradesh, Madhya Pradesh, Bihar, Gujarat and Maharashtra, although Muhajirs now occupy and control the three main cities of Sindh: Karachi, Hyderabad and Sukkur. They want to link these cities to create their own internal state in the heart of Sindh, leaving the native Sindhis the barren countryside. The plight of the Biharis who were driven out of Bangladesh after its creation, and that of other Indian Muslim emigres to Pakistan, have convinced most of the 140 million Indian Muslims who remain in India that their future lies in India, even if many may cheer for Pakistan during India–Pakistan cricket matches.

Again, the shifting nature of ethnic or national identity may be seen in the variations of Bengali nationalism in the twentieth century. At what point did 'Muslim' Bengalis who had identified with Pakistan, become 'Bengali' Muslims who would accept nothing less than an independent Bangladesh?[2] After all, as mentioned above, during the 'Pakistan' movement that paralleled the Indian nationalist movement, some Bengali leaders had toyed with the idea of a united Hindu–Muslim Bengal state, separate from the proposed independent states of India and Pakistan. A united Bengal concept may have briefly crossed the minds of some Bengali nationalists on either side in West Bengal and East Pakistan during the struggle for Bangladesh in 1971. Although Indian military intervention helped create Bangladesh, the possibility that Hindu Bengali nationalists in West Bengal may also want to join this 'Bengal Nation' must have surely worried Indian policy-makers as well. Underlying this outlook for a greater Bengal state was the belief that language and culture superseded religious differences. India's West Bengal has a population of 60 million, of whom about 10 million are Muslims. The total Bengali-speaking population of both Bangladesh and West Bengal in India today number almost 180 million, and would have constituted a powerful state if a united independent Bengal had been forged in 1947. However, reunification schemes for a 'Greater Bengal' have not been heard since the creation of Bangladesh in December 1971. This may be because Bengali Hindus do not wish to be a minority, albeit a significant one, in a larger Muslim majority Greater Bengal. They would rather be a more insignificant linguistic minority but as part of a much larger Hindu majority India. Similarly, while Bengali Muslims may want a united Greater Bengal where they are a religious majority, they do not wish to be part of the Muslim minority in a Greater India with a Hindu majority.

When looking at the Kashmiri problem, it is important to recognize that the self-perceptions of Kashmiri Muslims have fluctuated between four identities over the last half century. The first identity may be found in the ideology of the 'Kashmiriyat' that incorporates Valley Muslims, Hindu

Pandits, Hindu Dogras and Ladakhi Buddhists into a regional whole.[3] This perception of a distinct Kashmiri identity has generated its own demands for separate nationhood. At one time or another, Hindu Pandits and Dogras and Valley Muslims have all sought an independent multi-religious state of Kashmir. The second Kashmir identity is marked by perceptions of the broader Indian secular heritage that prevailed among many Kashmiris. This outlook was best ennunciated and exemplified by the Kashmiri Pandit, Prime Minister Jawaharlal Nehru, but was also shared by other Valley Kashmiri Muslim leaders such as Sheikh Abdullah. The third identity may be found in the rise of Muslim nationalism in Kashmir that makes some Kashmiri Muslims feel more a part of Islamic Pakistan. This implies a return to the two nation theory of Jinnah. Kashmiri Muslims are Pakistanis because they are Muslims first. The fourth emerging Kashmiri identity arises from the spread of transnational Islamic fundamentalist values into the state that makes Kashmiris part of the broader Islamic world west of the subcontinent in West and Central Asia.

Transitions in a group's self-identity may also be seen in the milder Sikh resistance to being classified as a subdivision of Hinduism, that eventually turned into a clear-cut rejection of Hindu absorption, and then to the newer identification of being a separate religious group that needed to live within an independent state. Indeed, the dramatic turnaround in the mid-1980s from Sikh perceptions of themselves as staunch Indian nationalists (together with Hindu perceptions of Sikhs as the 'sword arm' of Hinduism) into the subsequent state of Hindu–Sikh conflict in Indian Punjab, is quite revealing about the transforming nature of ethnicity and conflict in South Asia.

It is important to recall that the relations among Punjabi Muslims, Sikhs and Hindus were cooperative and cordial under the British Raj. Indeed, the Punjabis of all three religious persuasions constituted the bulk and the backbone of the British Indian Army. They had fought shoulder-to-shoulder in two world wars. Even during the mass slaughter and migration of Hindus, Muslims and Sikhs in the Punjab, after the province was partitioned in 1947, members of the three religious communities in the British Indian Army remained disciplined despite the emotional stress produced by the havoc in the Punjab. Since Partition, Indo–Pakistani wars have in some ways tended to resemble a civil war among Punjabis since the Pakistani armed forces are about 80 percent Muslim Punjabi, and the Indian armed forces have been almost one-third Hindu and Sikh Punjabi. From one ethno-regional group, Punjabis have become three separate religious ethnic groups.

The above examples indicate that religious antagonism may override racial, cultural and linguistic ties. However, the past record of cooperation and goodwill among Hindus, Muslims and Sikhs in Bengal, Kashmir and Punjab suggest that these positive ties may also be restored given the right attitudes and conditions.

TERRITORIAL SECESSIONS AND RECOGNITION OF NEW STATES

All the states of South Asia may fulfill much of the broader concept of nation most of the time, but in the narrower sense they constitute a political conglomeration of several nations bounded by individual states. They all fulfill the criteria of a state, albeit multi-ethnic ones. However, today there are several 'nations' in South Asia such as the Muslim Kashmiris, Sikh Punjabis, Hindu Assamese, mainly Hindu Tamils, and Muslim Sindhis all demanding separate independent states. Except for the Assamese and Sindhis; nationalism and the demand for separate nationhood is derived from a combination of language, culture and religion. In the case of separatist demands in Assam, Sindh, Baluchistan and Pashtunistan; the separatist nationalism is based mainly in language and culture since their nationalism is not linked to their self-perceptions of being Muslim or Hindu, or from an anti-Hindu or anti-Muslim reaction. This tends to make their secessionist drives relatively weaker than those of Muslim Kashmiris, Sikh Punjabis, Christian Nagas and Mizos, and Hindu Tamils who tend to constitute hostile religious minorities in mainly Hindu India and Buddhist Sri Lanka. Belonging also to a religious minority accentuates their consciousness of being part of a separate nation requiring separate statehood.

The support and promotion in some international circles for an independent Kashmir could have grave consequences for the stability of South Asia. If Kashmir is separated from India under international pressure, it could lead to a weakening in the position of the 135 million Muslims left behind in India who will have to live through another partition on the Muslim question.[4] More likely, Kashmiri separation would unleash a Hindu–Muslim communal bloodbath in India that would be impossible to control. Kashmiri independence could be followed by independence being wrested by other Indian states. Aware of this possibility, India has determinedly resisted the Kashmiri independence struggle and is prepared to do so indefinitely. On the other hand, the hardcore Muslim insurgents seem determined to continue with their 'jihad' for its own sake whatever the hope and the outcome. With some exceptions in the extreme southern and eastern Indian states of Tamilnadu, Kerala and Assam; there is no indication among political leaders and parties in India of a willingness to compromise on the territorial status quo in Kashmir. While overseas supporters of an independent Kashmir may argue that India is exaggerating the prospects about its own disintegration if it gives up Kashmir, Indian leaders and the attentive public see things differently and act accordingly.

Indian Muslims, whatever their private sentiments toward Pakistan and Kashmir, publicly do not support the secession of Kashmir. But they are concerned about being held 'hostage' to the actions of Kashmiri Muslims.[5] The Hindu nationalist Bharatiya Janata Party has declared on many occasions that the Kashmiri Muslims' decision to leave India would reflect adversely on the loyalty of all Indian Muslims. Even some leaders of the Janata Dal and Congress party have made veiled references to such an interpretation. In response to some of these statements, the Imam Sayyid Bukhari of Jama Masjid in Delhi stated that Indian Muslims can do no more than support the Indian position on Kashmir.[6] To expect them to do more, or to be held responsible for the actions of the Kashmiris, would be unfair. However, the situation itself may be beyond any party or leader's control once frenzied Hindu–Muslim communal violence is unleashed.

On the other hand, any international decision to maintain the status quo in Kashmir will be resented in Pakistan. Pakistan feels that it was cheated at the time of Partition when it failed to acquire Muslim-majority Kashmir. Although Pakistan seems willing to maintain the territorial status quo on all other cases of secessionist demands, it insists on making an exception of Kashmir. However, the more important question today may be not what Pakistan considers its moral or legal right to Kashmir, but the probable consequences for the rest of the subcontinent in tampering with existing *de facto* international boundaries. Indeed, the resolution of the Kashmir issue by granting it independence or even merger with Pakistan, may prove fatal to Pakistan itself since its unity is largely fostered by its confrontation with India over Kashmir. Unlike the rationale for India which is based on its long existence, the rationale for Pakistan has never been so clear, either at the time of partition or today. Pakistan is the antithesis of India in that India does not have to justify itself while Pakistan does, and its search for a positive identity has not ceased.

The attempted creation of an independent Khalistan out of the existing Indian Punjab, as demanded during the 1980s by a segment of the Sikhs, proved to be no less complicated than the creation of Pakistan out of India in 1947. Thousands of Sikhs, especially in business and professional fields, are scattered throughout India outside Punjab. About 45 percent of the population of Punjab – 60 percent of most of its major cities – remains Hindu in spite of the second 'internal' partition of Indian Punjab in 1966 when the Punjabi Hindu majority areas were separated into the new states of Haryana and Himachal Pradesh. Since the Hindus remaining in Punjab did not want to be part of an independent Sikh state of Khalistan, there was the question of a third division of Punjab and the inevitable mass migration of millions of Sikhs and Hindus across new frontiers if Khalistan had become a reality. And it goes without saying that there would have been extensive communal bloodshed, as in the case of the division of Punjab in 1947 between India and Pakistan. In that partition, about 10 million Muslims, Sikhs and Hindus were caught on the 'wrong' side of the new frontier. Amidst widespread communal massacres, they were forced to migrate to the other side within a month. About half a million civilians lost their lives in the 1947 partition of the Punjab.

The potential loss of Assam would also be crucial to the Indian economy and for the political stability of India. An independent Assam would imply that the entire northeast sector of India would be cut off eventually from India. It would open a Pandora's box of new independent states – Nagaland, Mizoram, Meghalaya, Manipur and Tripura. Sikkim, located within the narrow corridor between China and Bangladesh, would be difficult to retain within India. Assam would also be the first Hindu majority state to gain independence and could trigger similar movements in the other Hindu majority states of Tamil Nadu, Karnataka, Telengana and elsewhere.

In Pakistan, the dilemma of Sindh is that democratization and decentralization may not resolve the problem of power-sharing among the Sindhis, Muhajirs, Pashtuns and Punjabis. It may instead lead to greater economic and political power for the Muhajirs and Punjabis resident in Sindh. On the other hand, an independent Sindhudesh may create a 'Bihari' problem that would be of greater magnitude than that which occurred in Bangladesh. Following the independence of Bangladesh in December 1971, over 4 million Urdu-speaking Muslims from the Indian state of Bihar who had migrated to East Pakistan in 1947, were accused of having fought with West Pakistan's military against independence. Bangladeshis considered them to be Pakistanis and asked that they be repatriated. By the mid 1980s, the Pakistan government had repatriated about 1.8 million Biharis to Pakistan, nearly all of whom joined the other Muhajirs in Sindh.[7] But the Sindhis resisted these new immigrants unsuccessfully. They have since refused to accept more Biharis as this implied a further addition to the Urdu-speaking Muhajirs in Sindh. According to unofficial estimates, there are still some 2.5 million Biharis in Bangladesh who wish to be repatriated. Thus, the existing 12 million Muhajirs are not likely to be absorbed easily in any independent Sindhudesh, and they are not likely to be accepted back into India either.

Partitioning Sri Lanka into separate Tamil and Sinhalese states may appear relatively simple since the Sri Lankan Tamils (not including the Plantation Tamils) are confined mainly to the northeast sector of the island. However, in the highly contested east–central sector which contains both Sri Lankan Tamils and Tamil-speaking Moors, the members of the two groups cannot be easily separated. The domino effect elsewhere in South Asia of a breaking up of Sri Lanka cannot, likewise, be underestimated. Most immediately, it could lead to a revival of separatist sentiments in neighboring Tamilnadu.

BALKANIZATION VERSUS CONFEDERALISM

The dilemmas posed by narrow versus broad concepts of nationhood, of state integration versus disintegration, must be confronted in South Asia. As in Europe where the recognition of new states led to the complete disintegration of the Soviet Union and Yugoslavia, the recognition of new states in South Asia could lead to even greater disastrous consequences. First, it would generate new problems arising from new boundaries and new minorities. Second, the recognition of the above states could lead to a chain reaction elsewhere leading to further instability in India and Pakistan and, to a lesser extent, Sri Lanka. Third, the level of inter-ethnic bloodshed and mass refugee flows would generate a humanitarian nightmare in South Asia that would exceed that in Europe in the early 1990s.

Countering the trend towards state disintegration arising from ethnic nationalism, are efforts to promote a regional confederation of states. Such an agenda may be seen as a method of inter-state conflict management and of optimizing economic development and growth through the consolidation of political systems and economic markets. Beginning in 1983, a regional organization, the South Asian Association for Regional Cooperation (SAARC), was created which was intended as a confidence-building system in South Asia, by encouraging greater economic and social cooperation, and eventually political cooperation. The more optimistic supporters of SAARC would like to see the organization grow into a larger confederation or 'super state' along the lines of the European Union. However, the 1983 New Delhi Declaration that formalized SAARC made it clear that this was essentially intended to be an intergovernmental organization, and not a supranational organization. The development of SAARC may well prove to be the necessary antidote to the growth of narrow nationalisms and the potential for territorial fragmentation in the existing states of South Asia.

One major obstacle to the development of SAARC has been the uneven distribution of population and resources across the participating states, a problem that is more acute in South Asia than in Europe or Southeast Asia. The 2000 population of India was one billion compared to 145 million in Pakistan, 125 million in Bangladesh, 22 million in Nepal, 18 million in Sri Lanka, 1.8 million in Bhutan and 0.3 million in Maldives. The ratio of the dominant state to the rest was one billion to 310 million in the SAARC group, compared to Indonesia's population of 200 million to the rest of ASEAN's population of 155 million. Consequently, the smaller states within SAARC have been concerned about domination by the largest state, India; and the largest state, India, had corresponding concerns that the smaller states would constantly gang up against it.

SAARC has confined its discussions to economic and social arenas only. As a matter of policy, it excludes all contentious security and political issues which might reduce its meetings to rounds of accusations and recriminations. Mainly due to India's insistence, SAARC also attempts to keep the military of major external powers away from the region, which is again quite unlike the ASEAN approach which perceives the role of external military powers in the region as essential to the maintenance of strategic stability.

The strategy of excluding all contentious political issues from the deliberations of SAARC may have been intended primarily to exclude the dispute over Kashmir between India and Pakistan. Inclusion of the Kashmir dispute almost certainly would have paralyzed the organization and led to its early demise. Issues regarding the Farrakha Barrage dispute between India and Bangladesh, the Tamil secessionist struggle in Sri Lanka, and Indo–Nepalese dispute regarding overland trade routes through India, were also precluded from the SAARC agenda. India's differences with these countries over these issues were resolved in the 1990s through bilateral negotiations.

In general, the inability of SAARC to address and resolve contentious security and political issues within the region may be one reason that it has remained relatively weak and ineffective. While economic and social cooperation was expected to mitigate security and political issues, the failure to address these questions effectively through bilateral negotiations has slowed progress on greater economic and social cooperation. The main obstacle to progress in SAARC has been caused by the Indo–Pakistani impasse on Kashmir. In order to bypass Indo–Pakistani diplomatic confrontations, faster 'subregional' cooperation is under way in the northeast among India, Bangladesh, Nepal and Bhutan as well as India and Sri Lanka.

Another major concern among the smaller members of SAARC is India's natural economic dominance. After all, India alone has a population that is about seven times the population of the next largest state in the region, with an economy that is also almost as large in relative terms. Thus, it may be argued by the other members of SAARC; especially Nepal, Sri Lanka, Bhutan and Maldives; that any attempt at regional economic integration through the removal of all trade barriers would cause the other economies to be overwhelmed by the Indian economy, much more than the Indonesian economy would in ASEAN. At the same time, Bangladesh, Nepal and Sri Lanka are anxious to exploit the large Indian market and have pushed for transforming the existing South Asian Preferential Trading Arrangement (SAPTA) into the South Asian Free Trade Association (SAFTA), a customs-free union.

In keeping with its belief that its identity lies west of the subcontinent, Pakistan prefers confederal arrangements with the Muslim countries of the Economic Cooperation Organization (ECO) bloc rather than with the multireligious countries of SAARC. The ECO began as a successor to the Regional Cooperation for Development, the economic wing of the Central Treaty Organization (CENTO) between Turkey, Iran and Pakistan. The ECO seemed lifeless until the Soviet Central Asian republics became free and became members. One Pakistani analyst projected the eventual formation of a 'United States of Hilal', a large Muslim confederation that would stretch from Pakistan to Turkey and encompass the newly independent Muslim states that emerged out of the former Soviet Union.[8] In a sense, this would be the logical extension of the concept of 'Pakistan' beyond the subcontinent, Pakistan itself having been created as a 'homeland' for Indian Muslims within the subcontinent.

But Pakistan's strategy of linking itself with the states of West and Central Asia also carries some weaknesses. Afghanistan needs to be stabilized in order to establish road and rail communications with the Central Asian states, a prospect that remains uncertain despite the overthrow of President Najibullah and the victory of the various factions of the Afghan mujahideen in April 1992 and, more recently, the Taliban.[9] As in Afghanistan, stability in Tajikistan remained uncertain at the end of 1999. The rivalry between Turkey, Iran and Saudi Arabia for influence among the new Central Asian republics has further undermined the prospects for unity. There are also other socio-economic and demographic problems, related to considerable variations in wealth and populations, that stand in the way of fostering an Islamic confederation that goes beyond loose economic ties.

If it is premature to establish a full-fledged confederation in South Asia, perhaps the countries of South Asia should agree on two fundamental principles: that the existing international borders, whether good or bad, legal or illegal are inviolable; and that none of the states in the region will aid and abet each other's separatist movements. India may find proposals for maintaining the territorial status quo in South Asia to its liking. Pakistan will surely insist on making an exception of Kashmir, especially since it feels that it had a moral right to Muslim-majority Kashmir at the time of independence. But the reality is that India can enforce the status quo in Kashmir by sheer weight of its military power. It has done so in the past and can continue to do so. To complicate matters, many Kashmiris who want independence aspire to a state that would include Azad Kashmir, the part of Kashmir currently under Pakistani control. Giving the latter up would hardly be acceptable to Pakistan after fifty years. Readjusting the complex ethnic distributions of South Asia through territorial changes is an impossible task. The goal of reconfiguring the countries in the region into several smaller states would inevitably carry an incalculably high human cost, a consequence that should be avoided in the interest of maintaining stability in the region.

NOTES

1 Since 1920, British India was legally a state separate from Great Britain and represented as such at the League of Nations and the United Nations.
2 Urmila Phadnis, *Ethnicity and Nation-Building in South Asia* (New Delhi and Newbury Park, CA: Sage Publications, 1989), 15. For an in-depth analysis of conditions and events leading to the creation of Bangladesh, see Richard Sisson and Leo E. Rose, *War and Secession: India, Pakistan and the Creation of Bangladesh* (Berkeley: University of California Press, 1990).

3 See Riyaz Punjabi's chapter, 'Kashmir's Bruised Identity,' in Raju G. C. Thomas, ed., *Perspectives on Kashmir: The Roots of Conflict in South Asia* (Boulder, Colorado: Westview Press, 1992).
4 See Ashutosh Varshney, 'Three Compromised Nationalisms: Why Kashmir Has Been A Problem', in Thomas, ibid., 191–234.
5 See Omar Khalidi, 'Kashmir and Muslim Politics in India', in Thomas, ibid., 276–284.
6 See Khalidi, ibid., 281–282.
7 See Hasan Askari-Rizvi, 'The Bihari Problem', *The Nation*, 21 November 1991.
8 This view was expressed to me during my conversation with a Pakistani journalist during my visit to Karachi in February 1992. He was at the time on his way to attend the conference of the ECO in Teheran. Even if much of this is wishful thinking, there is an influential group of politicians, bureaucrats and intellectuals who feel that Pakistan's ultimate destiny lies in this direction.
9 A much more optimistic assessment than my own is provided by Maqbool Ahmad Bhatty, 'Prospects for Cooperation with Central Asia', *The Nation*, 8 October 1991. Bhatty points out some of same obstacles mentioned here – the instability of Afghanistan and uneven levels of per capita incomes – but feels that these problems can be overcome eventually. See report by Hugh Pope, 'Rudderless Tajikstan Heads for the Rocks', *Independent* (London), 27 June 1992.

PART III

DEVELOPMENT

Chapter 10

Economic Crisis, Momentary Autonomy and Policy Reform: Liberalisation in India 1991-95

Ronald J. Herring and N. Chandra Mohan

LIBERALISATION AND POLITICAL POWER

The politics of liberalisation is the politics of moving the boundary between authority and market as allocative mechanisms. Any existing pattern of state intervention must in some sense represent a vector sum of political forces that have been operative over time. Therefore, whatever the source of economic reform, moving the boundary towards markets logically produces new configurations of economic power, and thus indirectly political power in society.[1] Moreover, economic liberalisation can be expected to redistribute political power as a consequence of the redistribution of economic power. India fits neither scenario clearly.

Analysis of shifts in political power must distinguish between structural power and the consequences of political behaviour. What Charles Lindblom called the 'privileged position of business' – the structural power of capital in Marxian discourse – is clearly different from the ability of business groups to lobby for particular policies.[2] Indeed, structural power means having one's interest served without having to make a fuss politically. Liberalising governments often invest so much in the success of reform – to legitimate the pain of adjustment – that the structural power of capital increases. 'Business confidence' becomes a meta-agenda of regime praxis. At the same time, incorporation of business associations in the policy process and business purchase of influence through political contributions, for example, are clearly separable from structural power. However, electoral politics in India are unlikely to reflect class power in any direct way. Instead, factional and individual rivalries, primordial divisions, and local distributive issues remain typically more important than particulars of national economic policy.

This essay argues that no redistribution of political power caused the redirection of economic policy in India. Nor is there evidence of so significant a redistribution of wealth that class-political forces have been realigned. However, the structural power of both domestic and international capital have increased because of the legitimating practices of a liberalising regime. Simultaneously, a weakening of the Centre through economic liberalisation has altered the distribution of power between Delhi and the states – a process which is likely to sustain liberalisation politically.

Instead of a redirection of economic policy due to new political coalitions or political power shifts, in India it was a severe external payments crisis which opened a political space for a technical redirection of economic policy. This space was occupied most prominently by the Finance Ministry with a significant infusion of personnel and ideas – along with pressure – from international financial institutions. International transfusion counted more than a popular mandate or realignment of active political forces. Subsequently, as the crisis ebbed, the ensuing dynamics began to exhibit the common dialectic of technical and popular politics of the form predicted by Karl Polanyi – of society placing constraints on the market as the final arbiter of life chances.[3]

Liberalisation in India is politically problematic because interventionist developmentalism was the master narrative of state–economy relations from the beginning. In a genuine democracy, state autonomy is always difficult to come by. Halting and modest attempts at liberalising reform in the 1980s were largely stalled by societal resistance. Crisis-induced momentary autonomy changed these exploratory initiatives into a serious national agenda in 1991. As the resulting policy changes evoked both perceived and real opposition to the effects of adjustment, policy retreat indicated shifts of power within the state – from the Finance Ministry to the Prime Minister's Office. The pressures of electoral politics on a vulnerable regime and intra-party challenges to the prime minister's position weakened the reform initiative. Rather than reform redistributing power, at this stage (roughly 1993–1995), politics began redistributing the reforms.

We will first discuss the conceptual and methodological conundrum of assessing redistribution, then analyse the origins of liberalisation, and finally discuss the politics of reform over the fairly brief period of 1991–1995. To the extent that one can draw a broad picture from this period, it would be true to say that the major structural redistribution of power in India since liberalisation efforts began in the 1980s was from politicians to technocrats and back to politicians.

CAVEATS: CONCEPTUAL AND TEMPORAL

Delineating specifically political effects of structural adjustment in India presents two problems: one generic and one specific to the national case. On the specifics, it is premature to assess effects of structural change in the political economy when the presumed causal force is more process than end state. The process itself is subject to the political vicissitudes of competitive democracy. Liberalisation in India is not the holistic 'neo-liberal package' often condemned by the left and promoted by the 'Washington consensus'.[4] The very distance between India's extensively controlled political economy and neo-liberal orthodoxy assured that the national incarnation would be a hybrid. A reform package was cobbled together, put in place piecemeal and modified over time, as a result of shifting political dynamics. The autonomy of the reform process as causal force is thus in doubt; it belongs as much to the left side of the equation as to the right side.

Political practice indicates how fluid the reform process has been. Former prime minister of India Narasimha Rao, for example, constantly reassured foreign investors that the 'changes are permanent'. Though nothing is permanent – certainly not policy, especially in a vigorous and volatile democracy – the linkage to ideational structural change was critical. If no one believed the reforms were permanent, they would not be.[5] Changes in ideational structure, to the extent they remain in place, will be the most important enduring consequences of liberalisation. That is, whatever the short-run movements of political power configurations, the long-dominant assumption of the appropriateness of a planned and regulated economy has been undermined. The 'great transformation' ideologically has been to depoliticise public policy about the economy, at least relative to the pre-existing levels.[6]

Secondly, even in the minimal temporal sense, we need to allow for enough time for the dust to settle in India. The prime mover of reform, Finance Minister Manmohan Singh, stated in a press interview in 1995 that 'We have completed 60 percent of the agenda, though we have a lot of unfinished business.'[7] Reforms had been on the agenda since at least 1980, but actual policy change was limited.[8] Since 1991 there has been relatively more commitment to a coherent and comprehensive package of change. But the stress is on relativity: liberalisation in India remains contested, limited in objectives, and subject to subtle shifts in regime tactics. Distributive effects across sectors, regions, classes and households are not yet clear. To the extent that distribution of political power is derivative of changes in the structure of the economy, such changes are difficult to assess before significant economic change has taken hold.

The political praxis of oppositional forces likewise has assured the reformation of reforms. The strategy has been one of continually searching for vulnerabilities in the government's policy in the hope of finding exploitable weaknesses – of feared, imagined or real pain in society. To the extent that rational opportunism describes political behaviour, this testing the margins of liberalisation for niches is likely to be a more permanent characteristic than any structural re-alignment.

These points are not merely excuses based on the youth of the reforms, but rather an assertion of the importance of process. Certainly not everything is up for grabs; meta-themes such as 'business confidence' constrain certain avenues of change in ways neither fully apparent nor subject to political referendum.[9] Nevertheless, as noted by Anthony Downs, the political process surrounding policy change produces new coalitions and new mobilisation.[10] In a democratic polity, a permanent redistribution of power is unlikely. As Atul Kohli has argued, the earlier Indian reforms were blunted by the reassertion of political populism.[11] The reforms of the 1990s are likely to remain suspended between agents asserting technical rationality and those wedded to situational and conditional populism as political practice. In comparative terms, this outcome is a function of the deep institutionalisation of democracy in India and the pluralist power base of the Indian state.

ORIGINS OF LIBERALISATION

Liberalisation came to India not through electoral endorsement of an 'open economy', as in the case of Sri Lanka, but as crisis response.[12] Nevertheless, even in crisis there is choice; the Rao government's choices reflected the accretion of pressures and ideas which made the old regime untenable. The origins of the reform episode then reflected less social choice than crisis management; as a result, the reforms were more technocratic than democratic. The crisis allowed the triumph of a policy discourse – quite limited in distribution, but gaining ground – which held the Nehruvian consensus on planning in a closed economy as less and less tenable. Popular receptivity to the new policy was heavily dependent on a negative verdict on the previous system. The currently hegemonic theory-in-practice bemoans independent India's weak historic economic performance and attributes the causes to an overly interventionist state.[13]

There are two logics of state economic interventionism: one a rationalist planning mode, the other a defensive reaction mode. The 'license-permit-quota *raj*' to which liberalisation was a response was built in both modes. Intervention in the defensive reaction mode follows Karl Polanyi's historical observation that 'market and regulation grew up together'.[14] In Polanyi's vision, societal vulnerability drives intervention to 're-embed' markets in society. It is clear that a political economy of extensive intervention may be built on precisely this base, through the politics of protection from market dynamics and responses to 'market failure'.[15]

A positive theory of intervention was consonant with India's historical political development. The attraction of the developmentalist argument for intervention – including central planning – seemed clear in the formative period of mobilisation for independence. The success of the Soviet Union at a time when the capitalist world was sunk in depression, combined with the dominant views on economic development (before Gershenkron), indicated that planning was the way to catch up. Colonialism added two important elements: a pervasive strong state and – the legacy of backwardness – an acute awareness of national inferiority in a hierarchical world system. Moreover, opposition to colonial rule had symbolically, politically and economically centred the concept of *swadeshi* (self-reliance). It was understood that dependence on imports from England was a linchpin of subordination. The 'imperialism of free trade' provided a counter to the attractiveness of an open economy.[16] The Keynesian revolution in theory and policy in the 1930s further legitimated the notion of state responsibility for aggregate economic outcomes at the normative level, even in capitalist societies, and bolstered the accepted efficaciousness of the tool kit of intervention by the modern state.

Self-reliance as policy objective meant that India was notoriously tough on transnational corporations (TNCs) in the post-independence period, leading to low rates of foreign direct investment which were infinitesimally small until 1980, and meagre in comparative terms thereafter. The strategy was one of import substitution in a virtually closed economy.[17] The closed economy was legitimated not only by developmental logic, but was consonant with holdovers from the colonial period, especially the administrative apparatus created during World War II. With low internal rates of savings, this relative absence of external investment was almost certain to depress growth rates in most models, whether Marxist or classical. Likewise, the Indian government's commitment to self-reliance resulted in very conservative international borrowing behaviour until the 1980s, further restricting the capital circuit. Despite impressive achievements in industrialisation, protection allowed infant industries the luxury of never growing up and soaked consumers with monopolistic high prices and shoddy products by international standards.

Though the Nehruvian consensus on planning proved historically robust, even in the heyday of Congress party hegemony there were cracks. Nehru's vision was contradicted by first the powerful faction in the Congress party associated with Patel, then the Swatantra (Freedom) Party, and finally by Kamraj and regional bosses of the Congress in the states. There were always dissonant voices.[18] When Nehru died in 1964, these contradictions asserted themselves: Congress electoral success declined, first in the states in 1967 and finally at the Centre. As modest growth failed to deliver on the noble promises of the founders, much of the 'developmental' activity of the state became politically necessary public consumption – in effect a political consequence of the failure of the growth state. Prospects for growth dimmed as populism consumed resources at the expense of investment.[19]

The weakening hegemony of Nehru's party did not translate automatically into political support for dismantling the 'Nehruvian consensus'. Resistance to reforming the state's relation to industry was not all irrationality, inertia and statism, but was rooted as well in contestatory democratic politics. Indira Gandhi's split of the Congress party in 1969 relied on populist imagery to reinforce her central claim to distinctiveness and socialist credentials – 'abolish poverty' (*garibi hatao*). Nationalisation of banks and restrictions on monopoly practices and use of foreign exchange tightened the regulatory regime significantly. The victory of the Janata coalition in 1977 gave a boost to the notion of propping up village industries, handicrafts, and traditional small-scale sector activity. Janata's industrial policy in 1977 engaged the state in active promotion of decentralisation, arguing that previous policy had concentrated industry in the metropoles.[20]

When Indira Gandhi returned from electoral exile in 1980, she expressed growing concern with evidence of India's international and comparative failures. Industrialisation in particular had slowed down. The incentive structure in industry was clearly working backward: entrepreneurs were trading licenses rather than producing anything. The large and affluent expatriate community was critical to the feedback loop as well. Their perspective was comparative, and they found India a bad place to do business in comparison to the rest of the world. Mrs. Gandhi demonstrated a clear intent to reform in the composition of the committees she set up, but little was accomplished. There were no serious trade reforms until 1985, nor a significant export initiative and import licensing remained restrictive until the crisis of 1991.

Serious attempts at liberalisation began with her son, Rajiv Gandhi. Like his mother, Rajiv Gandhi was assassinated before his liberalisation initiatives bore fruit, but retreat was forced in any event by vigorous reaction of popular political forces, particularly labour.[21] Rajiv Gandhi's modernisation mandate ended when the specifics of liberalisation became matters of political discourse and the Congress lost key elections. Domestic political dynamics persistently weakened the gradual retreat from interventionism that was gaining adherents within the state.

The momentary autonomy necessary for these elements within the state to assert their agenda was provided by the external payments crisis of 1991, not electoral redistribution of power.[22] The financial crisis reflected the conjunctural effects of the Gulf War: its US$ 3.3 billion shock, increased debt servicing from the expansionary 1980s, and erosion of confidence of international bankers – which together left India with enough hard currency for thirteen days of imports officially (compared to 5.2 months a decade earlier, in 1980–81) – and less unofficially. The balance of payments deficit as a percentage of GDP increased from 1.7 in 1980–81 to 3.5 in 1990–91 and in dollar amounts from $2.1 billion to an official $8 billion (the reality being closer to $10 billion).[23] Perceptually, there were no options beyond the controversial sale of gold and turning to the IMF.

The external nature of the payments crisis that brought India to reform and the external source of the policy model both served to give international ideas, actors and forces primacy in explaining reform. Internationalisation of the policy dialogue had been increasing for at least a decade, however.

To both politicians and bureaucrats, international comparisons, particularly to South Korea, provided legitimation for reform.[24] India had once exported machine tools and steel to South Korea, but by the 1980s found itself importing the same items from South Korea. South Korea had become a major force in the markets in United States, while India remained marginal. More generally in comparative terms, India's share of world trade had declined from around 2 percent in 1950 to 0.5 percent in 1989, while Korea's had risen to 2.1 percent. China, likewise, surpassed India in terms of share of world trade.[25] The comparative perspective illustrated that unlike other Asian nations, India's industrial products were not competitive in price or quality in the international market.

Perestroika in the Soviet Union simultaneously delegitimised the primary model of state-led industrialisation, autarky and planning. As important, the decline, desertion and eventual demise of the Soviet Union removed for India an external market and source of imports which was sustained not by competitiveness but by geopolitical alliance.[26] The shift in worldview was thus supported by structural logic in the periphery. With the disintegration of the communist bloc and reintegration of its parts into the global market economy; India correctly perceived that marginalisation, particularly with regard to foreign direct investment, was a real threat.[27]

At the level of ideas, then, the Nehruvian consensus eroded under extraordinary external pressures at the end of the decade of the 1980s which culminated in the payments crisis of 1991. With regard to the change in ideas, the notion that India was doing badly in comparative terms was crucial. It is useful to consider that record as an independent cause of liberalisation. No new specifically liberal coalition is necessary[28] to explain reform if the economy does so badly that virtually any change from the status quo ante will draw support or quiescence from erstwhile veto blocs in the political economy.

Leaving aside the unmeasurable underground economy,[29] the famous 'Hindu rate of growth' (a phrase that originated with the late Raj Krishna) of 3.5 percent per annum from 1950–80 was comparatively weak but not catastrophic. The 'Third World' was growing at about 4.9 percent per annum over the same period, and the world economy at 4.1 percent per annum. India's figures in per capita terms look weaker comparatively because population growth has been relatively high. Industrial growth from 1950–1965 was a robust 7 percent per annum. Concern that the 'license-permit-quota *raj*' was stifling growth focused on the drop in the rate of growth in industry after 1965 – to 3.5 percent in the 1965–1980 period. Yet with roughly the same state and a tighter regulatory regime, the industrial growth rate increased in the high-spending 1980s to 7.9 percent per annum.[30]

A very rough periodisation makes evident, then, that India did reasonably well in terms of growth until the mid-1960s over a period when the world economy was anomalously robust, experienced a decline after 1965, especially in industrial growth, and experienced a boom in the 1980s due to unsustainable fiscal deficits, external debt and a balance of payments crunch which in 1991 constituted the proximate causes of liberalisation. Unlike the boom states of Latin America, India was conservative in its international financial behaviour before the 1980s. The 1980s look very much like Reaganomics in the United States: rapid expansion built on an unsustainable expansion of debt, both internal and external – effectively a Keynesian boom.[31] However, the result in India, unlike the US (which mints its own foreign exchange reserves), was a genuine financial crisis in the international sector. When the state was fiscally conservative, growth rates were fairly low, but the economic crises of more aggressive states were also absent. When the state became more profligate, growth rates increased, but so too did symptoms of crisis. Since liberalisation in 1991, the economy's performance has only marginally deviated from the Hindu rate of growth, maintaining a growth rate of 4–6 percent per annum. It would be difficult to deduce any major derivative structural changes from so small an aggregate change in so large a political economy.

THE MORAL ECONOMY OF LIBERALIZATION

In the 'moral economy' model of mass acceptance of elites, what concerned subordinates was not how much was taken from them, but how much was left: the subsistence threshold. What we now call 'safety nets' were a sine qua non condition for elite legitimacy. Karl Polanyi's analysis of the politics of market society was that despite greater average wealth, 'society' would reject the insecurity of the market in favour of public guarantees of security. Prime Minister Rao anticipated the mass critique, 'When we started liberalisation, everyone thought this is going to throw thousands and lakhs out of employment in this country and what is called hire and fire will become the order of the day ... this has not happened in this country. This has not been allowed to happen in this country.'[32] For this reason, despite the loss of relative power on the part of labour, there continues to be no 'exit policy' – firms cannot unilaterally decide to shut down or fire workers. Populist rhetoric ameliorates the reform project: adjustment will have a 'human face.'

What political coalition then sustained liberalisation, if there were vociferous critics and little difference in aggregate growth rates? The answer must lie more within the state than in society, and primarily at the level of ideas rather than blunt calculation of knowable interests in which each individual counts for one. For a project of this magnitude to succeed, there must be in some sense a reformulation of policy discourse such that going back becomes unthinkable. The ideological praxis of liberalisation has been to delegitimise both the state and statist developmentalism. Much as the reformist regime of Narasimha Rao desired to project a continuity with Nehru, the period after 1991 saw fundamental shifts at the cognitive-normative level. The finance minister of a Congress government called the Nehru edifice 'functionless capitalism', rather than the long positively valenced 'socialistic pattern of society'.

One piece of this emergent discourse was an attack on the state as dysfunctional and parasitic. Rajiv Gandhi's attacks on the Congress party and on the Indian state were illustrative of an emerging consensus in elite circles. In his famous 'Bombay Speech' to the Congress party, he said:

> and what of the iron frame of the system ... the myriad functionaries of the state? They have done so much and can do so much more, but as the proverb says there can be no protection if the fence starts eating the crop. This is what has happened. The fence has started eating the crop ... We have government servants who do not serve but oppress ... they have no work ethic ... no comprehension of the values of modern India. They have only a grasping, mercenary outlook, devoid of competence, integrity and commitment.[33]

For reforms to have their legitimating effects, actors inside and outside the system must believe that there has been a permanent shift in policy logic, whatever the short-term reverses on levels of budget deficits or the failure to evolve an 'exit policy' for firms. The prime minister summarised:

> Reform is a continuous process. Elections come, elections go. What reassures me is that just as in foreign policy, economic policy has become a matter of consensus. We'll not have any of the existing parties saying that these economic reforms are bad, that if we come to power we will scrap them. You will not find this in their manifestos any longer.[34]

To believe that this shift is truly ubiquitous and permanent, given the diversity and volatility of Indian political life, is a leap of faith. However, the example most often used to illustrate the cognitive-shift proposition is that even the powerful left communists, the Communist Party of India (Marxist), as ruling party in West Bengal since 1977, have accepted the need to court foreign investment and placate capital.[35] When the last viable political party on the left rejects the struggle against market society as futile, it is reasonable to assume that a new consensus has taken hold. Of special importance is the fact that as the left buys into the reforms, political power is de facto redistributed because the choice set for voters is narrowed. There is then in an electoral sense no real alternative to the reform project. In this sense, the economic structural effect of reform is mirrored by and in some ways productive of a political structural effect: the withering of subjectively viable alternative anti-liberal political projects.

Though it is most striking to see West Bengal's communist government's 'new industrial policy' stressing worker discipline and productivity, no-strike agreements, and abject solicitations of foreign capital, the phenomenon has been general. Opposition parties rhetorically resist policies selling out the nation and decimating the 'poor', but when in power at the state level, the new consensus is apparent. The *Far Eastern Economic Review* noted that in the only state ruled by the 'nationalist' and 'Hindu fundamentalist' Bharatiya Janata Party (BJP) – Rajasthan – the first building you reach on the national highway from Delhi is a Stroh's beer factory.[36] Karnataka, ruled by the nominally leftist Janata Dal, which had been critical of reform, pursued foreign investment more vigorously and successfully than other state governments. After the Enron power project was scrapped in Maharashtra, the state government assiduously pushed for the clearance of Cogentrix's 1,000 MW power project. In Uttar Pradesh, the lower caste leftist coalition government was among the leaders in privatising public sector enterprises.

Nevertheless, the consensus on reform has been partial and qualified. In particular, the political salience of the security nexus mitigated orthodox adjustment. The National Renewal Fund as a safety net was announced in 1992, with support from the World Bank, before the reemergence of populism discussed below. Not only the ubiquitous 'weaker sectors', but capital as well looked to the state for protection from the market – specifically international capital and competition. The prime minister's office stated that 'predatory practices' by TNCs would not be allowed. Commerce Minister Pranab Mukherjee said in 1994, 'We simply cannot allow a situation where our industry is wiped out.'[37] The idea behind floating the Indian Investment Promotion Board (IIPB) reflected a Polanyi-esque constraint on the market to protect (mostly symbolically) domestic businesses from hostile take-overs by MNCs. Likewise, there is a Foreign Investment Promotion Board (FIPB) to screen approvals for FDI proposals on a case-by-case basis.[38]

Drawing lines between 'predatory' and 'hostile' business practice and the ordinary *jungli* laws of the market is a new normative project for the Indian state. Likewise, it is difficult to know where 'adjustment with a human face' ends and where populism, subsidies and backsliding begin. The technical and nominally neutral economic discourse of the early period of reform had no definitive answers; the operative answers lie in ordinary political practice.

POLITICS OF REFORM

Taking a longer view of liberalisation (roughly 1980 to 1995), there was a discernible redistribution of power from politicians to technocrats and back to politicians – but on a different policy trajectory. In the period of significant reform, roughly 1991–1995, there were significant short-term shifts within this broader pattern. For rough periodisation, we consider the fiscal years of 1991–92 and 1992–93 the high point of technocratic direction. Politics reasserted its autonomy against the technical agenda of reformers beginning in 1993–94.

Reform began in 1991 under the auspices of a minority government, necessitating support both from disparate power bases within and outside the Congress party. The party's manifesto did not offer sweeping liberalisation. After Rajiv Gandhi's assassination, Narasimha Rao ascended within the Congress party in 1991 as a compromise candidate. The powerful factions that united behind Rao were predominantly from the South (as was Rao), but included Sharad Pawar's faction in Maharashtra. The traditional heartland of the Congress in the Hindi-speaking states of Uttar Pradesh, Madhya Pradesh, Rajasthan and Bihar had by then collapsed. Intra-party power struggles had been papered over, but the ambitions of Sharad Pawar and Arjun Singh for leadership of the party created open fissures over time.

What gave Prime Minister Rao space for reform was not an overwhelming electoral mandate, nor a unified party, but economic crisis. The reform was technocratic in its support base and widely associated in political practice with an IMF-sponsored program of fiscal consolidation and structural reform. The finance minister, Manmohan Singh, was the architect, assisted by a team of economic advisors such as Montek Singh Ahluwalia and Ashok Desai (who was later replaced by Shankar Acharya).

Finance Minister Singh and his advisors, some of whom had considerable experience working with the IMF and World Bank, had virtually a carte blanche in terms of authority from the prime minister, particularly during 1991–92 and 1992–93. The national currency was quickly devalued in two steps. Import liberalisation reduced controls and simplified procedures. Tariffs, which had been among the highest in the world, were also dropped in steps. The fiscal deficit proved to be more difficult, but in the first year shrank from a high of 9.1 percent of GDP in 1990–91 to 5.7 percent in 1992–93. Inflation reached a double-digit peak in August 1991 but subsided to single digit levels the following year. Union budgets of 1991–92 and 1992–93 bore the authoritative stamp of a coherent economic team led by a technocrat, Manmohan Singh. The results were initially impressive: the fiscal deficit shrank and devaluation boosted exports. Imports were sluggish because of recession in Indian industry. As a result, there was dramatic improvement in the balance of payments and foreign exchange reserves began accumulating.

Transition from a coherent technocratic process of economic reform to something more akin to politics-as-usual became apparent in fiscal 1993–94. The coherent economic team witnessed the abrupt departure of a key advisor, Ashok Desai, who was the architect of important trade policy reforms. Speculation in Delhi was that he left because of dissatisfaction with the slowing pace of reforms and his steady marginalisation in the finance ministry. In resigning, Desai said that 'the game of snakes and ladders, which those around played with such ferocity, such guile, such subtlety, such flair' was inconsistent with his reasons for joining the government.[39] The finance minister acknowledged that the power conferred on him and his ministry by the structural crisis of 1991 was subsequently diluted by the resurgence of pork-barrel politics. In an interview with *Forbes* magazine, when asked what worried him, Singh replied, 'Now that things are normal in India, now that the immediate crisis is past, we have our ministers wanting to spend more money, to resume projects. In the time of crisis, I was far more influential and far more powerful than I am today.'[40]

The salience of reform declined not only because the financial crisis passed, but because of more threatening political dynamics outside economic policy. The revival of Hindu fundamentalism at Ayodhya, communal carnage, and the Bombay bomb blasts preempted central government attention. Moreover, Prime Minister Rao faced internal challenges to his leadership, in part on questions about the moral economy of the adjustment's 'human face'. In the campaigns preceding elections to four crucial states, fiscal discipline of the previous two years predictably began to slip, reflecting the predictable electoral business cycle. The fiscal deficit jumped to 7.3 percent of GDP. Inflation headed back to double-digit levels, and industry remained sluggish. Increased public expenditures did not salvage the elections for the Congress party however. Setbacks to the Congress in state elections in Karnataka and Andhra Pradesh (the prime minister's home state) undermined Rao's position in the party and were widely perceived as a repudiation of the liberalisation agenda.[41]

Prime Minister Rao remained publicly committed to reform after the electoral disasters, but clearly began to drift away from the technocratic direction of policy – significantly increasing rural public spending and delaying structural reforms urged by the technocrats (such as allowing labour markets to function by permitting the hiring and firing of workers). Lay-offs and mass unemployment remained boundary conditions of reform. The prime minister's frequent description of a 'middle path' which represented 'adjustment with a human face' was indicative of the power shift from the finance ministry to the Prime Minister's Office.

Populist compulsions operated more in the anticipatory political tactics of the prime minister than in the streets. Forces within the party and government also pressed Rao to be politically efficient, not theoretically reformist. The national elections of spring 1996 introduced new compulsions. In his Independence Day speech on 15 August 1995, Prime Minister Rao announced social assistance spending of Rs 50 billion – covering an old-age pension scheme, mid-day meals for primary school children and an insurance scheme for the rural poor. 'We are spending Rs 18,000 crore on these programs of rural development and social services as against Rs 8,000 crore in 1991. So this money that we are providing is meant to reach every village, to provide relief to the rural people ...' The Government conceptualised these schemes as social progress, not simply boondoggles and subsidies berated by the technocrats.

Polanyi's view of societal resistance to the dominance of the market provides an important insight into the electoral politics of liberalisation. In India, much of the dynamics have been pre-emptive, not only through politicians reading the tea leaves of off-term or local elections, but through competition and division within the party leadership itself. Insecurity politics drives retreats from or preemptions of economic reform which induces further insecurity.

THE EMPIRICAL PROBLEM OF SORTING WINNERS AND LOSERS

Delineating winners and losers in an on-going process over a short duration is problematic. In structural terms, it is highly likely that the proprietary classes of Bardhan's model of the political economy have taken the major benefits of reforms; control of assets, surplus resources and connections should shelter holders from threats and enhance opportunities in accelerated economic change. The losers will be those with insufficient resources to weather short-term disruptions of accelerated economic change. In terms of the structure of federalism, states are likely to win at the expense of the Centre, and advanced states at the expense of backward states.

Agriculturists, particularly the surplus-producing farmers, have been perhaps the major beneficiaries of the reform period, but not because of liberalisation. The terms of trade (the ratio of agricultural prices to industrial prices) have tilted in their favour through major hikes in procurement prices of rice and wheat relative to the pre-reform period.[42] These shifts transfer surpluses or intersectoral resource flows to the country at the expense of the city. The higher prices of agricultural goods have naturally resulted in a persistent inflationary bias since reforms were initiated.[43] Agriculture remains heavily subsidised and largely untaxed even after the reforms of 1991. For a sense of perspective, the share devoted to agricultural services and subsidies (fertiliser, electricity, irrigation and credit) has grown from 37 percent of central government expenditures in 1985–86 to 58 percent in 1992–93 according to the World Bank's Country Economic Memorandum for India, 30 May 1995. State governments, which are responsible for 60 percent of public expenditures on agriculture, crucially depend on the rich peasantry for political support.

While prosperous farmers benefit from higher product prices, agricultural labourers who have to purchase costlier grain from the market lose. As the public distribution system does not have a broad reach in rural areas, higher food prices erode the real wages of agricultural labourers. This appears to have happened since 1991-92. The electoral setbacks faced by the ruling Congress party in Andhra Pradesh, Karnataka, Maharashtra and Gujarat in fact were attributed by Rao's opponents in the party to adverse effects on the rural poor. Large-scale distress, in terms of worsening poverty and unemployment, which influenced electoral outcomes seems to have been conceded by Congress tacticians.

Stabilisation really began to bite in 1991-92 and 1992-93. The consumer price index for agricultural labourers (CPIAL) rose by 21.9 percent in 1991-92. The rate of increase in prices then came down to 0.7 percent in 1992-93 and an up-trend began in 1993-94 and 1994-95 – 11.6 and 10.6 percent respectively.[44] Such sharp swings in consumer prices for agricultural labourers may adversely affect rural wages and poverty. Manmohan Singh in his union budget speech for 1995-96 conceded that trends in real wages were adverse during 1991-92 but argued that they improved soon thereafter: '... total employment is expanding much faster than three years ago. Real wages of agricultural labourers had declined in 1991-92 during the crisis. They had increased above pre-crisis levels by 1993-94.'

The ongoing debate on rural poverty can be taken further if one looks at minimum-wage data for agricultural labour. Any person who is employed under the Jawahar Rozgar Yojana (Employment Assurance Scheme) has to be paid the statutory minimum wage. A series from 1990-91 to 1994-95 indicates that nominal wages rose by 83 percent – from Rs 15.24 to Rs 27.93. When deflated by the CPIAL, the trends are slightly different from those suggested by Singh. Real wages dropped by 5 percent to Rs 1.93 in 1991-92 and 1992-93, then fell by another 2.6 percent in 1993-94, then rose sharply to Rs 2.24 in 1994-95.[45] Unlike official claims, these data indicate that rural poverty may have worsened during the first three years of reform, before catching up by 10 percent in 1994-95. The wage rate is, however, only part of the calculation; what matters is annual *income*, that is, days of employment times the wage rate. Increased economic activity in time should increase demand for labour. The common assumption that the poor are more vulnerable to liberalisation than to the dynamics of *dirigiste* is to date unproven.

One would expect that differential access to foreign direct investment – on which the strategy depends – would create shifts in benefits and political power across regions, given the strategy's dependence on attracting investment. The evidence is not yet in. There is some data suggesting that inter-regional disparities in incomes across India widened after reform. In the reform period of the early 1990s, the poorer states in the Hindi-speaking belt such as Bihar, Uttar Pradesh and Madhya Pradesh experienced an even sharper deceleration in overall growth than the nation, widening disparities in social well-being and human development. By contrast, prosperous states like Maharashtra and Gujarat cornered the bulk of investment proposals. In 1994, Maharashtra saw $1.19 billion of FDI approved, more than a quarter of the total for India. Since 1991, $30 billion of investment had been approved in the state out of which $7 billion was FDI. Next in line was Gujarat with $23 billion of investment proposals since 1991. Such trends exacerbated existing regional disparities.

The bureaucracy potentially loses as liberalisation threatens loss of discretionary authority – and thus the potential for rents. Simultaneously, the potential rents are much larger in international transactions. Moreover, globalisation opens new opportunities for individuals. Income and perks in global as opposed to national jobs clearly attract sections of India's bureaucracy. The stampede towards job opportunities in the Asian Development Bank (ADB) or World Bank is illustrative. A couple of years ago, ADB advertised four positions in the *Economist* magazine. No fewer than thirty-eight applicants comprising senior government officials were interviewed in New Delhi. The aspirants were key officials involved at the highest levels of government: comprising senior economic advisors, joint secretaries and officials from the Department for Economic Affairs. They were privy to the formulation of sensitive policies in a country which was undertaking an ambitious reforms agenda. They were a strategic resource which the country could ill afford to lose. One explanation for the exodus holds that frustration increased within the bureaucracy because its powers were being steadily eroded as the license-quota-permit *raj* was dismantled. Simultaneously, Indian officials were in greater demand from outside as globalisation proceeded. Reforms especially undermined the position of ministries such as of industry and commerce relative to that of finance. Bureaucrats thus felt increasingly irrelevant and were eager to get out and simultaneously improve their personal positions.

It is more difficult to generalise about industrialists. Winners could now win much bigger, and it was still not so easy to lose as in the theoretical market economy. Triggered by the same self-reflective critique that spawned liberalisation, the Indian state began to take industrial associations – especially the Confederation of Indian Industry (CII), but also the Federation of Indian Chambers of Commerce and Industry (FICCI) – into closer confidence in policy making. This change was in large part a response to India's dismal record in relation to the successful developmental states, where collusive arrangements are routine and institutionalised. In sharp contrast to the overt hostility shown in the past to businessmen by the state, Prime Minister Rao began to take a planeload of Indian industrialists with him on foreign tours. Indian capital appeared not to be as divided as was once popularly thought. The big business groups that prospered in the protected home market were understandably reluctant to support the opening up to foreign capital, but the newer and faster rising industrial groups supported reform. The earlier fears of Indian capital that it would be swallowed up by TNCs – especially among family-owned combines such as the Bajajs, Thapars, Tatas, and Singhanias – continued to persist. This led to the formation of the so-called Bombay Club meeting of industrialists who complained, among other things, of the lack of a level playing field. Interestingly, such fears were not allayed despite the willingness of the Indian government to address most of their concerns.

This shift toward a more corporatist (but without labour) political economy was not the direct result of liberalisation, but rather of a new understanding within the state of the structural power of capital and the paradigmatic power of the developmental state model.[46] Without bringing capital in, much of the reform effort would not bear fruit in terms of growth. This understanding was less the 'Washington consensus' than the one usually associated with Tokyo.

FEDERALISM, REGIONALISM AND NATIONALIST POLITICAL NICHES

Just as central planning was born in a nationalist critique of foreign economic dominance and a perceived need for nation-building, liberalisation opened the door to a nationalist counter-critique and responses to regional disparities. To the extent that the nationalist program resonated politically, a niche for a new political formation emerged.

Reform meant a gain of power by the periphery vis-à-vis the Centre in economic policy. Rather than a Benthamite panopticon state directing a subordinate periphery, the states began exerting initiatives which de facto became national policy. Individual states began to aggressively pursue the global integration which was the centrepiece of Delhi's strategy. The deals struck by individual states de facto become constitutive of economic policy – or absence of same. This change is likely to be difficult to reverse, as reimposition of interventionism from the Centre is difficult to imagine with so unstable a Centre.[47]

This new form of federalism became most apparent in policy toward foreign direct investment (FDI). India's explicitly protectionist regime had been one of the most restrictive in the world. Foreign investments, like foreign products, were severely restricted. One expected liberalisation to redistribute power toward those sectors, industries and firms which were globally competitive, at the expense of those which were critically protected by the license-quota-permit *raj*.

The new strategy depended on FDI; so multinational firms and investors may eventually be the winners in the process. Power, roads, telecommunications networks and other infrastructure remain critical constraints on growth. Ironically, the populism of the response led to a situation in which continued growth of necessity depended on foreign investors – the fiscal crisis of the populist state insured that basic infrastructure improvements awaited foreign direct investment. The fear was that under conditions of political uncertainty, finance would go elsewhere. As symbolically important projects were cancelled or delayed, markets attached risk premiums to India which restricted the inflow of capital.

Reforms in the FDI regime were greeted with initial enthusiasm abroad, but domestic politics disrupted Delhi's announced position, leading to more international caution. A tension began to emerge between the demands of globalisation and the nationalist priorities of the political process. After the Mexican turmoil, such tensions jeopardised India's standing in the emerging market stakes. The earlier scrapping and subsequent renegotiation of the $2.8 billion Enron power project by the Hindu nationalist BJP and the primordialist and regionalist Shiv Sena in Maharashtra is a case in point. The question uppermost in the minds of foreign investors became whether or not they were indeed welcome to invest in India. The tendency of state governments to review deals struck by their predecessors also triggered serious doubts among international firms about whether the reforms were indeed 'irreversible', as commonly claimed in Delhi.

Similar fears were expressed by foreign investors when the Congress party was routed in the state elections in Andhra Pradesh and Karnataka, which were widely interpreted as referenda on the new economic policy. But the political leadership allayed their fears regarding the continuity of policies on FDI. Karnataka's new chief minister, in fact, provided that assurance at the World Economic Forum in Davos. The fact that even communist-run West Bengal aggressively courted FDI also assured investors. Parties might change at the state level but there was a sense that reforms would continue in accord with the policy of the Centre.

This optimism evaporated with the scrapping of the Enron and Thapar power project in Maharashtra, the review of AES Transpower's power project in Orissa, besides many others.[48] Reinforcing fears of a second wave of nationalist hostility against TNCs – resonating with the deep official suspicions of the late 1970s – was the targeting of Kentucky Fried Chicken outlets and the relocation or scrapping of the Japanese industrial township in Haryana, among many other examples. Some firms, such as the US power company CMS and a brace of British telecom companies like Vodaphone, publicly announced their intention of rethinking or putting on hold their investment plans until uncertainty surrounding the 1996 elections resolved itself.

Politically, the correlates of such trends was the emergence of the Bharatiya Janata Party. The BJP ruled or shared power in the states of Maharashtra, Gujarat, and Rajasthan. Once a party of shopkeepers and traders, it emerged to assiduously cultivate the constituency of big industrialists who were insecure with reforms and the threats that TNCs would assimilate or destroy their family-run enterprises. There was, however, a tension within the party on what should be its line on economic nationalism or *swadeshi* (self-reliance). The hard core RSS (*Rashtriya Swayamsevak Sangh* – the militant activist wing of the BJP) together with certain hard liners who group themselves under the *Swadeshi Jagran Manch* (Self-reliance Consciousness Movement) have been extremely jingoistic about foreign investment in consumer goods such as Pepsi, Coca Cola, and Kentucky Fried Chicken. On the other hand, there was a moderate tendency within the BJP which favoured a broader interpretation of *swadeshi*. According to this view, foreign investment would have to meet the criterion of essentiality – 'we need micro chips rather than potato chips'. Which of these two tendencies would ultimately prevail was a critical question to foreign investors.

The BJP/Shiv Sena's decision to scrap the Enron project resonated with domestic industrialists who privately railed against 'mindless globalisation'. Prime Minister Rao sought to capture nationalist space by conceding the demands of the so-called Bombay Club. The Foreign Investment Promotion Board began to turn down controversial deals such as the Tata-Singapore Airlines venture, suggesting a defensive stance towards foreign investment. This sort of backlash was also felt by the Japanese entrepreneur Suzuki in its thwarted efforts to secure majority control over the highly-profitable automotive giant Maruti Udyog Ltd. Suzuki's ambitions to secure control over another motorcycle venture were also blocked when the affected Indian industrialist directly appealed to the PM's office.

Widening regional disparities and increased insecurity had implications for identity politics – of communal, nationalist or regionalist forms. Based on interviews with party leaders of the BJP, P. Raman reported that the BJP strategy became one of doing less on the overtly anti-Muslim front and taking 'full advantage of the anti-reform backlash from the weaker sections ...' Moreover, '... the RSS clan has realised that in the current atmosphere of globalisation, self-respect and self-reliance make the essential ingredients of Hindu resurgence.' Identity politics not being totally reliable, the RSS and BJP understood that '... pleading for the common man and weaker sections is unavoidable to counter the regional and Mandal-based parties and to blunt their competitive populism'. If this economistic slant did not work, Raman reported, hardliners in the BJP planned to resort to communal riots, as they had data that indicated increases in their support after riots.[49]

It would be a stretch to attribute direct causal power to economic reform in the resurgence of identity and communal politics. Nevertheless, scapegoating of 'others' and reassertion of national identity resonate with perceived increases in economic insecurity, inequality of conspicuous consumption, and threats of decadence from a kind of Gresham's Law of culture (the MTV critique). Globalisation typically combines just these elements.

THE ELUSIVE DELHI CONSENSUS

Knowing what to call liberalisation is half the analytical and comparative battle. India's reforms are not of the scale or depth of economic changes in China or Poland. The 'middle path' was in effect the 'mixed economy'. Prime Minister Rao himself said, 'We have always been a liberal democratic society with a mixed economy. The mix may have to change from time to time, but we have never needed convincing that a mix was needed. So was change.'[50]

India's reforms have been incremental and hedged by political opposition. The most substantial change was at the external boundary with the international system. Import duties were lowered, the rupee was devalued and made convertible on current account; foreign direct investment became less restricted and actively courted. Given the extraordinarily closed nature of the political economy before 1991, the changes were significant and clearly advantaged those firms and industries which were either internationally competitive or offered attractive joint-venture opportunities.

Changes in domestic policy proposed from the high ground of technical neutrality were more subject to problems of implementation and political opposition – more within the ruling party than on the streets. Delicensing unfettered capital but was partial; case-by-case deals remained important. Despite rhetorical disparagement, public sector units remained public sector. Privatisation has been stalled until an 'exit policy' (to permit firms to unilaterally shut down) emerges; as N. Chandra Mohan consistently writes, exit is still a four-letter word in Delhi. Projections of fiscal austerity were countered politically. Fiscal laxity meant an increased debt burden; interest payments consumed more than half of government revenues. The Agriculture Ministry protected farmers from announced cuts in fertiliser subsidies. Control of the financial sector remained significant. The government itself increased in size and cost despite liberalisation. The direction of reforms was neo-liberal, but there were dimensions of continuity and contradiction as well as change.

Rather than the reforms redistributing political power, it seems that political power redistributed the reforms. Absence of an exit policy is quite extraordinary in a market economy. Large farmers were able to protect their subsidies and escape an income tax (a state subject). Subsidy targets were consistently exceeded. After 1991–92, the government was not able to meet targets for fiscal deficits as a percentage of GDP. Budget deficits in turn drive inflation, which generally redistributes income upwards and claims the poor as its first victims. There was not all that much privatisation by the Centre, and insurance-sector reforms stalled. However, subsidies for export promotion, food and fertiliser remained.

The dominant dynamic was, as Polanyi predicted, of episodes of privileging the market versus those of reactive or anticipatory protection of 'society' from the disintegrative and punishing forces of unconstrained market forces. It was from this logic that Prime Minister Rao justified major initiatives to protect the rural poor, on whom the brunt of liberalisation pain was projected to fall. When the finance minister was asked why the government restricted cotton exports when prices were beginning to rise, he tellingly replied, 'These are the contradictions which come in. Our concern was the problem of handlooms. These are also genuine problems. When starvation death news started coming in, something had to be done about the hardships.'[51]

The relative losers of liberalisation in class terms were the same as the losers under the license-permit-quota *raj*. The winners also were no different from the broad 'proprietary classes' Bardhan saw as the power behind the throne of the Indian state.[52] One clear set of winners of the reform period, but not of liberalisation per se, were the surplus-producing farmers: despite higher crop prices, subsidies for inputs (fertiliser, water and power) and continuation of de facto exemption from income tax were protected.

Significant shifts in political power are difficult to find. At the level of power of business associations, the internationalist Confederation of Indian Industry (CII) benefited at the expense of older associations such as the Federation of Indian Chambers of Commerce and Industry (FICCI). Its integration with the state marked a departure from the particularism of generally hostile state–business relations and resembled in form more the developmental state than traditional practice. Liberalisation's contribution to attracting foreign investment advantaged firms with something to offer international capital; simultaneously, open access to markets and imported inputs probably advantaged their less well-connected competitors. Labour was almost certainly the largest institutional loser, but labourers may have benefited over time from the general economic change. As in all economic change, the worry is about those least able to adapt. There is some evidence that the poor were hurt first, as is often the case but that is to be expected: the Washington consensus is based on the belief that inducing a recession is a necessary step for stabilisation – after which comes recovery.[53] There was some evidence of recovery (see above), at least for the rural poor.[54] Certainly politicians believe that a pro-poor stance was tactically necessary to win the support of the electorate. Liberalisation thus reinforced populist praxis.

In the distribution of power in federalism, the states almost certainly gained. The attractiveness of foreign direct investment, and the assiduousness with which states have pursued it, together make it unlikely that a weak Centre will or can reverse openness in the foreseeable future. Differential gains among states exacerbated regional inequalities.

In the third proprietary leg of Bardhan's class triangle – the professional knowledge-holders – there was an internal shift to the benefit of those with foreign contacts and knowledge, production skills and access to information.[55] In some ways, despite the obvious opening of opportunity in the course of marketisation, particularistic contacts remain important even after liberalisation. In privatisation, political contacts may prove even more valuable than economic entrepreneurship. The same is true of joint ventures brokered by the state. Far from destroying particularism, which is a dominant feature of the statist political economy, liberalisation may reinforce the basic mechanisms and importance of particularism and connections.[56]

With regard to the generalisation that the distribution of economic and political power become more skewed under liberalisation, the evidence is mixed. Economic inequalities probably increased. But a concentration of political power – beyond the definitional increase in the structural power of capital – was not in evidence. The pre-reform regulatory regime did not distribute perquisites randomly or consistently in the direction of the less powerful; to have done so would have violated one of the core principles of political economy.

Structural power shifts – as opposed to electoral advantage – are by definition part of liberalisation: social control yields to private power. The Rao government invested so much in the success of reform that the structural power of capital almost certainly increased;[57] without investment, the project would certainly fail.[58] This particular structural shift was mirrored in institutional development: incorporation of business associations in the policy process marked a significant departure from earlier practice – from surreptitious and particularistic access to open consultation. Simultaneously, the structural power of labour resisted a full-scale transition to market society. Electoral politics, on the other hand, was part of a dialectic and ephemeral process, constrained in so large a nation by the specificity of the local. If 'all politics is local', factionalism, primordial divisions and local distributive issues remained more important than particulars of national economic policy. Whether the tensions created by globalisation will open a permanent niche for new forms of nationalist political practice – most directly evidenced by the BJP so far – remains to be seen.

At the ideational level, there was a phenomenal shift in what counts as a powerful discourse.[59] Intellectual support for regulatory regimes was decisively undermined. This shift, and the reflexive disappearance of a coherent alternative political project, may have been the most important political effects. Support for liberalisation as ideology was augmented by the deepening of a consumer culture based on metropolitan lifestyles and presumably a 'middle-class' voting identification. To the extent that economic reforms can be portrayed as, or were perceived as, a necessary condition for continuing participation in global consumerism, the support base became broader and deeper. Though there were losers, the losers were in all likelihood predominantly poor people who never counted for much in national politics. And though consumerism remains more illusion than reality for the bulk of the population, the illusion is important: it is something like a lottery, where one sees tickets being redeemed and wants to have a chance, even knowing (but subjectively discounting) the odds.

Finally, sustaining this shift amidst political turbulence does not depend on simple political arithmetic. Rather, a trajectory once established obeys a kind of social inertia – unless opposed by an equal and opposite force, the direction remains unchanged. A particular constellation of forces in the international system produced a momentary autonomy for crisis management which shifted policy direction significantly. The social mechanics of putting together an equal and opposite force present almost insurmountable problems of collective action at this point in history.

NOTES

Abbreviations
BI: *Business India* (New Delhi)
BS: *Business Standard* (New Delhi)
EPW: *Economic and Political Weekly* (Bombay)
FEER: *Far Eastern Economic Review*
IT: *India Today*

1 Ronald J. Herring, 'Explaining Sri Lanka's Exceptionalism: Popular Responses to Welfarism and the "Open Economy"', in John Walton and David Seddon, eds, *Free Markets and Food Riots: The Politics of Global Adjustment* (Oxford: Blackwell, 1994).
2 Charles Lindblom, *Politics and Markets* (New York: Basic Books, 1977).
3 Karl Polanyi, *The Great Transformation* (New York: Farrar and Rhinehart, 1944).
4 John Williamson, 'What Washington Means by Policy Reform', in John Williamson, ed., *Latin American Adjustment* (Washington: Institute for International Economics, 1990); Thomas J. Biersteker, *Dealing with Debt: International Financial Negotiations and Adjustment Bargaining* (Boulder: Westview Press, 1993). On the neo-liberal orthodoxy more generally, see Walton, *Free Markets and Food Riots*, chapters 1 and 2.
5 See interview with Narasimha Rao, *FEER*, 2 February 1995, 45. In an interview with CNN on 1 February 1995, a spokesperson for the World Bank said that the 'bailout' of Mexico, then expected to be about US$40 billion, was necessary to 'preserve the credibility of market reforms on a global scale'. Much of the politics and policy of economic reform is a game of convincing investors that the risks are lower than they subjectively are. For an example of the press coverage of 'permanence' of the reforms as a major issue, see *BS*, 4 February 1995.
6 Of course, liberalisation even in the most liberal societies has not depoliticised the economy. Ronald Reagan asked to be elected president of the United States on the grounds of a simple question to the electorate: Are you better off now than you were ten years ago? Reagan's political strategy proceeded as if the government were responsible for individual welfare, a proposition familiar in the political economy of the developmentalist state, but curious in a liberal one.
7 *IT*, 15 October 1995, 28

8 For an especially detailed history of the individuals and dynamics of early efforts at reform, and eventual liberalisation, see Vanita Shastri, 'The Political Economy of Policy Formation in India: The Case of Industrial Policy', PhD dissertation, Cornell University, 1994, chs 4–5; on the 1980s, see Atul Kohli, 'Politics of Economic Liberalisation in India', *World Development* 17(3), 1989, 305–28.
9 See, for example, Charles Lindblom's 'Market as a Prison', which takes a more structuralist position (as in the Marxian notion of the 'structural power of capital') than his better known 'privileged position of business' in *Politics and Markets* (New York: Basic Books, 1977).
10 Anthony Downs, 'Up and Down with Ecology: The Issue-Attention Cycle', *Public Interest* 28, summer 1972: 38–50.
11 Kohli, 'Politics of Economic Liberalisation in India', op cit.
12 Herring, 'Explaining Sri Lanka's Exceptionalism', op cit.
13 A succinct and articulate expression of this now-common view is contained in Surjit Bhalla, 'Freedom and Economic Growth: A Virtuous Cycle?' in Axel Hadenius, ed, *Democracy's Victory and Crisis* (Cambridge: Cambridge University Press, 1997). For the classic statement that launched the 'rent-seeking' theory of weaknesses of state intervention, see Anne O. Krueger, 'The Political Economy of the Rent-Seeking Society' *American Economic Review* 64(3), 1974.
14 Polanyi, *Great Transformation*, op cit.
15 Herring, 'Explaining Sri Lanka's Exceptionalism', op cit.
16 Finance Minister Manmohan Singh, derided fears of openness as 'the East-India-Company mentality'. Yet even the internationalist Confederation of Indian Industry began to raise these fears as legitimation for selective control of foreign investment.
17 The export pessimism that dominated development planning resonated with the theories and experiences of Latin America as filtered through ECLA, Prebisch et al. This is not surprising on the periphery. The puzzle may be why the East Asian nations, receiving similar signals of peripheral inferiority, were less pessimistic. The impossibility of autarky must have been a conditioning factor; self-reliance was thinkable in continental India, but not in Japan or Korea.
18 Francine Frankel, *India's Political Economy, 1947–77: The Gradual Revolution* (Princeton: Princeton University Press, 1978), 201–45.
19 Pranab Bardhan, *The Political Economy of Development in India* (Oxford: Blackwell, 1984).
20 Shastri, 'Political Economy of Policy Formation in India', op cit.
21 Kohli, 'Politics of Economic Liberalisation in India', op cit.
22 The argument that the reforms represent a 'silent coup' as hypothesised in Prabhat Patnaik, 'International Capital and National Economic Policy: A Critique of India's Economic Reforms', *EPW*, 19 March 1994, is weak on several points. First, specification of the reasons for the increased power of the liberalisers is problematic. Secondly, the weakening of the reform initiative in response to electoral and party politics, which is consistent with the momentary autonomy argument, is not explained.
23 On both the days' worth of reserves and level of deficit, the official figures attempted to put the best face on the situation. The unofficial figures are from Jayanta Roy, who was then advisor to the Finance Ministry, on loan from the World Bank.
24 Mrinal Datta-Chaudhuri, 'Market Failure and Government Failure', *Journal of Economic Perspectives* 4 (3), Summer 1990.

25 As an inevitable correlate, India's imports as a share of GDP were very low in 1989, just over 8 percent compared to a world norm closer to 20 percent, which is even higher in the Asian NICs.
26 The Trilateral Conference on Trade and Development held in Delhi in 1989 is illustrative. Abid Hussein and Manmohan Singh were both present. The German delegation described a future in which there would be two important blocs: Japan-China Inc. and Fortress Europe. The German ambassador headed a faction in the delegation that openly called for a further reaching of *ostpolitik*, centred on India as an 'export platform' to counterbalance Japanese influence in the region. The other faction in the German delegation favoured a pull-back from Asia, to Eastern Europe, where there were advantages of 'geography and history'. In neither scenario did India figure as anything but a location for strategic moves of others' capital. The Indian delegation made the now-familiar pitch that India's middle class is in marketing terms the size of several large European nations and deserved serious consideration by international capital. [Herring was a member of the American delegation.] On the Soviet connection, see Shastri, op cit., 241. The USSR represented 30 percent of India's trade.
27 To take but one example, net foreign investment in China in 1989 was about $1.4 billion, or 0.3 percent of GDP; in India it was, less than one-tenth that amount, $125 million, or 0.05 percent of GDP.
28 Contrary to Robert Bates, *Markets and States in Tropical Africa: The Political Bias of Agricultural Policies* (Berkeley: University of California Press, 1981).
29 It seems likely that there is a positive relationship between extensive regulation and under-reporting of economic activity.
30 Comparative growth data from World Bank, *World Development Report*, annual; Dilip S. Swamy, *The Political Economy of Industrialisation*, (New Delhi: Sage, 1994), ch. 1; Shastri, 'Political Economy of Policy Formation in India' op cit., 18 et passim.
31 External debt tripled between 1980 and 1989 in absolute terms and as a percentage of GNP from 11.9 to 24; the debt service ratio increased from 9.1 to 26.4. India's credit rating fell from A2 to Ba2.
32 *BI*, 11–24 April 1994, 51. One of the suggested remedies was to boost rural public spending to alleviate rural unemployment. The partial success of this strategy after 1993 resulted in a tightening of rural labour markets.
33 Inaugural Speech at Congress Centenary Session, Bombay, 28 December 1985, 13. See also discussion in Shastri 'Political Economy of Policy Formation in India' op cit., 168 ff. The metaphor of the fence eating the crops is part of village agrarian discourse.
34 *FEER*, 2 February 1995, 45.
35 Recognizing, as good Marxists should, the structural power of capital. See Ross Mallick, *Indian Communism: Opposition, Collaboration and Institutionalisation* (Delhi, New York: Oxford University Press, 1994). Mallick documents the attempts of the communist state government in Bengal to move faster and farther than Delhi in attracting foreign capital and the more extensive concessions to capital on the part of labor since communists came to power.
36 *FEER*, 2 February 1995, 46.
37 *BI*, 9–22 May 1994, 50.
38 See Mallick, *Indian Communism*, op cit., 51, as well as *BI*, 9–22 May 1994, 50. Though in the early stages of reform, no proposals were turned down, later certain big-ticket FDI proposals did not meet FIPB approval: e.g. Reebok shoe manufacturers, Wrigley's chewing gum, Quaker Oats, and a proposal for whisky manufacture. The FIPB rejection rate fell from 40–50 percent prior to

1991 to under 10 percent in 1993; about 30 percent of approvals since reform have been through the automatic route, International Monetary Fund, *India: Economic Reform and Growth*, (Washington, DC, Occasional Paper no. 134, 1996), 43.
39 *BI*, 25 April–8 May 1996, 52.
40 *Forbes*, 24 April 1995. The finance minister registered similar views on the crisis and his own power in an interview with *IT*, 15 October 1995, 28–29.
41 This political interpretation had force even though a closer look at the elections illustrates that the particulars of liberalisation policy were not really at issue. Nevertheless, the party read popular responses to the opposition's attack on Congress's pro-poor image as a rejection of liberalisation.
42 The ratio was 116.4 in 1991–92, 113.3 in 1992–93, 111.5 in 1993–94 and 114.5 in 1994–95 and 113.3 in 1995–96 (up to December) [base: 1981–82 =100]. Government of India (GOI), Ministry of Finance, *Economic Survey 1995–96* (New Delhi, 1996), table S-66.
43 The mid-term appraisal of the Eighth Five Year Plan (1992–93 to 1996–97) done by the Planning Commission observed that during the reform period, 1991–92 to 1993–94, inflation was 10.7 percent per annum, compared to pre-reform period 1985–86 to 1990–91 average of 7.8 percent per annum.
44 From *GOI, Economic Survey 1995–96*, table S-65, authors' calculations. The figures refer to the last month of the year rather than the average of months.
45 Unpublished data; real wage numbers provided by then Secretary, Ministry of Rural Development, B.N. Yugandhar, who is currently Secretary to the Prime Minister.
46 The term 'developmental state' as used in academic discourse originated with Chalmers Johnson, *MITI and the Japanese Miracle: The Growth of Industrial policy, 1925–1975* (Stanford: Stanford University Press, 1994). See also Jung-en Woo, *Race to the Swift: State and Finance in Korean Industrialisation* (New York: Columbia University Press, 1991); Alice Amsden, *Asia's Next Giant: South Korea and Late Industrialisation* (New York: Oxford University Press, 1989); Robert Wade, *Governing the Market: Economic Theory and the Role of Government in East Asian Industrialisation*, (Princeton: Princeton University Press, 1990). All of these models locate East Asian success in engagement of the state with the business community as opposed to either the classical *laissez-faire* approach or the antagonistic (and selective) regulation of capital characteristic of the Indian regulatory system.
47 The elections of 1996 and 1998 produced no clear claimant to formation of the government. The BJP was asked to form a government, but proved incapable of doing so. A loose united front of regional parties and the left was the next candidate. This coalition was less friendly to liberalisation than the Congress, which pledged it unconditional support from outside. The government fell when the Congress withdrew support, leading to the election of the BJP-led National Front Coalition. Like its predecessors, the new government also remained fragmented in ideology and program.
48 The Enron deal was most important symbolically. The American corporation claimed it was losing $250,000 a day between cancellation of the project by the new state government and its renegotiation. The project was renegotiated at a lower aggregate price, leaving the clear political impression that the original contract had been predatory. The controversy served to reinforce the worst fears of India about MNCs and MNCs about India. On the ramifications of Enron and views of India in corporate boardrooms, see John F. Burns, 'Second Thoughts on India', *NYT*, 9 January 1996, 47–48.

49 *Business Standard*, 6 February 1995.
50 *BI*, 11–24 April 1994, 50.
51 *IT*, 15 October 1995, 29.
52 See Bardhan, *Political Economy of Development*, op cit.
53 John Walton and David Seddon, eds., *Free Markets and Food Riots,* op cit.
54 Economic theory is simply too divided to tell us how ominous or promising are the underlying structures that are changing rapidly in India. For a well-argued pessimistic view, stressing industrial retrogression, lower capital formation, reliance on 'hot money' (portfolio investment) and other variables, see Prabhat Patnaik, 'International Capital and National Economic Policy: A Critique of India's Economic Reforms', *EPW,* 19 March 1994.
55 Bardhan, *Political Economy of Development*, op cit.
56 For example, in a speech by Manmohan Singh of 28 January 1995, the finance minister said: 'We should be careful not to replace an inefficient public sector by a regime of crony capitalism,' *BS,* 6 February 1995. Presumably something real prompted this public expression of concern.
57 A high-level advisor to the government said in Herring's presence that the prime minister told him, 'Find out what the CEOs want and we will do it.'
58 Patnaik and Chandrasekhar argue that 'during the period of structural adjustment the pace of capital formation in the economy has gone back to what it was approximately a decade ago': Prabhat Patnaik and C.P Chandrashekhar, 'Indian Economy under "Structural Adjustment"', *Economic and Political Weekly,* 25 November 1995:3001–3013.
59 Shastri, 'Political Economy of Policy Formation in India', op cit.

Chapter 11

Liberalising India's Economy: Context and Constraints

Vanita Shastri

This paper argues that economic reform is a process. In many countries, like India, liberalising the economy has been spread over a number of years so that varied factors have influenced the pace and rigor of the reforms. Rather than adopting the strategy of 'shock therapy', India has introduced economic reforms gradually. While this path has had its setbacks, as shown below, the recent economic crises in South east Asia and Latin America have vindicated the Indian path for its reformers. This paper argues that although economic reforms have appeared to be intermittent at times, they have been passed continuously since 1991, and have carried forward a process of reforms initiated in the 1980s. Secondly, the paper explores the Indian economic reform process and the constraints it has faced in proceeding at a faster pace. Thirdly, the paper demonstrates that the economic reforms have spread to the states and to various sectors and developed a sustainable character. Yet, as I conclude, the Indian state is faced with various domestic pressures and needs to address an important dilemma: how to market the economic reforms with a political discourse that neither jeopardises the reforms nor undermines the democratic strength of the Indian polity.

CONTEXT OF REFORMS

Soon after independence, India adopted an import-substitution model of development with an emphasis on self-reliance, through which it attempted to achieve both growth and social justice. While this model did not result in noteworthy growth rates, it did result in India becoming one of the most closed economies of the free world. India settled for what has come to be called the 'Hindu rate of growth' – a fairly steady 3.5 percent per annum. The industrial growth rate has been more varied: averaging 7 percent during 1950–65, falling sharply thereafter to 3.5 percent between 1965–80, and rising again to 7.9 percent during the period 1980–89.[1] Although the numbers are not so impressive, India's industrial policy did achieve in creating a large industrial base with domestic production accounting for approximately 95 percent of the supply of manufactured goods and almost 100 percent of consumer goods until the 1980s.[2]

The Change Team

Disagreeing with the view that economic liberalisation in India began with the fiscal crisis of 1991, I have argued elsewhere that the process of economic reforms was initiated during the 1980s.[3] In those early years, during the Rajiv Gandhi period (1984–89), the crucial change that took place was a shift in policy discourse with the introduction of new ideas to shape economic policy. Rajiv Gandhi, himself a critic of the earlier economic model, began a critical review of the old policy. The most crucial aspect of the changes of that decade was the introduction of new ideas and the putting in place of a *change team* to carry forward the task of economic reform.

The new ideas that emerged from a critical inquiry of the earlier model of development generated a counter model. While a complete conversion of ideas did not take place, a crucial shift in the dominant ideas governing economic policy did begin. What remained was actual forging of a new consensus around these ideas. The elements of this new discourse were in sharp contrast to that of the Nehru–Mahalanobis period (1950–80). It laid emphasis on technology, exports, profits, quality, competition and market signals as opposed to the earlier concerns regarding self-reliance, protection, licensing and prevention of the concentration of wealth.[4]

In India no key pilot agency can be pinpointed as having driven the economic liberalisation process. Instead, a group of policy entrepreneurs, or the change team,[5] were installed in positions which made it possible for them to play a key role in the liberalisation process. Elsewhere I have detailed the composition and nature of the work of this change team. Suffice it to say here that it was comprised of both political and bureaucratic members.[6] The latter included members from the permanent civil service and laterals who were economic advisors appointed from outside the administrative career pool of the bureaucracy.

The Indian model of economic reform that has emerged is one of the change team playing a crucial role in the liberalisation process. Having experience in working within the Indian system, this group of individuals was familiar with the pressures and pulls of introducing change in India. Their work can be seen as a three-fold process. The first has consisted of the preparatory work: that is, writing policy papers, doing the research work, making new lists of industries for decontrol, and detailing the sequence of liberalisation. The second has consisted of remaining sensitive to the political situation in the country, especially after 1989 when political instability and coalition governments have been the norm. As A. N. Verma, Principal Secretary to Prime Minister Rao (1991–96) admitted, 'In evolving our proposals we took note of what was politically sensitive.'[7] As the change team consisted of both politicians and bureaucrats, a two-way self-reinforcing process began to operate in which the bureaucrats needed a political leadership supportive of reforms, just as the latter needed the detailed policy work of the administrators. Third, ready with proposals, the change team pushed reforms whenever a window of opportunity emerged. The change team has thus been able to maintain a basic commitment to liberalisation and has continuously worked on the strategies for change.

The change team has identified the core areas of reform and made public statements about them. In recent budget documents, apart from announcing changes, the government has set the direction and pace of reforms. In 1996, for example, the government announced that it would set up expert committees to recommend changes in key areas. The latter included insurance, disinvestment in public sector enterprises (PSEs), management of public expenditure, a Tariff Commission, and a new bill for a Board for Industrial and Financial Reconstruction (BIFR). While progress has not been achieved on all fronts so far, work has started with the Disinvestment Commission and an insurance bill. The latter was very close to being passed by Parliament in May 1999 but became a victim of the ongoing politics and governmental instability.

Economic Crisis and Political Instability

The process of implementing reforms in India, as in many others countries, has shown that new ideas and a change team by themselves do not lead to the successful passage of substantial reforms. Carrying them to fruition also depends on the electoral mandate that a government enjoys, the capacity of a state to implement new policies, and pressures from opposition political parties or other groups in society. The stalling of reforms from within state institutions can be pervasive, especially in an administrative context in which the bureaucracy enjoys substantial power in relation to the sector that is being reformed. Moreover, if the process of policy change is long and drawn out, encompassing different leaders and a number of years, it is likely that other influences will work their way into the process. New technical options may be induced by economic pressures, or there could be active pressures from external actors such as international financial institutions.

The severe balance of payments crisis of 1991, in which India was left with foreign reserves to cover only two weeks of imports and reached a situation of near default on external payments, created a political window of opportunity in which some reforms were rapidly pushed through. The economic crisis also forced India to seek help from the International

Monetary Fund (IMF) and agree to external conditionalities. The crisis created a context in which selling reforms to various domestic constituencies became much easier for the Rao government (1991–96). The stabilization and structural adjustment program of the government implemented by Finance Minister Manmohan Singh during 1991–96 encompassed various measures to deal with the crisis. Among the first were measures to curb inflation, which was brought down from 17 percent in 1991 to around 8–10 percent in 1992–93. Growth figures also went up, rebounding from 0.8 percent in 1991 to 5.1 in 1992–93, and reaching 6.3 percent in 1995–96.[8]

Despite measures to control and manage India's macro-economic stability, public finances have turned adverse and expenditures have overshot targets. All governments since 1991 have had a difficult time reigning in fiscal deficits which have continued to hover around 5–6 percent. The budget estimate of the fiscal deficit for 1997–98 was 4.5 percent of GDP, but that rose to 6.1 (the highest since 1993–94) and may need further revision owing to the bounty of the government with regard to urea prices and reduction of import duties across the board. The internal debt burden has consequently soared to 9.7 percent of GDP (*Economic Survey*, 1997–98). Exports have suffered a slowdown as well, after doing very well during the early 1990s. From 20 percent annual growth rates, they have fallen to 14 percent during 1994–97, and plunged further to 2.6 percent in 1997–98.

In the thirteen months that the BJP-led coalition government was in office it passed two budgets. Soon after presenting its second budget, the government lost a no-confidence vote in Parliament. While the budget was passed regardless, the political turmoil in the country has put the reform process in a limbo at a time when the economy was already in a downturn. The annual rate of growth has fallen from 7 percent and more that was achieved in 1994–97 to 5 percent, and was likely to fall further according to information put out by the Center for Monitoring the Indian Economy, a reliable source for data on India. Sectoral growth rates have declined as well with agriculture falling to -2 percent in 1997–98 from 7.9 percent in 1996–97, and industrial growth going down to 5.7 percent after recording a simple average of 8 percent between 1992–93 to 1996–97. Thus, the reform process has been affected by the recurrent political instability and economic slowdown.

Democratic Compulsions

What seems to have emerged as the Indian model of reforms is one of reforms in a consensual mode. In the Indian case, the democratic context makes leaders acutely aware and sensitive to possible political opposition that economic reforms may bring. Hence, they are 'careful not to administer too great a shock to the domestic economy', tailoring reform policies to suit the political mood. This became clear when Prime Minister Rao, returning from the Earth Summit in 1992, said that in his talks with other leaders also involved in reforming their economies, it emerged that a gradual approach to reform worked better. The politicians have repeatedly pointed out that reforms are a process which would be spread over a number of years. The gradual approach to reforms also has supporters outside government. Tarun Das, Director-General of the administrative wing of the Confederation of Indian Industry (CII), a major industry association that is playing a new role in influencing the government,[9] states that, unlike the East Asian economies, 'India is not a tiger' and would rather pursue a steady process of reforms.[10] Hence, the political leaders have constantly emphasized building consensus for the reforms. When a Mexican or a South east Asian economic crisis occurs, they point to how the cautious approach has in fact served India better.

Interestingly, the annual IMF–World Bank meeting in Washington in October 1998 highlighted this when officials of the international financial institutions were all praise for China and India. They pointed to the fact that both India and China have held steady and been able to maintain growth at a time when other countries are facing the effects of the East Asian turmoil. IMF director, Michael Camdessus, said after the meeting, 'They [India and China] are proceeding at their own pace and of their own volition toward a more open market economy, dismantling regulations and controls that are recognized as impediments to growth'.[11]

Yet, in the 1998 *Global Competitiveness Report* India ranked fiftieth out of fifty-three countries in overall competitiveness. As Nirupam Bajpai and Jeffrey Sachs point out, this has not changed much from India's position as forty-ninth in the 1997 report.[12] India's strengths are in five areas: a vibrant stock market, strong science and engineering capabilities, relatively strong business schools, a vast labor force and judicial independence and rule of law. Alongside, there are significant areas of weakness as well: deficient financial markets, numerous administrative regulations which still exist despite reforms, numerous state subsidies, poor availability and quality of infrastructure, ineffective labor markets, prevalence of irregular payments (i.e. bribes), and poor facilities for research and development with little success at commercializing new technologies. These weaknesses all point to areas in which further reforms are required.

After the initial sweep of reforms in 1991, it is alleged that economic reforms have slowed down, or at least have not maintained a pace which has gained the approval of foreign investors. The knowledge that the immediate dangers of economic crisis and bankruptcy have declined and that foreign reserves had gone up, especially after 1992, has possibly contributed to the slow down in the rate of implementation of reform measures. Time and again, Indian officials point out, the Indian system works well in a crisis but once a sense of normalcy returns, then action slackens. It should be pointed out that, apart from a few politicians who have supported and stood at the forefront of the reforms, the majority do not support them enthusiastically either because they do not want to hurt powerful lobbies or are unsure of the repercussions on their electoral constituencies. Thus, domestic politics, with the emergence of coalition governments, weakening of party institutions and political instability have decreased the conditions of state autonomy.

Variable Sensitivities to Reform

Yet, these very conditions contain both opportunities and constraints for economic reform. This becomes clearer if, for purposes of analysis, we divide reforms into two sets: *high-profile* and *low-profile* reforms. High profile reforms are those that are more visible and affect mass politics. They typically require strong government, higher state capacity, and/or astute political management. Examples of these include *exit* policy, privatization of public sector enterprises, ending government subsidies, and insurance sector reforms. These reforms are politically more sensitive, affect public opinion, and hence have a more difficult time being passed. Low profile reforms are those that are invisible to the public eye and hence go unnoticed or do not affect mass politics. They may be just as important for the economy but are either not easily understood by the general public, or they do not create the same political upsurge and hence can be more easily passed by a smaller section of the political and bureaucratic elite. Successive governments have routinely undertaken such reforms. Examples are capital market reforms, converting the Industrial Credit and Investment Corporation of India (ICICI) and the IFLC into a corporation which can raise capital in the market, changes to the National Mineral Policy in 1993 which included removing restrictions on foreign nationals holding equity in mining companies and numerous others.

Thus, low profile programs like the stabilization program, rationalization and lowering of import duties, rationalization of domestic indirect taxes, freeing the foreign exchange regime and current account convertibility have been consistently spread over numerous budgets. Fiscal deficits have been slowly brought down to 5 percent and 4.5 percent since 1991. Likewise, there has been progress on other routine reforms, which have been consistently passed during this period.

The implementation of high profile reforms have, predictably, proved difficult to implement. In the early Rao period, although the government promised to reduce subsidies, it was only able to reduce export subsidies and carry out a partial decontrol of fertilizer prices in 1992. However, because of political pressure emanating largely from the farm lobby and its representatives in Parliament, the fertilizer subsidies were restored in 1993.

Social sector spending which was reduced in the budget of 1991, was also pushed up later, and has been increasing in subsequent budgets.[13] A 32 percent increase was made in the plan size in 1993–94 to give a fillip to development programs. India is one of the few examples of a country that has increased social sector spending during its structural adjustment program under pressure from its rural lobby and left political opposition to reform policies.[14]

This has led to comments along the following lines, 'India's economic reforms of the 1990s while having achieved a distinct beginning, have not demonstrated sustainability. After the initial set of actions the speed of reform slowed down. ... The main problems seem to be continued ad-hocism and a lack of well-integrated policies, non-transparent nature of selected policies and political uncertainty'.[15]

Even in those areas where changes have been made, there has been some degree of zig-zag on reforms, giving a distorted picture to the outside world. Key examples of these are the decisions to open telecommunications and power to the private sector. The National Telecom Policy, passed in May 1994, followed what the then Secretary calls a 'homeopathic approach' – one of nibbling at reform by opening services first in select cities and circles. He would rather the government had opened all circles simultaneously, made entry transparent, and restructured the relevant government departments (namely, the Department of Telecommunications and the Mahanagar Telephone Nigam Limited).[16] Similarly in the case of power, the outline policy for private investment was published in 1992, but the details were brought out only two years later. Moreover, the case by case approach is troubling as it creates greater scope for corruption. The Enron case is a good example of the dangers of political involvement in approving projects. The subsequent judicial inquiry and settlement have provided a learning experience to those in power, albeit at the high cost of negative exposure and delay in project completion.[17]

In contrast, the government has referred the case of public sector reforms to the BIFR for consideration and recommendation. Although slow, since 1996 a number of changes have been put in place.[18] Among these an autonomy package for the *navratnas*, or the nine blue-chip PSEs, has been approved. This policy was extended to 97 small PSEs, called *mini-ratnas* in September 1997. The government publicly committed itself once again to public sector reforms by stating in the 1998 budget that its share-holding in PSEs would be brought down to 26 percent.[19]

To further reforms in sectors that have been doing well over the last decade, the government declared certain areas as 'thrust areas'. One such sector is software, which earns a sizable share of India's exports earnings. The software industry in India has been growing at over 50 percent per year since 1991. While exports in other areas slowed down recently, this sector remained buoyant with software export earnings totaling more than

Rs 65,300 million in 1997–98 and an overall growth rate of 70 percent in 1998–99, as reported by the National Association of Software and Service Companies (Nasscom). The government set up a Task Force on Information Technology (IT) headed by the deputy chair of the Planning Commission, Jaswant Singh, to formulate a national informatics policy. With the dynamic and IT-savvy Chief Minister of Andhra Pradesh Chandrababu Naidu as the co-chair, the task force exhibited keenness to remove obstacles to the fast growth of this sector.

State Governments and Economic Reform

There has also been a shift in the site of reforms from Delhi, the nation's capital, to various state capitals. Taking their cue from the center, a number of state governments have come forward with reform polices at the state level. While the Congress Party carried out the reforms in the Center; elections to state legislative assemblies in 1993, 1994 and 1995 brought a variety of opposition and regional parties to power in the states. The fact that most of these governments have shown commitment to reform by carrying forward their own programs of reform provides evidence that a broader based consensus on economic reforms has been building.

However, it should be noted that this process has been aided by a longer process which has involved the central government putting pressure on state governments to control state budget deficits. The demand that states pay their share of bills to the public sector had begun to be made by the governments of Mrs. Gandhi and Rajiv Gandhi in the late 1980s. Threats that either state governments pay their dues or the central government would deduct the sums owed from their plan grants and cut off credit to them, began to be implemented under the Rao government. Facing a finance crunch on transfers from the center, states found it increasingly difficult to implement election promises, especially populist measures like free school lunches or subsidized rice which had helped the parties get elected to office.

The tighter fiscal situation compelled many state governments to undertake initiatives for fiscal reform. On the revenue front, some states have undertaken to reform sales tax administration (namely Kerala, Maharashtra, Punjab and Uttar Pradesh); privatise the collection of octroi tax (an interstate tax charged on the movement of goods; a course followed in Maharashtra, Rajasthan and Punjab); reform the taxation of property (Andhra Pradesh); establish new luxury taxes and modifying existing state excises (Punjab, Maharashtra and Rajasthan); and pass legislation to permit tolls on bridges, highways and overpasses designed to attract private sector participation in public infrastructure development (Rajasthan, Tamilnadu, Punjab and Madhya Pradesh).

Realizing that it is up to them to improve the climate for industry, a number of states have undertaken economic reforms to attract private sector industrial investments. Most states have created a single window agency for approving investments, both foreign and domestic. A number of states have established special software technology parks or industrial parks for the promotion of exports, providing these with comprehensive infrastructural facilities and tax exemptions. Noteworthy in this regard are Karnataka, Andhra Pradesh and Haryana.

With the central government allowing private sector involvement in infrastructure, a number of state governments have finalized agreements with private parties on power projects and the development of roads. Noteworthy among these are Maharashtra, Madhya Pradesh, Gujarat, Orissa, Kerala and West Bengal. Coastal states are also looking at private participation in the development of ports. In power sector reform, Orissa led the way with a comprehensive program adopted by the state in 1993.[20] The ultimate objective of the Orissa government is to completely withdraw from the power sector as an operator of utilities and limit its role to policy making and regulation. Toward that end, it has set up the Orissa Electricity Regulatory Commission with jurisdiction over setting tariffs, licensing and monitoring performance standards. The Orissa State Electricity Board has been replaced with three corporate entities in 1995 with authority to generate, transmit and distribute electricity.

A number of states are also involved in the disinvestment of equity, closure, reorganization and/or selling state enterprises, in order to cut losses and raise funds for investment. Noteworthy are Kerala and Uttar Pradesh. While the former has the most formally articulated strategy, the latter is making faster progress on implementation. In Gujarat, reorganization has taken place with retraining of labor. While a coherent national exit policy is shrouded in politics; at the state level the selling of state resources, retrenchment of labor, and retraining are being pursued in a piecemeal manner by state public enterprises.

An attempt is being made to isolate and abolish those laws that are retrograde. For example, in Madhya Pradesh the need to renew licenses under the Factories Act have been abolished. In Maharashtra, the district collector's permission to convert agricultural land to industrial use is no longer needed. Industrial location policy has also been revised to permit the setting up of industries that are non-polluting, non-hazardous and hi-tech within the municipal zone of Greater Bombay.

In the last few years, competition between states to woo foreign investment has also started, with chief ministers going abroad to invite investors to their 'investor friendly state'. Noteworthy are the trips by the chief ministers of communist West Bengal, Jyoti Basu, and Chandrababu Naidu of Andhra Pradesh, to the US. Table 1 gives a state-wise break-up of approved foreign investment in India.

Table 1: Foreign Collaboration & Foreign Direct Investment Proposals Approved In The Reform Period (August 1991–January 1997), by State

State	Technical	Financial	Total	Amount of FDI Approved*	% of Total
A & Nicobar Islands		5	5	9.8	0.0
Andhra Pradesh	1,144	295	439	25,112.7	2.5
Arunachal Pradesh	na	2	2	110.6	0.0
Assam	6	4	10	15.0	0.0
Bihar	42	27	69	1,307.5	0.1
Chandigarh	2	12	14	724.6	0.1
Dadra & Nagar Haveli	32	16	48	698.3	0.1
Daman & Diu	9	7	16	57.2	0.0
Delhi	54	458	512	1,173,303.6	17.1
Goa	33	35	68	2,823.9	0.3
Gujarat	297	251	548	37,625.4	3.7
Haryana	146	268	414	17,884.0	1.8
Himachal Pradesh	48	22	70	3,296.8	0.3
Jammu & Kashmir		1	1	80.1	0.0
Karnataka	255	434	689	54,938.9	5.4
Kerala	38	66	104	5,209.2	0.5
Lakshadweep	na	1	1	5.0	0.0
Madhya Pradesh	82	110	192	52,683.3	5.2
Maharashtra	523	832	1,355	126,763.9	12.5
Meghalaya		1	1	25.0	0.0
Nagaland	1		1		0.0
Orissa	28	49	77	37,907.9	3.7
Pondicherry	22	30	52	2,529.1	0.3
Punjab	39	66	105	8,212.0	0.8
Rajasthan	65	128	193	6,054.7	0.6
Tamilnadu	269	543	812	54,687.5	5.4
Tripura		1	1	6.8	0.0
Uttar Pradesh	176	219	395	24,445.2	2.4
West Bengal	92	179	271	52,495.5	5.2
Others (state not indicated)	2,142	1,752	3,894	325,926.7	32.1
Total	4,545	5,814	10,359	1,014,940.2	100.0

Note: * in Rupees million

Source: Government of India, Ministry of Industry, Secretariat for Industrial Approvals, *Newsletter*, February 1997.

While these are healthy developments, a lot remains to be done. As industrial enterprises are set up at the local level; they continue to face difficulties in getting land, water, telephone and electricity connections. It is at this level, of procedural and administrative reforms, that a lot remains to be done. Jaswant Singh, a prominent member of the BJP, chaired a committee of chief ministers, which met regularly to discuss reforms that could be passed or implemented across the states. Key to these were changes in excise duties and sales taxes.

Some states have been more proactive than others. Both in terms of state level reform and FDI, some states have done better than others. In terms of foreign investment inflows; Maharashtra, Gujarat, Tamilnadu, Delhi and Andhra Pradesh are leaders; while Uttar Pradesh, Madhya Pradesh, Rajasthan, Bihar and Assam are laggards. The latter group are also more populous and poorer in fiscal resources. While the Bihar government has been notorious for its fiscal mismanagement, Assam has been troubled by law and order problems. Although there are a wide variety of changes taking place, available information indicates that states with higher incomes and greater levels of political stability have been able to attract more foreign capital than the ones who are poorer or have politically unstable state governments.[21] And, states that lag in reducing the 'license-permit-quota *raj*' and 'inspector *raj*' continue to lose industrial investment and employment in favor of those that do.

Foreign Direct Investment

The foreign investment regime in India has been liberalised since 1991, making it easier to bring in foreign investment with up to 51 to 100 percent ownership in a number of industries. Although foreign direct investment (FDI) was allowed in high priority industries first, since liberalisation FDI has been slowly allowed into almost all areas including infrastructure (such as mining, roads, ports, and telecommunications). There is a very short list of industries from which it is excluded now, that are perceived as sensitive with regard to the environment or defense. The Foreign Investment Promotion Board (FIPB) was set up in 1992 to approve foreign investment proposals. In addition, the Reserve Bank of India (RBI) has also been granted the power of automatic approval for foreign investment in a number of cases specified in the annual budgets. As such, FDI in India has increased significantly after 1991 to a little over $2.9 billion in September 1998.[22]

However, although the government has repeatedly stated that it welcomes FDI, there are still a number of issues that need attention for the inflow of FDI to increase further. These include the adoption of a clear and transparent policy regarding foreign investment rather than the granting of approval on a case by case basis; allowing investment in the small-scale sector, and making the process of approval faster and easier.

Often the government has sent mixed signals to foreign investors (as in the Enron case, and in that of the Singapore-Tata Airlines joint venture). As a result, India, which received 0.1 percent of the global FDI between 1985–1992, has been merely able to increase its share to 0.6 percent after 1993. This is minuscule compared to China which received 5 percent of global FDI in 1985–92 and 9 percent after 1993.[23]

CONSTRAINTS ON THE REFORM PROCESS

Reforms are Anti-Poor

In the democratic political system of India with its large poor population, the politician has generally been perceived as the savior of the poor and downtrodden. As the liberal press and certain political parties have painted the reforms as pro-rich and pro-urban, the public has been swayed by what it has heard in the short-term, and not by what they might expect in the long-term.

Reform advocates argue that with long term growth and a larger GDP, the benefits of reform will slowly but certainly trickle down to the entire population, including the poor.[24] However, in the interim high growth rates have not been consistent, as the figures since 1997 show. Overall exports have also slowed down from 20 percent growth to about 2.5 percent since 1997. This is compounded by various fiscal corrections that have been undertaken, with the result that the situation for the poor has worsened. Recent studies on the effect of reforms have found that since liberalisation; food prices have risen, inflationary pressure has lowered real wages, and the contraction of public sector spending in areas like health, education and public works have all meant that the poor are directly hurt much more. While the latest available estimates in 1993–94 point to the fact that incidence of poverty or the proportion of people living below the poverty line has gone down since 1987–88, Rao asserts that the consumer price index for agricultural laborers has increased by 50 percent over the five years ending 1993–94. This has been due to the effort to reduce food subsides which has led to a steep increase in the issue prices of foodgrains under the public distribution system (PDS).[25]

These conclusions are based on studies of the immediate or short run macro economic measures as the full impact of economic reforms on the poor over the long term is yet to be ascertained. As discussed here the more difficult 'high profile reforms', including reforms in agriculture, have not been undertaken as reformers in India have so far been cautious about hurting any large group in a big way. Furthermore, the left parties and other critics of economic liberalisation have viewed the opening of the economy and efforts to attract foreign investment as a sell-out to multinationals, as hurting national interests, and leading to lay-offs. All of this is well understood by a public that has been bred on socialist rhetoric for four decades, and has made a speedy implementation of the reform package all the more difficult.

Hence, the reforms have been generally perceived to be anti-poor. As this counter discourse affects elections, there has been a slowing down of reforms prior to elections. Instead, populist measures are promised to gain quick support of the public.

Electoral Realignments

The dominance of one party over Indian politics between 1950–80 led analysts to call the party system in India the 'Congress system'. However, the increasing de-institutionalization of the party, rise of personalistic politics, and resort to populist rhetoric have led to an overall secular decline of the Congress at both the Centre and the states. This became especially evident in the elections of 1989, 1991 and 1996 when the traditional support bases of the Congress, particularly those concentrated in the minorities, such as Muslims, and the Scheduled Castes and Tribes; abandoned it for other parties.[26]

The electoral experience of the Congress party in 1996 was dismal. Having ushered in economic reforms the Congress party faced a debacle in the state elections of 1993 and was voted out at the Centre in 1996. The opposition parties emphasised in their rhetoric that the economic reforms had led to scams, making the rich richer. Consequently, there is a strong perception that any party identified as the champion of reforms will reap a poor electoral fate.

The decline of the Congress party and re-emergence of caste and religious mobilization have colored the political landscape in India in recent years. Hindu religious sentiments have been whipped up by the Bharatiya Janata Party (the BJP, or the erstwhile Jan Sangh) and led to mass politicization around religious issues. The secular opposition parties, who have relied on an alliance of backward castes since 1967, have attempted to convert this coalition into a more stable base of support by mobilizing the Other Backward Castes (OBCs) and Dalits. Such mobilization reached its high-point in 1989–90, when Prime Minister V.P. Singh decided to implement the Mandal Commission Report and reserve a proportion of government jobs for the OBCs.

The political developments of the late 1980s and early 1990s have defied simple electoral arithmetic, forcing all parties to accept some realignment of their constituencies. While the Congress party has proved unable to retain all of its traditional supporters, the opposition parties (grouped around the Janata Party as the United Front) have been unable to coalesce the groups they were aiming toward. Meanwhile, the Hindu vote has remained too unstable to make the BJP feel politically secure, as the conditions under which Hindus vote as Hindus are different from when they vote on caste, class or issue lines. The gravitation of the backward castes and Dalits in Bihar and UP to political parties (such as the Rashtriya Janata Dal, Samata Party and Bahujan Samaj Party) that are regional, has added to the state of flux. The re-negotiation of electoral bases, given the caste and religious polarization, signifies that electoral fortunes have become more and more unpredictable.

Coalition Politics

Given the political instability and the increasing difficulty in any one party forming a majority government, the formation of coalition governments, begun in 1989, has ushered in a new era in Indian politics. Prior to that year, electoral pressures only built up during the last year or two of the five-year term of a parliament. But with the advent of coalition governments, the political elites have become preoccupied with the more immediate issues of politics, leaving little time for matters of long-term policy and developmental projects which could risk short-term gains for the sake of long-term benefits to the country.[27]

Conventional political wisdom states that, as a rule, coalition governments signal the erosion of state autonomy. Economic policy, especially corrective policy that needs strong measures, is not a priority for political elites at such times. Rather, soft policies that help build political bridges and sustain politicians' power bases become more important.

Yet, in the Indian case, an anomaly to such conventional wisdom took place when the liberalisation process received its major push in 1991 under a minority government. The immediate context of a severe economic crisis enabled the Rao government to push through a wide set of reforms for which the details had been worked out earlier. In addition, as Varshney has argued, the rise of triangular politics in India since 1989, in which the task of keeping the BJP out of power has surpassed the importance of obstructing economic reforms by center-left parties, made the passage of economic reforms much easier.[28] 1991 may have been an exceptional period, as the experience of subsequent coalition governments comes closer to the conventional wisdom outlined above.

The experience of the coalition government of the United Front (UF), during 1996–98, is one such example. Comprised of fourteen parties with varied ideological commitments, the UF government faced contradictory pulls on numerous occasions, with little central control being exercised with regard to economic reforms. This led to a situation where individual decisions in different ministries affected the pace and progress of reforms. A number of reform measures were passed in early 1997 largely because of the direct intervention of Prime Minister Deve Gowda himself. Under pressure from business, Gowda prodded the bureaucrats into action, who 'drew up a list of policies that had been put on the back-burner' by the earlier administration. Virtually none of these policies were conceived from scratch: all of them were already in various stages of completion. Gowda had to pursue reforms while managing his political colleagues, a difficult task given the diverse interests present.[29]

The BJP-led government had a short stint of thirteen months in power. The pressures of keeping a thirteen party coalition together proved difficult from the very start as threats from the AIADMK constituent from Tamilnadu continuously plagued the Vajpayee government, leading to its downfall in April 1999. Despite its political problems, a number of important economic bills which the government had deemed as 'second generation reforms' like, the Foreign Exchange Management Act (FEMA), creation of a insurance regulatory authority, a money laundering bill, and others were introduced.

The BJP government gave emphasis to its *swadeshi* plank from its manifesto. In order to appease businesses it imposed an across-the-board custom duty of 8 percent in 1998 (later reduced to 4 percent) arguing that it was providing a level playing field for domestic businesses. In its second budget it sought to reduce fiscal deficits, revive the economy by giving concessions to the housing sector, to agriculture, and to lowering interest rates.[30]

Financial Scams

A number of financial scams have emerged since the start of economic liberalisation raising doubts about reforms in the financial sector. These scandals have come to imply that reforms lead to corruption, and that there is a need to go slow on reforms. The spate of scandals has created the impression that deregulation gives unscrupulous operators opportunities to amass riches quickly. The financial crimes have included a major securities fraud involving Harshad Mehta in 1992, the MS Shoes scandal, ITC, and the CRB Capital Markets collapse in June 1997. However, supporters of reform point out that these incidents highlight the need for greater transparency, better corporate governance, and faster reforms. Nevertheless, these scandals have slowed down the process of financial sector reforms since the government of the day has had to deal with the public wrath and add teeth to regulatory authorities like, the Securities and Exchange Board of India (SEBI).[31]

Ambivalence of Big Business

In the early liberalisation period, domestic industry was euphoric and willing to support the rationalization of rules and decontrol of certain sectors. There was broad agreement that radical changes were needed in licensing procedures to ease entry, making rules transparent, to reduce day-to-day clearances, the cost of making business trips, and of maintaining 'industrial embassies' in the capital.[32]

However, differences within business groups over various issues have led to the business community giving government conflicting signals. The business class has been particularly divided on the issue of foreign investment. This became clear when top business groups met in Bombay in late 1993 and voiced their reservations about liberalisation. Their main complaint was that the effects of liberalisation would be uneven, especially for Indian companies in contrast to their foreign counterparts. They argued that they were not anti-reform or asking for protection, but wanted a level playing field to face unequal competition from abroad. It is unequal because foreign companies have larger resources, are able to access international capital markets at lower interest rates than Indian companies, have better technology and managerial resources. Rahul Bajaj, a spokesperson for the 'Bombay Club' (as this group has come to be known) said, 'It is a matter of time, but after all time is everything. Let more Tiscos, Telcos, Reliances and Bajaj Autos be formed, and then Indian industry will be ready to compete with every one.'[33] While they favor liberalisation in general and the opening of infrastructure to foreign companies they are resisting the latter in sectors in which domestic industry has a presence. Such ambivalence is to be expected from a class that has been protected for so long, especially as the government sought to extend liberalisation to areas about which they were sensitive. The support by the BJP to such ideas, in its call for swadeshi, points to a slowing down of the reforms.

Bureaucratic Stalemate

The constraints stemming from the bureaucracy can be divided into three different sources. First is the fear of inconsequence and loss of control. Officials who have had control over economic decisions for many years are not able to live with the notion that their powers and influence will decrease. As economic reform entails freeing the economy of controls, there is an attempt to find new ways of keeping control. In a number of cases, there has been a withdrawal from declared reforms which can be taken as examples of unfriendly acts by bureaucrats who are not sure of their own position at the end of reforms. These include a change in the airline policy, putting the Tata-Singapore Airline deal in jeopardy; scuttling the Bangalore airport deal by using the argument that it is against 'national interest'; the arbitrary manner in which the Direct Home TV was banned; doling out quotas in the power sector; and constituting the board under the Prasar Bharati Bill.

Second, there has been a lack of confidence in taking a decision and getting sucked into controversy. Bureaucrats often refuse to take strong pro-reform decisions because of a lack of direction from the government. This has compounded in the Indian context of political instability, coalition politics, and the recurrent fall of governments. The possibility of getting sucked into a controversy involving a probe by the Central Bureau of Investigation (CBI) is often enough for some to lie low and delay taking decisions.[34]

Third, many bureaucrats judge the political situation and slowdown voluntarily. The bureaucratic policy elites (such as those part of the 'change team') have come to understand the working of the Indian system well. The political and ideological reality in India resists to speedy changes, especially after socialist ideology has held sway for forty years.

Understanding this reality the bureaucratic policy entrepreneurs have themselves often recommended slowing down the reform process. Instead, they developed a strategy for sequencing the liberalisation program by preparing detailed papers and pushing for change whenever a 'window of opportunity' opened.

Yet, at the same time, it is useful to remember that the literature on economic reform points to an increasing rather than decreasing role for the bureaucracy.[35] Though some departments have closed, such as the Director General of Technical Development (DGTD), in general new roles emerge as a result of reform. These require the officials to get 'market savvy' and to re-invent themselves as the government's role as regulator does not end, but takes on new forms. In the Indian case, the setting up of the Securities and Exchange Bureau of India (SEBI), the Telecom Regulatory Authority of India (TRAI), and numerous state regulatory organizations, point to the fact that officials continue to play important roles, albeit in different garbs.

While some ministries have lost power, other institutions have gained. There has been a shifting around of power, leading to the emergence of stronger institutions as a result of economic reform. The case of the RBI is a crucial example of a state institution whose powers and role in the economy has increased since the reform process began. With the easing of foreign investment and automatic approvals in select industries, the work of the RBI has increased as it is responsible for numerous clearances, approvals and registration.

Democratic Pressures

Democracy in India has been hailed as an exception, compared to most other developing countries where democratic experiments periodically gave way to authoritarian and military dictatorships.[36] However, are democratic pressures in India a constraint or an opportunity to make policy changes? The influence of regime types on policy making has been the focus of research for some time.[37] In statistical terms, the results of these studies have proved to be at best 'mixed', and at worst 'inconclusive'.[38] Yet, they seem to show that democracies do present more obstacles in the path of change than other types of regimes because it is impossible for political parties to build popular support by sacrificing current consumption to secure a 'bright future'. The dilemma between distributing goods for legitimisation and delivering development for accountability pulls a democratic polity in opposite directions, lowering overall growth.[39] Being a democracy, India faced these dilemmas, which made it difficult to change, especially as distributive politics became intertwined with vested interests wanting to maintain the system.[40] Political parties and their leaders realized early enough that a skillful use of socialist and populist promises, even if only in rhetoric, constituted a rewarding electoral strategy. This rhetoric had its counterpart in fiscal policies which influenced the use of state resources. The burgeoning of government expenditures in the context of shrinking revenues and declining ability to tax, along with the 'inability of the state to restrain the acquisitive tendencies' of dominant groups, led to a situation in which the state's capacity to implement declared policies was reduced even further.[41]

The issue of democracy is important because most political leaders have been sensitized to this fact and to the need to build a consensus and carry all the people along with the reforms. Consequently, gradualism has become the hallmark of Indian reforms which has been cited as an achievement by Indian political leaders. By going slow, India has so far avoided a major economic crash, like Mexico or Southeast Asia, or a major political upheaval, akin to the Soviet breakup. On the other hand, India could be faulted for proceeding too slowly. As Isher Ahluwalia pithily said, 'While China was busy reforming its economy and doubling its national income since 1979, India has been debating the process of economic reforms and building a consensus!'[42]

Nature of the State

Issues related to the nature of the state are closely related to those of autonomy and capacity, the extent of intervention in developmental tasks, mobilization of groups, and the ability to shape goals. While the Indian state enjoyed periods of autonomy in which extensive intervention and control of economy and social relations were introduced, over time its capacity to attain its objectives has been seriously eroded.[43] Its overextended administrative structures, with tasks that became too unwieldy for its state apparatuses to keep track of, made relations with government tedious for the common man. In certain cases, state institutions were captured by societal groups that narrowed its capacity and autonomy even further.

Periodically, economists, labor leaders, ex-bureaucrats and intellectuals have attacked the liberalisation program as hurting the 'vulnerable sections of our population ... because of high inflation, concentrated mostly in prices of food and necessities'. They assert that 'the stabilization and adjustment program has stalled economic growth'. Regional and opposition parties have also used the rhetoric of losing sovereign decision-making to outsiders and made populist promises to the electorate to oppose the Congress governments' reform agenda successfully.[44] However, once elected, the fiscal realities have led state governments to embrace the new reform ideology.[45] With erstwhile socialist and communist parties shedding their strident anti-market stance, acceptance of the reform program promises to strengthen in the future.[46]

While a counter-discourse against liberalisation has continued, consensus on the pro-market liberal alternatives has widened, especially after the economic crisis in 1991. Successful consensus building around a new set of ideas that work well with market reforms may well become responsible for the success or failure of the reform package itself. This is because the process of reform is inevitably intertwined with the politics of interest groups. Since the benefits of reform lie in the future and are unknown, interest groups often oppose reforms in the short run, even if they might benefit from them at a later date. Hence, reforms are inevitably faced with a strong status quo bias in the presence of individual specific uncertainty. Regimes that are able to discuss the effects of policy changes and muster domestic political support for those changes are more likely to implement a reform package successfully.[47]

NEED FOR A NEW POLITICAL DISCOURSE ON ECONOMIC REFORMS

To my mind, the next spate of economic reforms could come when the economic reform proposals are conveyed in a language that can demonstrate that reforms will benefit the common man and can help provide opportunities for the poor. According to N. Vittal, former Secretary of the Department of Telecommunications, the language and/or selling of reforms should include some benefits for the politician as well – not in terms of kickbacks, but in emphasising to the public that the politician who supports reforms is bringing specific benefits to his constituency in the process of economic reform.[48] Similarly, Jaswant Singh, the BJP MP, points out that the language used in reform discourse is very important. In the Indian case, the use of words like 'disinvestment'/privatization or 'exit policy' have negative connotations, and it may be more worthwhile to use different words. For example, instead of exit policy, it may be more fruitful to talk of 'new labor laws'.[49] At any rate, some creative thinking is needed so that the political vocabulary is able to effectively communicate the benefits from reform to the people. The party that can effectively achieve fiscal prudence, privatization and build a conducive environment for business; even while it helps to create more jobs, better and larger facilities for education, health, and higher incomes; will be better able to rally mass support for economic reforms.

The current unpredictable outcome of elections and unstable political coalitions seem to indicate that in the near future, one party dominant majorities are unlikely. Hence, reforms will have to be undertaken by coalition governments. In such circumstances what kind of political coalitions can best create constituencies for furthering the cause of economic reforms in India? The most favourable scenario may be if centrist parties form a coalition at the center, for example under the Congress party. A coalition under the BJP sent mixed signals to foreign investors with its swadeshi, but saw a continuation of administrative and procedural reforms. However, in order to succeed, the BJP also had to behave like a centrist party by the time it left power in mid-1999.

The worst case for reforms would be a coalition of parties that sees the expansion of state sectors and public expenditures as best supporting its constituency. This must be understood in relation to the large-scale political democratization of depressed classes and castes that has taken place in the 1990s. By coincidence, the process of economic reforms and an aggressive campaign for their rights by the depressed classes and castes have become synchronized. This politicization has led to the break up of the traditional voting pattern of every political party and has had its effect on the pace of economic reforms as well. The tension between a shrinking state presence in various sectors as required by the reforms, and the assertive use of state power by this section to fulfill its political and economic aspirations is a crucial issue in present-day Indian politics. One way to accommodate the reform process with the aspirations of the newly mobilized classes would be by focusing on the importance of social-sector spending, especially in education and health. Thus, there is a need for creative leadership that can link economic reforms to more basic issues like education, employment and health.[50]

In any case, as highlighted above, some economic reforms will continue owing to the work of the economic bureaucracy or 'change team', which will continue to provide the specialized papers and recommendations for reforming specific sectors. Specific recommendations will be implemented, in an intermittent manner, as and when political 'windows of opportunity' become available. In addition, the role of business associations pushing for reforms has also increased, and their continual pressure for more economic changes will also have an influence on policy.

NOTES

1 Isher Ahluwalia, *Industrial Growth in India: Stagnation since the Mid-Sixties* (Delhi: Oxford University Press, 1985).
2 World Bank, *India: An Industrializing Economy in Transition* (A World Bank Country Study, 1989), 7.
3 Vanita Shastri, 'The Politics of Economic Liberalisation in India', *Contemporary South Asia* 6 (1), 1997; and 'The Political Economy of Policy Formation in

India: The Case of Industrial Policy, 1948–94', Ph.D. dissertation, Cornell University, 1995.
4 For a detailed schematic representation of the two models, see Shastri, 'Politics of Economic Liberalisation in India', ibid., 35.
5 This term is used by John Waterbury to describe the technocrats who manage the reform process and the sequential shift in public policy. As the 'brain trust of the political leadership', they 'require the visible and consistent support of the head of state'. However, in his usage, Waterbury expands the notion to include political leaders involved in the reform program. It is in this broader sense that the concept is used here – to refer to the small but cohesive group that initiates, rationalises, and carries forth the reform agenda, thus including bureaucrats, technocrats and political leaders. See John Waterbury, 'The Heart of the Matter? Public Enterprise and the Adjustment Process', in Stephan Haggard and Robert Kaufmann, eds, *The Politics of Economic Adjustment: International Constraints, Distributive Politics, and the State* (Princeton: Princeton University Press, 1990), 191.
6 Shastri, 'Politics of Economic Liberalisation in India'.
7 This meant that politically sensitive issues were not taken up: A. N. Verma, interview, New Delhi, September 1997.
8 For details on this period, see Ronald J. Herring's chapter in this volume.
9 See Shastri, 'Political Economy of Policy Formation in India', op cit., chapter 6, 322–371.
10 Tarun Das, interview, *India Abroad*, 10 October 1997, 26.
11 *Times of India*, 6 October 1998.
12 See Nirupam Bajpai and Jeffrey Sachs, 'Strengthening India's Strategy for Economic Growth', *Economic and Political Weekly* (EPW), 18 July 1998.
13 *Economic Times*, 15 March 1993. See also Special Budget Section of 1995.
14 For a discussion of the role of different lobbies on economic reform, see Prem Shankar Jha, 'Political Freedom and Economic Reform', paper presented at Center for International Affairs seminar, Harvard University, 3 March 1995; and Atul Kohli, 'Politics of Economic Liberalisation in India', *World Development* 17 (3), 1989, 309–21, for the earlier period.
15 Parthasarathi Shome and Hiranya Mukhopadhyay, 'Economic Liberalisation of the 1990s', *EPW*, 18 July 1998, 1925.
16 N. Vittal, former Secretary of Department of Telecommunications, interview, New Delhi, 20 August 1996.
17 The Enron power project was approved by the Congress government in Maharashtra under the scheme for fast-track power projects set up by the central government in 1993. However, the BJP-Shiv Sena coalitions, which formed the state government after the elections of 1995, canceled the Enron deal in a highly politicized and dramatic manner. Subsequently, faced with a legal battle with Enron, the BJP government at the state renegotiated the project with an agreement from Enron to lower the per unit cost of power for consumers.
18 For a background of public sector reforms, see Shastri, 'Political Economy of Policy Formation in India', op cit., 404–423.
19 Government has typically owned majority shares in public sector enterprises, but since the economic reforms process in 1991, the share of government and governmental financial institutions is being brought down slowly. The first such case was that of Maruti Udyog in which the government allowed the foreign partner (Suzuki) to increase its stake to 51 percent in 1992.
20 Material for this section is taken from the 'Economic Survey' of various years, especially 1995–96.

21 'Economic Liberalisation and Federalism: The Case of India', *Contemporary South Asia*, forthcoming.
22 *Economic Times*, 23 October 1998.
23 N. S. Siddharthan, 'Industrial Deceleration and 1998–99 Union Budget', *EPW*, 18 July 1998, 2018.
24 C. H. Hanumantha Rao and Hans Linnemann, eds, *Economic Reforms and Poverty Alleviation in India* (New Delhi: Sage Publications, 1996); Smitu Kothari, 'Whose Independence: Social Impact of Economic Reform in India', *Journal of International Affairs* 51 (1), June 1996, 85–115; Madura Swaminathan, 'Structural Adjustment, Food Security and Systems of Public Distribution of Food', *EPW* 31 (26), 1996, 1065–72; and World Bank, *India: Achievements and Challenges in Reducing Poverty* (Washington, D.C.: World Bank, 1997).
25 C. H. Hanumantha Rao, 'Agricultural Growth, Sustainability and Poverty Alleviation: Recent Trends and Major Issues of Reform', *EPW* 18 July 1998, 1945. Also see V. M. Rao, 'Economic Reforms and the Poor', *EPW* 18 July 1998, 1949–1954; J. Mohan Rao, 'Food, Agriculture and Reforms', *EPW* 18 July 1998, 1955–1960; and S. Mahendra Dev, 'Public Distribution System: Impact on Poor and Options for Reform', *EPW* 29 August 1998, 2285–90.
26 See Stanley Kochanek's chapter in this volume.
27 E. Sridharan, 'Leadership Time Horizons in India: The Impact on Economic Restructuring', *Asian Survey* 31 (12), December 1991, 1200–13.
28 Ashutosh Varshney, 'Mass Politics or Elite Politics? India's Economic Reforms in Comparative Perspective', Harvard University, December 1996, mimeo.
29 George Skaria and Rohit Saran, 'Reforms 97: The Inside Story', *Business Today*, 7–21 March 1997, 74–89.
30 Special Issue on the 1999 Budget, *Frontline* 16, 13–26 March 1999.
31 After the Harshad Mehta stock market scam, new laws for monitoring and preventing insider trading and manipulations of stock prices were put in place. See Percy Mistry, 'Financial Sector Reform in India', in Robert Cassen and Vijay Joshi, eds, *India: The Future of Economic Reform* (Delhi: Oxford University Press, 1996); L.C. Gupta, 'What Ails the Indian Capital market?' *EPW*, 18 July 1998;, 1961–66; and Shalendra D. Sharma, 'Democracy, Neoliberalism and Growth with Equity: Lessons from India and Chile', *Contemporary South Asia*, forthcoming.
32 Surinder Kapoor, businessman, interview, New Delhi, 16 July 1992.
33 *Economic Times*, 22 August 1997, 3.
34 In the last few years a number of top officials and senior politicians have been caught in cases of corruption which have allegedly resulted from reform in some sectors. The most telling example was in the field of telecom in which the Minister of Communications, Sukh Ram, and officials in the Department of Telecom were found to have been involved. In the face of political uncertainty and unstable governments, numerous decisions are not taken or are postponed because officials are not willing to take the risk of being punished later.
35 Miles Kahler, 'Orthodoxy and its Alternatives: Explaining Approaches to Stabilization and Adjustment', in Joan Nelson, ed, *Economic Crisis and Policy Choice* (Princeton: Princeton University Press, 1990).
36 Jagdish Bhagwati, 'Democracy and Development', *Journal of Democracy* 3 (3), 1992; Atul Kohli, 'Democracy and Development', in John Lewis and Valeriana Kallab, eds, *Development Strategies Reconsidered* (New Brunswick: Transition Books, 1986), 153–182.

37 See 'Symposium on Democracy and Development', in *Journal of Economic Perspectives* 7 (3), summer 1993, 45–94.
38 Of the 21 findings, eight were in favor of democracy and authoritarianism, while five discovered no difference. The studies before 1988 show that authoritarian regimes grew faster while none of the studies since 1988 can substantiate this finding. Moreover, there is a greater variance in the performance of authoritarian regimes than democratic ones: Adam Przeworski and Fernando Limongi, 'Political Regimes and Economic Growth', *Journal of Economic Perspectives*, ibid., 61–65.
39 Pranab Bardhan, *Political Economy of Development* (Oxford: Basil Blackwell, 1984), 47.
40 As shown by Bardhan, ibid.
41 Jayati Ghosh, 'Development Strategy in India: A Political Economy Perspective', in Sugata Bose and Ayesha Jalal, eds, *Nationalism, Democracy and Development: State and Politics in India* (New York: Oxford University Press, 1997), 165–83.
42 Comment made by Isher Ahluwalia, Conference on 'Bureaucracy and Economic Reforms', New Delhi, June 1996.
43 Bardhan, *Political Economy of Development*, op cit.
44 Since the reforms of 1991, regional parties in the south and the Bhartiya Janata Party (BJP) have attacked the Congress for selling out to international business. BJP has clearly stated that it does not agree with the easing of foreign investments in the country.
45 Opposition governments elected in 1994 and 1995 in the states of Karnataka, Andhra Pradesh and U.P. have begun to woo foreign and domestic capital into their states by reforming state laws and dropping restrictions: *India Abroad*, 10 March 1995, 26.
46 Consensus on reform ideology got a boost when the West Bengal government began to change its economic policies as well: *India Abroad*, 10 March 1995, 20–23.
47 Stephan Haggard and Steven Webb, 'What Do We Know about the Political Economy of Economic Policy Reform?' *World Bank Research Observer* 8 (2), July 1993, 143–68.
48 N. Vittal, interview, New Delhi, 20 August 1996.
49 Jaswant Singh, BJP leader, speaking at a seminar 'India's Democracy at Fifty', Washington D.C., 24 September 1997.
50 I would like to thank Amita Shastri for some of these ideas that emerged in our discussions.

Chapter 12
Institutional Impediments to Human Development in Pakistan
*Christopher Candland**

... contradictions abound in a country of weak institutions and strong individuals, of economic growth without human development, of private greed and lack of social compassion, of election rituals without real democracy.

Mahbubul Haq[1]

Within two decades of its independence, American economic advisors declared Pakistan's economic development a resounding success.[2] Since its creation in August 1947, Pakistan had achieved and maintained high rates of growth of gross national product (GNP), averaging more than 6 percent per annum. According to dominant economic thought when Pakistan was in its formative years, the key to development – defined as growth of GNP per capita – was the concentration of capital. Thus, Pakistan's economic planners aimed to achieve high growth rates by concentrating capital, and diverting a minimum of resources to social welfare. Inequality was an explicit component of Pakistan's strategy of economic growth through 'functional inequality'.[3] Given the emphasis placed at that time on the 'social utility of greed', it seems a little strange that many now regard Pakistan's combination of high gross domestic product growth rates and low levels of human development as 'enigmatic' or 'paradoxical'.[4] In view of the low priority given to human development in the past, it is not surprising that Pakistan currently suffers some of the lowest rates of literacy, life expectancy, infant and maternal survival in the world.

What calls for explanation is why performance in the social sectors has not improved recently with greater professed public commitment and financing. The institution of electoral contest for public office, which was

---

*I am grateful to Syed Abu Ahmad Akif for perspective on the administration of public health and education in Pakistan and to Pranab Bardhan, Philip Oldenburg, Asad Sayeed, Amita Shastri, and Akbar Zaidi for comments on earlier drafts.

never very firmly established in Pakistan, returned in 1988 with the death of President Ziaul Haq. This return to electoral politics coincided with a new economic era and International Monetary Fund (IMF) structural adjustment agreements. Particularly important was the Social Action Program (SAP) which has been the umbrella program for government investment in education, health, sanitation, water supply, and population planning since 1992. It appears that since 1988 social spending in real terms and as a proportion of total government expenditure initially shrunk (1988–91) and then increased (1992–98). The effectiveness of those funds, however, seems to have declined. Public debts, internal and foreign, also increased and constricted economic policy options. Competition between rival political parties – parties which are themselves weak – does not seem to have reduced political abuse of social sector spending.

Why does Pakistan suffer such serious levels of deprivation in its social infrastructure and social opportunity? The concept of social infrastructure refers to a network of publicly accessible programs and services involved in the promotion of the public's education and health. As Jean Dréze and Amartya Sen have elaborated, the concept of social opportunity is identified not with specific indicators of development, but with the expansion of choice for individuals. Health, education, and literacy are conceived as the goals and the means to greater social opportunities.[5] Descriptive accounts on the failings of Pakistan in the sphere of human development typically attribute it to a lack of public responsibility and accountability, a weak civil society, corrupt governments, parasitic politicians, and avaricious industrialists. In this chapter, I argue that there are three major institutional impediments to the resolution of Pakistan's poor performance in human development. One, pervasive discrimination against girls and women. Two, unaccountable, unrepresentative, and unresponsive government with its control of the administration of education, health, water, and sanitation. Three, the fiscal crisis of the Pakistani state, the full impact of which on social sector development has been held at bay for the time being by external financing.

Accordingly, I analyse below why the operation of public institutions in Pakistan has not created greater social infrastructure and opportunity. The first section of this chapter briefly assesses Pakistan's record on human development. Trends in government expenditure on social sectors such as education and health are then examined. The next section discusses the situation of pervasive gender discrimination and statist development practices. These are related to the poor performance in the recruitment and retention of teachers and health professionals and to poor government management of development administration. Next, the performance of the Social Action Program is assessed. Analysis of the reasons for the failure of the SAP to implement its projects helps to clarify how institutional arrangements in the administration of social welfare and infrastructure impede human development. The final section of the chapter considers the economic requirements of governance in Pakistan.

SOCIAL INVESTMENT

Pakistan's record in human development and provision of social infrastructure and opportunity is miserable, and compares unfavorably even to countries with lower real per capita income. Pakistan devotes a smaller percentage of central and provincial government revenue to education, social welfare, health, and community services than all other economies in the group of countries the World Bank classifies as poor, or that the United Nations Development Program (UNDP) classifies as being at a low human development level. The national and provincial governments in Pakistan devote only 2.7 percent of GNP to education and only 1.8 percent to health.[6] Nearly one in ten Pakistani infants die before the age of five. Maternal survival rates, the single best indicator of human development, are low. One reliable survey found maternal mortality rates ranging from 281 deaths per 100,000 live births in Karachi to 673 deaths per 100,000 live births in rural Baluchistan.[7] The figures for Baluchistan are on par with those of the Central African Republic and Sudan, countries with half of Pakistan's per capita purchasing power parity estimates of GNP.[8]

Access to education and the quality of educational opportunities are poorer in Pakistan than in all other economies of similar per capita income levels. Pakistan has a 62 percent adult illiteracy rate and, by some accounts, is the only country in Asia to suffer a decline in educational achievement.[9] Nearly 20 million children of primary school age, equal to almost half of the country's primary school age children, do not attend school. Children of poor families are prevented from attending school by the prohibitive cost of uniforms, books, and supplies. Others are repelled by the poor conditions of the schools. A majority of students reported being regularly beaten at school.[10] Drop-out rates, more accurately termed 'push-out' rates, are among the world's highest.[11] Nearly one half of the country's first grade entrants did not complete fifth grade.[12] Studies of school continuation rates found the lack of teachers to be the most significant factor for low male enrollment and the lack of both teachers and classrooms to be the most significant factor for low female enrollment.[13] Even where there are teachers and schools, the education which is available is of wretched quality, further discouraging children from attending or continuing.

Available comparative statistics on development, such as those reported by the UNDP's *Human Development Report* or the World Bank's *World Development Reports*, are poor. The data is typically manipulated by reporting agencies for political purposes. The UNDP figures are originally provided by government officials, such as district education officers and public health officers, who report exaggerated numbers to their superiors to meet mandated targets. These, of course, must be exaggerated over past years' exaggerated figures. Table 1 should be read with scepticism for comparability. This is especially true for the figures for primary school enrollment and female primary school enrollment.

Pakistan compares poorly with its neighbors India, China, and Sri Lanka on a number of significant indicators of human development. As the table highlights, comparatively it performs the worst with regard to infant mortality, primary school enrollment and female school enrollments, literacy and female literacy, access to health care and family planning services. Sri Lanka has one fifth of Pakistan's infant mortality rate. Pakistan's female adult literacy is one third that of China and Sri Lanka. These poor socio-economic conditions set in motion a vicious cycle in human development in which parents are poorly placed to make the necessary investment in their children's education and their future social opportunity.

In the 1980s Pakistan made steady progress against poverty largely through remittances sent home by Pakistani workers in the Gulf economies. As a result, the proportion of the population living in poverty declined from 46 to 34 percent between 1985 and 1991.[14] However, when these remittances declined between 1991 and 1995 an additional 18 million

Table 1: Pakistan's Social Development in Comparative Perspective

	Pakistan	India	China	Sri Lanka
Infant Mortality Rate (per 1,000 live births, 1996)	95	73	38	17
Primary School Enrollment (percent of school age population, 1997)	46	102	121	107
Female Primary School Enrollment (as percent of male school age enrollment, 1997)	45	82	98	98
Adult Literacy Rate (percent of population, 1995)	38	52	82	90
Female Adult Literacy Rate (percent of female population, 1995)	24	38	73	87
Population w/o Access to Health Care (percent of population, 1990–95)	45	15	12	7
Population Growth Rate (per annum, 1970-1995)	3.0	2.1	1.6	1.5

Sources: UNDP, *Human Development Report 1998* (New York: Oxford University Press, 1998), 148–149, 162–163, 128–129, 132–133, 146–147, 176–177; and Social Policy and Development Centre, *Review of the Social Action Program* (Karachi: Social Policy and Development Centre, June 1997), i.

people were ground into poverty, although the economy grew at 4.5 percent.[15] Currently, more than 45 million Pakistanis survive below subsistence levels of caloric intake. The structural adjustment measures initiated in 1988 have helped to drive subsistence farmers, low wage workers, and their dependents into poverty because basic social infrastructure is lacking. Allocations to education and health by provincial governments, which largely fund the social sectors, dropped precipitously between 1988 and 1991, both in constant prices and in per capita terms.[16] Only when large amounts of external funding were obtained for Pakistan's SAP did expenditure on human development improve. Provincial governments now spend more than half of their budget on social sector development. Their approach, however, is largely an expansionary one – to build new schools and clinics, rather than to staff or supply them or to improve the operation of existing ones.[17] There may be a notably higher level of public and governmental expression of concern for human development today than there was ten years ago, but there are institutional lacunae that prevent that concern from being implemented in practical terms.

GENDER DISCRIMINATION

Gender discrimination is a pervasive feature of the social environment and perhaps the more intractable institutional impediment to human development. Three interrelated points about it are noted. First, the discrimination against girls and women is pervasive and extends from birth to grave. Second, girls and women are more readily entrapped in vicious cycles than boys and men. Third, the under-development of girls and women undermines the development of all.

Human development indicators reveal pervasive and severe discrimination against girls and women. In a reversal of global trends, in the one year to four-year age group, 12 percent more girls die than boys. Girls die in greater numbers because of pervasive discrimination: they typically eat less and last, are schooled only if their brothers are and often not even then, and are the last to be taken for or receive medical attention. Women giving birth face unclean water, infection, non-sterile implements for severing umbilical cords, and a dearth of medical professionals and practitioners. The lower standards of care received by girls and women has altered even the national balance of males and females. Using female-male ratios found in Sub-Saharan Africa, the Pakistani female to male ratio reveals millions of missing girls and women. The female to male ratio in Pakistan indicates that approximately four million girls and women have died prematurely (that is, in comparison to their male counterparts) due to gender discrimination.[18]

Female literacy (age 25 years and above) is half that of males. While only half of Pakistan's adult male population can read a newspaper, only a quarter of Pakistan's adult females can.[19] Men (age 25 years and above) received an average of fewer than four years of schooling; women (age 25 years and above) received an average of slightly more than one year of schooling.[20] Primary school attendance among girls is roughly half of that of boys.

Girls and women are simultaneously more adversely affected by and more constrained by the vicious human developmental cycle. School completion rates, for example, are much worse for girls. At the same time, one of the strongest influences on girl's primary school completion rates is literacy of their mothers.[21] Uneducated girls are more likely to grow up to be illiterate mothers whose girl children will be less likely to complete primary school.

Discrimination against and the denial of basic human rights to girls and women poisons the entire process of expanding social opportunity. For example, outside of urban affluent areas such as Islamabad, Lahore, and Karachi pervasive discrimination against women's employment outside of the home prevents women from being educators and contributing to the educational advancement of a younger generation. Most government teachers in Pakistan are men. Female teachers are dissuaded by the prospect of postings in inhospitable and discriminatory rural areas. This contrasts with the situation in many other countries where women were prevented from employment in most professions but teaching was one profession that was open to women.

ADMINISTRATION OF PUBLIC WELFARE

Many of the political institutions that have a negative impact on the implementation of public policy are of colonial vintage. On the lines of the colonial Government of India Act 1935, Pakistan's constitution permits the executive branch of government to promulgate ordinances that vie in authority with laws passed by representative assemblies. Moreover, the system of training and promotion that was employed by the Indian Civil Service in colonial times continues within the District Management Group today and insulates the bureaucracy from society. As in colonial times, the district remains the basic administrative unit. The district commissioners in the former 'settled areas' of Punjab and most of Sindh, and political agents in the agencies or 'tribal areas' of Baluchistan and Northwest Frontier Province control local politics and the administration of human development. In each district, government departments have district officers. The two principal departments involved in human development in Pakistan are the Department of Education and the Department of Public Health Engineering. Principals and teachers report directly to the district educational officer. Doctors and other health professionals report to the district health officer.

Provincial governments are responsible for agriculture and irrigation, local government and rural development, health, education, police, courts, and highways and roads. A member of the provincial assembly, the minister of the relevant provincial government ministry, appoints educators and health professionals throughout the province. These appointments are typically made on a political basis. Appointees are not necessarily interested or capable in the profession for which they receive a salary, but accept these appointments as political rewards. Parents do not have influence over the provision of these public goods. The assessment of teachers and health care professionals is also not made locally and does not involve the communities where these teachers and health care professionals work.

Teachers face an array of disincentives. Working conditions, living conditions, pay, and social stature are extremely poor. Teachers typically teach a number of subjects and classes of different grades concurrently. There are no established avenues for promotion.[22] The facilities are poor: one fifth of the country's primary schools have no facilities other than a chair, a mat, and a blackboard.[23] Teachers in Pakistan often earn less than a living wage and receive an embarrassingly low rank as a government employee.[24] As one scholar comments, 'Teachers salaries are frequently almost at par with domestic servants. Indeed, a driver can earn more.'[25] Teachers receive no medical or transportation benefits, and there are no pension plans for teachers. They are also not permitted to form unions. Thus, there is a lack of social status associated with the profession, and many chose it because it offers them their only chance at regular employment. Subsequently, provincial governments have difficulty filling teaching positions with qualified individuals and there is high rate of absenteeism among working teachers.

Many government schools, especially primary and secondary schools, are even fictitious. Ministers may contract construction that does not take place and arrange for kick-backs and inadequate facilities. In fact, tiny villages are known to have more than one 'ghost school'. Like their government schools, many government teachers also exist only on paper. The former governor of Sindh, Moinuddin Haider, estimated in December 1998 that the province had 19,000 'ghost teachers'[26] – teachers who exist for pay-roll purposes only.

In the early 1990s, the proportion of students in private schools increased even while total enrollment and completion rates declined nationally. Studies conducted by the Social Policy and Development Centre found that 'the public is both willing and able to pay for [education and health] services.'[27] Constraints to education are overwhelmingly in its supply, not in demand. Survey evidence confirms that poor parents have an especially strong interest in educating their children. While their disposable income is low, poor parents spend a larger proportion of their income and resources on education than do parents with higher incomes. Yet, due to the network of established interests, they remain excluded from exercising pressure to ensure an effective delivery of the promised services. The weak provision of public education thus cannot be ascribed to weak demand. Shifting the power to locate, plan, and monitor quality education into the hands of parents is essential for effective educational reform in Pakistan.

Public health faces similar institutional impediments. Rural health centers and basic health units are often not staffed, even though salaries are paid. The appointment of health care workers, like teachers, are often made to pay debts incurred while campaigning for office and/or to secure future political support. Marshalling substantial evidence, Akbar Zaidi has argued that the underlying flaw in public health care in Pakistan is its class bias.[28] The government allocates 80 percent of public health expenditure to urban areas. Only 18 percent of the country's hospital beds are found in rural areas where 70 percent of the population lives.[29] In rural Sindh, there is one doctor for every 57,000 people.[30] Health professionals are trained in government medical colleges to hone their professional skills in curative care and the ailments of the rich; while parasites, infections, and other easily preventable illnesses cause most of the deaths in the country. 250,000 persons die annually of tuberculosis in Sindh province alone; yet there is no coherent plan for treatment or control. Lack of facilities, low pay, poor management, and lack of social status dissuade even those doctors who would like to serve in rural areas.[31]

THE SOCIAL ACTION PROGRAM

The shortcomings of the SAP throw further light on the reasons for Pakistan's low level equilibrium trap in social investment. The Pakistan People's Party (PPP) government initiated the SAP in 1992, and the first phase was completed in July 1997. The program aims to make major advances in and create synergies between four social sectors: primary education, primary health, water supply and sanitation, and family planning. The financing of the SAP is largely external. The World Bank, Asian Development Bank, Government of Netherlands, and Overseas Development Agency of UK committed more than US$ 4 billion to the program. The program was intended to increase financing for social services, to correct flaws in the delivery of these services, and to reform the institutions involved in social services.[32]

The failings of the SAP are well known. In most sectors, no comprehensive plans were devised. Thus, although education was stated to be a priority of the program, no clear policies on primary education were formulated. The SAP did assist provincial governments in formulating water policies, but did not prevent the diversion of water to homes of friends of members of the provincial assemblies. No clear policies were formulated for sanitation or for health. It is not clear how much of the SAP was undertaken on the initiative of the government of Pakistan, and how much of it was promoted by the international donor community. It is clear that without major external financing, however, it would be unlikely to survive.

The SAP lacks community participation to counter the political consumption of human development expenditures. The participation of community-based organizations, such as parent–teacher and school management committees, was to be one of the essential institutional innovations of the SAP. Instead, 'community organizations' were created by government fiat and have been inactive or ineffective.[33]

The provision of social investments is highly politicized. Local politicians, members of the provincial assemblies and of the National Assembly occupy seats on district social action boards and in district development advisory committees. These politicians typically use their position to direct the funds handled by these committees to their political supporters. Ministries and departments related to the social sector are particularly vulnerable to misappropriation in part because the press pays greater attention to wrong-doing elsewhere in government.

The principal impediment to human investment is the dearth of structures that can monitor the use of public resources. The hierarchy of Pakistani officialdom prevents community-based organizations from forging productive relations with government agents. Some implementing agencies have experienced debilitating levels of interference from the provincial bureaucracy. The renewed harassment and arrests of journalists and newspaper editors – an effective deterrent to political abuses of development funds – further restricts public oversight as well as freedom of speech.

The institutional impediments to greater human development in Pakistan are to a large degree promoted and enabled by the state. State action in the adoption and implementation of development models and economic policies and administration of public education and health bear this out.

STATIST ORIGINS AND LEGACIES

Regardless of the government in power or its economic ideology, the Pakistani state has played a dominant role in economic development and in Pakistani society. A once stable and homogenous group of senior state mangers were nurtured on the colonial pattern by the Pakistan Administrative Service. Civil servants held positions as governor general, president of the senate, and prime minister; and proclaim an ideology for Pakistan committed to its survival and to the state's exercise of effective authority. The government increasingly relied on a professional and technocratic approach to economic development, so that a significant feature of Ayub Khan's self-proclaimed 'development decade' of the 1960s was his reliance not only on Pakistani economists who had been trained in the United States, but also US economists and advisors. As one senior Pakistani economist put it, '... to him [Ayub Khan] the economic profession has reasons for remaining profoundly grateful because of the honor he has conferred on it, and the responsiveness he has shown toward professional advice.'[34]

Pakistan's early economic development strategy was designed to engineer rapid economic growth and capital accumulation. Indeed, it was explicitly based on the doctrine of functional inequality, and viewed the concentration of capital not as a social danger but as a necessity for rapid growth. The centerpiece of its industrial strategy was investment in a public sector that would serve to develop the private sector – not a public sector based on an ideological commitment to state ownership in the collective interest, as in India. Capital concentration and economic inequality were central components of the strategy, Western economic advisors to the Pakistan government in the 1950s and 1960s argued that there was an unavoidable trade-off between 'development' (or economic growth) and equitable distribution. Pakistan planners believed that economic growth required the concentration of wealth.[35] In 1963 Mahbubul Haq, Chief Economist of the Planning Commission, underscoring Pakistan's 'need for a growth economy', summarized Pakistan's development challenge, in a manner he later regretted:

> It would be tragic if policies appropriate to a Keynesian era were to be tried in countries still living in a Smithian or Ricardian world ... the best (and, perhaps, the only) form of social security is ... through the creation of sufficient capital by some. There exists, therefore, a functional justification for inequality of income ... The road to eventual equalities may inevitably lie through initial inequalities.[36]

As a result of this strategy, the state became increasingly dependent on foreign funds for development.[37] Private capital ownership became concentrated in the hands of a small group of industrial families.[38] Regional and economic disparities fostered their own tensions that eventually led to the break up of Pakistan.[39]

Opposing Ayub's strategy of economic development, his former foreign minister Zulfikar Ali Bhutto campaigned on a platform of Islamic socialism in 1969. Once in power, however, he exercised dictatorial powers and violence against workers and middle class opposition to control their protests in the midst of the severe economic crisis of the early 1970s. He also proceeded to nationalize a whole range of industries and firms, provoking the wrath of the business class. Bhutto's variety of inward-looking statism ended in July 1977 when his hand-picked Army Chief of Staff, General Zia ul Haq, took over power.

Interestingly, the intervention of the military in 1977 did not cause a turn away from the state-dominated pattern of economic development which had characterized both Ayub Khan's and Bhutto's governments. Following the Soviet invasion of Afghanistan in December 1979, Pakistan became the front-line state opposing Soviet aggression and obtained billions of dollars in economic and military aid from the US. The Zia government also benefited from the export of unskilled and semi-skilled labor to the oil-producing Gulf states. Through the 1980s, remittances from Pakistani workers in the Gulf amounted to 6.5 percent of GNP,[40] peaking in 1984 at 8 percent.[41] The military diversified into an economic organization involved in the consumption, distribution, and production of various goods. Patronage between individual business people and elected officials and bureaucrats continued to drive economic performance, and the local bodies established by Zia strengthened local political leaders. The early 1980s saw the rise of a more politically-influential industrial and business class, especially in the Punjab. Yet, broader state-society relations remained attenuated by the arrest of political opponents, press censorship, intimidation of journalists, intolerance of public dissent, and manipulation of Islamic ideology to legitimize authoritarian ordinances and practices. Thus, the state continued to occupy the dominant role in society.

Pakistan's neo-classical economic ideology helps obscure that Pakistan's public sector, until the post-1988 structural adjustment measures, was very large. Until 1987–88, investment in the public sector constituted 57.9 percent of total investment.[42] Government-owned companies and firms existed in the automobile, banking, cement, chemicals, engineering, fertilizer, iron and steel, oil exploration and refining, and agricultural processing industries. The government held monopolies in telecommunications, power, railways, and air transport services.[43] The dismantling of the statist economic structure only began after General Zia's death in 1988 to avoid a serious balance of payments crisis.

A noteworthy pattern in Pakistan's economic adjustment program since 1988 has been the role of military-approved and appointed 'caretaker' governments as the signators to IMF commitments to adjustment measures. The 1988 IMF structural adjustment program loan of US $1.2 billion to Pakistan, which spurred adjustment, was negotiated and signed by the interim government of Ghulam Ishaq Khan. On two subsequent occasions again, in 1993 and 1996, it was interim governments of former World Bank vice president Moeen Qureshi and Meraj Khalid who arranged adjustment measures with the IMF. The subsequently elected governments of Benazir Bhutto and Nawaz Sharif respectively were forced to implement the measures negotiated.

Thus, in important ways, the return of elected representative regimes has not promoted greater political participation in the definition of economic policies or in their implementation. Instead, they have been constrained to implement the policies of liberalization of imports, cutting of fiscal deficits and government spending, widening the role of the private sector, reform of pricing and tax policies, and the elimination of subsidies – placing them in a difficult position to gather popular support in the short and medium term. While the two PPP governments were more effective in controlling fiscal deficits, the high proportion of the budget that was siphoned off to cover interest on the public debt and spending on the military placed tight constraints on what any government could accomplish. The military, for instance, was scheduled to grow by over 8 percent and consume nearly 25 percent of central government expenditure in 1998–99. Rather, privatization has formed the mainstay of reforms under both the Pakistan Peoples Party (PPP) and Islami Jamhoori Ittehad (IJI) governments alike. It has allowed each government to finance deficit spending and to dispense public assets, especially the most profitable units, to political supporters.

GOVERNMENT REVENUE

As revenue is only superficially rooted in domestic corporate or personal income taxation, the Pakistani state faces a fiscal crisis. While Pakistan is not on the verge of falling into the ranks of 'failed states', state capacity is in serious decline.[44] The state has not been able to establish an effective claim on public income. As state revenue is only superficially effective in taxing domestic corporate or personal income, it faces a severe fiscal crisis. The relationship between the government's ability to extract resources from society, approximated by effective taxation, and responsive governance, as gauged by government commitment to social infrastructure development, is unstable and based on flawed institutions. The proportion of government revenue derived from direct taxes, which approximates 14 percent of total government revenue, is among the lowest in the world, and is declining. In a country of more than 140 million people, there are fewer than 800,000 income taxpayers. Various regressive forms of taxation, such as retail taxes and trade taxes, are increasing along with non-tax revenue, which largely consist of proceeds from privatization.

Business–state relations show signs of deep instability. Higher levels of revenue require an increase in state capacity to collect direct taxes. This is possibly stifled by the poor legitimacy of the state's claim to operate in the public interest. Pakistan's Central Board of Revenue announced in April 1998 that it would identify 200,000 new tax payers that year. In response, newspaper editorials asked why the Pakistan citizens should pay for government expenditures that do not benefit them. Before the arrival of foreign heads of state and dignitaries, the business community resorts to strikes to compel the government to abandon plans to increase direct corporate taxation. As a result of public resistance, the pool of tax-payers has not increased.

However, the crisis facing Pakistan is not merely a fiscal problem. More seriously, the state suffers from a deep legitimation crisis. In effect, the

Pakistani state is not seen by its tax payers, both actual and potential, as capable of delivering public goods. Repeated ill-conceived attempts by governing parties to project their Islamic credentials indicate the low level of public support that exists for the Pakistani state, regardless of the party in power. Continuing a practice begun by Ziaul Haq, both PPP governments under Benazir Bhutto and IJI and Muslim League governments under Nawaz Sharif have sought to use religion, and to ostensibly promote religious practices to collect public resources. For purposes of distribution for social welfare, the government collects *zakat* (a donation to the deserving poor). The Zakat and Ushr [a tax on landed wealth] Ordinance of June 1980 permits the government to deduct 2.5 percent from bank deposits and stock market earnings. Thirty-two thousand local zakat committees distribute funds meant for Muslim widows, orphans, and disabled people (*mustahiqeen*).[45] Although one of the pillars of Islam is that Allah's generosity should be shared with the poor, the public widely resents being forced by the government to perform what should be a voluntary article of faith, and objects to the misappropriation and highly politicized use of the funds by the local zakat committees. This has led to mass withdrawals from savings account before zakat deductions are made before *Ramadan*.

The economy, however, faces more serious economic and social problems. These include a low and rapidly declining savings rate – 14.6 percent in 1995, down from 23.9 percent in 1985. It is also weighted down by the high illiteracy rate, which will not improve much with the next generation.

THE ECONOMICS OF GOVERNANCE

Pakistan['s] ruling elite, divorced from the aspirations of the masses, is supremely indifferent to the provision of basic social services to the people. Without basic reforms in Pakistan's political and economic system, its prospects for economic and social progress appear somewhat clouded. Yet the question persists as to how and when such fundamental reforms will be engineered and who will engineer them.

Mahbubul Haq and Khadija Haq[46]

Governments that can generate significant revenues from external sources, such as from oil exports or from military allies, do not feel obligated to negotiate with the public for access to its wealth. During Ayub Khan's government as well as during the Soviet war in Afghanistan, when Pakistan received large amounts of foreign economic and military assistance, Pakistan took on some of the characteristics of a *rentier* state. The government was to a substantial degree relieved from negotiating with significant social groups – consisting of the higher income groups, large land-holders and business classes – for access to public funds. The actual situation since 1988, in contrast, has been that the Pakistani state does not have the possibilities – other than the one based on labor remittances – of operating as a rentier economy based system of revenue. The state needs to generate greater domestic tax revenues which requires more public responsiveness.

State formation in the present international configuration involves not only the development of a near exclusive legitimate exercise of physical power over a territory, what Max Weber referred to as a 'monopoly over the legitimate use of physical force'.[47] State formation also requires the development of a stable revenue system to finance the machinery of the state. A critical challenge faced in the course of state formation and legitimacy creation is maintaining popular support even while it extracts revenue. There is little evidence that the Pakistani state has persuaded the Pakistani public that it should have access to its income. The reinstitution of electoral competition for public office may well have heightened the fiscal crisis.

Even though the state needs access to greater domestic revenue, potential taxpayers do not feel government programs are meaningful or effective for them. The tax-evading public in Pakistan is, thus, large and growing and shows little inclination to contribute to public finances. The poor provision of physical and social infrastructure and misuse of public funds does not inspire confidence in the revenue collection and distributive capacity of the state.

The impediments to human development in Pakistan are, thus, not merely economic, but political and social as well. Economic reforms would be more productive if they focused on building social infrastructure rather than reducing government expenditure and promoting industrial deregulation and trade. While government payments of interest on debts and expenditure on the military alone is greater than government revenue, human development expenditure has not merely been crowded out by such expenditure. Social institutions, such as community oversight bodies and medical associations, which might have a positive impact on the implementation of public policy, are missing. Indeed, there is a dearth of social institutions, such as public associations and community-based law enforcement, that can mediate between society and the state to permit an effective formulation and implementation of public policy.

Elections may have made less effective an already ineffective and graft-prone set of institutions related to human development. The involvement of politicians in the process of development administration, such as in the selection and retention of teachers or appointment of health practitioners, has not produced better performance in human development. Elected members of provincial assemblies often have even greater incentives than insulated district officers to use education and public health funds for private gain, so that the institutions for development administration lack sufficient responsiveness to social need. If the Pakistani state is to extricate the country from its low level human development trap, the institutions of development administration will have to be reformed.

Pakistan is not in a state of regress – a condition in which governance and human development drag each other into a cycle of decline – but it is also very far from having replaced anti-developmental institutions with pro-developmental ones. Two great obstacles to higher levels of human development is the pervasive discrimination against girls and women as well as an unaccountable and unresponsive government. An analysis of the failures of the Social Action Program points to a critical need for greater decentralization and community management.[48] The structural adjustment measures initiated in 1988, which proponents revealingly refer to as policy reforms, are inadequate to Pakistan's development challenges. They do not aim to reform social and political institutions, but are merely intended to create greater macro-economic stability and micro-economic efficiency.

A poor human capital base and flawed institutions for the administration of human development promote a self-limiting state. The military admits that the greatest security threat is the prevailing climate of corruption and civil violence. Military expenditure is widely considered to be out of line with the country's security needs. The most significant threats to Pakistan's security as a united and sovereign state are thus not external but internal and exacerbated by government neglect of social sectors and flawed institutions for human development. Without reforming Pakistan's perverse institutions for human development and restructuring its expenditure, its overall performance in human development is unlikely to improve.

NOTES

1 Mahbubul Haq, *Human Development in South Asia 1997* (Oxford: Human Development Centre, 1997), 37.
2 On Pakistan's successful experiment with the 'social utility of greed', see Gustav Papanek, *Pakistan's Development: Social Goals and Private Incentives* (Cambridge: Harvard University Press, 1967). Papanek was an advisor to Pakistan's Planning Commission.
3 On the option of functional inequality in early Pakistani economic strategies, see Angus Maddison, 'The Social Impact of Pakistan's "Functional Equality"', *Class Structure and Economic Growth in India and Pakistan* (Oxford: Oxford University Press, 1973), 136–163.
4 The quotations are from Iftikar Malik, *State and Civil Society in Pakistan: Politics of Authority, Ideology and Ethnicity* (Basingstoke: Macmillan, 1997), 163; and Omar Noman, *Pakistan: Political and Economic History Since 1947* (London: Kegan Paul International, 1988), 167.

5 Jean Drèze and Amartya Sen, *India: Economic Development and Social Opportunity* (New York: Oxford University Press, 1995), 6–16.
6 UNDP, *Human Development Report 1997* (New York: Oxford University Press, 1997), 187. The figures compared were for 1980, the latest available; and Mahbubul Haq and Khadija Haq, *Human Development in South Asia 1998* (Oxford: Human Development Centre, 1998), 180–181. Figures are for 1993/4 and 1990 respectively.
7 I. Olenick, 'Poor Socioeconomic Status Is Linked to High Maternal Mortality in Rural Pakistan', *International Family Planning Perspectives* 24 (2), June 1998, 96–97
8 UNDP, *Human Development Report 1997*, 214.
9 Sophia Swire, *Old Roads, New Highways: 50 Years of Pakistan* (Karachi: Oxford University Press), 230.
10 Donald Warwick and Fernando Reimers, *Hope or Despair?*, 19.
11 Myron Weiner, *The Child and the State in India* (Princeton: Princeton University Press, 1991), 7175.
12 Warwick and Reimers, *Hope or Despair?*, 22.
13 Social Policy and Development Centre, *Review of the Social Action Program*, June 1997, vii.
14 World Bank, *Pakistan: Poverty Assessment*, Country Operations Division, South Asia Region, interview, 25 September 1995, 68–69.
15 Mahbubul Haq reports an increase in the poverty rate over the period from 20 percent to 30 percent of the total population: *Human Development in South Asia 1997*, 17.
16 World Bank, *Pakistan: Poverty Assessment*, ibid.
17 Aisha Ghaus-Pasha, et al, *Social Development in Pakistan* (Karachi: Social Policy and Development Center, 1998), 40.
18 Haq, *Human Development in South Asia 1997*, 24. On female–male ratios and missing women in India see Jean Dreze and Amartya Sen, *India: Economic Development and Social Opportunity*, 141–178.
19 Ghaus-Pasha et al, *Social Development in Pakistan*, 18.
20 Ibid., 130.
21 The strongest predictor of female primary school completion rates in Pakistan is mother's literacy. Warwick and Reimers, *Hope or Despair?*, 23.
22 Ibid., 29 and 40.
23 Ibid., 34 and 41.
24 Ibid., 31.
25 Omar Noman, 'Primary Education in Pakistan', in Myron Weiner and Omar Noman, *The Child and the State in India and Pakistan: Child Labor and Education Policies in Comparative Perspective* (Karachi: Oxford, 1995), 258.
26 'Sindh has 19,000 ghost teachers', *Dawn*, 1 December 1998, 3.
27 Social Policy and Development Centre, 'User Charges in Education', policy paper 3, (1994) and Social Policy and Development Centre, 'User Charges in Health', policy paper 5, (1994). The quotation is from Ghaus-Pasha, et al, *Social Development in Pakistan*, 50.
28 Akbar Zaidi, *The Political Economy of Health Care in Pakistan* (Lahore: Vanguard, 1988).
29 Zaidi, 'Issues in the Health Sector in Pakistan', in *Political Economy of Health Care in Pakistan*, 1–11.
30 Zaidi, ibid.
31 Zaidi, 'Why Medical Students will not Practice in Rural Areas', in *Political Economy of Health Care in Pakistan*, 59.
32 Ghaus-Pasha et al, *Social Development in Pakistan*, 58.

33 Asad Sayeed, 'Squander in the Name of Social Development: The Story of the Social Action Programme', *News*, 10 [month] 1998; and Ghaus-Pasha et al, *Social Development in Pakistan*, 59–60.
34 Habibur Rahman, *Growth Models and Pakistan: A Discussion of Planning Problems* (Karachi: Allies Book Company, 1962), 5.
35 Akmal Hussain, *Strategic Issues in Pakistan's Economic Policy* (Lahore: Progressive Publishers, 1988), 367–373.
36 Mahbubul Haq, *The Strategy of Economic Planning* (New York: Oxford University Press, 1963), 1–3.
37 Foreign loans, which constituted only 1.1 percent of GNP in 1954–55, rose to 8.7 percent of GNP by 1964–65.
38 Mahbubul Haq, 'A Critical Review of the Third Five Year Plan', in M. A. Khan, ed., *Management and National Growth* (Karachi: West Pakistan Management Association, 1968), 27. Cited and quoted in Maddison, *Class Structure and Economic Growth*, 158.
39 On the negative consequences of economic concentration under Ayub, see Keith Griffin and Azizur Rahman Khan, eds, *Growth and Inequality in Pakistan* (London: Macmillan, 1972); Stephen Lewis, Jr., *Economic Policy and Industrial Growth in Pakistan* (London: George Allen and Unwin, 1969); and Stephen Lewis, *Pakistan: Industrialization and Trade Policies* (Karachi: Oxford University Press, 1970).
40 S. Akbar Zaidi, 'Health, Well-being and Adjustment: The Case of Pakistan', paper prepared for the Conference on the Impact of Structural Adjustment on Health, Jawaharlal Nehru University, New Delhi, 1997, 7.
41 Noman, *Pakistan: Political and Economic History*, 161.
42 Government of Pakistan, Ministry of Finance, *Pakistan Economic Survey 1990* (Islamabad: Government of Pakistan Printing Press, 1991).
43 World Bank, 'Pakistan: Country Economic Memorandum FY93: Progress Under the Adjustment Program' (Washington, DC: World Bank, 23 March 1993), 49.
44 Jean-Germain Gros, 'Towards a Taxonomy of Failed States in the New World Order: Decaying Somalia, Liberia, Rwanda and Haiti', *Third World Quarterly* 17 (3), 1996, 455–471.
45 Afzal Iqbal, *Islamisation of Pakistan* (Lahore: Vanguard, 1986), 108. Zakat collections have increased steeply since their inception in 1980, from a rate of 5.2 percent in the 1980s to 17.4 percent in the 1990s in real terms. In 1993–94, the Government of Pakistan collected Rs 1.75 billion in zakat. Asad Sayeed and A. F. Aisha Ghaus, 'Has Poverty Returned to Pakistan?' Social Policy and Development Centre, July 1996, 11, citing the *Pakistan Economic Survey* and the *Annual Reports* of the State Bank of Pakistan.
46 Haq, *Human Development in South Asia 1997*, 37.
47 Max Weber, *From Max Weber: Essays in Sociology*, trans. H. H. Gerth and C. Wright Mills (New York: Oxford University Press, 1958), 78.
48 Social Policy and Development Centre, *Review of the Social Action Program* (Karachi: SPDC, June 1997).

PART IV

SECURITY

Chapter 13

Creating a Common Home? Indo–Pakistan Relations and the Search for Security in South Asia

Vernon Hewitt*

Indo–Pakistan relations present the analyst and the policy maker with one of the most intransigent cases of mistrust, suspicion and threat to be found in the contemporary world. The early 1990s witnessed a series of diplomatic expulsions, mutual accusations of spying, the closing of consular offices, and allegations of covert support for separatist groups and militants operative in Kashmir, Sindh (especially Karachi), India's northeast and Baluchistan. In March 1993, a series of bomb explosions in the Indian city of Bombay killed 250 people, and led to the accusation that Pakistan was behind the carnage. In early 1996, a bomb explosion in Lahore led to similar accusations by the Pakistanis against India. In mid-1999, following incursions from the Pakistani side, the two countries fought a short war in the Kargil area of Kashmir.

Within both India and Pakistan, political competition for national power had, by the end of the 1980s, heightened foreign policy rhetoric considerably. Between 1993 and 1995, New Delhi denounced the foreign policies of the Benazir Bhutto government on a number of occasions as interventionist and irresponsible, aggressive and conspiratorial, while Islamabad utilised a number of election rallies and campaigns to 'expose' Indian human rights violations (especially against Kashmiris) and against Indian Muslims in general. In this atmosphere of growing recrimination, cultural and economic exchanges were substantially reduced, despite outstanding bilateral and regional commitments to improve them. There were virtually no high-level bilateral political contacts between 1994 and 1996.

Furthermore, it was increasingly clear that in the realms of defence expenditure and arms procurement, India and Pakistan continued to match

---
*I would like to thank my colleagues Eric Herring and Richard Little for reading over this chapter and making various comments and suggestions. Both brought my attention to a particularly useful set of articles and books.

each other's capabilities, seeing each other as the major threat to peace within the region. Most dramatically, in May 1998, Indo–Pakistan relations were radically transformed by a series of nuclear tests, initiated by India and reciprocated by the Pakistanis, in clear defiance of emerging international norms against proliferation. On 11 and 13 May 1998, the Indian government detonated five nuclear devices at a site in Rajasthan, close to the Pakistan border. These dramatic events broke the nation's self-declared moratorium on such tests announced in the wake of the so-called Peaceful Nuclear Explosion (PNE) of 1974. Earlier in the year, for the first time in the history of independent India, the Hindu nationalist Bharatiya Janata Party had formed a national coalition and assumed power in New Delhi. The BJP's 1998 electoral manifesto had stated categorically that the party was committed to 're-evaluate the country's nuclear policy and exercise the option to induct nuclear weapons'.[1] Despite international condemnation, India reiterated its commitment to weaponise a nuclear deterrent through its own indigenous missile system, and lay claim to the status of a nuclear weapons state (NWS).[2] Despite huge US pressure, Pakistan carried out its own tests, initially to widespread public support. In a public broadcast to the nation, Prime Minister Sharif stated that India had left Pakistan with no other option than to respond in kind. Addressing an audience at the Pakistan National Defence College, Sharif stated, 'Now nuclear deterrence is indispensable to our security doctrine. We will preserve this deterrence, under all circumstances. We shall not compromise on our security and survival.'[3]

How has such a serious and complex situation arisen? It has been widely recognised that, given the initial vulnerability of any nuclear deployment, and the absence of any assured second strike capabilities, the nuclear balance between India and Pakistan will encourage a pre-emptive military strategy. The possibility of a nuclear war in South Asia is already determining the rhetoric of the region's senior politicians. How can the genie be put back into the bottle? Can the states of India and Pakistan ever learn to trust each other? How do the other states of South Asia perceive the tone of Indo–Pakistan relations? What, if anything, can or should be done by the international community to improve bilateral relations between the two and persuade them to participate within current and prospective international non-proliferation regimes? This chapter will present a brief historical overview of Indo–Pakistan relations, before moving on to look at specific areas of divergence, notably attitudes towards nationalisms and legitimacy, contested borders (Kashmir exemplifies both of these), their broader security perceptions, and the scope and extent of economic and political regionalism.

In circumstances where the distinction between domestic and foreign policy is hard to maintain, it will be argued that the degree of mistrust and insecurity between India and Pakistan is generic and not issue-based. It is due to the historic nature of state formation itself and not to specific, easily identified areas of contention. As such, confidence-building measures between the two states are difficult to initiate and sustain because they must reconcile opposing (and competing) policies covering a wide range of issues. The causes of Indo–Pakistan mistrust are complex and interrelated. Attempts to explain it usually end up in tautological reasoning. For example, it is often maintained that while Indo–Pakistan relations would benefit from the presence of a robust regional organisation capable of facilitating cooperation and dialogue, but the very tenacity of Indo–Pakistan mistrust prevents such an organisation from emerging in the first place. Likewise, it is often argued that only when the Kashmir crisis is solved can Indo–Pakistan relations improve, but it is equally plausible that a solution to the Kashmir crisis can only come about when the overall tone of Indo–Pakistan relations is itself improved.

Similar arguments can be made with regard to almost every facet of the bilateral relationship and have become, in part, the excuse for postponing serious attempts to resolve Indo–Pakistan hostilities. Yet if the present situation is allowed to continue, or even to escalate, not only is there an increased likelihood of another war in the region, there is a considerable risk that it could be nuclear. The recognition of the probability of a nuclear exchange is not premised on some form of racist conception of South Asians or their political leadership which sees them as 'irrational and excitable' actors, unable to comprehend the significance or gravity of the current situation. As I argue in this chapter, the probability of such an exchange lies in the intensity of the insecurity felt by these two states, the extent of the historical legacies, and the current flashpoints built into almost every facet of Indo–Pakistan relations. Yet even if the current stand-off is normalised in a way familiar to students of the old East–West Cold War, a continuation of the Indo–Pakistan stand-off sustains a climate which stunts the political and social development of these two great nations. The chapter concludes with some tentative suggestions towards constructing a 'common home' for South Asia as a whole, in which all the states of the region will feel secure. I believe that the reasons for doing so now are compelling.

LEGACIES OF PARTITION AND STATE FORMATION

The mutual mistrust that lies at the heart of Indo–Pakistan relations has been historically and politically constructed in the minds of specific elites, and although these elites have changed since Independence, they remain profoundly influenced by the trauma of partition. Partition created two states, born in animosity, out of the common socio-cultural threads of British India. Perhaps in few other places in the world is the so-called 'burden of history' so present or so relevant. Pakistan was created, intentionally or otherwise, as a consequence of the 'two nation theory' advanced by the Muslim League, the Muslim nationalist political party, which stated that the Hindu and Muslim communities within the Raj constituted two separate nations. In 1940, the Muslim League argued that, '... those areas in which the Muslims are in a numerical majority, as in the north-west and the north-eastern zones, should be grouped to constitute independent states in which the constituent units shall be autonomous and sovereign'.

This argument, confused as it was by intra-Muslim competition, was resisted by the Indian National Congress, the main source of Indian nationalist opposition to the British. Under the leadership of a liberal intelligentsia, the Congress claimed to represent all Indians regardless of their religion, language or race, evolving a unified state-centered ideal of 'the nation' and upholding an associated democratic and secular state ideology. The ideology of secular nationalism allowed the Indian National Congress to present itself as the successor to the entire territorial configuration of British India, including the princely states.

For the League, the articulation of a religious nationalism contested the Congress' secular enterprise by laying claim to represent a transcendental God-given constituency-the Muslims of South Asia. In the context of faltering British resolve and Congress hostility, the 'two nation' theory resulted in the balkanisation of British India, and the creation of a 'moth-eaten Pakistan' state consisting of a two-winged nation, one in the northwest, the other in the northeast. Over one million people are said to have died following independence, as Muslims left for Pakistan from the Muslim-minority areas of northern India, and Hindus and Sikhs left for India. Widespread rioting and communal violence occurred in the western sector, especially in the wake of the partitioning of the provinces of Punjab and Bengal.[4]

The spectre of social and territorial disintegration remains in both India and Pakistan to this day. Given Congress' reluctance to sanction its creation, Pakistan was immediately conscious of India's animosity to its survival. The existence of Pakistan questioned the ability of the Indian state to deal fairly with religious minorities, especially of the Muslims who stayed back in India or lived in the regions of northwest India (notably Kashmir). It persisted in alleging that Indian secularism was merely a type of Hindu reformism, a white-wash for Hindu dominance. Such a perception of India has been considerably reinforced by the emergence of the BJP as India's largest party, and its ideology of Hindutva, which envisages a national identity premised on Hindu culture and profoundly hostile to Indian Muslim identities.

In turn, the existence of secular India questioned the ability of Pakistan to identify Muslims adequately, given the high degree of social and cultural pluralism that existed within the Muslim majority areas. Many of the Muslims who found themselves within Jinnah's state defined themselves primarily through linguistic, regional, and other aspects of their identity-often at odds with the state-favoured Koranic, Sunni traditions. There were many non-Muslims in the new state as well, especially in East Pakistan. The refusal of the Pakistani elite under Jinnah to endorse a confessional, theocratic state merely deepened the confusion implicit in the concept of the Pakistani state and heightened its competition with India.

As a result, both states contested the premise of the other's existence and sought to defend themselves. The fact that both India and Pakistan were large, multi-ethnic and multi-linguistic states, with relatively high levels of domestic unrest and instability, provided ample opportunities for each to intervene covertly in the domestic politics of the other. Many linguistic and cultural identities cross-cut the hastily improvised borders between them. The demarcation of the international border, carried out by the Radcliffe Boundary Commission and published the day after Independence, left many serious anomalies, especially in and around the Chittagong Hill Tracts of East Bengal, the Rann of Kutch area in the West, and in certain parts of the Punjab. Partition created a Pakistan with a 1,400 mile border with India in the west, and a 1,300 mile border with Afghanistan. The so-called Durand Line inherited from the British cross-cut numerous tribal groups in the North-West Frontier Province (NWFP), and was not officially recognised by the Kabul government.[5] The location of East Pakistan-situated a thousand miles to the east of Karachi-created a logistical nightmare for Pakistan's post-independence socio-economic and security arrangements.

Along with the ideological dispute which in turn had generated a fight over territory, Partition also involved a protracted dispute over how the physical assets of the Raj were to be divided between the two dominions. The speed with which the British moved to disengage from South Asia did much to contribute to the crisis. In her work on the Pakistani state, Jalal noted that 'The Partition machinery set up to determine Pakistan's share of the assets of undivided India had seventy-two days in which to dismantle a government structure it had taken the British over a hundred years to construct. Settling who was to get what ... took place against a backdrop of an unprecedented communal carnage.'[6]

It had been provisionally agreed that all physical assets would be divided on the basis of a one-third/ two-thirds split, but since the territories of the new state of Pakistan constituted some of the most backward areas of British India, Pakistan was significantly disadvantaged. Most of the industrial centres, such as Bombay and Calcutta went to India. The only area of industrial significance bequeathed to Pakistan was the port of Karachi, and this too had been relatively neglected. Serious infighting took place over the balance of payments. The Raj's contribution to the British war effort, paid off by the British treasury in 1946 left New Delhi in possession of a large amount of sterling. Pakistan was to be given 17.5 percent of the financial assets of the Raj, most of which was held back by India until

1948–49. Ultimately, Pakistan did not receive in full the Rs 750 million that should have been paid to Karachi. Following the outbreak of violence in Kashmir, India suspended payments after only Rs 200 million had been transferred. Such actions convinced the Pakistani leadership that India was determined to 'strangle' the new state at birth.

Indo–Pakistan mistrust was intensified by India's successful intervention in the Pakistani civil war of 1971, which culminated in its loss of East Pakistan and the creation of the sovereign state of Bangladesh. India's support for the Awami League and the Bengali militants, or Mukti Bahini, convinced the Pakistani leadership that India remained unreconciled to the fact of Partition. Even after New Delhi had called a unilateral cease-fire in December 1971, many Pakistanis believed that an all-out offensive in the Western sector had been averted through international pressure on New Delhi, and not by any specific self-restraint on the part of the Indian leadership. At the moment of triumph, Indira Gandhi had been quick to note that the independence of Bangladesh had totally discredited the two nation theory once and for all, since Jinnah's state had systematically failed to meet the cultural requirements and expectations of the Bengali-speakers in the east. Such a statement merely confirmed for Pakistan's Punjabi–Muhajir elite the image of a calculating, implacably hostile India. Sajjad Hyder, Pakistan's high commissioner in New Delhi in the run-up to the Bangladesh crisis, notes in his latest memoirs that, 'Our perceptions of India are that, beneath a thin veneer, the Indian leadership and a sizeable segment of Indian opinion continue to regard the formation of Pakistan as an historical error and that given the opportunity they would wish in some way to redress the situation.'[7] More recently, a Pakistani academic noted in a public lecture that 'it is significant that many Indians, when they speak of the *Indian* land mass cannot refrain from making it clear that what they are really talking about is the entire South Asian region.'[8]

THE KASHMIR CRISIS

The extent to which the tensions between India and Pakistan go back to the communal conflicts of the pre-independence period and the dynamics of partition, is best illustrated by the continuing conflict over the control of the former kingdom of Jammu and Kashmir. The integration of the princely states of India into the successor dominions of India and Pakistan was a huge and complex undertaking, involving the transfer of sovereignty from the feudal multi-ethnic states to either New Delhi or Karachi. In 1947, two-fifths of the Indian sub-continent was administered through indigenous rulers, constituting over 600 individual states and principalities scattered throughout the Raj.

By late 1946, the British had devised a scheme in which the princely rulers would themselves decide which dominion to join. The first step consisted of a Standstill Agreement which would be an interim measure whereby a princely state, uncertain about the exact future conditions of its membership within India or Pakistan, could provide for the continuation of essential services until a final decision was made. The second step would be the Instrument of Accession, which would be a permanent agreement through which a prince would join the state of India or Pakistan and immediately concede external affairs, defence, finance and communications to the new central government. Princely fiat was the deciding factor in this process. Although in reality it would be moderated by considerations of geography and, in some cases, the religious sentiments of the people, these latter elements were absent from any formal British consideration of processes deployed to resolve the future of Princely India.

The majority of the princely states decided their fate by August 1947. Yet a few, including the state of Jammu and Kashmir remained undecided. One of the largest and most magnificent of the princely states, the kingdom of Jammu and Kashmir had a predominantly Muslim population, but its Dogra ruling dynasty was Hindu.[9] Jinnah and the Muslim League claimed the kingdom of Kashmir on the basis of the two nation theory, and because of its physical proximity to the Muslim majority provinces of NWFP and Pakistani Punjab. Nehru and the Congress claimed it on the legal basis of the Instrument of Accession. This document was signed by the Maharaja *in extremis*, in October 1947, following the onset of a tribal invasion from across the newly established border with Pakistan. Assessing that the Pakistani government had organised this armed attack, the Maharaja requested Nehru's immediate assistance and acceded to India. Along with the Instrument of Accession, the Congress government in Delhi also claimed Kashmir on the grounds that a majority of Kashmiri Muslims identified with the secular agenda of the Congress party and did not endorse the League's emphasis upon Islam.

This last point – regarding the popularity of the Congress and its Kashmiri ally, the National Conference – were an important part of Indian claims to Kashmir. Despite initial talk of holding a plebiscite to clarify whether the Kashmiris wished to join India or Pakistan, and efforts at mediation by the UN, the former Dogra kingdom was in effect partitioned by the hostilities of 1947–48. Pakistan gained control over and continues to administer the former Poonch jagir (now known as Azad Kashmir), and the northern territories of Hunza and Gilgit: a combined area of approximately 30,503 square kilometres. India retained possession of the valley of Kashmir, Jawanee, and the Ladakh areas of Leh and Kargil. Both India and Pakistan continue to claim the territory in its entirety as part of their wider nationalist ideology. India considers its administration of Muslim-majority Kashmir integrally consistent with its view of itself as a secular state. Pakistan claims Kashmir in the belief that, despite its loss of East Pakistan, it is the leading protector of South Asia's Muslims.

Despite a ceasefire in December 1948, Kashmir was the focus of a second Indo–Pakistan war in 1965, and witnessed heavy fighting during the 1971 war over East Pakistan. In the 1965 conflict, the Pakistani offensive, code-named *Operation Gibraltar*, was preceded by the widespread infiltration of Pakistani-trained Kashmiri agents across the ceasefire line in the belief (erroneous as it turned out) that the Indian Kashmiris would see them as liberators. While the 1948 ceasefire line was modified in 1965, and converted in 1972 at the Simla Conference into a 'soft border' otherwise known as the Line of Control (LoC), the stalemate over Kashmir has continued. The Simla Conference, with its recognition of the LoC as an international border, appeared to herald a new era in Indo–Pakistan relations. Yet by the late 1980s, the Simla Accord came under dispute in the changed context of domestic instability on the Indian side of the LoC, and of the Kashmiri insurgency. In 1994, Benazir Bhutto and Narasimha Rao made statements referring to Kashmir as the 'unfinished' business from the days of Partition, and stressed their determination to resolve the matter.

The political situation within the Indian state of Jammu and Kashmir deteriorated rapidly from 1987 onwards. By 1990, the state constitution stood suspended and the administration was being run from New Delhi through the office of the governor. The marginalisation of the established political parties (especially the National Conference, a Kashmiri party linked to Sheikh Abdullah, the initial architect of the Indian political settlement) and increasing intervention in the affairs of the state by New Delhi indicated an undermining of India's commitment to uphold the special status of Jammu and Kashmir within the Indian federal system. The changes throughout the Islamic world following the Iranian revolution and the inflow of arms and Muslim fighters for the Afghanistan conflict also led to the growth of insurgency in Kashmir against what many saw as the Indian 'occupation' and demanded widespread political change. New militant groups articulated pro-Pakistani or pro-independence agendas against the formula supporting provincial autonomy of the National Conference, and fought against the Indian administration and each other to gain political ascendancy. The growing communal tensions and violence forced the majority of the Hindu community to flee from Srinagar in the winter of 1990–91.

Confronted with its own problems of socio-cultural integration, the break-down of political order in Jammu and Kashmir revived Pakistan's old hopes that the disputed territory might well wrest itself from the Indian Union. The Pakistani leadership, under Nawaz Sharif and later Benazir Bhutto, publicly supported the causes of various Kashmiri groups, especially Islamic ones such as the Jamaat-i-Islami. Furthermore, in the context of intense intra-party competition within Pakistan, both Benazir Bhutto and Nawaz Sharif used the Kashmir dispute to rally anti-Indian support to politically legitimate themselves in their bid to gain power in the 1990 and 1993 election campaigns.

In India, the extent and suddenness of the Kashmir crisis raised anxieties about the process of nation building and the degree of Pakistani intervention. The need to 'teach the Pakistanis a lesson' became common in the rhetoric of the right wing political parties, such as the BJP, in the 1996 election. The arguments over Pakistani involvement created fear in the Congress leadership that attempts to discuss the matter openly with Benazir would be interpreted as appeasement by their political opponents. By 1994, India deployed a large number of troops to isolate the various (and multiplying) militant groups from the Kashmiri population and to seal the border with Azad Kashmir and Pakistan. At one stage over 400,000 troops were deployed in the vicinity of the LoC. From 1995 onwards, the Indian government also embarked on the dangerous tactic of releasing insurgents back into the field to fight for the Indian cause, once they had offered loyalty to the Indian security forces while in detention. These often criminalised militants turned to extorting the Kashmiri population through elaborate protection rackets or mere intimidation. New Delhi charged that Pakistani assistance was the primary cause for the breakdown in law and order, and that weapons and supplies were finding their way from the Pakistan army to irregular units fighting a jihad on behalf of their fellow Muslims. India released a large amount of documentation detailing Pakistani training camps in Azad Kashmir.

Internationally, while India stressed that Kashmir was a bilateral affair, the Pakistanis attempted with some success to keep the Kashmir issue on the international agenda. India denounced Pakistan for interfering in its internal affairs, and with an eye to Pakistan's links to the US, accused it of supporting Islamic fundamentalism, a euphemism for terrorism. Indian accusations against a 'foreign hand' in the affairs of Kashmir mirror Pakistani accusations of Indian help to Baluchi separatists in 1973–74, and Sindhi nationalists in 1983–85. However, the Indians base their arguments on their actual experience in the 1965 war in which the Pakistanis did make use of infiltrators prior to a full-scale military attack, and the controversy surrounding Pakistan's official involvement in the tribal invasion in 1947. The Indian leadership finds it difficult to accept that Pakistan's widely known identification with the causes of Islamic groups in Kashmir does not translate into material support. These arguments are historically constructed, highly emotive and difficult to verify.

The main culprit, as far as India is concerned, is the Pakistani intelligence service known as the Inter Services Intelligence (ISI) Unit, and the position it has within the Pakistani state as a whole. Little, if anything, is known with any certainty about this organisation. Between 1983 and 1987, the ISI was headed by General Akhtar, the most senior politician in Pakistan after Zia, and concerned itself with the surveillance of internal opposition to Zia's regime, and key aspects of foreign policy, with particular reference to Afghanistan. While the restoration of an elected government to Pakistan in

1988 may have constrained the ISI's role in internal security gathering, it does not appear to have constrained its influence over Pakistani foreign policy generally. Disputes, initially with Benazir Bhutto after 1988 and then with Nawaz Sharif in 1993, centred over who could make senior army appointments, and who was in charge of Pakistan's Afghan policy. While Benazir and the PPP as a whole favoured supporting moderate factions of Kabul's Mujahiddeen government, the ISI continued to favour Gulbuddin Hekmatyar's radical faction, a group favoured by the late General Zia. There were also wider issues of constitutional importance that were in dispute, such as the lines of accountability between the ISI and the National Assembly, its links to the Prime Minister's Office, and the powers of the national president. From early 1993 onwards, various right-wing research groups in the US, supported to some extent by leaks in the Pakistani press from retired military officers and ex-politicians, revealed that in 1992 the ISI had established an organisation calling itself the Markaz-Dawar, to co-ordinate Islamic militant activities in Kashmir and elsewhere under the leadership of one Maulvi Zaki. With 'secret' headquarters situated in Peshawar, the Markaz-Dawar was preoccupied with training fighters and re-directing weapons left over from the Afghan conflict to Kashmiri militant groups, above all, the militant wing of the Jamaat known as Hizbul Mujahideen.

Many of the sources of this information are in themselves dubious. Even if true, it was not immediately clear that such actions were sanctioned, or even known, by the Pakistan government. In 1993, in response to direct American pressure and the threat that the US would formally designate Pakistan as a terrorist state, Nawaz Sharif stopped ISI support for Kashmiri militants by sacking General Javid Nasir, the then head of the organisation and dismissing over twelve of his assistants. On the face of it, it seemed that Pakistan was as alarmed as the Indians and Americans to discover that the ISI had been spending about US \$3.3 million a month on training and weapons supplies.[10]

Although there is some reliable evidence that ISI activities do respond to direct parliamentary and prime ministerial pressure, especially following the appointment of a PPP president in 1993, there are good reasons for believing that the ISI constitutes an unaccountable institution operating within the Pakistani state. The probable autonomy of the ISI is an important factor when it comes to accusing the Pakistan government of openly assisting Kashmiri rebels. One enduring feature of Pakistan politics since independence has been institutional factionalism and the existence of 'parallel' lines of command, especially between the military and the civilian authorities, complicated by periods of military rule. Such a problem, the product of a long history of military involvement in national politics, has clearly persisted into the 1990s, even if it may fluctuate in intensity.

By late 1997 there was some evidence that the ISI was being controlled by a more assertive political leadership. The emergence of Sharif's Muslim

League in the February 1997 elections with a commanding majority in the National Assembly, and its subsequent abolition of the Eighth Amendment – which had earlier inverted a prime ministerial form of government into a presidential-executive one – seemed to open the way for greater control and accountability to the legislature and the civilian branches of state. Yet the associations between the military, the civil service and the politicians, forged during the long years of martial law, were not easily separable. The creation of a National Security Council, in which members of the military would sit alongside the prime minister and other senior civilian politicians, was widely interpreted as an attempt by the Pakistan military to maintain parallel authority to civilian institutions, retaining direct access to the executive on matters of defence and internal security. The military was keen to retain its autonomy in Kashmir and its pivotal role in the administration of the northern territories.

The complex interaction of civilian and military interests within Pakistan has resulted in a degree of duplication and confusion within Pakistan regarding its Kashmir policy. From the Indian perspective, this creates the possibility for 'plausible deniability' over any direct involvement by the Pakistan government in the Indian Kashmir problem. For other less partisan observers, it creates the worrying possibility that Pakistan has often proved unable to reign in foreign policy adventurism originating in the military's concern with national security and implemented without civilian or legislative scrutiny. These fears seemed fulfilled when in May 1999, Indo–Pakistan relations lurched to the precipice of war when Indian intelligence located over 400 Pashtun-speaking insurgents on the Indian side of the LoC, in the vicinity of the town of Kargil. The Indians blamed Pakistan for supplying and supporting the insurgents, to the point of providing a protective umbrella of heavy shelling and other mortar fire. The Pakistanis denied any formal involvement in what they claimed was an independent tribal action. The incident, by far the most serious since 1971, was in many ways a curious echo of the original crisis of 1947. In 1999, as in 1947, the question for many was to what extent did the Pakistanis support the tribal action? Could such a large number of persons have passed through Baltistan and into the Indian side of the LoC without detection?

In answer, one has to take into consideration the geographical isolation of some of these border areas, and the difficulties that arise preventing covert movement across the LoC, from both the Indian and the Pakistani side. The Kashmir valley and the high *margs* on either side of the LoC, are incredibly isolated. Severe winter weather makes surveillance of the area very problematic. Part of India's intelligence failure in Kargil in 1999 stemmed from the simple fact that the border could not be monitored for almost six months of the year because of snow. The near-by town of Drass has recorded some of the lowest temperatures on the planet. The northern territories, especially Hunza and Gilgit, are in many ways 'beyond the pale' of the Pakistani government and the concept of Pakistan is itself vague and submerged by more immediate local identities. Indian sources claim to have identified up to seventy-two routes used by militants to cross from the western side of the LoC, mainly in the vicinity of the Haji Pir Pass, the Tosha Pass, and across the LoC from Baramula to Srinagar.[11] This area is difficult to patrol and hazardous to move around on. At certain times of the year it is virtually closed off from the outside world.

It was possible that militants initially crossed the LoC without the Pakistani government being aware, or indeed without the blessing of the ISI. The Pakistani Rangers, a paramilitary group entrusted to guard the border areas, traditionally suffered from poor training and high levels of corruption. They were replaced by regular Pakistani troops only in 1990. Certainly private organisations linked to the Jamaat carried out substantial collections on behalf of Kashmiri militants, calculated by one writer to be of the order of one million US dollars. Moreover, the extent to which the Afghan war has militarised tribal society should not be under-emphasised. It is possible in the NWFP to buy AK-47s and Kalashnikovs on the open market, with an AK-47 costing about $870. Other weapons, including Stinger missiles and multiple rocket launchers, have also leaked into the local bazaars from what is referred to as the 'Afghan' pipeline. Yet such sales in themselves have little, if anything, to do with official Pakistani policy.

India's ability to disarm the militants, to disrupt their arms supplies, and to capture weapons stocks directed to the 'front line' are not in themselves evidence of Pakistani complicity, although they present a case which Pakistan needs to address satisfactorily. There have been considerable arms confiscations by India. Between 1990 and the end of 1992 alone, its Border Security Force (BSF) gained possession of 7,000 AK-47s, 150 machine guns of various makes, 500 rocket launchers (some of Chinese design), 1,500 rocket grenades, and several tons of explosives.[12]

Indian accusations of Pakistani intervention (and to a lesser extent, vice versa) illustrate one aspect of the tragedy of Indo–Pakistan relations that has cost both states dearly. The existence of a ready-made foreign security threat too readily detracts attention away from domestic causes for the political alienation of Kashmir from the mainstream of Indian politics, and indeed to many other political failings of India and Pakistan towards their own citizens. Recent analyses have drawn attention to how, in the context of regional insecurity, Pakistan's elite has feared the consequences of sanctioning a federal system and sought to build a centralised, bureaucratic state 'robust enough' to stand up against India. The Indian elite too, has proved reluctant to extend autonomy and to further democratise the Indian federal system, especially in the case of Kashmir, because of entrenched fears that such devolution will weaken the state in the face of Pakistan hostility.[13]

INDO-PAKISTAN RELATIONS AND NATIONAL SECURITY

The present and continuing impasse over Kashmir remains likely to maintain a low in Indo–Pakistan relations, and to be the most likely context in which a crisis could lead to a war. Many commentators have argued that if some solution could be found to this particular morass, Indo–Pakistan relations would be radically transformed. Yet the same people also observe that the problem of Kashmir will only be resolved if Indo–Pakistan relations improve. There are some reasons, however, for doubting this prognosis, despite the salience of the Kashmir issue. While Kashmir best exemplifies the competitive and conflictual nature of the Indian and Pakistani states, this dynamic is to be found at work in other issues also, especially in the perceptions that each state has about its regional responsibilities and its wider international image.

India's political elite inherited from the British Raj a strategic view of India's importance. They actively promoted the new state as the legatee of the Raj from which, as the Congress clarified from the British, the Muslim-majority provinces seceded in 1947. From the outset, despite its image as a large and poor state, India conceived of itself as an influential actor in international affairs. Throughout the 1950s, India was particularly active regarding the outstanding issues of decolonisation and global disarmament. Determined to remain aloof from the cold war, India was co-founder of the Non-Aligned Movement, and sought to use this forum to influence the emergent post-colonial world. Such influence was initially moral – a belief in mutual respect and trust and the belief that the toleration of ideological pluralism could largely avoid conflict. Yet in the wake of the 1962 Sino-Indian war, India's convictions about its future status changed. By the time of Nehru's death in 1964, and certainly by the end of the third Indo–Pakistan war in 1971, India's political elite had come to define power and influence along more conventional, even military, lines.

By 1972, India believed that it alone should maintain the regional order of states in South Asia with respect to its defence requirements and foreign involvement, and that internationally it should be treated as a regional power with great power potential. In contrast to its earlier neglect of a standing army and the military establishment generally, India began to give importance to power projection capabilities. As analysts noted in the wake of the Indo–China war, an involution of preoccupations took place. India became less concerned about having a high international profile in various fora, and more concerned about strengthening the components of its national power. Non-alignment became, more or less, a loose synonym for a tradition *realpolitik* approach.[14]

Beginning with various bilateral arrangements with Nepal and Bhutan, and more dramatically with the Simla Accord in 1972, and again with the Indo–Sri Lankan Accord of 1987; India has acted as the dominant power within the South Asian region and has sought to be recognised as such by the international community, especially the United States. P. N. Haksar, one-time principal private secretary to Indira Gandhi, renowned statesman and writer, commented in the wake of the third Indo–Pakistan war that, 'The events of 1971 in our sub-continent sent a message across the chanceries of the world – that Indira Gandhi's India, with its triumph over Bangladesh, was emerging as a power in its own right.'[15] In the early 1980s the clearest indication of an Indian 'Monroe doctrine' for the region was given by a foreign policy analyst working at the Centre for Policy Studies in New Delhi, 'No South Asian government must ask for extensive military assistance with an anti-Indian bias. If a South Asian country genuinely needs to deal with a serious internal conflict it should ask for help from neighbouring countries, including India.'[16]

In keeping with this doctrine, India embarked upon a process of military modernisation. In 1997 India had the fourth largest standing army in the world, numbering over one million men. The actual figure of 1,145,000 compares to 2,840,000 for China (1997) and 1,240,000 for Russia. In 1996–97, the Indian airforce consisted of 870 combat aircraft, including the latest Mig-27 and a squadron of Mirage 2000 jets. By 1994, the Indian navy numbered 47,000 men (excluding the 5,000-strong manned airforce wing and 1,000 marines). The fleet consisted of over 25 principal surface vessels, including two aircraft carriers, 5 destroyers, 21 frigates and 15 operational submarines. The 1997–98 lease-back arrangements with the Russian federation marginally increased the Indian navy. In 1998 the BJP government confirmed that India would begin building its own indigenous aircraft carriers by 2001.

In 1989 it was announced that India planned to construct its own nuclear submarine, and a series of aircraft carriers. There has already been some moderate success in building frigates. Moreover, as noted earlier, India has pressed ahead with an ambitious and comprehensive missile development programme. Following the establishment of the Integrated Missile Programme in 1983, India has also been able to research and develop an indigenous missile system made up of a mobile short range missile and an intermediate range missile, known as the Prithvi and the Agni respectively. By 1995, the Integrated Missile Programme had developed and started to test up to five different missile systems. By 1998 both India and Pakistan had successfully test-fired their intermediate range missiles; the Pakistani Ghauri-I, with India carrying out another successful test of the Agni missile in the spring of 1999. Thus both states have the delivery systems capable of striking deep into the other's territory. Since the early 1970s India has also undertaken independent satellite production which has involved extensive collaboration with the former Soviet Union (and continued with Russia), the European Space Agency, and increasingly NASA.

India's view of its power and status, made manifest in the modernisation of its military as well as through various statements by its leading politicians, run counter to Pakistan's image of itself as India's equal with its own legitimate defence requirements. An emphasis upon parity, and the refusal to concede Indian supremacy are considered essential by Pakistan's military establishment and a majority of its civilian leadership, to ensure its own autonomy of action and to guarantee its survival. Yet it is this claim that irritates Indians who see it as unrealistic for a state of Pakistan's size, and if Pakistan's intentions are peaceful, unnecessary. As they point out, India commands 72 percent of the territorial area of South Asia, 77 percent of its population, and approximately 78 percent of the region's natural resources.

Pakistan's concern of 'matching' India appears to be, in part, a type of strategic culture forged in the context of Partition. Its anxieties over security seem to go back to Partition and the way in which the British Indian army was divided between the two states. Pakistan's share of the undivided British Indian army came to over 30 percent (140,000 out of 410,000 men), 40 percent of the navy, and 20 percent of the airforce. Of sixty-seven battalions in British India, only thirty-five, after being stripped of their Hindu and Sikh companies, went to Pakistan. However, much of the military infrastructure, such as air bases, ordnance factories and supply depots remained in India. Once the prospects of war loomed up with relation to Kashmir, India refused to allow any further transfer of military stores or hardware into the hands of the Pakistani army. From the onset, Pakistan sought to build up a modern army capable of defending its borders against Indian aggression. Such a commitment, given the relative poverty of Pakistan at the time of Independence, was an arduous undertaking. Moreover, the difficulties of retaining a military balance with India were underscored by its own geo-strategic narrowness, in which the western Indo–Pakistani border ran close to the main north-south lines of communication between Karachi and Islamabad. In terms of industrial and economic might, Pakistani strategic thinking has long feared India's size and the advantage this gives India in any protracted military campaign.

Pakistan's response to its perceived strategic vulnerability was to look for extra-regional allies and access to foreign 'off-the-shelf' weapon systems. Only with extra-regional guarantees – or nuclear weapons – did it feel it could adequately defend itself. In the 1950s Pakistan was quick to turn to the United States and, as Sino–Indian relations deteriorated in the 1960s, to China. In a balance of power strategy, it sought to create close alliances with both states and to ensure that they would come to its assistance in the eventuality of a war with India. Using the cold war to justify US assistance, in the 1950s, 1960s and in the wake of the Soviet invasion of Afghanistan in 1979, Pakistan received large amounts of sophisticated weapons which New Delhi feared would be used ultimately against India.

By 1994, Pakistan had assembled a powerful and well integrated army of approximately 520,000 personnel (excluding reserves), and an airforce made up of at least 430 combat aircraft. In contrast to India, most of these are Western (American, British and French) and have been imported into Pakistan under various international security arrangements. The Pakistan navy, partially to off-set Indian developments, has also increased dramatically in the last decade. In 1994 it consisted of eleven main surface combatants and nine submarines, a small reduction from previous years. In the succeeding year purchases and leaseback arrangements with the United States and Britain have doubled the tonnage of the Pakistan fleet. In 1994, the Pakistanis signed a deal with France for the purchase of four Agnosta class diesel submarines. Pakistan insisted that the deal ought also to include a clause forbidding the French to sell the same class of submarines to the Indians. In 1995, the Chinese agreed to a credit deal which allowed Islamabad to buy Chinese weapons at concessional rates. In 1998, China denied that it had provided Pakistan access to its own nuclear technology, or facilitated the development of Pakistan's nuclear weapon capability. It also denied providing Pakistan with access to M-11 intermediate missiles.

On the face of it, Pakistan's defence strategy has paid off well, but it has violated one of the central premises of India's security perceptions: that any external involvement in South Asia must be with India's agreement. Moreover, the fear that an external power, even one formally committed to guarantee its territorial integrity, might actually lack the political will to do so at a critical moment in its history has encouraged the belief that the only secure Pakistan is a nuclear one, capable of levelling Indian conventional capabilities. Recent arms embargoes against Pakistan, under both the Bush and Clinton administration, have reinforced this fear.

A CONVENTIONAL ARMS RACE

The asymmetry between Indian and Pakistani conceptions of their legitimate security requirements have resulted in an arms race in South Asia.[17] This has manifested itself in the high ratio of defence expenditures to Gross Domestic Production, in contrast to that of welfare and social services. This is especially true for Pakistan whose arms expenditure has often been higher than state expenditure on education or public health since 1947. While the debate amongst economists over the 'development cost' of arms expenditures in poor countries remains inconclusive, it is clear that defence budgets have diverted scarce resources from other urgent priority areas such as education, and the provision of public health facilities such as hospitals and clean drinking water. High levels of spending on defence are also, arguably, inflationary since they create rigidities in cost and production over time which governments are compelled to pay for. In 1994 India spent US$ 8.1 billion on its armed forces, of which about US$ 4 billion went to the army. Pakistan's military expenditure was US$ 2.63 billion.[18] As a proportion of Gross Domestic Product, Pakistan's expenditure on the military is about three times that of India's. Despite budget cuts in 1989 by the Rajiv Gandhi government, the defence estimates were increased by 8.9 percent by V. P. Singh in 1990 because of increased tension along the Kashmir border with Pakistan. Similarly, despite increased austerity measures, both India and Pakistan increased their defence budgets by 6–7 percent in real terms in 1994–95. In the wake of the 1998 nuclear tests, both states hiked their defence spending, India by 17 percent in real terms and Pakistani by 11 percent. While both states were initially placed under sanctions, the effects on the Pakistani economy were more serious and led to an immediate capital scarcity.

There has been no serious attempt by either India or Pakistan to discuss arms control measures in South Asia, or to discuss the possible elimination of specific types of weapon systems. India has attempted, unsuccessfully, to prevent the US from providing Pakistan access to advanced fighter bombers or night capability targeting technologies for its tanks and APCs. With specific reference to conventional weaponry, Pakistan has long acknowledged that the only way it can match India's size and industrial base is through importing off-the-shelf technology, an expensive procedure to follow. Many analysts argue that in the long run Pakistan cannot match India, weapon system for weapon system without bankrupting its economy.

It has been argued that India's reference point for military power within international relations is not Pakistan; but greater powers such as China, the now weakened Russian Federation and even, arguably, the United States. Why else would India be interested in the development of a blue water navy or the development of carrier battle groups? While it remains concerned about Pakistani capabilities, Pakistan is seen as a regional irritant, a distraction from the wider and more important councils of foreign affairs. Yet for Pakistan, India remains almost the sole focus of its foreign policy and security doctrine. As Mohammed Waseem noted, 'Ever since the emergence of Pakistan, India has been our greatest preoccupation in the context of international relations.'

A NUCLEAR SOUTH ASIA: COSTS AND CONSEQUENCES

Nowhere is this asymmetry in conceptions of security between the two countries clearer than in their positions on the nuclear 'option'. While the Pakistani bomb has evolved in the regional context of growing Indian conventional superiority and Pakistan's cynicism in the 1970s over US nuclear guarantees; India's nuclear ambiguities are part of its wider search for potential great power status and part of its wider rivalry with China. It was of particular interest that, in the run up to the 1998 nuclear tests, the

Indian Defence Minister, George Fernandes, cited China – not Pakistan – as the prime security concern for India.[19]

While the nuclear issue is a matter of bilateral relations for Pakistan, for India it is of much wider import. Many in the Indian elite discuss nuclear weapons symbolically, as an attribute of a powerful state with global responsibilities. It has, relatively consistently in the post-Nehru era, reserved the right to develop and deploy nuclear weapons until the nuclear powers renounce their use and move towards ensuring their total elimination. This position was articulated afresh at the NPT review treaty in New York in 1995, and in the various discussions over the Comprehensive Test Ban Treaty (CTBT), which India refused to sign. In 1995 India deeply regretted the failure of the existing nuclear weapon states (NWS) to take seriously the concerns of the non-NWS with reference to the renewal of the Non-Proliferation Treaty (NPT), which India refused to sign, that the treaty merely froze in a nuclear advantage for the NWS. Likewise, when the US announced in 1996 that it would be working towards a CTBT, without reference to the existing stockpiles of weapons in the hands of the NWS, India protested vehemently and accused the NWS of practising 'nuclear apartheid'.[20] India was particularly outraged when the US listed India as one of the forty-four states whose ratification was needed for the treaty to enter into force after three years, a move designed to put the maximum pressure on the Indian government.[21] After the 1998 tests, India argued somewhat paradoxically that only India as an acknowledged nuclear weapons state could force the issue of global nuclear disarmament back onto the agenda of the on-going conference for disarmament at Geneva.

It could be argued that India's wider moral stance on global nuclear disarmament is bogus and disguises the extent to which India's political elite have undergone a re-thinking about the utility and importance of possessing nuclear weapons. What is so revealing about the official language used to 'spin' the Indian tests of 1998, in contrast to India's Peaceful Nuclear Explosion (PNE) in 1974, is the explicit linkage made between the ability to test a series of differing devices and the will to weaponise and deploy them. The prime minister's principal private secretary stated that the tests gave India 'a proven capacity for a *weaponised* nuclear programme'.[22] In May 1998, Defence Minister George Fernandes assured Indians that the government was serious in claiming India as a nuclear weapons state, '... without weaponisation, this whole question of being a nuclear weapon state doesn't make sense: weaponisation is necessary'.[23] Statements throughout 1998 confirmed that India was thinking along the lines of developing a strategic nuclear force under the command of a newly re-constituted National Security Council (NSC).[24] However instrumental the Indian argument is about the need for total nuclear disarmament, it is clear that there is still a widespread attachment within the NWS to the symbolic power of these systems. As such a recognition does not condone India's decision to test (or indeed Pakistan's determined response), it makes the consequences of a nuclear South Asia all the more compelling. India and Pakistan are now nuclear states. They have the delivery systems and the skills to deploy. The debate has moved onto arms control.

INDO–PAKISTAN RELATIONS AND SAARC

S. Gangal noted in the late 1980s that 'India and Pakistan have more in common, river systems, climates, languages, cultures and religion than perhaps any two nations anywhere else'.[25] In different circumstances these commonalties would have facilitated joint economic ventures and a healthy balance of trade. However, in the context of deep seated distrust and suspicion, these very commonalities became a further source of insecurity. Furthered by India's emphasis upon self-reliance and a planned economy, trade relations between India and Pakistan, and between the various states of South Asia as a whole, have remained incredibly small, about 4 percent of South Asia's US$ 54 billion trade total in 1993. Indo–Pakistan trade was less than 2 percent of India's total trade by value in 1994. Provisional figures for Indian trade in 1995 show Pakistan's share of imports below Nepal, Bangladesh and Sri Lanka.

The economic strategy of India and Pakistan became, like many facets of their domestic policies, competitive towards each other and exclusive to each other's interests. While certain bilateral agreements facilitated the continuation of shared water resources in the northwest (such as the Indus River Treaty); differing fiscal policies, and even embargoes set up during hostilities, disrupted the jute trade in the Northeast. Partition had left the jute fields in East Pakistan but most of the jute processing mills in India. Mutual hostility has prevented any further cooperation over ecological management of shared regional resources.

Attempts to improve trade relations between India and Pakistan have long been seen as a prerequisite for improving bilateral relations generally. Recent economic changes in India and Pakistan towards economic liberalisation and the opening of domestic markets to direct foreign and portfolio investments, arguably create opportunities for fresh initiatives to encourage bilateral economic activities. What, realistically, can be done in such circumstances? Much of the current literature identifies two problems for pressing ahead with in-depth economic co-operation. One, drawn from development economics, highlights the similarities of the Indian and Pakistani economies in their developing status, and their import and export requirements. Both economies are seeking to export similar goods to third markets, and have similar import requirements in intermediate, manufactured and capital goods. Both states are also competing for capital, concessional aid or soft loans from the international community as a whole. As such, it is argued that their economies are incompatible.

The second argument returns to the tone of Indian and Pakistani relations as a whole, and argues that where a rationale exists for increasing economic activities, such as through the creation of economies of scale in new industries, or pooling expertise and infrastructure, creating commodity price support schemes, the advantages would almost certainly accrue to Indian economic interests. Given the size of the Indian economy, and the relative efficiency of Indian industry in some leading sectors such as computer software, semi-processed goods and light manufacturing, Pakistani companies would be at risk in their own markets without state protection. Evidence from other areas of economic co-operation, most notably the Central and East African Federations,[26] reveal the potential inequalities stemming from common market strategies.

The economic incompatibility between the Indian and Pakistani economies can be overdrawn, however. Both states could provide markets for goods that have, following the events in Eastern Europe and the former Soviet republic, lost their traditional outlets. A recent conference on South Asian security noted that at least five or six areas of potential co-operation existed, provided that the political will was there. Yet like so much in Indo–Pakistan relations, initiatives that will benefit Indo–Pakistan relations are discouraged because of mistrust and scepticism. Casting the net slightly wider, many believe that regionalism is the answer, both to the successful economic integration of India and Pakistan, and to wider confidence-building measures generally.

Until the mid 1980s, South Asia was one of the few regions in the world not to have any regional security or economic organisation. One explanation for this absence was the tenacity of Indo–Pakistan hostility. In 1980, Ziaur Rahman, President of Bangladesh, issued a draft for what came to be called the South Asian Association for Regional Co-operation (SAARC), to both reconcile his own regime with Pakistan and to construct a viable framework to cement Indo–Pakistan co-operation. Rehman recognised that without Indian goodwill such an organisation would be still-born, but he also recognised that the creation of a regional forum, in which all the states of South Asia were granted the same rights, would contradict the essential bilateralism of Indian foreign policy.

However, New Delhi's anxieties about the possible rise of an anti-Indian coalition of the smaller states were moderated by the acceptance of the only condition that India placed on the table – that bilateral issues would not be brought up at SAARC meetings. The organisation would confine itself to general matters and not discuss political issues. India was determined to prevent Pakistan from using the SAARC forum to bring up issues such as a South Asian Nuclear-Free Zone initiative or Kashmir. The Dhaka Declaration, signed in 1985 by India, Pakistan, Bangladesh, Sri Lanka,

Nepal, and Bhutan stated that SAARC was formed to 'co-operate on a regional basis, to accelerate the pace of economic development, and to enhance national and collective security'. Sections Four and Five of the Charter outlining the objectives of SAARC note explicitly that it would work to promote 'mutual trust, understanding and appreciation of each other's problems, and promote active collaboration and mutual assistance in the economic, social, cultural, technical and scientific fields'.

The success of SAARC has been mixed. Given the deep divergence between the two main South Asian protagonists, it is not surprising that SAARC has failed to facilitate a major break-through in Indo–Pakistan relations, or develop an effective collective decision making process. Although the organisation initiated a series of common action programmes covering telecommunications, rural development and meteorological forecasting, its avoidance of political issues has led to non-action. Attempts to define terrorism and work towards its successful elimination have failed in the wake of mutual recriminations regarding support for and assistance to 'militant' organisations. Several summits have been disrupted because of deterioration in bilateral relations, such as the 1991 summit due to Indo–Sri Lankan hostilities. The 1993 summit had to be postponed because of Hindu–Muslim violence in India in the wake of the Ayodhya mosque crisis. To some observers, SAARC is merely a rhetorical exercise, neither an economic union nor a collective security arrangement.

Such an assessment, however, fails to recognise the success in SAARC surviving at all. It fails to note that SAARC managed to keep alive the commitment to cooperation, even if the organisation has failed to substantiate specific policies. Such tenacity is by itself impressive. For example, once the 1993 summit managed to get underway, SAARC pressed ahead with discussions over the possibility of setting up a regional development bank, various commodity agreements, and discussed arrangements for setting up preferential trading agreements (SAPTA). In 1995, the Eighth SAARC summit identified twenty-two items of trade that would benefit from a common market, while at the same time seeking to assure member states that their national economic security would be guaranteed. Since 1996, SAARC has increasingly sought to address the compulsions of greater regional co-operation, while at the same time recognising that many, if not all, the states within the region are in competition for foreign capital. In 1998, the SAARC summit in Sri Lanka provided an opportunity for the Indian and the Pakistani prime ministers to meet informally in their hotel to try and re-start some Indo–Pakistan dialogue. Although SAARC cannot provide a forum in which the bi-lateral tensions of India and Pakistan can be addressed, the fact that the entire summit of 1998 was overshadowed by this event is indicative of the unfortunate centrality of Indo–Pakistan relations to the successful future of SAARC.

UNRESOLVED DILEMMAS

In his novel *Shame*, Salman Rushdie turns aside from his narrative to confess, directly to the reader, how difficult it is to write accurately about Pakistan without appearing absurd. For Rushdie, fiction often appears the only way in which one can adequately convey the sheer insanity of politics. Nowhere is this insight more useful than in attempting to come to terms with the dismissal of Sharif in October 1999, and the restoration of military rule after eleven years of political bickering, increasing corruption and sectarian violence. Sharif sacked General Pervez Musharraf after sending him to Sri Lanka, and then, when Musharraf returned in anger, tried to prevent his plane from landing at Islamabad international airport. This was done by authorising the parking of fire engines on the runway. Rather like a lesser Roman emperor, once it became clear to Sharif that he had lost the loyalty of his praetorian guard, he allegedly started stuffing his belongings into a holdall and called for his private plane.

Apart from revealing the continuing failure of democracy in Pakistan, the incident in which a prime minister with a two-thirds majority in the national assembly was removed to public acclaim reveals the centrality of the Kashmir issue to the future stability of the Pakistani state. For it was Sharif's apparent abandonment of the Kashmir issue that had sealed his fate. As the Kargil crisis continued to develop through May 1999, the US became increasingly critical of Islamabad's denial that it was involved in the incident at all. On July 4, Sharif had been called to Washington to hear demands from President Clinton that he withdraw his forces immediately from 'Indian territory', and withdraw all technical support to Afghan militants operating in the Dras sector. Sharif denied any involvement or support, but was contradicted in a statement issued by Musharraf that Pakistan would not withdraw unless India withdrew as well. Such a remark, issued by the commanding officer not far from the field of battle was somewhat baffling, given that Pakistan had, in the words of the prime minister earlier, nothing to withdraw except moral support. If Pakistani troops were involved in Kargil, as they undoubtedly were, who had authorised their use?

This dilemma – of who was running Pakistan's foreign affairs – confronted Clinton's analysts with the extent to which the parallel government of the ISI and its senior military leaders had hoodwinked an elected government in Pakistan. The logic for such adventurism remained obscure. Was this an attempt to internationalise the Kashmir issue? Did it have anything to do with the nuclear tests of the previous year? If the former, as seems most likely, the attempt backfired badly. Such a provocative gesture by one nuclear state against another gave the latter (India) a huge public relations advantage – one it did not fail to use to the full. It allowed New Delhi to move closer to the US by pointing out the extent to which the

Pakistani state was flouting international law. It enabled India to portray Pakistan as a rogue state, in league with terrorists, the sort of state that the US should have no truck with. Even China was reportedly nonplussed by the event and called upon Islamabad to resolve the matter peacefully. India's moral outrage was also useful in detracting public attention away from its own security failure and subsequent heavy losses – officially given at around 590, but put as high as 1000 by external commentators.

Sharif's decision to give in to US economic and political pressure, lit a slow fuse under his prime ministership. In the face of India's military embarrassment, the Pakistani military preferred to argue that their strategy was actually beginning to work, and that the politicians had betrayed them. The ISI was astounded to hear that Pakistan's political leaders had capitulated, not to the Indians, but to the Americans. Grudgingly, they complied with Sharif's decision, despite General Musharraf's central involvement in the campaign. Disengagement on the ground was agreed to by July 11. Sharif appeared visibly shaken by events. He faced protests from Islamic organisations, several of whom renounced the agreement as a sell-out, an abandonment of Pakistan's interests in Kashmir. The United Jihad Council, headed by Sayid Salahuddin, called upon Pakistanis to reject Sharif's deal with the US and continue with the struggle, while the Jamaat organised protests in Lahore and Islamabad. Such protests were not new, but the scale of such public unrest was surprising. Such anti-Americanism visibly embarrassed Pakistan's sophisticated and cosmopolitan elite, but they seemed increasingly marginalised and directionless. Although not directly involved in these incidents and having little time for Islamicist sentiments, Musharraf slowly emerged as a national focus for opposition to Sharif. His professionalism as a soldier and his identity as a muhajir, reinforced his image as that of a man capable of leadership.

Two other factors sealed the fate of the civilian government in Pakistan. One was the sheer economic chaos generated by sanctions in the wake of Pakistan's nuclear tests. The economy had shrunk and foreign debt servicing had grown dramatically, making the country acutely vulnerable to US pressures over Kargil. Combined with this, the degree of political corruption, close to and within the prime minister's family, incensed the average Pakistani suffering inflation, capital scarcity and unemployment. Despite the promises of 1988, democracy had not brought any material gains or any apparent advantages. It had – in the form in which it had emerged – simply made matters worse. Had not both Benazir and Nawaz emerged at the centre of two mafia-like networks of corruption, kick-backs and vendettas? Where was any clean political force to be found? With Sharif incarcerated and Benazir still exiled in England, the civilian landscape was bleak and unconvincing. Despite the possibility that Benazir could mend fences with the military, she seems a spent force and her restoration would merely be another symptom of democratic failure.

Creating a Common Home?

Like Generals Ayub Khan and Ziaul Haq before him, Musharraf found himself using the broadcast media to berate the civilian politicians for turning Pakistan into a haven for criminals and racketeers. Yet, unlike Ayub or Zia, Musharraf was heading a state situated in a radically different international context, one in which the apparent necessity of military government was no longer accepted and in which international support, regardless of the nature of domestic or regional policy, was no longer the rule.

As such, Musharraf was forced, under the compulsion of international politics, to confront the domestic mayhem of Pakistan at a singular disadvantage. He had to promise the restoration of democracy in a state that seemed incapable of institutionalising it and a civilian leadership incapable of promoting it. He could attempt to democratise a state in which the military believes that it has a right to be powerfully represented, despite its woeful failure in the past to deliver the economic and social security that the Pakistani people so desperately needed. But then every other institution seems to have failed as well, and the real horror is that they look as is they could go on failing.

The real fallout of the Kargil misadventure was that it allowed the Indian government of 1999 – a coalition headed by the BJP – to move closer to the US despite the very considerable differences that remained over trade, nuclear proliferation, and the UN. India was spared the embarrassment of killing the CTBT when the US Congress voted the initiative down in September 1999 but, as was made clear by Clinton on his visit to India in the spring of 2000, differences remained. Clinton reiterated the need for India to comply with the 'norms' of the international non-proliferation regime and to use its technology for the purpose of eliminating poverty and achieving economic growth. Pakistan's adventure in Kargil and the coup came at just the right moment to give validity to Indian claims that the security environment within South Asia was such that New Delhi needed nuclear weapons to enhance its security and to defend itself from covert intervention.

There is, as yet, no US tilt towards India. Clinton's visit was important and reveals the extent to which the two countries are trying again to use their many social and political similarities to forge a closer relationship. But such an attempt has been made before and has usually faltered on a combination of Indian intransigence and US impatience. There is no clear evidence as yet that the numerous discussions between Strobe Talbot and Jaswant Singh over the ill-fated CTBT have led to a US endorsement of India's nuclear deterrent, no matter how sympathetic the interaction. Talks were held between Vajpayee and Clinton on matters ranging from the WTO to issues of direct investments by US private companies, but it was what was *not* said, not agreed upon, that still counts. Four billion US dollars worth of deals may well have been signed between Indian and US corporate interests, but a number of trade issues still remained to be addressed. This is not to imply that the visit was not a success, or indeed historic, but merely to argue that it marks only the beginning of a long and difficult process.

To conclude, the real significance of the Clinton visit was what it revealed about US–Pakistan relations. On March 25, 2000, on Pakistani state television, Clinton issued a stark rebuke to the Pakistanis for Kargil. He was visiting Islamabad on what was commonly referred to as a 'stop over'. He stated that Pakistan must stop trying to redraw the map with blood and called on the state to respect the LoC. More bluntly, in clearly ruling out US mediation over Kashmir, Clinton stated that 'there is no military solution to Kashmir'. No US President had ever been quite so direct or hectoring. No joint declaration was issued between Clinton and the Pakistani leadership, leaving no ambiguity about US sentiments towards the military. There is no military solution to Kashmir, but this may be less evident to the Pakistanis than to the Americans. The idea of a common home is not dead, but it is as remote and as far away as it must have seemed to the Soviets in the late 1950s.

TOWARDS A COMMON HOME: CONFIDENCE-BUILDING IN THE FUTURE

This chapter has argued that Indo–Pakistani relations have been structured by the historical experience of Partition, and the creation of competing nationalist ideologies. Analysts such as Gowher Rizvi have frequently noted that the ideological basis of state–society relations in India are incompatible with those of Pakistan, and vice versa. Nowhere is this conflict more obvious than in the case of Kashmir. Added to this is the profound insecurity that Pakistan has experienced in its attempts to match Indian power and status, and its determination to attain parity with India through the use of external alliances and support, primarily China and till recently the USA. Such linkages have been perceived as deeply offensive to India, and to Indian regional policy generally. These fears and concerns have led to three wars, supported a conventional arms race with a nuclear dimension, encouraged economic chauvinism, and created a climate in which Indian and Pakistani leaders criticise and accuse one another of conspiracy and war mongering. How can this circular process be broken?

Most suggestions soon run into problems. One common argument starts with the need for both India and Pakistan to recognise each other's security requirements, and thereby create the necessary condition to assure each other that neither will start a conventional war. As discussed above, both states see each other's security arrangements as excessive and hostile. Yet with the change in the international system since 1989, perhaps India could tolerate an external power acting both as the guarantor of Pakistani security (through treaty rights securing territorial sovereignty) and being a friendly power to India. During the cold war, both India and Pakistan used their respective super power allies to engage in military and political competition. With the collapse of the USSR, the US could now under-write a collective security doctrine for the region as a whole. Such a process would involve Indian acceptance of external mediation, something it has largely spurned in the past. Obviously, it would also involve some pretty complex negotiations between India and the US over New Delhi's attitude towards the bomb, which remains part of its psychological claim to being a great power. India could secure recognition of a US-sponsored collective security arrangement in South Asia in return for American recognition of India's wider international ambitions, such as a place on the United Nation's Security Council, and access to American technology for India's economic restructuring.

There are two main stumbling blocks with this proposal, however. Firstly, on the face of it, any US–Indian deal that appears to credit India with middle power/great power status creates an incentive for the Pakistanis to *not* comply, if they believe the US commitment to guarantee their territory and 'interests' are merely rhetorical. Even if such an agreement is cast in iron, compliance would certainly mean that the Pakistani elite would have to forego parity as a principal goal. Secondly, the proposition assumes that the Americans would want to add South Asia to their concerns, be willing to deploy and act in a crisis there. There is evidence that the Clinton administration, and even under his predecessor, George Bush, the United States was beginning to change its perceptions of India, and vice versa. A survey of US attitudes towards South Asia as a whole, and India generally, concluded that there is a growing recognition that South Asia's fate will increasingly influence the world in which the Americans and others live in. It is a region where the issues likely to dominate the twenty-first century come together. Such a view was dramatically underscored by the nuclear tests in 1998.

Many commentators have noted that the degree of social and cultural similarity across South Asia, and even the similarity between their respective political cultures, have been disguised and obscured by an emphasis on Partition, and the respective 'boxes' labelled India and Pakistan. In 1987, President Gorbachev made a speech in Prague, Czechoslovakia, in which he called for the return of Russia, and by implication Eastern Europe, into the greater European home. 'Europe from the Atlantic to the Urals is ... a cultural concept in a high, spiritual sense. Here, world civilisation was enriched with the ideals of the Renaissance and the Enlightenment.' It was a speech that had profound implications for the old East–West confrontation. Such a process could well be applied to South Asia, although it will require the leadership and the support of South Asians themselves.

Perhaps, in the short term at least, India will have to make the greatest concessions to improve Indo–Pakistan relations. In the long term, India's elites may well have to change much of their current thinking on what constitutes power and influence, both internationally and regionally. This will have to involve a turning aside from military, geo-strategic ideas towards concepts such as economic influence and moral influence, ironically more in keeping with Nehru's era than Indira Gandhi's. Finally, for the international community to refuse to consider improving Indo–Pakistan relations as a priority, and to believe that either state can be overlooked, is to court war and disaster. The international conditions are probably as favourable now as they have ever been.

NOTES

1 BJP, *Manifesto 1998: Vote For a Stable Government and an Able Prime Minister* (New Delhi: 1998), 31, 'Policies on National Defence'.
2 Perhaps the most revealing statement on the wider context in which the BJP-led government decided to test can be gleaned from Jaswant Singh's book, *Defending India* (New Delhi: Macmillans, 1998).
3 Text of PM's speech at http://www.clw.org/pub/...lition/sharif052099.htm.
4 For a fascinating study of the problems faced by the boundary commission, see R. J. Moore, *Making the New Commonwealth* (Oxford: Clarendon Press, 1987). Moore notes that 'the essential conditions of [Radcliffe's] brief [from the government] which he took up on 8 July was that he must exercise independent judgment to bring down the awards by 15 August (p. 25).
5 The Afghan claims on Pakistan primarily involved the province of Baluchistan. As late as 1969, the Afghan government issued a postage stamp that showed the borders of Afghanistan as incorporating Baluchistan and parts of the Pakistan tribal belt. See M. Z. Ispahani, *Roads and Rivals: The Politics of Access in the Borderlands of Asia* (Ithaca, NY: Cornell University Press, 1989).
6 Ayesha Jalal, *The State of Martial Rule: The Origins of Pakistan's Political Economy of Defence* (Cambridge University Press, 1990), 25.
7 Sajjad Hyder, *Reflections of an Ambassador* (Lahore: 1988), 75.
8 Z. A. Khan, *Pakistan's Security* (Lahore: 1990).
9 Space precludes a full discussion of the immensity of this subject. See Alastair Lamb's two books *Kashmir, A Disputed Legacy 1846–1990* (Roxford: 1992), and *Kashmir Birth of a Tragedy: Kashmir 1947* and my own *Reclaiming the Past: The Search for Political and Cultural Unity in Jammu and Kashmir* (1995) for a good overview of the controversies.
10 See Human Rights Watch Arms Project: *India: Arms and Abuses in Indian Punjab and Kashmir*, vol. 6 (10), September 1994, 1.
11 Ibid., 21.
12 'On the Kashmir Beat', *Jane's Defence Weekly*, 21 May 1994.
13 See Ayesha Jalal, *Democracy and Authoritarianism in South Asia: A Comparative and Historical Perspective* (Cambridge: Cambridge University Press, 1995).
14 A. Vanaik and P. Bidwai, 'India and Pakistan,' in R.C. Karp, ed., *Security With Nuclear Weapons? Differing Perspectives on National Security*, (London: 1991), 263.
15 P. N. Haksar, *India's Foreign Policy and its Problems* (New Delhi: Patriot Publishers, 1989), 53.
16 Ibid.

17 While I recognise the vagueness of this term, it seems to me to convey the right sense of urgency about defence expenditure, and weapon system procurements currently witnessed in Indo–Pakistan relations. I am convinced that the current position between India and Pakistan fits both Martin Wight's definition of an arms race (in *Power Politics*, 239), and Colin Gray's discussion of an arms race in 'The Arms Race Phenomenon', *World Politics* 24, 1974, 41. Note Gray's fourth point that 'there must be a rapid increase in quantity and/or improvements in quality of weapons,' ibid.
18 IISS, *The Military Balance 1989–90*, (London: OUP, 1990). Put another way, however, India still spends less on defence as a percentage of her GNP (about 4 percent) compared to Pakistan's estimated 7 percent. There are difficulties in calculating or estimating China's defence expenditure, and quotes vary from 4–8 percent: see *Brassey's Asian Security* (London: 1989), 43.
19 See my mimeo 'Containing Shiva? India and the Politics of Nuclear Non-proliferation', in IISS, *The Military Balance 1998/9* (London: OUP, 1998).
20 The Indian position on the CTBT is also about access to technology. Given the advanced computing technologies of the NWS, actual testing is no longer necessary for improving their weapons system.
21 Jaswant Singh believed that such a move was against international law.
22 *Keesing's Record of World Events* 44 (5), 1998, 42240, emphasis added.
23 *Times of India*, 27 May 1998.
24 For George Fernandes' remarks, 'Weapons would not be Tactical', see *Indian Express*, 4 July 1998.
25 S. C. Gangal, *India and the Commonwealth* (Agra, India: Shiv Lal Agarwal, 1970), 63.
26 The East African Federation collapsed when Tanzania and Uganda realised that foreign investment was being attracted disproportionately to Kenya. Attempts to redirect aid led to recriminations and collapse of the common market strategy.

Chapter 14

The Flash-Point of South Asia: Kashmir in Indo–Pakistani Relations

Sumit Ganguly

The state of Jammu and Kashmir has been an object of dispute between India and Pakistan since their emergence from the detritus of the British Indian empire in August 1947. The two antagonists have fought three wars: in 1947–48, 1965, and 1971. The first two wars dealt directly with the question of Kashmir. Beyond the bilateral dispute, the Kashmir issue has three other important dimensions which will be dealt with in this chapter. The first deals with Kashmir's controversial status within the Indian Union since its accession to India in October 1947. The second concerns the exigencies of Indian domestic politics, which contributed directly to the rise of the violent ethno-religious secessionist movement that has wracked the state since 1989. In this so-called 'low-intensity' conflict, more than 35,000 individuals lost their lives since December 1989.[1] Finally, in the aftermath of the Indian and Pakistani nuclear tests in May 1998, the Kashmir dispute has attracted renewed international attention as a potential flashpoint in Indo–Pakistani relations.

This paper will explore three central questions. First, it will explore India's relationship with the state of Jammu and Kashmir and argue that this relationship is emblematic of the most extreme shortcomings of Indian federalism.[2] Second, it will examine the complex reasons for the inability of various national governments in New Delhi to deal with Jammu and Kashmir according to the widely accepted norms of a federal polity. Third, it will discuss various measures that can be taken to address the felt grievances of the Kashmiri population and restore Kashmir's autonomous status within the context of the Indian Union.[3]

THE CONTESTED ACCESSION

The weight of British colonial history shaped India's special relationship with Jammu and Kashmir.[4] The exigencies of British withdrawal from the subcontinent created a contest between the two nascent states of India and

Pakistan over the control of Jammu and Kashmir. Pakistan's claim to Kashmir was irredentist: its leaders, most notably Mohammed Ali Jinnah, sought to incorporate Kashmir to ensure Pakistan's 'completeness' as the 'homeland' of South Asian Muslims.[5] India, under the tutelage of its first prime minister, Jawaharlal Nehru, with somewhat lesser zeal, sought to persuade the ruler of Kashmir, Maharaja Hari Singh, to accede to India. Nehru's commitment to the construction of a secular polity underlay India's attempt to draw Kashmir into its fold. In the Nehruvian view, India's secular credentials would be bolstered if a predominantly Muslim state joined India, thereby repudiating Jinnah's 'two nation' theory.[6]

In this context it is pertinent to mention that Sheikh Mohammed Abdullah, the leader of the Jammu and Kashmir National Conference, the largest and most popular organisation in the state, had been drawn to the socialist outlook that had characterised segments of the Indian National Congress, the party that spearheaded India's nationalist struggle. More specifically, through his contact with Prime Minister Nehru, Abdullah had sought to transform his party into a secular multi-religious organisation seeking to represent all Kashmiris.

Maharaja Hari Singh harbored other plans, however. Even though Mountbatten had issued an explicit injunction against the option of independence, Hari Singh was unwilling to join either India or Pakistan. Accordingly, he signed a 'Standstill Agreement' with Pakistan (but not with India) and prevaricated on the question of accession.[7]

As Hari Singh vacillated on accession, in early October 1947 a tribal rebellion broke out in the region of Poonch, near the western reaches of his state. In an attempt to exploit the collapse of authority, Pakistan infiltrated regular troops disguised as local tribesmen to aid the insurgents.[8] In late October, as the rebels reached the outskirts of Srinagar, the capital, Hari Singh in a panic appealed to Prime Minister Nehru for assistance. Nehru agreed to help only if two conditions were met: the maharaja would have to accede to India and, given the inability to hold a referendum amid the chaotic conditions of the rebellion, the imprimatur of Sheikh Mohammed Abdullah, the people's leader, would have to be obtained for the accession. Only after Sheikh Abdullah gave his assent did Nehru accept the Instrument of Accession from the maharaja.[9] Nehru's decision to seek the sheikh's consent was significant. According to the terms of the transfer-of-power agreement between the princely states and the British, the maharaja had the legal right to accede to India or Pakistan. Nehru, however, was concerned with the issue of legitimacy, and thus felt compelled to devise some mechanism to ensure that the accession of Kashmir to India would be perceived as fair and just.

Shortly thereafter, in late October 1947, Indian troops were dispatched to Kashmir. They managed to halt the Pakistani onslaught, but not before the raiders had occupied one-third of the state.[10] Over the course of 1948 the two armies fought pitched battles in Kashmir but neither side proved successful in seizing significant portions of territory. In attempts to defuse the crisis, the United Nations passed two important resolutions on 17 January and 17 August 1948. The first resolution called on the two parties to refrain from the use of force in the disputed territory and to inform the Security Council of any material change in the situation there. The second resolution, which took cognisance of the presence of regular Pakistani troops in Kashmir, unequivocally stated that all further action towards settling the dispute would be conditional upon the withdrawal of those troops. Eventually, on 1 January 1949 a United Nations resolution brought about a cease-fire between the warring parties.[11] The territorial dispute, however, remained unresolved.

KASHMIR'S RELATIONS WITH INDIA

Even though Kashmir's accession to India was both legal and legitimate, its subsequent relations with New Delhi proved contentious. The difficulties stemmed from two conflicting drives: one, the interest of Sheikh Abdullah's organisation, the National Conference, to ensure the greatest degree of autonomy for Kashmir; and two, the concerns (and misgivings) of the political leadership in New Delhi about the country's unity and territorial integrity. This tension between demands for regional autonomy and increased devolution of power to the constituent states versus central efforts to control power has repeatedly manifested itself in the Indian political context and has yet to reach a clear-cut resolution.

The framers of the Indian constitution had sought to create a federal polity but with significant unitary provisions.[12] The decision to frame a constitutional dispensation that included compelling unitary provisions stemmed from both the centralised legacy of British colonial rule and the misgivings of the Indian nationalist leadership about the dangers of fragmentation of the nascent polity.[13] The tension between the federalising and centralising proclivities embodied in the constitution reached an apogee in the framing of Kashmir's special relationship with India.

Certain explicit conditions relating to Kashmir's future ties to India had been spelled out when the maharaja signed the Instrument of Accession. Three critical areas – defence, foreign affairs, and communications – came under the purview of New Delhi, leaving the state with a wide swath of residuary powers.[14] The leaders of the National Conference, however, saw the arrangements embodied in the Instrument of Accession as provisional and subject to ratification and possible modification under the aegis of a state-level constituent assembly. Most importantly, they argued that Kashmir, India's only Muslim-majority state, must have special provisions governing its relations with New Delhi. Accordingly, Sheikh Abdullah entered into negotiations with Prime Minister Nehru and Sardar

Vallabhbhai Patel, the Minister for State Affairs. The negotiations were tortured and difficult.[15] The principal objection of the National Conference leaders focused on the extension of certain basic constitutional provisions to Jammu and Kashmir. Eventually, the two sides reached an agreement, and on 25 November 1949 it was announced that the Constitution of India would be extended to Jammu and Kashmir, but with important qualifications embodied in Article 370 of the constitution. Article 370 allowed the state to set up its own constituent assembly to draft its constitution, limited the powers of the president of India to pass legislation concerning the stipulations of the Instrument of Accession, and prohibited Indian citizens from purchasing property in the state.[16] Further negotiations culminated in the Delhi Agreement of August 1952, in which the central government met most of the Kashmiri demands for autonomy but also extracted some significant concessions. Most importantly, the agreement extended the jurisdiction of the Indian Supreme Court to Jammu and Kashmir, gave the president of India the power to grant reprieves and commute punishments, vested residuary powers in the state government, and provided that the rule of Maharaja Hari Singh would be abolished and his son, Karan Singh, would be elected as the first president of the state.

Despite this agreement, Sheikh Abdullah and one of his closest acolytes, Mirza Afzal Beg, failed to promptly seek the assent of the state constituent assembly on the Delhi Agreement. Matters worsened in 1953, when the Sheikh and some of his principal advisers, most notably Maulana Sayeed Masoodi, the general secretary of the National Conference, made a series of intemperate statements and raised doubts about Kashmir's eventual accession to the Indian Union. In the aftermath of these statements, on 9 August 1953, on the advice of key members of the Intelligence Bureau (IB), Prime Minister Nehru dismissed the state government. An interim government was brought in under the leadership of another National Conference leader, Bakshi Ghulam Mohammed. Shortly thereafter, Bakshi steered the National Conference to accept the provisions of the Delhi Agreement. Sheikh Abdullah, Beg, and certain other National Conference leaders, all of whom had been incarcerated, could not participate in the proceedings. In May 1954, the president of India incorporated the recommendations of the constituent assembly, inserting Article 370 into the national constitution.

THE EXIGENCIES OF POLITICS: INTERNATIONAL, REGIONAL, AND NATIONAL

The dismissal of the Sheikh Abdullah regime notwithstanding, the incorporation of Article 370 in the Indian Constitution should have addressed the misgivings of its Muslim population about their rights and status within the union. However, political forces at the international, regional, and national levels conspired to undermine the legal provisions that defined Kashmir's unique position within India.

At the international level, the Kashmir issue quickly became enmeshed in cold war politics. Among other matters, adroit Pakistani diplomacy, which emphasised the country's putative anti-Communist commitments, generated American sympathy for its position on the Kashmir question. Non-aligned India's concurrent diplomatic ineptitude, and an inordinate emphasis on the legal aspects of its case, ensured that the central issue of Pakistani aggression was overlooked in the UN. Instead the UN Security Council focused on the Pakistani allegations of widespread repression of Muslims in Jammu and Kashmir and pushed for a plebiscite to resolve the dispute.[17] In turn, although committed to a plebiscite, India insisted that Pakistan had to withdraw its troops from the areas that it had occupied before any plebiscite could be held. Pakistan, on the other hand, insisted that its forces would withdraw or remain depending on the outcome of the plebiscite. As both sides remained steadfast on their positions, little or no progress was made in the multilateral forum. By 1960, the UN had lost interest in the Kashmir question.

Bilateral attempts involving both diplomacy and the use of force also failed to settle the dispute. In the wake of the 1962 Sino-Indian border war and under Anglo-American pressure, India agreed to hold discussions with Pakistan on the Kashmir question. Accordingly, six rounds of bilateral talks were held between December 1962 and May 1963. These talks, which initially appeared promising, eventually proved to be futile.[18]

In the absence of an agreement with Pakistan, the Congress government in Delhi, during Prime Minister Nehru's last days in office, passed a series of legislative and presidential directives that eroded Kashmir's special status within the Indian polity. Two items of legislation that were passed to extend certain articles of the Indian Constitution to Kashmir deserve particular attention. Article 356 empowers the president of India to dismiss a state government when the president deems that the state government can no longer maintain law and order. Article 357 abolished the terms 'head of state' and 'prime minister', which had been specifically retained in the case of Jammu and Kashmir. Now, as in other Indian states, the two leading officials would be known as 'governor' and 'chief minister'. Although the extension of the latter provision was largely symbolic, its symbolism was freighted with considerable significance: Jammu and Kashmir was losing its distinctive status in the Indian polity.[19]

The failure of multilateral as well as bilateral negotiations, India's rearmament efforts in the aftermath of the disastrous Sino-Indian border war of 1962, and its legal measures to steadily integrate Kashmir into the Indian Union prompted the Pakistani military dictatorship of Mohammed Ayub Khan to resort to force to change the status quo in Kashmir.[20]

Two events, in particular, emboldened the Pakistani decision-makers. The first involved the outbreak of violence in the Kashmir Valley in December 1963 in the aftermath of the theft of a holy relic (putatively a hair of the Prophet Mohammed) from the Hazratbal mosque in Srinagar. Since the demonstrations had a markedly anti-Indian tenor, the Pakistani leaders erroneously construed them as supportive of Pakistan. Later, in early 1965, Pakistan undertook a limited probe of India's defence preparedness along a poorly delineated border in the Rann of Kutch, in western India. The Indians did not respond with vigour because they deemed the area to be of limited strategic significance. Again, the Pakistanis made a flawed assessment of the motivations underlying India's behaviour: they interpreted the lack of a firm military response as indicative of Indian military pusillanimity. These two fundamentally incorrect assumptions prompted the Pakistani leadership to launch an invasion of Kashmir. After full-scale war broke out in September 1965, the Pakistanis realised the error of their assumptions. The Kashmiris, though unhappy with Indian rule, did not rush to cooperate with the Pakistani infiltrators. Worse still, the Indian Army not only responded with vigour but sought to extend the war into the Pakistani Punjab.

The 1965 war ended for the most part in a stalemate. At a Soviet-brokered post-war settlement in Tashkent (in then Soviet Central Asia), the two sides agreed to return to the status quo ante and to refrain from the use of force in settling the Kashmir dispute. Simultaneously, despite the objections of several senior army commanders, Indian Prime Minister Lal Bahadur Shastri (Nehru's successor) returned the key Haji Pir Pass (captured in the war) to Pakistan.

SLOUCHING TOWARD SIMLA

The Tashkent Agreement did not bring about a genuine settlement of the Kashmir dispute, however. The Pakistani leadership remained unreconciled to the status of the state but realized that they lacked the military means to detach it from India. In 1971, India and Pakistan were at war again.[21] India trounced Pakistan in this war and played a key role in the creation of Bangladesh from the ruins of the former East Pakistan. The postwar settlement, the Simla Agreement of 1972, returned the territory held by each side to the status quo ante, and converted the 1949 UN Cease-Fire Line (CFL) into a Line of Actual Control (LoC). It also led to the repatriation of some 90,000 Pakistani prisoners of war. Finally, it reiterated that the two sides would abjure from the use of force to settle the Kashmir dispute.[22]

During the 1971 war again, much to the chagrin of the Pakistanis, the Kashmiris had shown no inclination to foment disturbances in the valley. Worse still, the sanguinary secession of East Pakistan demonstrated that religion alone could not be the basis of state-building and state legitimacy in South Asia. As a consequence of both factors, Pakistan's irredentist claim on Kashmir was rendered virtually meaningless. If Pakistan could not command the loyalties of its co-religionists in East Pakistan, what basis did it have to muster the weak loyalties of Kashmiri Muslims?

THE 1975 ACCORD

The clear-cut victory of 1971 over Pakistan led Prime Minister Indira Gandhi to focus her attention on the domestic dimensions of the Kashmir problem. She freed Sheikh Abdullah from internal exile and started negotiations with him to resume normal political activity in Kashmir. Initially, Abdullah was quite intractable and expressed little willingness to negotiate with Mrs. Gandhi. After much persuasion on the part of the prime minister's principal emissary, G. Parthasarathi, and the entreaties of Balraj Puri, a prominent Kashmiri activist, Abdullah changed his mind and allowed Mirza Afzal Beg to open negotiations with Parthasarathi. These negotiations culminated in the Beg-Parthasarathi Accord of 1975, under the terms of which Abdullah promised to end the plebiscite phase of the Kashmir question. Now the issue before the two parties would revolve around the 'quantum [amount] of autonomy'.

The Pakistani designs on Jammu and Kashmir and fears of an incipient secessionist movement led by Sheikh Mohammed Abdullah and other disaffected National Conference leaders propelled the government of India to pursue a two-pronged strategy in its dealings with the state. On the one hand, the central government was prepared to allow considerable latitude to state governments in Srinagar. On the other hand, the government made clear to the Kashmiri leaders they would not tolerate any hint of secessionist sentiment. This was in keeping with past practice in which Indian leaders from Nehru onward had overlooked the malfeasances of various regimes in Kashmir in order to maintain the support of the Kashmiri leadership. However, this was to have fateful consequences in that the process of political development, which followed a fitful course in most other parts of India, was stunted at a very early stage in Kashmir.[23]

Simultaneously, in attempts to co-opt the Kashmiri populace, the national government had provided significant developmental assistance to the state: building infrastructure, establishing and expanding higher education, and expanding mass communication to widen mass media exposure (in large part to counter hostile Pakistani propaganda). These efforts had one critical but unintended consequence: they produced an increasingly sophisticated electorate over the course of forty-odd years. Yet, thanks to the willingness of New Delhi to tolerate electoral and other political malfeasances on the part of the dominant National Conference, an honest opposition party failed to develop in the state. While political mobilisation increased dramatically, institutional growth failed to keep pace.[24]

Previous generations of Kashmiris had routinely countenanced every form of political skullduggery. The new process of political mobilisation, however, produced a different brand of Kashmiri who was unwilling to tolerate similar malfeasances.[25] Indeed, the elections in 1977 and 1983, which through a conjunction of specific circumstances were mostly free of electoral taint, whetted the appetite of the younger Kashmiri electorate for the proper functioning of a democratic polity.

The first of these elections, held in the wake of the 1975 Beg-Parthasarathi Accord, brought Sheikh Abdullah back to power in Kashmir with a dramatic majority. Unfortunately, Abdullah's days in office were numbered and he died in 1982. His son, Farooq Abdullah, a physician who had spent a significant part of his early career in London and a political neophyte, was the sheikh's hand-chosen successor. Despite Farooq's lack of political acumen, he led the National Conference to another clear-cut victory in 1983. Since he had inherited the sheikh's mantle, most Kashmiris were willing to repose some faith in him and his leadership. Their hopes, however, would rapidly evaporate.

FAROOQ'S DISMISSAL

In 1984, Indira Gandhi, in one of her last acts prior to her assassination, dismissed the National Conference government on specious grounds.[26] Her dismissal of Farooq's government was consonant with her general hostility toward various state governments that refused to bend to her will. She systematically denuded the greatest legacy of her father, Jawaharlal Nehru, who had self-consciously sought to embed democratic norms and practices in the Indian polity.[27]

Within two years, however, Mrs. Gandhi's son and successor, Rajiv Gandhi, signed a pact with Farooq that restored the National Conference to power. The Rajiv-Farooq pact, which promised significant developmental resources to Kashmir, cost Farooq dearly in the eyes of many Kashmiri Muslims. They felt that Farooq had become New Delhi's errand boy, to be dismissed and recalled as it suited New Delhi's political needs and vagaries. Against this growing backdrop of anti-National Conference sentiment, the state went to the polls in 1987.

In this election, the Congress government in New Delhi made an electoral alliance with the National Conference. Fearing a significant electoral challenge from the newly formed Muslim United Front, a loose agglomeration of Islam-oriented parties opposed to the National Conference, the Congress–National Conference alliance resorted to a variety of political malpractices. Their cadres intimidated voters, tampered with ballot boxes, and disrupted voting booths. Earlier generations of

Kashmiris would have been passive and quiescent in the wake of these events. The emergent generation however, more conscious of its political rights and privileges, acted otherwise. They were aware that routine electoral irregularities, with marked exceptions (in Bihar, for example), were not to be found in most Indian states. Consequently, they felt that the promise of a genuine federal relationship which appeared to have developed between the years of 1977 and 1983 between Srinagar and New Delhi, had vanished from the Kashmir Valley.

TOWARD INSURGENCY

In the aftermath of the flawed elections of 1987 which brought a Congress–National Conference government to power, the disaffection of the Kashmiris quickly spilled into the streets of Srinagar and beyond. Large numbers of young Kashmiris felt betrayed by the corruption of the electoral process and turned to extra-parliamentary means to register their grievances. Strikes, demonstrations and acts of random violence became common throughout the Kashmir Valley in 1988. These events led to the abduction of Rubiya Sayeed, the daughter of the then national Minister of Home Affairs, Mufti Mohammed Sayeed, from a bus stop in Srinagar in December 1989. The kidnappers, who belonged to the outlawed Jammu and Kashmir Liberation Front (JKLF), the largest (and ostensibly secular) secessionist organisation within the state, used her as a bargaining chip with the Indian government. For her release, they obtained the freedom of a number of jailed JKLF cadres. The seeming pusillanimity of the government in New Delhi emboldened the JKLF and various other insurgent groups. It also encouraged certain segments of the Pakistani military; in particular the Inter-Services Intelligence (ISI) agency; to recruit, organise, train, arm, and provide sanctuaries for various insurgent groups, most notably the decidedly pro-Pakistani Hizbul Mujahideen. Although the roots of the insurgency were quintessentially indigenous, Pakistan's active involvement in the insurgency enhanced its strength and viciousness.[28]

A mixture of significant repression coupled with elections at national and state levels in 1996 and 1997 brought about a modicum of political stability to Kashmir. The insurgents, though worn down by India's 'mailed fist' strategy, were yet to be completely vanquished. Outbursts of violence continued to wrack the valley.[29] More importantly, much of Kashmir's Muslim population remained disaffected from the Indian state.

THE KARGIL CRISIS

Around May 3, 1999, two local shepherds in the Kargil region detected that Pakistani troops, mingled with Kashmiri insurgents, had crossed the LoC. They immediately alerted the officers of the Indian 121 Infantry Brigade responsible for the security of the area. In turn, this information was passed on to the 3rd Punjab Battalion. Within the next several days, the Indian forces drawn from the 3rd Punjab Battalion launched a number of patrols to assess the depth and extent of the Pakistani military incursions. Over the course of the next few weeks, incursions were also detected in the Dras, Batalik and Kaksar sectors. The intruders were well-armed. Their principal weapons were AK-47 rifles, medium machine guns and automatic grenade launchers. They were also supported by mountain guns and mortars, had adequate thermostatic clothing, and were supplied with snowmobiles.

The Indian military and political authorities were caught completely unprepared for these incursions which took place along a most inhospitable terrain at altitudes ranging from 14, 000 to 16,000 feet. Despite their surprise, the Indian authorities responded with vigor and moved to stop further infiltration during the month of May. As India brought in military reinforcements and sought to dislodge the Pakistani intruders they encountered stiff resistance. In these attempts to force the intruders across the LoC, the Indian military had to call in airpower. This was the first use of airpower in an Indo-Pakistani conflict since the 1971 war.

The conflict dragged on through the month of June with the Indian forces making steady advances but at considerable human and material cost. Toward the end of June, they had succeeded in capturing most of the lost ground. As the Indian forces stepped up their attacks, Prime Minister Nawaz Sharif made an abrupt trip to the United States during the weekend of July 4, and sought American intervention to end the conflict. Unlike in the past, the US expressed a willingness to help bring an end to the conflict but categorically blamed Pakistan for having embarked upon this military misadventure.

Over the next two weeks, despite the chagrin of certain individuals and groups within the Pakistan army, most notably the chief of staff, General Pervez Musharraf, the Pakistani forces withdrew from their positions and the conflict de-escalated.

Unlike in the 1965 war, when India had promptly resorted to horizontal escalation, on this occasion, the Indian authorities carefully confined the conflict to the immediate areas of Pakistani egress across the LoC. It is widely believed that India refrained from crossing the LoC because of Pakistan's overt demonstration of its nuclear capabilities in May 1998.

The Kargil conflict thoroughly undermined the 'spirit of Lahore', as the BJP-led coalition government adopted a particularly tough stance toward Pakistan. Among other matters, in the aftermath of the Kargil conflict it mounted a concerted diplomatic campaign to isolate Pakistan. Simultaneously, it increased the Indian defense budget by some 28 percent. Finally, at a rhetorical level, key BJP leaders made clear that no negotiations with Pakistan would be possible until General Musharraf abjured from supporting the insurgents in Kashmir.

STRATEGIES AND OPTIONS

In order to restore peace to Kashmir, India must resolve problems both internally and externally. At one level, India has to undertake a series of political measures designed to bridge the centre–state divide. At another level, it will also have to engage Pakistan in a meaningful dialogue to prevent a renewal of hostilities between the two newly nuclear-armed neighbours. The domestic dimensions of the Kashmir issue are inextricably linked to its bilateral aspects. Despite important differences in organisation and ideology, political parties across the Indian political spectrum agree that under no conceivable circumstances will India relinquish the portion of Kashmir that it currently controls. This shared perspective is unlikely to change. Consequently, it serves little purpose for Pakistan or other members of the international community to dwell on the prospects of a plebiscite. No government in India will agree to a plebiscite to determine the future of the state. Nor are Pakistan's attempts to sustain a rebellion tenable. India's significant counterinsurgency capabilities, its willingness to expend vast amounts of blood and treasure, and its sheer political determination to suppress the Kashmir insurgency ensure that an armed insurgency is doomed to eventual failure.

A variety of proposals have been proffered to bring an end to the crisis in Kashmir. Virtually every one of these proposals, which range from a strategy of ruthless repression to the granting of independence to the state, fail to meet the demands of political feasibility.[30] Any viable solution to the Kashmir crisis must include the following key elements. Both India and Pakistan must agree to convert the LoC into a de jure international border. Consequently, both sides must retreat from their maximalist positions which call for complete control over the entire territory of the original princely state. Accepting the territorial status quo will be quite galling and politically costly to any Pakistani regime. The alternative, however, is a continuing standoff with a more powerful adversary. It is questionable that Pakistan has either the institutional or economic means to indefinitely sustain such a strategy. Currently, Pakistan, which is teetering on the edge of bankruptcy, spends 38 percent of its national budget on defence.[31] Instead, a settlement along the LoC would guarantee a legal and binding commitment on the part of each state to limit its territorial claims to the portion of Kashmir that it currently administers.

A settlement along the LoC would also assuage India's principal misgiving about Kashmir's status within the Indian Union. The majority of India's malfeasances in Kashmir have stemmed from the deep-seated fear that Kashmir has not been fully integrated into India. Once the territorial dispute with Pakistan is resolved, India should be able to grant the residents of the state the requisite degree of political space and autonomy without fear of the prospect of secession.[32] Under such a dispensation, the vast majority of Kashmiris, who to varying degrees are still disaffected with Indian rule, would be able to express their needs and grievances through institutional channels, thereby restoring the frayed legitimacy of Kashmir's bonds to the Indian state.

The overt nuclearisation of South Asia since May 1998 further underscores the necessity of settling the Kashmir dispute. The mutual possession of nuclear capabilities may contribute to stability in the region. In the foreseeable future, neither side can be confident of pre-emptively attacking and completely demolishing the other's nuclear arsenal.[33] Consequently, a form of crude deterrence is likely to prevail unless one or both sides make significant strides in the acquisition of new delivery capabilities and the accompanying command, control, communications and intelligence capabilities. Yet, the prospect of a quick breakthrough remains unlikely. The palimpsest of mutual distrust and even hatred weighs heavily on Indo–Pakistani relations.[34]

Finally, though the overt possession of nuclear capabilities may have reduced the likelihood of full-scale war, it may have also contributed to the 'stability/instability' paradox.[35] The political leaderships of both states, despite their tendency to resort to occasional intemperate rhetoric, recognise that war is no longer a viable solution to the Kashmir dispute. However, most states in South Asia are not monolithic unitary actors. Sub-state actors, including various governmental units, seek to pursue their own interests and accomplish more parochial goals. In the Indo–Pakistani context, Pakistan's Inter-Services Intelligence agency is widely believed to play a key role in supporting the Kashmiri insurgents. Similar allegations have been levelled at India's Research and Analysis Wing (RAW) about its involvement in the troubled Pakistani province of Sindh. Support for these internecine conflicts could lead to inadvertent escalation, especially along the tension-ridden border in Kashmir. Consequently, even though the overt nuclearisation of the region has significantly reduced the likelihood of full-scale war; the prospect of inadvertent war through a process of misjudgement, miscalculation and misperception still haunts the region.

NOTES

1 Although the roots of this crisis are indigenous, Pakistan's involvement has expanded its scope and enhanced its ferocity. For an extended analysis of the origins of the Kashmir crisis, see Sumit Ganguly, *The Crisis in Kashmir: Portents of War, Hopes of Peace* (Cambridge and Washington, DC: Cambridge University Press and the Woodrow Wilson Center Press, 1997).

2 Three distinct segments make up the Indian-controlled portion of the former princely state of Jammu and Kashmir. These are Ladakh, in the northeast, which is predominantly Buddhist; the Kashmir Valley, in the west-central area, which is predominantly Muslim; and Jammu, in the south, which is predominantly Hindu.

3 In making this argument, I readily admit a state-centric bias. I believe that it is neither desirable nor feasible to re-open the question of Kashmir's accession to India. The so-called third option, namely independence for Kashmir, I contend would create an economically unviable state. Moreover, the political arrangements in an independent Kashmir would place the 'nested minorities,' the Ladakhi Buddhists and the Jammu Hindus, in a retrograde position. For an excellent discussion of the dangers of ethnic self-determination see Amitai Etzioni, 'The Evils of Self-Determination', *Foreign Policy* 89, Winter 1992–93, 21–35.

4 At the time of British colonial withdrawal from the subcontinent, there were two classes of states in the Indian Union. The states of British India were directly ruled by Whitehall via New Delhi. The other set, the 'princely states', were nominally independent but recognised the British as the 'paramount' power in India. As independence and partition approached, Lord Mountbatten, the last Viceroy, declared that the doctrine of 'paramountcy' would lapse when the British departed from India. The rulers of the princely states were given two options: depending on their geographic location and their demographic composition, they could join either India or Pakistan. Thus, Muslim-majority states that were geographically contiguous would join Pakistan, the new 'homeland' for South Asian Muslims. Non-Muslim majority areas, by the same token, would join India. Independence as an option was firmly ruled out. The state of Jammu and Kashmir posed a peculiar problem because it shared borders with both emergent states, and had a Hindu monarch and a Muslim-majority population. On this latter point see the excellent work of Ian Copland, *The Princes of India in the Endgame of Empire, 1917–1947* (Cambridge: Cambridge University Press, 1997); for a legal analysis of the lapse of the doctrine of 'paramountcy' and its consequences for Jammu and Kashmir, see Mohan Krishen Teng, *Kashmir: Article 370* (New Delhi: Anmol, 1990).

5 On this point see Sumit Ganguly, *The Origins of War in South Asia: The Indo–Pakistani Conflicts since 1947*, 2nd ed. (Boulder: Westview Press, 1994).

6 The 'two nation theory' suggested that Hindus and Muslims constituted two distinct primordial nations in South Asia and, accordingly, in the wake of British colonial withdrawal two states, one Hindu and the other Muslim, should emerge. For a trenchant critique of this theory, see Ian Copland, 'The Abdullah Factor: Kashmiri Muslims and the Crisis in 1947', in *The Political Inheritance of Pakistan*, ed. D. A. Low (New York: St. Martin's Press, 1991).

7 For a discussion of the 'Standstill Agreements', see V. P. Menon, *The Story of the Integration of the Indian States* (Bombay: Orient Longman, 1956).

8 On this point see H. V. Hodson, *The Great Divide: Britain–India–Pakistan* (Karachi: Oxford University Press, 1985).

9 In recent years, the question of the legality of Kashmir's accession to India has come under considerable criticism. The principal challenge has come from a British author, Alastair Lamb, whose views are given in his *Birth of a Tragedy: Kashmir 1947* (Hertingfordbury: Roxford Books, 1994). For an attempt to rebut Lamb's charges see Prem Shankar Jha, *Kashmir 1947: Rival Versions of History* (New Delhi: Oxford University Press, 1996). It should also be mentioned that when the issue of Kashmir's accession to India initially materialized, Lord Mountbatten insisted that the views of the Kashmiri population be ascertained on the subject once the law and order situation in the state was restored. Nehru and his ministers agreed to this proposition. See Menon, *Integration of the Indian States*, 399.

10   For an Indian account of the military operations, see Lt.-Gen. Lionel Protip Sen, *Slender Was the Thread* (Bombay: Orient Longman, 1969); for a Pakistani account, see Maj.-Gen. Akbar Khan, *Raiders in Kashmir* (Karachi: Pak Publishers, 1970).
11   Damodar R. Sardesai, 'The Origins of Kashmir's International and Legal Status', in Raju G.C. Thomas, ed., *Perspectives on Kashmir: The Roots of Conflict in South Asia* (Boulder: Westview Press, 1992), 80–92.
12   For a comparative discussion of the concept of federalism, see Douglas V. Verney, 'Federalism, Federative Systems, Federations: The United States, Canada, and India', *Publius: Journal of Federalism* 25(2), Spring 1995, 81–97.
13   For a thoughtful discussion of the conflicting demands of centralisation and devolution, see Granville Austin, *The Indian Constitution: Cornerstone of a Nation* (London: Oxford University Press, 1966), 186–95. For a particularly dire vision of India's 'fissiparous tendencies' see Selig Harrison, *India: The Most Dangerous Decades* (Princeton: Princeton University Press, 1960).
14   On this point see the excellent discussion in Teng, *Kashmir: Article 370*, 44–78.
15   Ibid., 57.
16   This final provision is of considerable significance. Without it, any government in New Delhi could encourage settlement in the Kashmir Valley and thereby alter its demographic composition. In the wake of such 'ethnic flooding', India could easily hold a referendum on the future of the state and win it handsomely. On this point see the relevant excerpt from Nehru's speech to Parliament in Teng, ibid., 111.
17   For a thoughtful account of the Kashmir issue at the UN, see Joseph Korbel, *Danger in Kashmir* (Princeton: Princeton University Press, 1966). For a sophisticated discussion of the Indian position, see Sisir Gupta, *Kashmir: A Study in India–Pakistan Relations* (Bombay: Asia Publishing House, 1966). For a deft defense of the Pakistani position, see M. M. R. Khan, *The United Nations and Kashmir* (Groningen: J. B. Wolters, 1954).
18   For a discussion the talks and their outcome, see Dennis Kux, *India and the United States: Estranged Democracies* (Washington, DC: National Defense University Press, 1993), 181–225.
19   See Russell Brines, *The Indo–Pakistani Conflict* (New York: Pall Mall, 1968), 238.
20   For a discussion of the events underlying the Pakistani decision, see Sumit Ganguly, 'Deterrence Failure Revisited: The Indo–Pakistani War of 1965', *Journal of Strategic Studies* 13(4), December 1990, 77–93.
21   The roots of this conflict can be traced to the exigencies of Pakistani domestic politics. See Robert Jackson, *South Asian Crisis* (New York: Praeger, 1975).
22   This meeting took place at Simla, the summer capital of British India, between Pakistani President Zulfiqar Ali Bhutto and Indian Prime Minister Indira Gandhi. In the Simla Agreement (1972), in addition to agreeing to return to the status quo ante and reiterating their agreement to refrain from the use of force in resolving the Kashmir dispute, the two sides agreed to settle it within a bilateral context. Pakistan subsequently contested the principle of bilateralism, however, arguing that the treaty explicitly allowed for other mutually agreed means of peacefully resolving the conflict.
23   For an excellent discussion of the evolution of India's political development, see Jyotirindra Das Gupta, 'India: Democratic Becoming and Developmental Transition', in *Democracy in Developing Countries*, ed. Larry Diamond et al. (Cambridge: Harvard University Press, 1995), 466–88.
24   For a discussion of the two strategies and their effect on the electorate in Kashmir, see Ganguly, *Crisis in Kashmir*.

25 For the classic discussion of the dangers inherent in a situation characterised by political decay against a background of political mobilisation, see Samuel Huntington, *Political Order in Changing Societies* (New Haven: Yale University Press, 1968).
26 The matter of Farooq's dismissal is discussed in Ajit Bhattacharjea, *Kashmir: The Wounded Valley* (New Delhi: UBSPD, 1994).
27 For a particularly scathing indictment of Indira Gandhi's disregard for democratic norms and practices, see Paul R. Brass, *The Politics of India since Independence*, 2nd ed. (Cambridge: Cambridge University Press, 1994).
28 For evidence of Pakistan's involvement in the insurgency, see Edward W. Desmond, 'Pakistan's Hidden Hand', *Time*, 22 July 1991, 23.
29 See Ramesh Vinayak, 'Wireless Wars', *India Today* (international ed.), 14 September 1998, 26–27.
30 The features, merits and shortcomings of these proposals are discussed at length in Ganguly, *The Crisis in Kashmir*, 131–50.
31 On the parlous economic situation in Pakistan, see Zahid Hussain and Manoj Joshi, 'In a Holy Mess', *India Today* (international ed.), 18 September 1998, 13–18.
32 India has shown a willingness to offer a range of political arrangements designed to accommodate ethnic and ethnoregional movements in various parts of the country, as long as the leaders of such movements show a willingness to accept the territorial integrity of the country. See the analyses of the prospects of several new states in Farzand Ahmed et al., 'New States: Divide But Rule', *India Today* (international ed.), 13 July 1998, 18–20.
33 Sumit Ganguly, 'India's Pathway to Pokhran II: The Prospects and Sources of New Delhi's Nuclear Weapons Program', *International Security*, 23(4), Spring 1999, 148–77.
34 Lalit K. Jha, 'Lahore Trip compared to Fall of "Berlin Wall"', *India Abroad*, 26 February 1999, 9.
35 This point is elaborated in Sumit Ganguly, 'Indo–Pakistani Nuclear Issues and the Stability/Instability Paradox', *Studies in Conflict and Terrorism* 18 (4), 1995, 325–34.

Chapter 15

Pokhran II and After: Consequences of the Indian Nuclear Tests of 1998

Ashok Kapur

This chapter deals with the consequences of the Indian nuclear tests of 1998. It first highlights the impact the Indian tests had on thinking at the global level because there is considerable confusion in international strategic assessments about India's strategic motives. As the chapter demonstrates, there exists no consensus about the aims and methods by which to address the new reality that has been created by the probability of overt India nuclear weaponisation. The essay maintains that the Indian tests reflect a considered response to a pattern of Pakistani, Chinese and American provocations in the strategic sphere; and the problem of nuclear proliferation cannot be laid to rest in the Asian-Pacific region in which Chinese and Indian strategic interests and ambitions run counter to each other. In these circumstances, a non-binding nuclear non-proliferation regime does not provide an answer to the Indian security problem or the problem of stability in the Asian-Pacific region. The chapter points to a need to bargain restraints in the nuclear sphere with India and Pakistan, India and the Peoples' Republic of China (PRC) as well as India and the USA as the obvious bargaining partners. Time and space limitations preclude a discussion of the bargaining opportunities and the difficulties. This chapter, thus, seeks to challenge and stimulate further the quest for new thinking and new policy development with regard to nuclear non-proliferation efforts.

LIMITATIONS OF A NON-BINDING NON-PROLIFERATION REGIME IN ASIA

The Indo–Pakistani nuclear tests were not ad hoc actions by their ruling regimes but represented the culmination of a long history of inter-state diplomatic rivalries and military conflicts between China and India as well as India and Pakistan. The Indian tests were a deliberate response to the provocative behaviour by the Peoples' Republic of China and the Clinton administration with regard to their nuclear non-proliferation and disarmament policies as they related to the strategic situation in the Indian subcontinent. While the PRC supplied nuclear and missile aid to Pakistan in violation of its non-proliferation commitments, the Clinton administration repeatedly refused to accept the evidence of the CIA on these issues. Moreover, both insisted that the issue of their own nuclear disarmament lay within the province of the nuclear powers only. Before the tests of May 1998, there was a widespread belief in international policy circles and in Western scholarship that nuclear proliferation was not inevitable, and that a line in the sand could be drawn against further nuclear and missile proliferation. There was a belief that effective anti-proliferation arrangements could be developed; that the international system was increasingly embracing the non-proliferation norm; and that potential proliferators could be isolated and marginalised in regional and world affairs. There was, thus, a belief that a discriminatory or hierarchical world of nuclear-haves and their allies (the satisfied powers) on the one hand, and potential regional/middle powers (who were dissatisfied about arrangements concerning their security and prestige and were dubbed the 'rogue' or 'intransigent' states) on the other hand, could be created and maintained. These beliefs revealed a smugness and over-confidence about the centrality and durability of non-proliferation in international security affairs. The smugness lay in the belief that a stable set of strategic relationships could be developed solely on the basis of bargains between the P–5 (or nuclear) states. There was also over-confidence that while the Indians and Pakistanis talked repeatedly about unequal international and strategic arrangements and their security interests, they were unlikely to challenge the 'global' non-proliferation 'regime', that is, they lacked the staying power as distinct from a capacity to engage in Hindu-style discourse without closure.

The Indo–Pakistani nuclear tests shattered this smugness and over-confidence that, in hindsight, reflected limited success with the smoke and mirrors of non-proliferation activity since the Non-Proliferation Treaty (NPT) was approved by the US and USSR in 1968. It is obvious that the non-proliferation Regime worked the best where it was needed the least, and it did not work in regions where it was needed the most, i.e. in regions of conflict in South Asia, the Middle East and the Korean peninsula. The Regime looked good on paper. Over the years, it acquired many institutional faces: export control lists that were negotiated in the Zangger Committee in 1970 and revised periodically; the Missile Technology Control Regime (MTCR) set up in 1987 by the seven leading industrialised nations which is a norm or an inter-state agreement but not an internationally negotiated treaty (as is the NPT); regional nuclear weapon free zones in South America and the South Pacific; the treaties that imposed chemical, bacteriological and radiological weapons bans; and the Comprehensive Test Ban Treaty (CTBT) finalised in 1996. But parallel to the rise of the anti-proliferation norm was the growth of activities of the NPT parties (including the P–5 nuclear powers) that indicated a preference for what Madeline Albright, US Secretary of State, calls 'different strokes for different folks'. In the nuclear world, this meant that the internationally proclaimed non-proliferators followed three different but related policies. One, among the P–5 NPT/nuclear powers, it meant a commitment to the modernisation of their nuclear forces, to nuclear deterrence and to nuclear trade, viewing them as acceptable, beneficial and necessary. Two, between the nuclear powers and their temporary/permanent regional allies, nuclear proliferation was also acceptable; indeed it was aided or tolerated. British and European companies supplied sensitive technologies to Iraq, the US helped Israel, the Europeans and China helped Pakistan, while the US looked the other way. Russia and China helped Iran and India (China sold India heavy water when India had a shortage). I call this *selective proliferation* with regional allies. Three, in contrast, with regional hegemons and regional rivals, the preferred and standard practice is to insist on non-proliferation. This has been the basis of American and Chinese demands that India disarm itself in the nuclear and the missile spheres. According to traditional US policy in Asia since 1949, regional hegemons who were perceived as 'unfriendly to the US', amongst which India was viewed as one, were sought to be contained.[1] Here the strategic imperative in US policy has overridden the democratic imperative that ideally ought to have brought them together. Compared to the second set of policies above, this is *selective non-proliferation*.

The overall pattern of behaviour of the old nuclear powers (the P–5 states) has thus had three integrated faces or elements. The first required continued modernisation and nuclear missile trade and technology-sharing among themselves. The second required selective nuclear proliferation with friendly states. The third required selective non-proliferation with unfriendly regional hegemons.

WESTERN REACTIONS TO THE INDO–PAKISTANI NUCLEAR TESTS

This is the background against which Western reactions to the Indo–Pakistani tests must be understood. The emphasis in the discussion below is especially on the Indian tests because India's nuclear behaviour has been seen as the stimulus for the Pakistani tests. This section reviews the analytical merit and factual basis of different types of Western assessments. The sampling of Western reactions is not comprehensive but is representative of the main parameters of the Western debate and is done to illustrate the argument.

Official Western reactions to the Indo–Pakistani tests were generally condemnatory. Statements by the P–5, G–8 and other international groupings of states showed a mixture of emotion, a self-serving preoccupation with Western strategic interests, hype about non-proliferation, and ethnocentric judgements about Indian and Pakistani strategic and political behaviour. In contrast, the assessments of certain American thinkers and peace researchers showed clarity, balance and a forward-looking problem-solving approach. Simultaneously, the actions of various Western governments revealed a split amongst themselves in their responses. The US, Canada and Japan slapped on sanctions and opposed World Bank loans to India and Pakistan, while the Europeans and Russians sought engagement rather than containment of the two states. However, even this division was not free of ambiguities, For instance, the US was soon following a two-track policy: along with the sanctions which were mandatory under US law, the US initiated a high level dialogue between Strobe Talbot, Deputy Secretary of State, and Jaswant Singh, Vice Chair of the Indian Planning Commission. We now turn to a discussion of an important sample of Western judgements and actions and their analytical merit and factual basis.

The Canadian government judged India's tests, in the words of its Foreign Minister, Lloyd Axworthy, in the following way:

(a) Let me begin today by stating my firm belief that India's recent nuclear tests constitute a clear and fundamental threat to the international security regime and thus, to Canada's security.[2a]
(b) India has publicly justified its nuclear tests primarily on the basis of regional security concerns. But, it is not evident that any significant change in regional security took place in the period leading up to the tests and, until recently, India's relationships with both China and Pakistan were improving. India's action clearly worsens its own regional security situation and the global security equilibrium.[2b]

The reasoning in the Canadian policy statement rests on the premise that non-proliferation equals international security and Canadian security; and conversely a threat to the non-proliferation regime is a threat to Canada. The Axworthy statement is both intellectually dishonest and illogical. While Minister Axworthy railed against the *new nuclear realpolitik*, he conveniently ignored the fact that the government of Canada is an active and enthusiastic participant in the *old nuclear realpolitik*. Canada is a member of both North American Air Defence (NORAD) and NATO, two military organisations which subscribe to the nuclear deterrence doctrine and which rely on the legitimacy of nuclear weapons for national defence. In effect, Canada enjoys the US nuclear umbrella, so that Canada's security depends in part on nuclear weapons. The idea that Indian nuclear tests and missiles pose a threat to Canada's physical security is utter nonsense because Indian missiles cannot reach Canadian soil and, happily, there is no conflict of interest that creates a military necessity for India to attack Canada.

Axworthy's comments on India's regional security concerns betray a lack of understanding about the persistence of traditional inter-state security threats in India's strategic neighbourhood; and indeed in Northeast Asia including the Taiwan Straits, the South China Sea and the Middle East. The Canadian minister's fondness for 'soft power' or 'global norms' is not shared by many Ottawa practitioners.

India's relationship with China cannot be described as 'improving' when Indian practitioners have continuously, during the 1980s and the 1990s, expressed strong concerns about China's missile and nuclear supplies to Pakistan, contrary to PRC's obligations under the NPT and the MTCR. Annexures 1 and 2 set out the data. Annexures 1 and 2 show the nature, scope and seriousness of China's nuclear and missile supply to Pakistan because it is contrary to NPT/MTCR supply restrictions which China had accepted. Another reason for the seriousness is that the supply involved high technology items. Add to this the PRC's naval activity in the Bay of Bengal, as highlighted in Map 1. Finally, Map 2 outlines the scale of PRC military capabilities in Tibet, which can be used against India. So the Axworthy statement does not have a sound factual or analytical basis.

In contrast, it is pertinent to note that India's nuclear and missile development is mostly indigenous with some foreign technological inputs primarily from the US, France, Germany, Canada and the USSR. The USSR/Russian supply to India of conventional military hardware, as well as the supply in the field of space and atomic energy, also did not violate any international agreement. It has no doubt played an important role in the development of India's military strength.

Another example of Western reaction is expressed by Harold Müller. He makes two broad generalizations and a critique of American policy:

(a) The events in South Asia have changed the parameters of world politics, and in particular those of nuclear non-proliferation and disarmament, fundamentally. They are as significant as the fall of the Berlin Wall nine years ago. Unfortunately, they point us in the opposite direction: away from cooperation, arms control and disarmament, towards confrontation, arms racing and, eventually nuclear war. The world community must make its utmost efforts to stem this fateful tide.[3a]

(b) It is essential to seek the trigger to the events in the fundamentally changed character of the present Indian government – a precarious coalition headed by the Hindu nationalist Bharatiya Janata Party (BJP). These nuclear weapons are not for security, status or prestige in the first place, as is all too often assumed. They are instruments for political power, for dominating the subcontinent and achieving equality with China. They are instruments for increasing the tensions with Pakistan, so that the more radical elements within the BJP can enhance their influence within their party and in India at large. To expand the

Map 1: Location of Chinese Activity in the Bay of Bengal

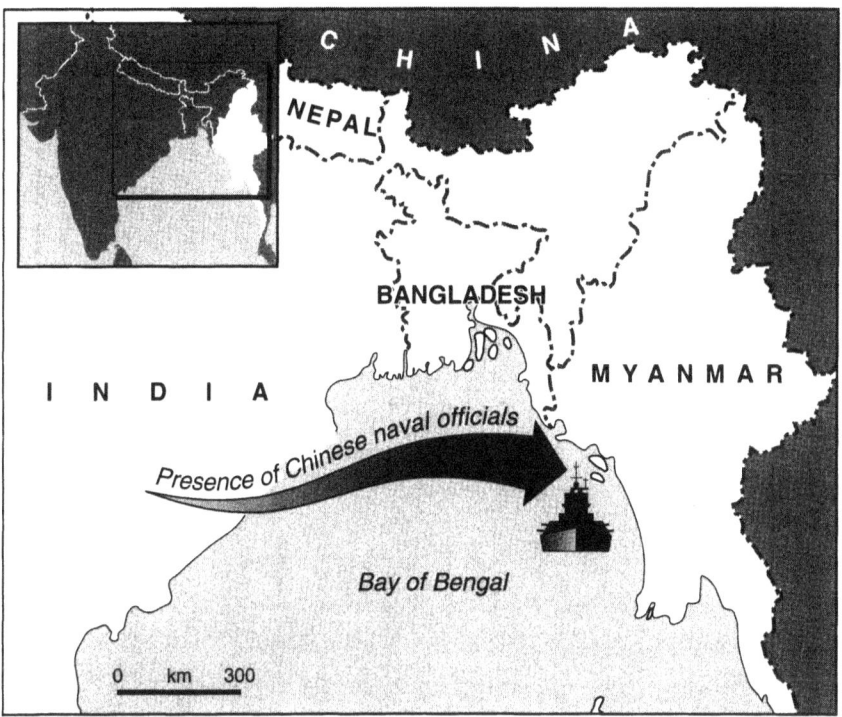

Source: Based on Indian press reports and author's interviews with naval officers and experts in Washington, DC, and Singapore, 1995–97

electoral basis beyond the tiny 26 percent of the last ballot, the BJP needs increased hostility with Pakistan. For this reason, a nuclear arms race is inevitable as long as this government prevails.[3b]

Müller's criticism of the USA's opportunistic policy is as follows:

> At the top, the lone superpower, the US is oscillating between a pragmatic continuation of past (pro-arms control) policies and the attitudes of Congressional conservatives (with some followers in the Pentagon and the Labs) that are the moral equivalent of rogue state views: contempt for multilateralism and international organizations, an opportunistic attitude to international law that is (ab)used when it is convenient, and refused if it demands compromise, a complete reliance on unilateral military strength, and the relentless pursuit of the national interest – egocentrically defined – without regard to the claims and interests of others.[3c]

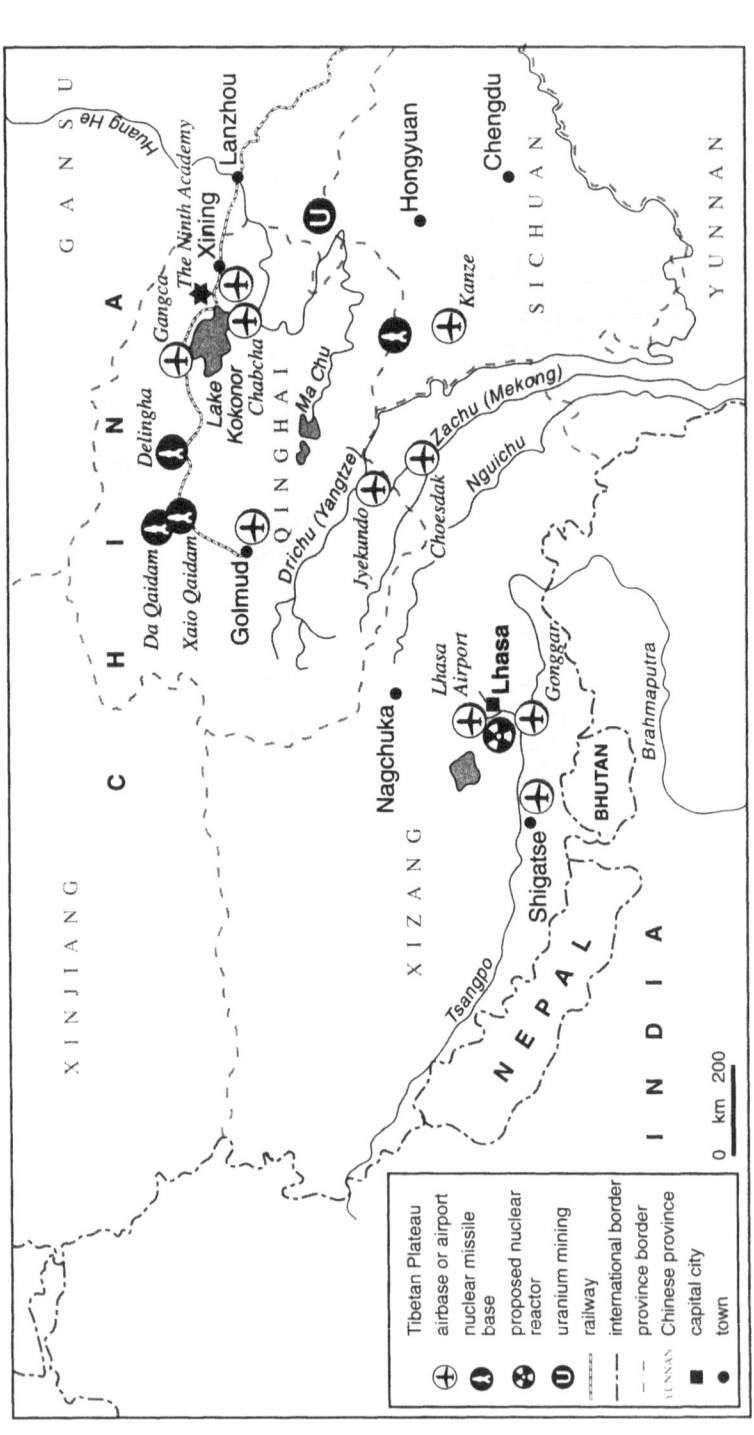

Map 2: Nuclear Facilities on the Tibetan Plateau

Source: *Nuclear Tibet: A Report by the International Campaign for Tibet* (Washington, DC: April 1993).

Muller's statement reflects the perception that the Indo–Pakistani tests were an important international event in the sense that the number of declared nuclear powers increased from five to seven and opened the door to further proliferation. However, it can only be seen as such in the context of the widespread but erroneous belief that the old P-5 states could build a Berlin wall of nuclear apartheid to keep new nuclear powers out. Clearly, the Indo–Pakistani tests shattered this belief and changed the parameters of non-proliferation policy (of drawing a line against further proliferation and protecting the international nuclear status of the P-5 powers). The US Secretary of State, Madeleine Albright, opposes the recognition of India and Pakistan as nuclear weapon states because it undermines the exclusivity of the P-5 nuclear club and the NPT philosophy. But the US position is absurd because unless the reality of Indian and Pakistani nuclear weapon status is formally recognised, and they are asked to join the NPT as nuclear weapon states, they cannot accept the legal obligations or responsibility of acting with restraint as nuclear weapon powers. The parameters have also changed in another way. With over one hundred hours of high level official talks in the period following the tests, the Indo–US strategic dialogue has two parameters: Indian security interests that relate to attitudes and policies of two unfriendly neighbours with whom India has fought wars and with whom there is a historical agenda of unsettled business on the one hand; and US non-proliferation policy on the other hand. Finding common ground or an area of negotiation so that conflicting interests and strategic concepts can be adjusted is the challenge before American and Indian practitioners.

Müller is right to point to the effects of the tests on the parameters, but he is wrong to emphasize the danger of a nuclear arms race and war between India and Pakistan as also India and China. Why should the subcontinental practitioners alone be seen as irresponsible political actors, and why should the domestic politics of the BJP be seen as the culprit when the BJP has had to secure consensus with its coalition partners? India has a system of checks and balances as the basis of its strategic decision-making. Indeed, a sign of the vitality of Indian democracy is that, on the one hand, there is an inter-party and public consensus that opposes nuclear apartheid which is inherent in the non- proliferation regime; but on the other hand, there is also a well-organised and vocal anti-nuclear movement in Indian policy circles and in Indian politics and society. In the West, the nuclear weapon is a political and a psychological weapon: it is meant to deter the enemy. It is the same in the Indian subcontinent. To insinuate recklessness to Indian or BJP practitioners, who are accountable as leaders in a democratic set-up, has the smell of racism and ethnocentricity. A peace researcher, Marcus Raskin, makes this point forcefully. To quote him:

> By the 1960s there were clearly many nuclear genies jumping out of national bottles. In the United States there was fear that 'Nasser might

get a bomb' in Egypt, just as later fears gripped American planners that 'Saddam might get the bomb' or 'Quaddafi might get the bomb'. One did not have to look too deeply to see that beneath these claimed fears was barely disguised racism. One did not hear the same concerns regarding Israeli, French, or British nukes. In fact, racist fear was an important element in creating support among the nuclear states to use the Non-Proliferation Treaty of 1968 as a substitute for an actual end to nuclear testing and serious disarmament.[4]

Statements by Indian and Pakistani practitioners confirm that the deterrent value of nuclear weapons is well understood in the subcontinent, and the prospect of war is fear-mongering by Western experts. Nuclear accidents can happen and do happen, but in the history of nuclear disasters the finger should point more to Ukraine and Russia for Chernobyl, to threats by the US to use nuclear weapons in the Korean and Vietnam conflicts, and to the actual use of US nuclear weapons against Japan in 1945, than to the Indian subcontinent.

In sum, Müller overstates the role of BJP's domestic politics, and understates the role of security and restraint as well as deliberation in Indian nuclear decision-making. External as well as internal considerations drive national decisions in India, as they do elsewhere.

A third sort of reaction comes from a Washington think-tank. It reflects a recognition of the new nuclear realities following the Indo–Pakistani tests. Cathleen Fisher of the H. L. Stimson Centre in Washington, DC, makes the following points:

(a) Only months after the Indian and Pakistani underground nuclear tests, the world shows every sign of adjusting to the new reality of seven, rather than five, admitted nuclear-weapon States (with Israel waiting silently, at least for now, in the wings.)[5a]
(b) The cornerstone of the non-proliferation regime – the NPT – lacks two essential requirements for a stable, effective and robust cooperative security regime: inclusiveness and legitimacy. ... the fault-lines in the NPT and non-proliferation regime have become more evident in recent months, but their existence predated the May nuclear explosions.[5b]
(c) The non-proliferation norm has been challenged – but also reaffirmed. While the May nuclear explosions overturned the nuclear status quo, they did not invalidate the non-proliferation norm, which has evolved over decades and is unlikely to be easily destroyed. ... although steps are now being taken to adapt to the new nuclear realities in South Asia, these actions have been undertaken within the context of the normative obligations created by the NPT. Negotiations with India and Pakistan seem intended to appeal to the sense of responsibility that *de facto* Nuclear Weapon States now share with the declared nuclear powers;

this approach stands in stark contrast with that used to deal with North Korea and Iraq, both of which are viewed as unabashedly rejecting non-proliferation norms.[5c]

A fourth sample of Western reaction reflects the forward-looking thinking of a peace researcher, Marcus Raskin. Raskin is critical of US policy and the 'do as I say, not as I do' approach. He points out the double standards as well as the contradictions and ambiguities in US policies, as follows:

> The Clinton Administration's general position is one that borders on foolishness unless the US changes its own nuclear stance. That is to say, the inherent asymmetry and discrimination embodied in the current US position are in fact a negotiating non-starter because they are based on the US view that it should not have to get rid of its own weapons.

The US calls on India and Pakistan to:

- 'stop all further tests, adhere to the Comprehensive Test Ban Treaty immediately and unconditionally' (the US has yet to do this)
- 'refrain from the manufacture of nuclear warheads and bombs or attaching them to ballistic missiles' (the US excuses itself from this admonition)
- 'halt the production of fissile material and participate constructively in negotiations on fissile material cut-off in Geneva' (the US has no clear policy for itself on fissile materials and their recycling)
- 'confirm policies not to export equipment, material or technology relevant to missiles or weapons of mass destruction and enter into ironclad commitments in that regard' (the US considers the export of nuclear, computer equipment and military assistance and sales on a case by case basis. It seeks to dominate the market in this regard.)
- 'refrain from threatening military movements or violations across the borders' (while the US itself carries out extra-territorial military movements in its own foreign and military activities as, for example, in Mexico, Columbia, etc.) 'And particularly the line of control [in Kashmir] or any other provocative acts or statements' (US representatives are careful to be sure that their language is diplomatic, but provocative acts in terms of covert operations in many parts of the world continue unabated)
- 'and reestablish direct communications between India and Pakistan with a view to addressing the basic cause of the tension between those countries, including the issues of Kashmir' (The General Assembly has taken a resolution about Kashmir that should open the way to external mediation. It should be noted that India considers Kashmir a domestic problem)[6]

Pokhran II and After

Raskin's moral reference point is Mahatma Gandhi's view, expressed after the US dropped atomic bombs against Japan, that the US had won the war but 'we will see whether it's to [sic, it has] lost its soul'. Raskin makes a compelling case against the NPT. It is discriminatory and the 'wrong course'. He concludes with a practical suggestion:

> The present stance of the United States, that India and Pakistan must sign the NPT as non-nuclear weapons states, must be reversed to acknowledge the reality of their new nuclear status, but in the context of a general disarmament program and renewed commitment of all nuclear states, new and old, to those commitments.[7]

This comparative sample of 'Western' reactions is not comprehensive, but is meant to illustrate a point: The Indo–Pakistani tests have opened up several channels of public discourse and discussion of new forward-looking strategies about nuclear proliferation, non-proliferation, nuclear disarmament, and American policies from the Kennedy to the Clinton eras. Scholars need to go beyond the official scripts to identify the new parameters of public discourse and to challenge the orthodox wisdom about the definition of the 'public international good' as distinct from the 'private national good'. My random sample of 'attentive governments and publics' reveals a surprising asymmetry in the distribution of blame and the action required of the players. Minister Axworthy and Madame Madeleine Albright assign blame exclusively to India and Pakistan (India more than Pakistan because Pakistan was seen as reacting to India's tests). They assign no blame to their own shortsighted policies. The actions they require entail significant Indian concessions, but none by the US and Canada. The fundamental problem with the discriminatory basis of the NPT is not acknowledged in the statements by the two North American states. Here Axworthy and the arms controllers in the Canadian Department of Foreign Affairs and Department of National Defence are maintaining in public a complete alignment with US nuclear and arms control policies. The only significant difference between the two governments is that the US is engaged in a strategic dialogue with India based on two parameters (Indian security and non-proliferation) but Canada shunned ministerial contact with the Indian government until May 1999.

The Müller approach has an element of finger-pointing against India–Pakistan (as in the US–Canada approach) but it also shares a growing concern with Raskin's analysis about the US's wrong and opportunistic course; but then Müller digresses highlighting the role of the BJP and domestic politics. Müller laments the lack of progress in the disarmament field but fails to recognise that the NPT was always intended to establish a two-tiered nuclear system. The policies of the P–5 states in the NPT system favour 'arms reduction' and modernisation of their nuclear forces, but not the elimination of P–5 nuclear weapons. Thus, the promise of nuclear disarmament in Article 6 of the NPT amounts to insincere rhetoric. The US cannot disarm in the conventional and the nuclear fields in the foreseeable future if it is to maintain its hegemony in world affairs.

From the other side of the spectrum of views, Raskin assigns blame to the US but also proposes an alternative approach. In a similar vein, Fisher seeks to secure a balance between the two worlds of nuclear renaissance and non-proliferation. Both analysts offer creative, forward-looking ideas, which seem to have escaped the thinking of governmental arms controllers in Washington and Ottawa.

There are, thus, considerable differences in Western reactions to the Indo–Pakistani tests. There is a wide gap between the 'new reality' and the orthodox approach adopted by Madeline Albright and Lloyd Axworthy. In contrast, the scholarly and peace research analyses reveal fresh thinking that responds better to the new reality.

CONSEQUENCES OF THE INDO–PAKISTANI TESTS

This section outlines the different types of consequences which, in the judgement of the author, point to the real impact or fallout of the Indo–Pakistani tests. The suggestion is that scholarly analysis and policy development has to be based on a consideration of the consequences which are outlined in this section, along with the insights of the scholarly views outlined above.

The tests had a major impact in a number of ways. The first of these was within India where they created a clear public identification about the importance of nuclear deterrence for the country. Widespread acceptance of the idea of nuclear deterrence represented a sea change in the history of Indian political and social thought. To appreciate this point, one has to examine the history of the Indian nuclear debate which gained ground in the 1960s.

On the one hand, India has had the full weight and tradition of Gandhi's focus on non-violence and Nehru's emphasis on peaceful diplomacy shaping its foreign policy outlook. The Nehruvian view had been the standard mantra in Indian diplomacy. On the other hand, the approach outlined by Bal Gangadhar Tilak before Independence has emerged as the post-Nehruvian basis of Indian diplomacy and military strategy. Tilak had argued that armed power was inevitably necessary to settle disputes – a view which Gandhi and Nehru did not accept. Yet, the tradition of recognising the value of paramount armed power as a means for settling disputes is a part of Indian political and social thought which competed with the Gandhian and the Nehruvian approaches.

From the 1960s, the debate within the Indian government and academics went three ways. One, there was the belief in peace and security through disarmament – a theme which is still there in Indian diplomacy. However, after the war with China in 1962, the parameters of foreign and defence policy were broadened: there grew a new belief that it was essential to have a strong conventional defence capability accompanying a quest for global nuclear disarmament. The emphasis in Indian policy continued to center on conventional rather than nuclear defence, even after the Chinese test in 1964 and the development of the NPT in 1968 pressured India and affected its interests and power. The third position in the debate emerged in the context of China's increasing nuclearisation and the growth of the NPT rules, which increasingly reduced India's maneuverability in international and regional strategic affairs. This position concerned the importance of nuclear deterrence in addition to the value of nuclear disarmament and a conventional defence capability. The debate continued from the mid-1960s to the late 1990s but the policy remained wedded to a fixation with a non-nuclearised India.

The first time we saw the word 'nuclear option' in an Indian government communique was in the context of the comprehensive test ban negotiations in 1996. This is significant because Indian practitioners choose their words carefully. I wrote a book on India's nuclear option in 1976 which reflected the academic debate. The official view at that time resisted the idea of nuclear deterrence as a matter of Indian policy, whereas now it has become common for the Indian government to use the previously shunned term 'nuclear deterrence'. The policy has now shifted in favour of nuclear deterrence and it rides on an essential point. There is an important distinction between the terms *defence* and *deterrence*. Defence implies fighting a war at a time and place of the enemy's choosing. Deterrence, in contrast, implies the possession of the means, the will, and the legal right to escalate the level of violence and to make this known to the other side – the purpose being to prevent enemy military action. This important distinction has now gained prominence in the Indian body politic, and Indian public opinion is enthusiastic about it. Thus, there is a major change both in India's nuclear behaviour and structure of Indian strategic thought.

The Indian tests also had a fallout on Pakistan. It is often said that the Pakistani tests in May 1998 were a response to the Indian tests, but this is not the fallout we have in mind. After the Gauri missile test of April 6, people like Mushahid Hussein, Minister for Information who has close ties with the military, and Prime Minister Nawaz Sharif made statements in Dacca and elsewhere that the Indians were weak, that they could not really stand up for their interests, and that they could be manipulated.[8] The Indian tests were thus meant to send a signal that the Indian government was not really weak and that it was quite capable of dealing with external provocations. The Pakistani element, in my mind, is not so important in terms of the subcontinental military balance or distribution of military power, but it is the psychological aspect that is important in Indian calculations. At the same time, there was a message to the Pakistanis – that

India could tolerate the higher costs of defence more than Pakistan can. So if Pakistan wants to escalate its expenditure on defence, if it wants an arms race with India, it should go ahead by all means but it must be prepared to pay the economic and social costs. The Indian tests have thus led to a process of enormous military engagement in the subcontinental neighbourhood.

The third consequence was in relation to China for whom the tests had an important message. It matters little how Western practitioners evaluate the tests. It is how India's rivals assess their technological and political importance. The Indian message to the Chinese was that direct or indirect Chinese military pressure against India, whether in the form of Chinese missile supplies to Pakistan or Chinese military modernisation in Tibet or Chinese deployment of naval personnel in the Bay of Bengal in the Coco Islands (a mere fifteen miles from the Andaman Islands), would not be tolerated and would be resisted. There is a further calculation which experts on the subject would appreciate, which is that China at this point does not have a military advantage over India. It has a slight advantage in terms of missiles, but it does not have an advantage in terms of naval power in the Indian Ocean or military strength in the Himalayas. Overall, the PRC does not have a military advantage over India, but it has strategic interests which clash with Indian interests and, if PRC's military modernisation continued unchecked, India could have been placed at a military disadvantage by, say, 2010 A.D. China, for instance, has interest in Sikkim, Arunachal Pradesh and in the Indian Ocean, along with two Indian strategic flanks, i.e. Pakistan and Myanmar. Changes in its military and nuclear doctrines and its on-going military modernisation reflect a PRC preoccupation with preparations to fight regional wars in the Asia–Pacific region. These changes could justify and enable the PRC intervention and hegemony in the Himalayan region that extends from Afghanistan across Kashmir and Tibet, up to India's northeast and the China–Myanmar–Bay of Bengal area.[9]

Chinese writings, including a discussion of a Chinese military commission in February 1993, emphasise the danger of regional wars in the Asia–Pacific region. The PRC strategists reviewed the entire Asia–Pacific situation and established a list of problem countries or threats to China. It is well to remember the cold war is over, countries are supposed to be normalising, and are supposed to be moving in the direction of peaceful cooperation and global economic interdependence. However, the Chinese noted that the Indian armed forces have modernised, that China could not easily win a war with India, and India was labeled as the 'largest potential' threat along with a few other countries.[10]

The Indian tests conveyed to the Chinese that provocations would not be tolerated, and that there would be a concrete military response. This points to a distinction in Indian behaviour. Up to that point, Indian diplomats had been directly and indirectly asking the Chinese about their military activities in Pakistan, to which the Chinese had given evasive replies. The Indian tests were meant to indicate to the Chinese that India was willing to raise the costs of defence for the Chinese. If PRC provocations persist, this means that now the Central Military Commission has to discuss the new situation with the Peoples' Liberation Army (PLA) and the PRC has to gear up its military modernisation. The PLA has been told that the Indian tests represent a threat to China, and it must increase its activities and pay the increased costs of Chinese defence vis-a-vis India.

The PRC and India are engaged in the nuclear field because now Indian missiles are known to be able to hit Chinese targets.[11] Currently, China's missiles can cover the entire Indian landmass, so at the moment China has an advantage in the missile sphere over India. However, Indian missile testing, and the prospect that eventually, within a few years, Indian missiles will be able to reach Beijing, Shanghai and Hong Kong, puts pressure on China to either increase its military preparations or to negotiate with India in a meaningful way. Recently, following Indian Foreign Minister Jaswant Singh's visit to Beijing, both sides agreed to participate in a 'security dialogue'.

The pressure of Indian nuclear, missile and naval development has to also be taken into account in the context of another pressure. The US–Japan decision to develop theater missile defence in East Asia (which presumably also includes Taiwan) will degrade China's nuclear and missile capability and China will either have to increase its nuclear and missile force or engage in a meaningful security dialogue with the US and Japan. Thus, taken altogether, the costs of China's defence preparations are likely to grow if China relies more on military capability and less on political diplomacy to achieve its strategic aims.

Of course, the costs will also grow for India, Japan and the US if these countries also rely exclusively on a military buildup for their security. Should the money go to poverty reduction and economic development in India, as Indian and foreign social activists and critics of Indian military development argue? Our answer is that the issue is not one of 'guns *versus* butter', it is one of 'guns *and* butter' because a country requires both economic and military strength and leverage to be taken seriously and to be able to give its people both material and psychological security.

The Indian tests also had a fallout in the Middle East. The Israelis, as is well-known, already possess a nuclear arsenal but they are still worried about the message the tests conveyed to the Iranians, who are already engaged in nuclear and missile activities though several years away from acquiring a nuclear bomb. Israel's concern is that the Indian and Pakistani tests will stimulate the Iranians. The Indian tests have already initiated rethinking in Egypt about its acceptance of the NPT. Egypt's statement at the UN General Assembly in 1998 shows the re-thinking. To quote:

Unfortunately, the Nuclear Weapon States lacked the genuine political will needed to fully and completely implement their obligations under the NPT.

The nuclear tests conducted recently in South Asia created a new reality, which had to be addressed by the international community. ... The tests demonstrated that both the NPT and the CTBT were inadequate instruments for maintaining the global non-proliferation regime and the international community had to address that at the regional and global level ... On the regional level ... it was important for more nuclear-weapon-free zones to be established, especially in regions of tension, such as the Middle East and South Asia. It was a matter of deep regret that the proposals for the creation of the Middle East zone, dating back to 1974, had so far failed....

Double standards in the pursuit of nuclear non-proliferation was dangerous and counter-productive ... His Government could not understand how certain countries could severely condemn and take strong action against one proliferator, while all but condoning the actions of another....[12]

If there were to be another shock to the non-proliferation system, the value of non-proliferation is likely to be degraded in the Middle East, and possibly in the Korean peninsula as well. These are the concerns which bother the United States. It is not simply the fallout of the tests in the subcontinent; it is also their fallout in the Middle East and Northeast Asia. North Korea's missile test in the Sea of Japan put the arms control arrangements in the Korean peninsula in doubt. Despite famine conditions and external diplomatic pressures, North Korea continues to develop its missile capability, and its nuclear capability is the object of bargaining with the US. Note that the bargaining is between North Korea, a 'rogue and isolated state', and on the other hand, the US, the sole superpower. So the fallout is not only in terms of India–Pakistan and India–China relations. It is also in relation to the Middle East and in relation to the non-proliferation regime in different parts of the world.

In relation to the United States which, of course, is the biggest player in this case, the Indian tests have also raised the costs of maintaining the credibility of the non-proliferation regime. As Joseph Cirincione points out

Hundreds of dedicated officials toil daily for these and other programs. Arms control officials genuinely feel that they are doing all that they can under the circumstances and that the system simply can't take any more.

The problem is that it just isn't enough. Non-proliferation work is in some senses like a pyramid scheme. It must keep expanding, bringing in new successes to satisfy the existing members of the plan. It can't stand still and maintain its structural integrity. If it falters, if members begin to doubt the success of the enterprise, nations will begin hedging their bets, doubting the wisdom of giving up weapons that others seem to be acquiring and the process could collapse.

Right now, despite the best intentions of many Administration officials and some members of Congress, the work being done, the resources being devoted and the amount of political capital being expended are simply not sufficient to deal with the problems presented.[13]

What are the costs for the United States, the only super power in the world? *Regime* really means maintaining the credibility of its different components. The components are the NPT, the IAEA, CTBT, MTCR and the export control arrangements. In relation to the above, the Indian messages were two-fold. First, when forced into the situation outlined above, India would raise the costs for the United States of maintaining the credibility of the regime. Second, the alternative is for the United States to negotiate with India in terms of Indian security interests. The message of the Indian behaviour to the United States was that the US would have to come to the diplomatic table; or that the Indian nuclearisation process, if continued, will lead to weaponisation, weapon production and eventual deployment, and the costs will keep on getting higher and higher for both the US and India. A related message was that the US cannot rely on past history (i.e. USSR's collapse) to assert its international status. *Status* represents 'present power' and presently the US is *a* leader but not *the* leader in Asia.

In assessing the different types of consequences, there was a marked contrast between the strategic behaviour of the present BJP government and previous Indian governments. Despite India's refusal to sign it, until recently the non-proliferation regime had deterred successive Indian governments, from those led by Indira Gandhi and after, from crossing the line against overt nuclearisation which were laid down by the regime. India talked against it but did nothing tangible to disrupt it. Indian nuclear behaviour from 1974 to 1998 was talk rather than action, and this was quite reassuring to the regime builders. After the 1974 test, which Indira Gandhi authorised, she did nothing towards overt nuclearisation. She had come under intense American and Russian pressure and she acted on the following basis: India would not go for bomb production beyond the 1974 nuclear test, India would not test again, and India would maintain its nuclear option in a theoretical and technical way.

To sum up, more generally, the message of the May 1998 tests was that when pushed to it India will engage hostile neighbours by military measures, that it will answer provocations by deeds and not simply through words, and that it will engage in a strategic dialogue through what is known as military diplomacy and not rely simply on polite diplomatic talk.

A second general message of the Indian tests was that regimes are like empires: they last as long as the 'natives' do not revolt. One can have enormous power on the side of regime and empire builders but once the natives decide to revolt, the moral authority of empires and regimes is susceptible to collapse. In this instance, the Indian natives have thrown a big stone at the non-proliferation regime, which could create a domino effect and severely degrade the pyramid structure of the regime.

A third general message connects with the lessons of international history. The history of international relations is about who is to have the legal and the moral right and the means to initiate and escalate the use of violence to maintain global and regional order. Historically, the great powers have claimed this right for themselves, and have denied it to the 'upstarts' or 'rogue' states. India's nuclear actions indicate that the monopoly of the right and means to initiate or escalate international or regional conflicts is not reserved to the big five countries, and that India will not accept a position of permanent military inferiority which is expected of a subordinate ally or a defeated power. India is neither. A defeated power can be required to disarm, as in the case of Japan, but India has not been defeated at the hands of big powers. It is a mystery why the Western establishment presumed that India would be amenable to being disarmed through the nuclear non-proliferation treaty like a dependent ally or a defeated nation. The implication of this point is that if the United States and China want Indian restraint with regard to non-proliferation, they cannot get it by crying a halt to the arms race for everyone else while upholding the determination of the P–5 states to continue their nuclear modernisation and their commitment to nuclear deterrence for their national security.

Restraint will now depend on negotiated solutions and political settlements. The Indian message is to set a clear priority. If the great powers want arms control or nuclear disarmament of independent-minded regional and middle powers, they will have to engage in a quest for political settlements with the regional players. The Indian tests provided a clear demonstration that Indians will not hesitate to create situations to avoid marginalisation and isolation in the regional sphere or the global sphere.

The pattern and style of the new Indian behaviour should be studied in the context of the emergent possibilities for a multipolar world. The American dream of a unipolar world with one super power is just that – a dream. It cannot justifiably be the basis of world order or nuclear non-proliferation or even order in the Indian subcontinent.

The discussion in this essay shows that the so-called international consensus against further (horizontal) nuclear proliferation has several serious fault lines. The issue of nuclear non-proliferation must be revisited in the context of the structure of conflictual relationships in the Indian subcontinental and Indian Ocean areas where the strategic interests and prestige of India, Pakistan as well as China, Russia and obviously the US are involved. But to discover the bargaining opportunities, the researcher and the policy-maker must use both in-depth research and imagination to locate the discussion in the realities of regional geo-politics so that global norms acquire a greater viability.

NOTES

1. 'The Position of the United States With Respect to Asia', NSC 48/1, 23 December 1949 (Top Secret), in T. H. Etzold and J. L. Gaddis, *Containment: Documents on American Policy and Strategy, 1945–1950* (New York: Columbia University Press, 1978), 252–3.
2. a, b Lloyd Axworthy, 'India's Nuclear Testing: Implications for Nuclear Disarmament and the Nuclear Non-Proliferation Regime', *Cancaps Bulletin*, no. 18, August 1998, 10.
3. a, b, c Harold Müller, 'The Death of Arms?' *Disarmament Diplomacy* (London), no. 29, August/September 1998, 2, 4.
4. Marcus Raskin, 'The US and the South Asian Nukes,' *Testing the Limits: The India–Pakistan Nuclear Gambit* (Amsterdam: Transnational Institute and Washington: Institute of Policy Studies), August 1998, 40.
5. a, b, c Cathleen S. Fisher, 'Parallel Nuclear Realities', *Disarmament Diplomacy* (London), no. 30, September 1998, 7–9.
6. Raskin, op. cit., 42.
7. Ibid., 40–43.
8. This was reported to the author by two reliable South Asian sources.
9. For aggregate comparison of Chinese and Indian military strength, see International Institute of Strategic Studies, *Military Balance*, annual (London).
10. 'Can the Chinese Army Win the Next War?' Summary of a secret meeting of the Central Military Commission, 1993.
11. 'Missile Encirclement: China's Interest in Missile Controls', *F.A.S. Public Interest Report* (Journal of the Federation of American Scientists) 51(5), September/October 1998, 1–2.
12. Statement of Egypt, UN General Assembly, *Disarmament Diplomacy*, no. 31, October 1998, 28.
13. J. Cirincione, 'The Paralysis of US Non-Proliferation Policy', *Disarmament Diplomacy*, no. 30, September 1998.

Annexure 1: China's Missile Exports and Assistance to Pakistan

Missile System	Characteristics	Areas of Reported Chinese Assistance to Pakistan
M-11 (also known as CSS-7; DF-11)	* Range: 300 km * Payload: 800 kg * Solid propellant * A few may be armed with nuclear warheads	Chinese transfer of M-11 missile transporter-erector launchers (TELs) (1991); Chinese provision of M-11 components and technology (1992, 1995); Chinese missile technicians visited Pakistan M-11 sites (1994); Reports of direct transfers of complete M-11s (1993, 1995); Chinese training of Pakistani M-11 army units (1995); Reports of Chinese assistance with indigenous Pakistani M-11 production (1996–97)
Missile factory for manufacture of medium-range ballistic missiles, likely the M-11 or a similar missile	* Located in Rawalpindi * Unclear whether this facility will be able to manufacture complete missiles, or only some major components	Chinese assistance, including blueprints and construction equipment (1996–97)
Hatf-1/1A	* Range: 80 km (Hatf-1A: 100 km) * Payload: 500 kg * Single stage; solid propellant	Developed with some Chinese aid
Hatf-2	* Range: 300 km * Payload: 500 kg	Developed with some Chinese assistance; uses Chinese technology; Reportedly an indigenous version of the M-11, but may be a modified Hatf-1
Hatf-3	* Range: 600 km * Payload: 500 kg	May be based on Chinese M-9 missile
Long-range ballistic missile	* Range: 600 km * Payload: 500 kg * Single stage * Possible nuclear role * Under development; details unknown	Chinese experts guiding Pakistani scientists in propellants, guidance, warhead technology (1996–)
Ammonium perchlorate	* Chemical used in rocket fuel	Alleged illegal Chinese shipment of 10 tons to Pakistan (1996)
Anza	* Surface-to-air missile * Under development (?)	Assistance from Chinese technicians

Source: Confidential sources, New Delhi; and US press reports.

Annexure 2: **China's Missile Transfers to Pakistan and U.S. Response**

Date of transfer or Report	Reported Transfer by China	Possible Violations	US Administration Response
Nov 1992*	M-11 missiles or related equipment	MTCR, AECA, EAA	Sanctions imposed on 8/24/93; waived on 11/1/94
July 1995	More than 30 M-11 missiles stored at Sargodha Air Base	MTCR, AECA, EAA	No sanctions
August 1996	Plant to manufacture M-11 missiles or missile components	MTCR, AECA, EAA	No sanctions
July to Dec 1996	DCI reported 'tremendous variety of technology and assistance for Pakistan's ballistic missile program	MTCR, AECA, EAA	No sanctions
Nov 1997	May have transferred technology for Pakistan's Ghauri medium-range ballistic missile that was flight-tested on 6/4/98	MTCR, AECA, EAA	No sanctions

* *Note:* Sanctions were first imposed on both China and Pakistan in June 1991

Key: AECA (Arms Export Control Act), EAA (Export Administration Act), MTCR (Missile Technology Control Regime)

Source: Congressional Research Service study, 15 May 1998.

Index

Abdullah, Farooq 318
Abdullah, Sheikh Mohammed 205, 290, 312–314, 317–318 see also Jammu and Kashmir National Conference
Acharya, Shankar 225
Adhikari, Man Mohan 135
adivasis 202
affirmative action see reservations
Afghanistan 211, 287
  civil war 49, 52
  war with Soviet Union 274, 277, 290, 294, 297
agriculture 227
Ahluwalia, Montek Singh 225
Ahmed, Abul Mansur 163
Ahmed, Fakhruddin Ali 25
Ahmed, Shahabuddin 79
Akali Dal 150
Akhil Bharatiya Vidyarthi Parishad (ABVP) 145
Akhtar, General 291
Alamgir, Mohiuddin Khan 82
Albright, Madeleine 328, 333, 336
Ali, Jam Sadiq 54
Aligarh Muslim University 150, 203
All Ceylon Tamil Congress (TC) 91–92, 94, 96
All-India Muslim League 200, 203, 286, 289
All Parties Conference (Sri Lanka) 109–110
All Parties Student Unity 74
All-Pakistan Muhajir Students Organisation 49
amendments, constitutional see constitutional amendments

Anglo-Mohammedan College see Aligarh Muslim University
Anjuman-e-Taraqqi-e-Urdu 149
Apte, Shiv Shankar 146
arms see weapons
army see military
Arya Samaj 142–143
Asian Development Bank (ADB) 229, 271
Assam 202, 206, 208
Awami League (Bangladesh) 45–46, 70–83, 161, 163–164, 167, 170–177
Awami National Party (ANP) 52, 57, 59
Axworthy, Lloyd 329, 336
Ayodhya movement 147–150 see also Babri Masjid
Azad Kashmir see Kashmir
Azad, Maulana 149
Azam, Golam 79, 170–171, 175
Aziz, A. 103

Babri Masjid 147–151, 166 see also Ayodhya movement
Bahadur, Surya 135
Bahujan Samaj Party 254
Bahuns 115–119
Bajaj, Rahul 256
Bajrang Dal 147–148
Baluchis 202, 206
Baluchistan 48, 58, 202, 206
Bandaranaike, Chandrika Kumaratunga 111
Bandaranaike, S.W.R.D. 90, 95, 97, 99–105
Bandaranaike, Sirima 97, 104–107

Index

Bandaranaike-Chelvanayakam Pact of 1957 (B-C Pact) 93, 102–103, 105
Bangladesh 2–13, 46, 69–87, 158–182, 196–211
 liberation war 70, 159, 170, 196, 288
 foreign relations
  with India 72, 75, 78–80
  with Pakistan 165
 national identity 158–182
Bangladesh Nationalist Party (BNP) 72–84, 166, 170, 172, 174–176
Bangladesh Rural Advancement Committee (BRAC) 79, 173
Bano, Shah 150
Basic Democrats 45
Basnyats 120
Beg, Aslam 52
Beg, Mirza Afzal 314, 317
Beg-Parthasarathi Accord of 1975 317
Bengali
 culture 161–166, 204
 ethnic movements 43, 161–163, 201, 204
 language 161–167, 204
Bhagwati, P.N. 28
bharadar 116
Bharadari 126
Bharatiya Janata Party (BJP) 22–24, 30, 34, 38, 147–148, 151–153, 206–207, 224, 231–232, 244, 253–256, 260, 284, 286, 290, 306, 320, 333, 342
Bharatiya Mazdoor Sangh 145
Bhashani, Maulana 72
Bhattarai, K.P. 132–135
Bhindranwale, Sant 150
Bhutto, Benazir 52–62, 274, 276, 290–292
Bhutto, Mir Murtaza 55–56
Bhutto, Nusrat 49
Bhutto, Zulfikar Ali 46–48, 273
Bihar 204
Birendra, King 124, 127–136
Biswas, Abdur Rahman 77, 85
BJP *see* Bharatiya Janata Party
Board for Industrial and Financial Reconstruction (BIFR) 243, 247
 see also business organisations
Bodos 202
Bombay Club industrialists 230, 232, 256
borders, international 196–211, 287, 321
Brahmans 115–119, 126, 128, 136–137, 142

Brahmo Samaj 142 *see also* communalism, organisations
British raj *see* Britain
Britain 88
 British colonialism 42, 91, 93, 141–143, 149, 205, 285–289, 311–312 *see also* colonialism
Buddhism
 India 142
 Nepal 115
 Sri Lanka
  patronage from the state 91–112, 183–192
  sangha (clergy) 97–98, 104, 110, 186–187
  schools 91, 187–188
bureaucracy
 Bangladesh 71, 78
 India 27–28, 153, 229, 242–243, 256–257
 Nepal 119–121, 127–130, 133, 137
 Pakistan 43, 45, 48, 63, 269–272
Burghers (Sri Lanka) 89
business organisations 229, 234–235, 243, 246, 256, 260

Camdessus, Michael 245
Canada 329–330
capital 216, 224, 229–230, 235, 273
caste
 lower castes 29, 144, 155, 253
 and elections 29–30, 155, 253, 260
 movements 35
 in Nepali political culture 115–119, 126–127, 136–137
 upper castes 29, 30, 144, 155
 violence 34
 see also Other Backward castes *and* reservations *and* scheduled castes
Central Bureau of Investigation (CBI) (India) 257
Central Intelligence Agency (CIA) (United States) 327
Ceylon *see* Sri Lanka
Ceylon Observer 102
Ceylon Workers Congress (CWC) 96–97, 103
chakari system 119, 128, 131
Chaudhury, A.Z. Azad 82
Chautaria family 120
Chelvanayakam, S.J.V. 92, 95, 97, 102, 104–105
Chettris (bahuns) 115–119, 126–129, 136–137 *see also* caste

348

Index

China 61, 305
  aid to Pakistan 297–298, 327–330, 340, 345–346
  nuclear weapons 298, 327, 330, 338, 343
  relations with India, 326, 330–344
Chinmayananda, Swami 146
chiti 144
Chittagong Hill Tracts (CHT) 81, 287
Chowdhury, Abdul Matin 176
Christian Affairs office (Sri Lanka)
Christianity 146 *see also* Christians
  missions 91, 142, 145
  patronage from the state 184, 189–190
  schools 91, 190
Christians *see also* Christianity
  India 141–142, 155
  Sri Lanka 91, 184, 189–190
Cirincione, Joseph 341
citizenship
  India 97
  Sri Lanka 92, 95–97, 100, 102–103
civil service *see* bureaucracy
civil war
  Afghanistan 49, 52
  Pakistan 46, 288
  Sri Lanka 109–112
  see also Bangladesh liberation war
class 39, 215, 260
Clinton, Bill 61, 304–307 *see also* Clinton Administration
Clinton Administration 298, 308, 326–327, 335 *see also* Albright, Madeleine *and* Talbot, Strobe
coalition governments 22–24, 30, 33, 254–255
cold war 33, 70, 297, 308, 315
colonialism 141–143, 186, 218
colonisation *see* colonialism *and* Sri Lanka, colonisation schemes
communalism 7, 35, 88–112, 141–156, 166, 232
  and elections 30, 253
  organisations 142–156
  violence 143, 102, 147–153, 206–207, 226 *see also* Babri Masjid
communist parties 22, 106, 130–132, 161, 164, 223
  Communist Party of India (Marxist)
  East Pakistan Communist Party (Marxist-Leninist) 164
  Marxist-Leninist party (ML) 135
  marxists 95, 104, 107

Nepal Communist Party (NCP) 132–134
  United Marxist-Leninists (UML) 133–137
Comprehensive Test Ban Treaty (CTBT) 300, 327, 342 *see also* nuclear weapons, non-proliferation
confederalism 208–211
Confederation of Indian Industry (CII) 229, 234, 245
  see also business organisations
Congress Parliamentary Board 21
Congress Party (India) 18–25, 27, 30–33, 148–153, 207, 219–220, 225–226, 248, 253, 260, 289–291, 318–319
Constituent Assembly
  India 18, 30
  Pakistan 44
Constitution of Bangladesh 71, 81
  1972 constitution 163, 165
  Fifth Amendment 166
  Eighth Amendment 168
  Article 38 170
Constitution of India 17–18, 29, 37, 155
  amendments to
    Forty-Second 20
    Sixty-First 29
  articles of
    Article 25 141
    Article 30 141
    Article 356 25–26, 32, 315
    Article 357 315
    Article 370 314
Constitution of Nepal
  1959 constitution 126
  1962 constitution 126–127, 130
  1990 constitution 133
Constitution of Pakistan 43, 46, 49–50
  1956 constitution 44
  1962 constitution 45
  1973 constitution 46–47, 49, 62
  see also Pakistan Provincial Constitution Order of 1947
  amendments to
    First 47
    Third 47
    Fourth 47
    Fifth 47
    Eighth 49, 53–54, 56–57
    Thirteenth 57
    Fourteenth 57–58
    Fifteenth 58–59
  articles of
    Article 6 49

Index

Constitution of Sri Lanka 90, 93, 99, 102–103, 106–107
  1948 constitution 183
  1972 constitution 108, 183
  1978 constitution 108, 184
  amendments to
    Thirteenth 112
  articles of
    Article 9 184
    Article 10 184
    Article 14 184
    Article 15 184
constitutional monarchy 124–125, 133
consumerism 235–236
cooperative federalism 31 see also federalism, India
Corea, Sir Claude 90
corruption 9, 19–23, 27–28,
coups
  Bangladesh 71–72, 84, 166
  Pakistan 41, 48, 61–64, 304

Dalits 25, 34, 253–254
Das, Tarun 245
de Silva, C.P. 106
defence see military
Delhi Agreement of 1952 314
democracy 3, 4–6, 11, 17–138, 187
  in Bangladesh 5–6, 69–87
  in India 4–5, 17–40, 257–258
  in Nepal 6, 114–138
  in Pakistan 5, 41–68
  in Sri Lanka 6, 88–113
Democratic Workers' Congress (DWC) 103
demotism 88–112
Department of Education (Pakistan) 269
Department of Hindu Religious and Cultural Affairs (Sri Lanka) 184, 188–189
Department of Muslim Religious and Cultural Affairs (Sri Lanka) 184, 189–190
Department of Public Health Engineering (Pakistan) 269
Desai, Ashok 225–226
deterrence, vs. defence 338
development 3, 8–9, 12, 215–280
  economic
    India 8–9, 36, 215–263
    Pakistan 9, 47, 264–278
  social (Pakistan) 9, 264–278
Dhaka Declaration 302 see also South Asian Association for Regional Cooperation

disarmament see nuclear weapons, non-proliferation
Donoughmore Commission 100
Drass sector 61 see also Kashmir
Dravidastan movement 201 see also regionalism
Durand Line 287

Economic Cooperation Organization (ECO) 210
economy 12, 215–280 see also development
  Bangladesh 70, 71, 75–77, 83
  India 215–263
  Pakistan 264–280
education
  Bangladesh 162, 168–170
  India 154–155
  Pakistan 266–271
  Sri Lanka 106–107, 111, 188–189
Egypt 340–341
Ehtesab cell (Pakistan) 57, 59, 62
ekatmata yatra (pilgrimage of unity) 147
Ekatturer Ghatok Dalal Nirmul Committee (Committee to Eliminate the Killers and Collaborators of 1971) 170
elections
  Bangladesh 70–79, 84, 86, 163, 170
  India 18–20, 29–32, 149, 151, 226, 253, 318–319
  Pakistan 44, 46, 48–49, 51, 55–56, 70, 277, 290
  Nepal 133
  Sri Lanka 96, 99–101
Emergency (India 1975–7) 20, 25, 28, 35, 37
emergency powers, India 20, 37
English language
  India 149
  Sri Lanka 91–92, 99, 101
Enron power project 224, 231–232, 247, 252
Ershad, Begum 79
Ershad, Hussain Muhammad 69, 72–74, 79, 82–83, 167–169
ethnicity 53, 63, 69, 88–112,
  and nationalism 158–159, 196–211
  ethnic violence 55, 102
executive
  India 18–24
  Pakistan 47, 55, 57
exports 225, 233

350

Index

external payments crisis of 1991 216, 220–222, 225, 242–244, 254

Farrakha barrage 80
fatwa courts (Bangladesh) 159, 172–174
federalism
  India 17, 30–33, 227, 230–232, 234, 294, 313, 317–319, 321–322
  Pakistan 42–47, 55–59, 63, 294
  Sri Lanka 109–111
Federal Party (FP) 92–98, 101–102, 104–106
Federation of Indian Chambers of Commerce and Industry (FICCI) 229, 234 *see also* business organisations
Fernandes, George 300
Finance Ministry (India) 216
Fisher, Cathleen 334, 337
foreign direct investment (FDI) 219, 224, 228, 230–231, 234, 249–252, 256
Foreign Exchange Management Act (FEMA) 255
Foreign Investment Promotion Board (FIPB) 224, 232, 251
Freedom Party (Bengal) 174

Gandhi, Indira 19–28, 32, 150, 219–220, 248, 288, 317–318, 342
Gandhi, Mohandas K. (Mahatma) 145, 187, 336–337
Gandhi, Rajiv 20–24, 28, 32, 109, 150–151, 220, 223, 242, 248, 299, 318
Gandhi, Sonia 23
gender 268–269 *see also* women
Giri, V.V. 25
girls *see* women
Golwalkar, M.S. 143
Goonetileke, Oliver Ernest 90
Gorkha 119, 202
Government of India Act of 1935 43–44, 269
governor-general of Pakistan 42–44
Governor's Rule 59
Gowda, Deve 80, 254
Grameen Bank 79
Gujral, I.K. 80
Gulf War, effects on Indian economy 220
Gurkhas 202

Haksar, P.N. 296

Haq, Fazlur 201
Haq, Khadija 276
Haq, Mahbubul 264, 273, 276
Haqiqis 56
health in Pakistan 266, 268–271
Hedgewar, Keshav Baliram 143
Himalayas 115
Hindi 143–144, 148–149 *see also* language
Hindu Code Bill 141, 146
Hinduism 142–144, 155
  ascetics 145–146
  and statecraft 117
Hindu Mahasabha 143, 145
Hindu nationalism 33, 141–156, 286 *see also* communalism
Hindutva movement 34, 143–156
Hindu Sangathan 143
history and nationalism 201
Hizbul Mujahideen 292, 319
Huda, Najmul 176
Human Rights Commission of Pakistan 58
Hussain, Zakir 25, 149
Hyder, Sajjad 288

IAEA *see* International Atomic Energy Agency
IAS *see* Indian Administrative Service
ICS *see* Indian Civil Service
identity 3, 6–8, 12, 141–212, 287–288
  in Bangladesh 158–182
  in India 141–157
  in Pakistan 287–288
  in Sri Lanka 183–195
illiteracy *see* literacy
Imam, Jahanara 170
imports 219, 225, 241
income tax *see* taxes
independence movements
  Bangladesh 70, 161–163, 199
  India 200
India 1–13, 17–40, 60, 141–157, 196–211, 215–240, 283–346
  civil society 35–36
  foreign relations
    with Bangladesh 72, 75, 78–80
    with China 299–300, 326, 330–332, 337–340, 343–344
    with Pakistan 60–61, 283–346
    with Sri Lanka 91
    with United States 304–307, 326–337, 342–344
  northeast 208, 339

351

Index

Indian Administrative Service (IAS) 27
  see also bureaucracy, India
  underepresentation of Muslims 153
Indian Civil Service (ICS) *see also*
  bureaucracy, India 27
Indian Independence Act of 1947 43
Indian Investment Promotion Board
  (IIPB) 224
Indian National Congress 200, 286 *see
  also* independence movements,
  India
Indian Trade Union Congress (INTUC)
  145
India-Pakistan war of 1971 46
Indo-Ceylon Agreement of 1954 100
Indo-Ceylon Agreement of 1964 (Sirima-
  Shastri Pact) 97
Indo-Ceylon Agreement Act of 1968 97
Indo-Nepal Trade and Transit Treaty 132
Indo-Pakistan war of 1947–48 289,
  311–313
Indo-Pakistan war of 1965 290, 311, 316
Indo-Pakistan war of 1971 288, 311,
  316–317
Indo-Sri Lanka Accord of 1987 109, 295
Industrial Credit and Investment
  Corporation of India (ICICI) 246
industrialisation 220–221
industry 220–221, 229–230, 241–242
inflation 225–226, 244, 252
infrastructure 230–231, 248–251
Instrument of Accession 289, 312–314
Intelligence Bureau (IB) (India) 314
Intergrated Missile Program 296
International Atomic Energy Agency
  (IAEA) 342
International Monetary Fund (IMF) 225,
  243–244, 245, 265, 274
Inter-Services Intelligence (ISI) 291–293,
  304–305, 319, 322 *see also*
  military, Pakistan
interventionism, India 35
ISI *see* Inter-Services Intelligence
Islam
  in Bangladesh 72, 158–177
  and education 154–155, 162, 168–170
  in India 141–156
  Islamic law 141, 150 *see also* shariah
    laws
  Islamisation movements 48, 50, 53,
    58, 72, 166
  and nationalism 71–72, 158–177,
    196–211
  in Pakistan 160–163

political parties 51, 70–72, 318
Shiaism 49, 53
Sunnism 49, 53, 287
Islami Chhatra Shibir 175
Islami Chhatra Sena (Student Soldiers of
  Islam) 172
Islami Jamhoori Ittehad (IJI or Islamic
  Democratic Alliance) 51–53,
  274, 276
Islamic Education and Research Act 1980
  (Bengal) 166
Islamic Universities Act 1980 (Bengal) 166
Iyer, V.R. Krishna 28

Jamaat-i-Islami (JI or Party of Islam)
  (Bangladesh) 70–72, 75–79, 161,
  164, 168, 170–176, 290, 305
Jamiat-i-Ulama 168
Jamiat-ul-Mudarresin 168
Jamiyat-ul-Ulama-i-Islam 164, 174
Jammu and Kashmir Liberation Front
  (JKLF) 319
Jammu and Kashmir National
  Conference 289–290, 312–314,
  317–319
Janata Dal 22, 24, 207
Janata Party 20, 24, 35, 220, 224
Japan 329
Jatiya Party (JP or National Party) 73–75,
  77–79, 83, 170
Jayatilaka, Sir Baron 90
Jayatilleke, Sir Edward 102
Jayewardene, J.R. 96, 99, 107–109
Jehangir, Asma 58
Jennings, Sir Ivor 90
Jinnah, Mohammad Ali 42, 200, 203,
  289, 312
jizya *see* taxes
judiciary *see also* supreme court
  of Bangladesh 173–174
  of India 18, 28–29
  of Nepal 133
  of Pakistan 47, 53, 55, 59, 64
Junejo, Mohammad Khan 49–50

Kakar, Abdul Waheed 54
Kalabagh Dam 58, 59
Karamat, Jehangir 56, 60
Kargil conflict 61, 293–294, 304–307,
  319–320 *see also* Kashmir
Karpatriji, Swami 146
Kashmir 10, 60–61, 204–207, 311–322
  see also Kargil conflict
  accession to India 289, 311–313

Index

in Indian-Muslim relations 207, 210–211, 288–295, 304–307, 311–322
separatist movements 196, 202, 205–207, 290–294, 317–321
Kathmandu 115–116, 119–123, 126, 137
Kathmandu valley 115, 120, 133–134
Katiyar, V. 147
Khalid, Meraj 274
Khalistan movment 196, 202, 205–207
Khan, Ali Liaquat 42, 44
Khan, Ayub 174, 272–273, 277, 315
Khan, Ghulam Ishaq 52–54, 274
Khan, Mohammed Ayub 45–46
Khan, Nooruddin 84
Khan, Sir Sayyid Ahmad 203
Khan, Yahya 46
Khilafat Movement 143
Kidwai, Rafi Ahmad 149
Koirala, B.P. 125–126
Koirala, G.P. 133–137
Koneswaran Temple dispute (Sri Lanka) 97
Kotelawala, Sir John 94, 98–100
Kshatriyas (Nepal) 115–116

labour 220, 222, 227–228, 234
labour unions 145
Lahore Resolution of 1940 163–164
language
  language education 149
  Language of the Courts Act of 1961 (Sri Lanka) 106
  movements 69, 99–106, 148–149, 162–163
  and nationalism 159–165, 198–205
  Official Languages Act of 1963 (India) 149
  official language issues
    Bangladesh 161–167
    India 143, 148–149
    Pakistan 161
    Sri Lanka 94–96, 99–106, 111
Left Front 23
Legal Framework Order of 1970 46
Leghari, Farooq Khan 55–56, 58
legislature
  India 17–33
  Nepal 126–127
  Pakistan 42–64
liberalisation 33–34, 36, 78–79, 215–236, 241–260, 301
  and coalition governments 254–255, 260
  and democracy 257–258

and populism 217–218, 225–233, 243–248, 252–253, 257–259
Liberation Tigers of Tamil Eelam (LTTE) 109–111
Line of Control (LoC) 61, 290, 293, 316, 321 *see also* United Nations Cease-Fire Line
literacy
  Bangladesh 69
  India 37, 154–155
  Pakistan 266–269, 276
Lok Sabha 26-27 *see also* parliament of India
  elections 26, 30
  under-representation of Muslims 153

madrasahs 162, 168–170, 189 *see also* education *and* Islam, and education
Mahaveli river valley scheme 108
Mahendra, King 123–129
Majlis-e-Shoora (Federal Consultative Assembly) 49
Mallas 120
Mandal Commision Report 34, 253
Manipur *see* India, north-east
Manju, Anwar 83
March to Kandy 104
Markaz-Dawar 292
marxists *see* communist parties
Maududi, Maulana 71, 174, 176
media 36–37
  censorship of 37
  expansion of 36–37
  and propaganda 306
Meenakshipuram conversions 147
Meghalaya 202
middle class 36, 235
Middle East
  economic support to Bangladesh 169
  and non-proliferation 340–341
  and Pakistan economy 267, 274
  religious/cultural link to Pakistan 200–201
  and South Asian economies 267
military
  Bangladesh 71–85, 160, 165–168
  China 330–333, 339
  India 295–299, 316, 319–320, 338–339
  Pakistan 9–10, 43–65, 274, 278, 291–294, 297–299, 304–306, 312–321
  Nepal 127, 129–130
  Sri Lanka 110

Index

military rule
 Bangladesh 71–74, 84–86, 165–168
 Pakistan 42–51, 60–65, 273–274, 304
Ministry of Buddha Sasana (Sri Lanka) 184, 191
Mirza, Iskander 44
missiles 296 see also weapons
Missile Technology Control Regime (MTCR) 327, 342 see also nuclear weapons, non-proliferation
Mizoram/Mizos 202, 206
modernity 114
modernisation 121
Mohammad, Ghulam 44
Mohammed, Bakshi Ghulam 314
monarchy 117–132
Mountbatten, Lord 312
Movement for the Restoration of Democracy 49
muhajirs 42–43, 59, 202–204, 208, 288
Muhajir Quami Movement (MQM) 49, 52–57, 59
Mukherjee, Pranab 224
mukhtiar 120
Müller, Harold 330, 336
multinational corporations (MNCs) 224 see also transnational corporations
Muluki Ain 121 see also law in Nepal
Musharraf, Pervez 41, 61–62, 304–306, 320
Muslim Bengal movement 163–177
Muslim League (Pakistan) 42–43, 161–162
Muslim League (Bengal) 168
Muslims see also Islam
 India 141–156, 206–207
 Sri Lanka 88, 95, 101, 110, 184
Muslim United Front 318

Nagaland 202, 206 see also India, north-east
Narayan, Jayaprakash 19, 35
Narayanan, K.R. 25–26
Nasim, General 85
Nasir, Javid 292
Nasreen, Taslima 76, 171–172
Nath, Digvijay 145
National Assembly (Pakistan) 44–46, 49–50, 54–57
National Assembly (Nepal) 124–127 see also Rashtriya Panchayat
National Awami Party (NAP) 48

National Democratic Alliance (NDA) 24
National Democratic Party (NDP) 133–135
National Front 22–24
National Government (Sri Lanka) 97
nationalism 196–211, 286–287
 Bengal 158–177
 India 141–156, 230–232
 Nepal 114
 Pakistan 199–204, 285–288 see also 'two-nation theory'
nationalities issue see identity and nationalism
National Renewal Fund 224
National Security Council (NSC)
 India 300
 Pakistan 293
National Telecom Policy (India) 247
Navaratnarajah, P. 102
Naxalite movement 19
Nehru, Jawaharlal 17–19, 24, 26, 100, 149–150, 155, 200–201, 205, 219, 289, 312–315, 337
Nepal 2–13, 114–138, 199
 cabinet 125–129
 central secretariat 128–129
 Hindu elite 115–118
 Janch Bhuj Kendra 129
 palace secretariat 128–129
 Revolution of 1990 132–133
 Tehri (tarai) area 117, 137
 traditions of governance 115–121
Nepal Communist Party (NCP) see communist parties, Nepal Communist Party
Nepal Sadbhavana Party (NSP) 135
Nepali Congress (NC) 125, 130–137
New Delhi Declaration of 1983 209
Newars 115–121, 126, 128, 136–137
Nizam-i-Islam 164, 174
non-alignment 33, 295
 non-aligned movement 295
non-governmental organisations (NGOs) 35–36
Non-Proliferation Treaty (NPT) 300, 327, 330, 333–342 see also nuclear weapons, non-proliferation
North Korea 341
Northwest Frontier Province (NWFP) 43, 48, 52, 58–59, 287
nuclear weapons 298–301, 306, 322, 326–346

354

Index

non-proliferation 300, 306, 326–344
  see also Comprehensive Test Ban Treaty *and* Non-Proliferation Treaty
  production 300, 342
  testing 60, 284, 299, 326–344

Oath of Offices (Judges) Order of 2000 (Pakistan) 62
Official Languages Act of 1963 (India) 149
Official Secrets Act (India) 37
Other Backward Classes (OBCs) 34, 253

Pakistan 1–13, 41–68, 160–163, 196–211, 264–280, 283–346
  creation 42, 196, 199, 285–286
  foreign relations
    with Bangladesh 165
    with China 61, 297–298, 327–330, 340, 345–346
    with India 60–61, 283–346
Pakistan Administrative Service *see* bureaucracy, Pakistan
Pakistan Democratic Party 164
Pakistan Muslim League (PML) 48, 52–54, 64, 276
  (Convention) 164
  (Council) 164
  (Nawaz) (PML-N) 55
Pakistan National Alliance 48
Pakistan Oppressed Nations Movement (PONAM) 58
Pakistan Peoples' Party (PPP) 46–48, 52–57, 64, 271, 274, 276, 292
Pakistan Provincial Constitution Order of 1947 43
panchayat system (Nepal) 124, 126–127, 131–132
Pandes 120
Panditharatne, N.G.P. 109
panjani 121
Pant, G.B. 149
parliament *see also* parliamentary system
  Bangladesh 73, 75–82
  Nepal 126–127, 133–137 *see also* National Assembly (Nepal)
  India 26–27, 33, 150, 153, 243
  Pakistan 49–62 *see also* National Assembly (Pakistan)
  Sri Lanka 95–97, 101–111
parliamentary system
  Bangladesh 85

India 33
Nepal 126–127, 133
Pakistan 42–43, 49
Sri Lanka 92–93, 100, 107
Parthasarathy, G. 109, 317
Partition 17, 70, 207, 285–288, 297
party system
  Bangladesh 71–72
  India 30
  Nepal 130–133
  Pakistan 49–50
  Sri Lanka 89
Pashtuns 202, 206
Patel, Sardar Vallabhbhai 313
Pawar, Sharad 225
Peiris, Denzil 102
Peoples' Republic of China (PRC) *see* China
People's United Front (MEP) 100
Pokhran tests *see* nuclear weapons, testing
police, under-representation of Muslims 153
political culture of Nepal 114–138
political leadership
  of India 18–24, 38
  of Sri Lanka 88–112
Political Parties Resolution of 1976 (Bengal) 167
polls *see* elections
Ponnambalam, G.G. 91–98
populism 217–218, 225–233, 243–248, 252–253, 257–259
poverty 29, 229, 234, 252, 266–268
  and elections 29, 228, 234
PPP *see* Pakistan People's Party
Prasad, Rajendra 25
Pratinidhi Sabha 126
Premadasa, Ranasinghe 110–111
president
  of India 18, 25–26,
  of Pakistan 44–45, 49–50
  of Sri Lanka 107–111
President's Rule 25–26, 32–33 *see also* Governor's Rule
press *see also* media
  India 37
  Nepal 122–123
  Pakistan 272
prime minister
  India 18–24
  Nepal 125
  Pakistan 42, 44, 46
  Sri Lanka 90–107

Index

princely states 288–299
privatisation 233, 247, 249, 275 *see also* liberalisation
public interest litigation 29, 37
Punjab
  Indian 207
  Pakistani 57
  partition of 205, 286–287
Puri, Balraj 317

quotas *see* reservations

Radhakrishnan, Sarvepalli 25
radio 37 *see also* media *and* telecommunications
Rahman, Muhammad Habibur 77
Rahman, Muhammad Mahbubur 85
Rahman, Shamsur 173
Rahman, Sheikh Mujibur 70–71, 85, 163–170
Rahman, Ziaur 69, 71–72, 165–168, 170, 302
raj *see* British
Rajiv-Farooq Pact 318
Rakhi Bahini 85
Ram Rajya Parishad 146
Ramshila pujan program *see* Ayodhya movement
Rana (Kunwar) family (Nepal) 116, 118–129
Rann of Kutch 287, 316
Rao, P.V. Narasimha 23–24, 32, 217, 222, 225–235, 245–248, 290
Rashtriya Janata Dal 254
Rashtriya Panchayat 126–127 *see also* parliament of Nepal *and* National Assembly (Nepal)
Rashtriya Swayamsevak Sangh (RSS) 143–147, 232
Raskin, Marcus 335–337
Reddy, N. Sanjiva 25
regionalism 30–33, 196–211, 230–232, 302
  regional movements 196–211
religion
  and nationalism 158–177, 196–211
  and the state 158–177, 183–192
  see also communalism *and* secularism
Representation of the People Act 151
Research and Analysis Wing (RAW) (India) 322
reservations 34 *see also* scheduled castes *and* scheduled tribes
Reserve Bank of India (RBI) 251, 257
Revival of the 1973 Constistution Order of 1985 49
Roy, Raja Ram Mohun 142
RSS *see* Rashtriya Swayamsevak Sangh
Rushdie, Salman 304
Russia 296

SAARC *see* South Asian Association for Regional Cooperation
sadhus *see* Hinduism, ascetics
Samarasinghe, G.V.P. 109
Samata Party 254
Sampurnanand, S. 148
Sanad of 1856 (Nepal) 121
sanctions 60, 299, 305
Sandypani Academy 146
Sangh parivar 145–155
Sanmilita Sangram Parishad 172
Sanskrit 143–144 *see also* language
Saraswati, Swami Dayananda 142
Sattar, Abdus 72
Saudi Arabia, assistance to Jaamat-I-Islami 175
Savarkar, Vinayak Damodar 143
sawals 121
Sayeed, Mufti Mohammed 319
Sayeed, Rubiya, abduction 319
Scheduled Castes 26, 29–30, 155
Scheduled Tribes 26, 30
schools *see* education
sectarianism 183–192 *see also* secularism
secularism 6, 33, 72, 141, 150, 155, 163–177, 183–192, 286
Securities and Exchange Bureau of India (SEBI) 257
security 3, 9–12, 283–346
  India 283–346
  Pakistan 278, 283–346
  South Asia 283–310
Senanayake-Chelvanayakam Pact of 1965 93, 96
Senanayake, Don Stephen 88, 90–94
Senanayake, Dudley 94–98, 104–105
Senanayake, Francis Richard 90
Senate (Pakistan) 46, 59
Shah dynasty (Nepal) 115–116, 119–120, 126
Shah, Sajjad Ali 55, 58
Shankara 142
Shariah Bill (Pakistan) 53, 58–59 *see also* Constitution of Pakistan, Fifteenth Amendment
shariah laws 150, 160, 168, 171, 176 *see also* Islam, Islamic law

Index

Shariat (Muslim legal code) *see* shariah laws
Sharif, Ahmad 173
Sharif, Nawaz 41, 52–62, 274, 276, 284, 290, 292, 304–305, 320
Sharma, Shankar Dayal 25
Shastri, Lal Bahadur 24, 26, 32, 316
Shekar, Chandra 22
Shiaism *see* Islam, Shiaism
Shiv Sena 151, 231
Shukla, R.S. 148
Sikhs 196, 202, 205–207
Sikkim 339 *see also* India, north-east
Simla Accord 290, 295, 316
Simla Conference 290, 316
Sindh 43, 49, 52–59, 199, 204, 206, 208, 322
Sindhis 53, 199, 201–202, 204, 208
Singh, Arjun 225
Singh, Ganeshman 133–134
Singh, Jaswant 248, 251, 259, 306, 329
Singh, Karan 314
Singh, Maharaja Hari 289, 312–314
Singh, Manmohan 217, 225, 228, 244
Singh, V.P. 22, 34, 253, 299
Singh, Zail 21, 25
Sinhala Only Act 106
Sinhala
   ethnic group 88–112
   language 90–91, 94–95, 98–104, 106
   Sinhala Buddhists 88–89, 91
Sino-Indian war of 1962 295, 315, 338
Siraikis 202–203
Sirima-Shastri Pact *see* Indo-Ceylon Agreement Act of 1964
Social Action Program (SAP) 265, 268, 271–272
social development *see* development
social infrastructure in Pakistan 265–268
socialism 19, 34, 71, 273 *see also* communism
software industry 247–248
Soulbury, Viscount 90, 94
South Asian Association for Regional Cooperation (SAARC) 8, 80, 209–210, 301–303
South Asian Free Trade Association (SAFTA) 210
South Asian Preferential Trading Agreement (SAPTA) 210, 303
South Korea 221
Soviet Union 196, 209, 218, 221, 316, 327

Sri Lanka 1–13, 88–113, 183–195, 208
   colonisation schemes 93, 95, 102–103, 106, 108
   district councils 97–98, 109
   Eastern Province 91, 93, 95, 101–103, 106, 108, 110
   ethnic civil war 109–112
   national flag 92
   Northern Province 91, 93, 95–96, 101–103
   Northeastern Province 111, 208
   relations with India 91
Sri Lanka Freedom Party (SLFP) 89, 95, 99–111
Srinagar 290, 312, 319
Standstill Agreement 289, 312
state governments 227, 230–232, 248–251
strikes 56, 73–77, 82–83, 94–95, 319
students 79, 145, 175
Suhrawardy, H.S. 201
Sunnism *see* Islam, Sunnism
supreme judiciary *see* supreme court
supreme court
   Bangladesh 77
   India 26, 28–29, 150–151, 314
   Nepal 135
   Pakistan 44–45, 47, 54–59
   Sri Lanka 185
swadeshi movement and lobby 34, 219, 232, 256
Swadeshi Jagran Manch (Self-reliance Consciousness Movement) 232
Swatantra (Freedom) Party 219
Syndicate 31–32

Talbot, Strobe 306, 329
Tamil
   ethnic movements
      India 201
      Sri Lanka 88–112, 206
   language 92, 95–96, 99–104, 201
   see also Tamils, Tamil Eelam movement, *and* Sri Lanka, ethnic civil war
Tamil Eelam movement 106–111, 202
   see also Tamil, ethnic movements
Tamil Language (Special Provisions) Act of 1958 97, 104
Tamil Regulations of 1966 97, 104, 106
Tamil United Liberation Front (TULF) 108–109
Tamil plantation workers 92

Index

Tamils *see also* Tamil
   Ceylon Tamils 88–112
   Indian Tamils 88–112, 201–202, 206
Tarar, Rafiq 58
Tashkent Agreement 316
Task Force on Information Technology 248
taxes
   India 233, 248–251
   jizya (Bangladesh) 160
   Nepal 137
   Pakistan 275–277
teachers *see* education
Tehri (Tarai) 117, 137
telecommunications 247
Telecom Regulatory Authority of India (TRAI) 257
television 37
Thapas 120
Thondaman, S. 103
Tibet 330, 332
Tilak, Bal Gangadhar 337
Tiruchelvam, M. 97
trade
   Bangladesh-India 80
   India-Pakistan 301–302
   regional trade 301–302
transnational corporations (TNCs) 219, 224, 230–231 *see also* multinational corporations
Treaty of Peace and Friendship of 1972 78–79
tribals 34
Tribhuvan, King 123
Trincomalee Convention 102
'two nation theory' 200–205, 286, 288, 312

ulema 48, 174
United Front (UF) (India) 23–24, 253–254
United Front (Sri Lanka) 106
United Jihad Council 305
United Marxist-Leninists (UML) 133–137
United National Party (UNP) 88–89, 93–101, 103, 104–111
United Nations 289, 313, 315
United Nations Cease-Fire Line (CFL) 290, 316 *see also* Line of Control

United States (US) 60–61, 284, 296, 304–307, 320, 326–337, 340–346
   aid to Pakistan 274, 297
untouchables *see* Dalits
Urdu
   language education 149, 162
   marginalization 148–149
utilitarianism 142 *see also* British colonialism
Uttar Pradesh 148–149

Vaddukoddai Resolution 106
Vaithianathan, Sir Kantiah 98
Vajpayee, Atal Bihari 24, 306
Vanavasi Kalyan Ashram (VKA) 145
Venkataraman, R. 25
Verma, A.N. 243
Vishva Hindu Parishad (VHP) 145–150

Wajed, Sheikh Hasina 71, 76–83, 86
war *see also* civil war
   Afghanistan war 274, 277, 290, 294, 297
   Bangladesh liberation war 70, 159, 170, 196, 288
   Gulf War 220
   Indo-Chinese war 295, 315
   Indo-Pakistan wars 288–290, 304–305, 311–322
   Sri Lankan ethnic civil war 109–112
   World War II 287
weapons 294, 296, 297–299, 338–340
   see also nuclear weapons
West Bengal 80, 223–224
Wijetunga, D.B. 111
Wijewardene, D.R. 90
women 79, 171, 173, 266–269
World Bank 95, 224, 229, 245, 271

Zakat and Ushr Ordinance of 1980 (Pakistan) 276
Zamiruddin, General 176
Zangger Committee 327
Zardari, Asif 57
Zia, Begum Khaleda 72, 75–78, 82–83, 86
Ziaul Haq, Mohammed 48–50, 273–276
Zinni, Anthony 61

GPSR Compliance

The European Union's (EU) General Product Safety Regulation (GPSR) is a set of rules that requires consumer products to be safe and our obligations to ensure this.

If you have any concerns about our products, you can contact us on

ProductSafety@springernature.com

In case Publisher is established outside the EU, the EU authorized representative is:

Springer Nature Customer Service Center GmbH
Europaplatz 3
69115 Heidelberg, Germany

www.ingramcontent.com/pod-product-compliance
Lightning Source LLC
LaVergne TN
LVHW041618060526
838200LV00040B/1334